GOVERNING THE FEMINIST PEACE

COLUMBIA STUDIES IN INTERNATIONAL ORDER AND POLITICS

Stacie E. Goddard, Daniel H. Nexon, and Joseph M. Parent, series editors

The Columbia Studies in International Order and Politics series builds on the press's long tradition in classic international relations publishing while highlighting important new work. The series is founded on three commitments: to serve as an outlet for innovative theoretical work, especially that work which stretches beyond "mainstream" international relations and cuts across disciplinary boundaries; to highlight original qualitative and historical work in international relations theory, international security, and international political economy; and to focus on creating a selective, prominent list dedicated to international relations.

States and the Masters of Capital: Sovereign Lending, Old and New, Quentin Bruneau

Making War on the World: How Transnational Violence Reshapes Global Order, Mark Shirk

GOVERNING THE FEMINIST PEACE

THE VITALITY AND FAILURE

of the

WOMEN, PEACE, AND SECURITY AGENDA

PAUL KIRBY AND LAURA J. SHEPHERD

Columbia University Press
New York

Columbia University Press
Publishers Since 1893
New York   Chichester, West Sussex
cup.columbia.edu

Library of Congress Cataloging-in-Publication Data
Names: Kirby, Paul (Research fellow), author. | Shepherd, Laura J., author.
Title: Governing the feminist peace : the vitality and failure of the women, peace,
and security agenda / Paul Kirby and Laura J. Shepherd.
Description: New York : Columbia University Press, [2024] |
Series: Columbia studies in international order and politics |
Includes bibliographical references and index.
Identifiers: LCCN 2023041807 (print) | LCCN 2023041808 (ebook) |
ISBN 9780231205122 (hardback) | ISBN 9780231205139 (trade paperback) |
ISBN 9780231555852 (ebook)
Subjects: LCSH: Women and peace. | Women and human security. | Security,
International. | Women—Violence against—Prevention—International
cooperation. | Women—Political activity.
Classification: LCC JZ5578 .K57 2024 (print) | LCC JZ5578 (ebook) |
DDC 327.1/72082—dc23/eng/20231101
LC record available at https://lccn.loc.gov/2023041807
LC ebook record available at https://lccn.loc.gov/2023041808

Cover design: Milenda Nan Ok Lee
Cover image: Poster created by Barbara Klunder for the Toronto International
Women's Day 1979. Used with permission of the artist.

CONTENTS

TABLES AND FIGURES

⸻

A NOTE ON REFERENCING

The primary analytical focus of this book is a set of documents we have curated, which we examine as one empirical manifestation of the WPS ecosystem. These documents were published in the period 2000–2020. The ecosystem dataset is introduced and explained fully in chapter 3 and a full list of the documents is available in appendix 1. These documents are referenced parenthetically throughout the book using bespoke abbreviations, as explained in appendix 1. Where a policy document falls outside of our collection period, it is cited in an endnote and listed in the bibliography following standard referencing conventions.

ACKNOWLEDGMENTS

I t is hard to know where to start with acknowledgments in a project of this magnitude. We have been trying to write this book in one way or another for several years, starting with the germ of an idea in early 2018. We have received invaluable support and assistance along the way, all of which has improved what follows immeasurably (mistakes and omissions, of course, etc.).

Paul's work on this research was primarily supported by the UKRI GCRF Gender, Justice, and Security Hub (AH/S004025/1). Laura's contribution was enabled by an Australian Research Council Future Fellowship (FT1791100037) and parallel funding from the University of Sydney Deputy Vice-Chancellor (Research) portfolio. The book also draws on data collected under the auspices of two earlier Australian Research Council Discovery Project grants (DP130100707 and DP160100212).

Data visualizations were provided by Chao Sun and the team at the Sydney Informatics Hub, for which we are extremely grateful, and adapted for publication by the team at KnowledgeWorks Global.

We have benefited enormously from research and data-processing assistance undertaken by Caitlin Hamilton, Caitlin Biddolph, Kit Catterson, Evelyn Pauls, and Nyibeny Gum Naam. What you are about to read was also shepherded into life by Caelyn Cobb, Monique Laban, and Marisa Lastres, our editors at Columbia, and improved by the sharp eye of Ryan Perks. We also give thanks to Barbara Klunder, who so kindly gave permission for us to reuse her art from Toronto International Women's Day 1979 for the front cover.

Throughout its years in development, we presented aspects of this research at various conferences and workshops, and we are grateful in particular for feedback from Sarai Aharoni and Marsha Henry at two such events. We would also like to thank those who have provided a supportive cradle, our scholarly coconspirators and interlocutors, for provoking our thinking more indirectly: Toni Haastrup, Caitlin Hamilton (again), Aiko Holvikivi, Muriel Kahane, Megan MacKenzie, Anna Stavrianakis, Nicole Wegner, Hannah Wright, and the Gender, Justice and Security Hub crew. There are many others whose support and scholarly companionship has been and remains invaluable.

Without compromising anonymity, we cannot thank by name those we interviewed and on whose experiences we draw in the pages that follow, but we are deeply and profoundly grateful for their time and their willingness to share their insights and expertise. We can, however, and do thank most effusively those who provided intelligence or leads: Sanam Anderlini, Christine Chinkin, Henri Myrttinen, Anna Stavrianakis (again), and Katharine Wright.

From Paul: This book is the culmination of seven years of collaboration, none of which would have been possible without Laura's support, dedication, and trust. From her willingness to take the risk with a WPS novice in the early days to her patience with the many, many iterations of this text, she has somehow been a friend and mentor as much as a coauthor. Aggie Hirst was there throughout, a source of endless joy and life, each day the vitality anew.

And from Laura: Above all, I am grateful to Paul for his commitment, his patience, his attention to detail. Working with Paul makes me a better writer and a better thinker, and I deeply appreciate our collaboration. Without his vision and his determination, this book would not exist.

ABBREVIATIONS

ATT	Arms Trade Treaty
CEDAW	Convention on the Elimination of all forms of Discrimination Against Women
CoACT	Coalition for Action on Resolution 1325
CSSF	Conflict, Stability and Security Fund
CWINF	Committee on Women in NATO Forces
DPKO	Department of Peacekeeping Operations
EAPC	Euro-Atlantic Partnership Council
ECOWAS	Economic Community of West African States
E10	Ten elected members of the UN Security Council
EU	European Union
FET	Female Engagement Team
FFPU	All-female formed police units
GBV	Gender-based violence
G8	Group of Eight
GNWP	Global Network of Women Peacebuilders
IDP	Internally displaced persons
IEG	Informal Experts Group
IR	International Relations (referring to the academic discipline, as distinct from "international relations" in lowercase, referring to interactions across boundaries of state)

ISAF	International Stability and Assistance Force
LAP	Local action plans
LGBTQIA+	Lesbian, gay, bisexual, trans, queer, intersex, and asexual people, and others of minoritized genders and sexualities
MIFTAH	Palestinian Initiative for the Promotion of Global Dialogue and Democracy
NAP	National Action Plan
NATO	North Atlantic Treaty Organization
NGO	Nongovernmental organization
OAU	Organisation of African Unity
P5	Five permanent members of the UN Security Council
R2P	Responsibility to Protect
PSVI	Preventing Sexual Violence Initiative
SADC	Southern African Development Community
SEA	Sexual exploitation and abuse
SRHR	Sexual and reproductive health rights
SRSG	Special representative of the secretary-general
SysAP	System-Wide Action Plan
TEWPA	Teso Women Peace Activists
UN	United Nations
UNDP	United Nations Development Programme
UNFPA	United Nations Population Fund
UNICEF	United Nations Children's Fund
UNIFEM	United Nations Development Fund for Women (now known as UN Women)
UN PBC	United Nations Peacebuilding Commission
UNSCR	UN Security Council resolution
WHRD	Women human rights defenders
WIDF	Women's International Democratic Federation
WILPF	Women's International League for Peace and Freedom
WPS	Women, Peace, and Security

1

THE IMPOSSIBILITY OF WOMEN, PEACE, AND SECURITY

To see a World in a Grain of Sand.
And a Heaven in a Wild Flower.
Hold Infinity in the palm of your hand.
And Eternity in an hour

—WILLIAM BLAKE, *AUGURIES OF INNOCENCE*, CA. 1803

. . . when you get there, there isn't any there *there.*

—GERTRUDE STEIN, ON OAKLAND, CALIFORNIA, 1934

~~The Women, Peace and Security agenda is . . .~~
~~Adopted in 2000 by the United Nations Security Council, resolution~~
~~1325 is the foundation of . . .~~
~~With its title derived from the thematic agenda item of 'women and~~
~~peace and security' at the UN Security Council, the Women, Peace and~~
~~Security agenda comprises . . .~~

———— ✺ ————

How do we introduce the subject matter of a book when our purpose is to show the illusion of that subject's singularity and coherence? To show the impossibility of capturing within a single term the enormity of that subject, the multiplicity of its *subjects*—in the sense of both its concerns and the protagonists pursuing them—and the ways in which even the most basic description of our field implicates us in subject-*making*, generating narratives of gendered agency and identity? Gertrude Stein remarked wistfully, regarding the possibility of returning to her native Oakland, California, and her longing for a sense of recognition, of home-coming: "there isn't any *there* there." We feel much the same about the ephemeral qualities of the subject in which we have invested much of our combined and separate careers. This is not to say that there is a lack of energy, a lack of effort, a lack of embodied and lived experience invested in feminist peace projects—quite the opposite. As we show in this open-ing chapter, the complex constellations of objects and subjects and rela-tions between them that make up the field of policy and governance called "WPS" are notable for their vitality, and are proliferating wildly, with the diffusion and diversity of the agenda often held up as evidence of both its success and its shortcoming.

The Women, Peace, and Security (WPS) agenda is typically introduced as an ambitious and coherent gender equality architecture conceived at the United Nations Security Council and with an exact birth date: Octo-ber 31, 2000 (see chapter 4). This was the "*first* time the Security Council devoted an entire session to debating women's experience in conflict and post-conflict situations . . . [and] it is the only Security Council resolution that has an anniversary celebrated by a growing constituency of practi-tioners and advocates."[1] The agenda exists to "ensure that gender is main-streamed throughout all conflict prevention and peacebuilding activi-ties, and reaffirms women's rights to be involved in decision-making and to access and take on leadership positions."[2] It is the global governmental expression of the "simple, yet revolutionary idea . . . that peace is only sus-tainable if women are fully included, and that peace is inextricably linked with equality between women and men."[3] The agenda is so celebrated as a rarity because it was driven from below: "a pragmatic attempt on the part of women's rights activists to address the significant violence and inequality that characterizes conflict, particularly women's experience of it."[4] Over more than two decades, WPS has been almost universally under-stood as a reconfiguration of prior logics of peace and security, involving a novel form of governing practice, and resulting in a more just global order: in short, the feminism of war and peace.

But the above paragraph represents a conventional—and, we will argue, limited—account of the agenda. In this book we offer an alternative historiography of WPS as a heterogenous collection of policy documents, political discourses, institutional guidelines, varieties of professional practice and expertise, dedicated aid programs, and not least (though these are often left out) activist and community mobilizations. This sprawling entity is indeed a gender equality project of great scope, but its exact terms are contested and diverse. This simple insight leads to a different vantage point on feminist governance. Practically every sympathetic scholarly account to date presumes the existence, somewhere, if only in principle, of a coherent WPS agenda that could—if the conditions were right—be made to succeed, to live, to transform the reigning forms of patriarchal war and peace. And yet the agenda is everywhere observed to be partial, stalling, inadequate, incremental, neglected—failing to thrive. Taking our cue from the persistence of promise and complaint, in this book we follow the trails of vitality and failure to explore the shifting manifestations of WPS.

Under scrutiny, the singular Women, Peace, and Security agenda turns out to be a chimera. WPS is multiple, available in radical and conservative variants, an expansive list of demands that lends itself to selective adoption, pliable but also laden with history. As the agenda has developed—growing in scope and depth and energy—it has diverged and converged anew. The pluralism of the agenda is much noted, often explained as a break between Western and local expectations or as a welcome branching into new themes in ways that don't necessarily disturb the coherence of WPS as a project.[5] We take a different perspective, however, and conceptualize the plurality of WPS in terms of ecology, rather than the replication of a singular organism. The complexity and dynamics of contestation ensure uneven growth, with some aspects of the agenda benefiting from significant resources and investment while other areas are comparatively silenced or starved. Parallel and competing initiatives produce truths of the agenda that are impossible to reconcile, as in the clash between the antimilitarist vision of the agenda and the desire to realize its promise by increasing the number of women in armed and defense forces. The making, unmaking, and remaking of WPS commitments and principles over time in turn mean that "the WPS perspective" on a given issue is always in the process of becoming. Though the imagery of chimera is mythological, our point is historical and sociological: grounded in the conditions that initiated the agenda, the contingencies of how it was taken up and applied, and the relations between the agencies that today collectively constitute it. The chimera is many-faced, a collision of bodies, imaginary and threatening, in later scientific terms a hybrid or fusion of botanical specimens. Though there are precursor species, there is no essential form. The idea that the WPS agenda exists, simply waiting to be implemented, is likewise an illusion. There is no *there* there.[6]

We develop the concept of a *policy ecosystem* to reveal the relational multiplicity behind the slick superficiality invoked by "the WPS agenda." The ecosystem is an analytical model prompted by our dissatisfaction with norm theory as the predominant framework in global gender governance research, and in the discipline of International Relations (IR) more broadly (as explained at length in chapter 2). The norm perspective emphasizes the establishment of robust standards of conduct, their diffusion by socialization and emulation, alternatively their failure or hybridization in the "local," and more recently their contestation by rival actors. From the vantage point of policy ecology, the sum of WPS interactions is more fruitful, less stable, and only ambiguously related to international "rules" that are everywhere flouted. The ecosystem presumes dynamic interaction and a diversity of practices along a continuum of efficacy, with norms incorporated as one, but by no means the only or even predominant, vector of meaning.

The ecosystem comprises both a *circuit*—a network of agents, individual and collective, who interact with each other to produce the range of texts and effects associated with WPS—and a *field*—the less distinct atmosphere of WPS, its discourses and topics, the flow of debates and desires for change, taken up by the circuit but exceeding it.[7] In our study, we will have cause to specify both the identity and motive of participants in the circuit and to consider the emergent qualities of the field. There is also a pleasant echo in our insistence that each arrangement or artifact within the agenda must be apprehended as relationally constituted, connected, and, importantly, always produced within these broader conditions of possibility, and our own collaborative engagement in this inquiry, which simultaneously produces a "we-subject"/writer within a broader ecosystem of intellectual endeavor. We reflect on this below, where we present an overview of the bricolage method, with which we try to fix, for a moment, the ecosystem to be studied.

To provide a foundation for our investigation, in the rest of this chapter we summarize the layers of our approach, beginning with an explanation of the motifs of vitality and failure we use to illuminate aspects of the WPS ecosystem that we analyze. We go on to situate debates about "the agenda" in a wider field of feminist entanglements. Though the agenda can sometimes appear as narrowly technical, even depoliticized, with its daily language of implementation measures and donor funding, it is laced with many of the same tensions that animate gender politics at large, from the relationship between feminism and nationalism to the discourse of rights and representation and the terms on which sexual and gender identity are recognized and negotiated. Part of our motivation is to bring questions of feminist peace back into conversation about, and with, WPS. We then engage with theories of governance to draw on ideas about the "rules, structures and institutions that guide, regulate and control social life" in the field of the WPS agenda, to situate the policy documents within their circumstances and relations of production by examining the arrangements and agents that enact WPS.[8] In the analysis presented in the following chapters, we address the policies, protocols, and guidelines that *codify* WPS, which are both produced by/through governance arrangements and actions, and which condition the possibilities of those same arrangements and actions. The book moves across these layers, taking in politics and critique, practice and policymaking, arrangements and artifacts. This chapter therefore concludes with a brief discussion of how we make sense of the layers and an outline of the structure of the book.

Let us, then, try again to provide an introduction . . .

VITALITY AND FAILURE

Over the last two decades, feminist activists and at least partly sympathetic policymakers have nurtured a system of peace and security governance anchored in, but extending far beyond, a series of United Nations Security Council resolutions adopted under the title of "women and peace

and security." The basic history has become rote. The first of these resolutions was adopted in 2000 (S/RES/1325); its identifying number, "1325,"
has become an icon as much as a policy object, a touchstone for feminist
engagements from formal peace negotiations and political settlements to
the protection and assurance of women's rights during war. Subsequent
resolutions expand on the substance of resolution 1325 in various (and
variously satisfactory) ways, and together the sequence of resolutions
adopted under this title is the supreme architecture of what has crystal-
ized as the Women, Peace, and Security agenda (commonly abbreviated
to "the WPS agenda" or simply "WPS"). In addition to the resolutions,
and the international governmental organization under the auspices of
which they are adopted, there is an abundance of related policy guidelines,
protocols, and plans interpreting the provisions of the agenda, along with
a mass of advocacy coalitions and networks, government programs and
representatives, think tanks and research centers, experts, diplomats,
community groups, and practitioner organizations. The agenda has
become part of the repertoire of international peace and security, its claims
repeated by officials otherwise distant from the traditions of feminist
thought.

The magnitude and complexity of the agenda is a testament to its success, and the energies devoted to the feminist peace. The success itself
poses a question: How did "one revolutionary idea [become] the official
policy of the highest body tasked with the maintenance of international
peace and security?"[9] How has a seemingly antimilitarist feminist project made such progress in traditionalist institutions of state, in councils
for security and ministries of war? Students of the agenda have offered a
number of answers: That WPS is but one face in a changing culture of
security prompted by the collapse of bipolar Cold War antagonisms. That
diligent activism by transnational networks and concerned publics has
opened a channel, albeit a tentative one, to mitigate and redress the violence that remains endemic to global politics. Or that the agenda was
never, or is no longer, properly feminist and antimilitarist at all, but has
instead been co-opted and instrumentalized to serve the war system it
once promised to transform. Each of these explanations has some purchase, and in their different ways all draw attention to the *vitality* of WPS,
a locus for marshalling energies. Most obviously this is so for the energies of women's groups, civil society organizations, activists and advocates

who continue to make the case for WPS as a vector of progress or a means of survival. Despite a pervasive sense of disenchantment with the bureaucratization and dilution of the more radical elements of the agenda, feminists from around the world continue to mobilize in the name of WPS, to make demands on its terms, and to reinforce the contract through accountability mechanisms and legal guarantees. Others are moved in more mundane ways. Bureaucracies have been spurred to conduct scoping studies, revise protocols, set quotas, commission experts, and form working groups. Parliamentarians have debated, advocated, and challenged governments of various stripes to live up to the rhetoric of gender equality increasingly expressed in WPS terms of art. Academics have defined their vocation in relation to the agenda, an investment that often brings them into dialogue and dispute with others on the WPS scene.[10] Even for those most critical of the securitization or colonial resonances of the agenda, the naivety of WPS advocacy lends energy to hegemonic forces, who are able to manipulate that resource for other ends.

The liveliness of WPS is expressed most immediately in the profusion of policy documents, offices and initiatives, and political opportunities flowing from resolution 1325. As we document in chapter 3, there are now several hundred high-level policy directives devoted to the agenda issued by a panorama of actors. The pace has at times been almost frenetic, with Security Council resolutions passed mere months apart (see chapter 4). Yet the energies of the agenda are not intrinsically beneficent, as the more celebratory accounts of feminist progress might imply. The field shimmers with potential, both power *and* danger, to adopt the diagnosis of Dianne Otto.[11] The potentiality of WPS is everywhere invested with feeling: hope for expanded equality and security; national pride conveyed in government plans and ministerial speeches; bitter frustration at Security Council intransigence; rage in the face of atrocity; excitement at new alliances and mobilizations. The vitality of activism is integral to the memory work of transnational feminist networks, in which the landmarks of the agenda often feature prominently (see figure 1.1).

The labor of generating and sustaining WPS policy is emotional as well as intellectual.[12] This terminology is fraught, of course. "Emotion" is too easily read as belittling women's groups and "women's issues"; in more philosophical terms, the juxtaposition of emotional and intellectual labor enshrines a distinction between feeling and thought that has a long and

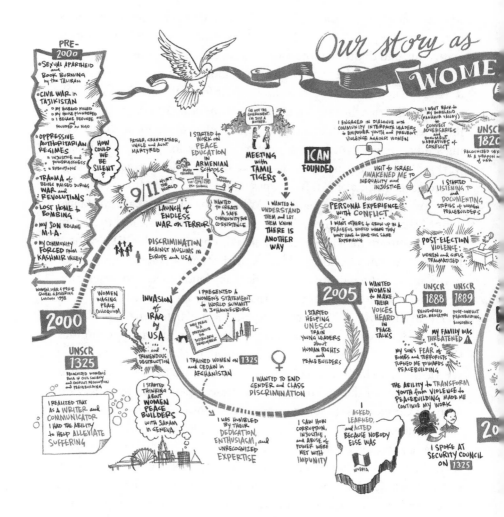

FIGURE 1.1 "Our Story as Women Peacebuilders, 2000–2020," a visual narrative produced by seventy peacebuilders from thirty-eight different countries.

Source: International Civil Society Action Network, *ICAN Annual Report 2019* (Washington, DC: ICAN, 2019), https://icanpeacework.org/wp-content/uploads/2020/07/ICANAnnual Report2019final-1.pdf.

troubled history.[13] Following critical scholarship on the politics of emotion, we therefore highlight the force of affect in our explorations of vitality: the "flow of resonances"; the intensities of "mood, intuition, temperament, attachment, disposition, and even memory" as animating the WPS field.[14] "Affect" connotes a range of investments and responses not

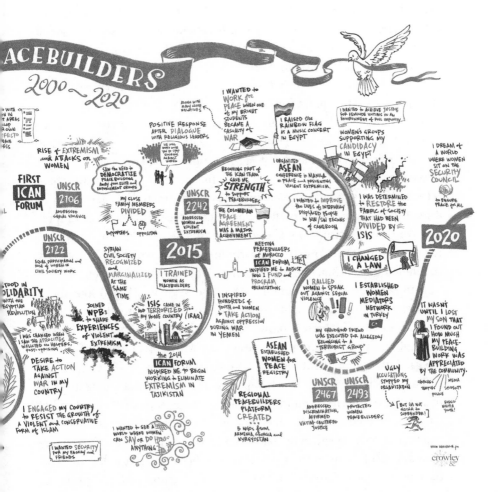

reducible to psychological interiority or somatic reflex. In the simplest terms, affect is a feature of the social world. Politics is always affectual, but the relations between feeling, knowing, and acting are more pronounced, more explicitly recognized and reasoned about, in feminist thought. Moreover, feminist entanglements with governance institutions require affective *skill*; Anna Elomäki and colleagues describe this as "affective virtuosity," which "entails not only the competence to analyse and negotiate the conflicting emotions in the room but also within oneself," arguing that this virtuosity is needed in particular as "feminist knowledge producers negotiate their relationship with neoliberal governance."[15]

Feminist investments are also powered by what Clare Hemmings has called "affective dissonance": the gap between a sense of self and social conditions that politicize, generating new ways of thinking and acting in relation to others.[16] Dissonance produces movement, an energy of becoming that also unsettles: "it is this *question* of affect—misery, rage, passion, pleasure—that gives feminism its life."[17]

WPS is, then, full of life: vibrant, thriving through successful propagation. And yet failure, even the threat of death, stalks the feminist peace. The WPS origin story may be of "a revolutionary outcome," but it is "yet to trigger revolutionary change."[18] In its most common expression, there is the failure to properly implement the agenda; practically every study of it identifies major and persistent underachievement. The most comprehensive and significant single evaluation to date was the 2015 high-level review commissioned by the UN secretary-general, which diplomatically concluded that "obstacles and challenges still persist and prevent the full implementation of the women, peace and security (WPS) agenda."[19] Though scholarly analysis of the agenda (sometimes) identifies (moderate) successes, the central shared research puzzle has been how best to account for the shortcomings of the agenda, with a predominant focus on the gap between political rhetoric and national action.

The culprit is typically "lack of political will," a complaint heard with increasing regularity as more states adopt the agenda. This is a kind of failure contained within the agenda's success. In similar terms, advocates and practitioners speak of the fatigue induced by the passage of ever more thematic resolutions in the United Nations Security Council, adding little to what came before and, in some cases, undermining it. Fatigue lasted at least until the stream of resolutions ran dry (see chapter 4). Then there is the neglect of some part of the agenda, the abandonment of promises to prevent conflict in favor of simply making war safe for women.[20] A near universal refrain is the lack of understanding of, or resistance to, the "true" WPS principles that ought to be prioritized and thus operationalized. The "norms" at the heart of WPS are at once a marker of achievement—brought into being by demands placed on the Security Council—and a yardstick of failure—because the standards are observed principally in the breach (as we discuss in chapter 2). There is an underlying, and often implicit, assumption that if the tensions could be ironed out, then the agenda could be effectively implemented; if the agenda could be properly resourced, with the investment of high-level leadership, and actors could agree on fundamental or original principles, then the implementation gap would be eliminated, and feminist peace realized. The slow progress in meeting targets for even the most uncontested forms of participation, the chronic underfunding of the agenda, and the often unrecognized and unvalued labor of advocacy exhausts and exasperates activists. Lack, fatigue, neglect, exhaustion, betrayal.

A second charge of failure comes from another direction: not the failure of states to implement WPS, but the failure of the agenda itself *as a feminist project*. Though the agenda is about women, this does not by necessity make it feminist, nor does it resolve the vexed question of what is entailed in a feminist politics today. For many critics, "WPS" articulates a problematic figure, a collective feminine subject assumed to share an identity and interest. The "woman" being added to "peace" and "security" is a victim, usually of sexual violence, who is at the same time invested with powers of reconciliation and peacemaking ultimately derived from a maternal archetype.[21] This image of the woman—in need of saving but also offering a kind of salvation—damns the agenda to reproduce a binary model of gender (men as always already perpetrators, women as victims), and to facilitate racial hierarchies in gifting the role of benevolent hero to the liberal states of the Global North.[22] In the theater of WPS, individual women are expected to perform accordingly, to appear in front of a Security Council represented overwhelmingly (and often only) by male ambassadors, to recount their trauma and plead for assistance.[23] The logic of WPS as a policy frame stands in stark contrast to the trajectory of feminist theory away from essentialism and against treatments of "gender" in isolation from its imbrication with the political categories of race, nation, class, sexuality, citizenship, and (dis)ability.[24] The critique is not only one of scholarship. Contemporary feminist movements frequently reject undifferentiated conceptions of womanhood, instead acknowledging the diversity of women's experiences and sometime privileges, committing to intersectional feminism, and/or queering conventional masculine/feminine distinctions. In short, the category *woman* is not a solidaristic identity to be assumed, but a construct to be critiqued and replaced, a task at odds with the prevailing gender scripts of the WPS agenda.

We have ourselves participated in both these discourses of failure, separately and together, proposing ways to do WPS better or pointing out the reductivism of the interventions designed in its name.[25] But there is also a third sense in which WPS is failed, this time *by academic feminism itself*. For practitioners and activists invested in WPS, the interest taken by scholars—as either a topic of expertise or an object of critique—is too often detached from the urgent use to which resolution 1325 is put by women activists during and after conflict. Whether national plans match the resolutions in all particulars, and whether some actors promote essentialist ideas of femininity, is on this account less important than the maneuvers, tactics, and compromises that create new realities. Academic feminism, which becomes closely linked to the positions of semiprofessional and professional women of privilege who are often the graduates of feminist university courses in the Global North, faces its own "implementation gap," unable to forge solidarities with women's groups that articulate their struggles in different terms, and which adapt the tools at hand—including resolution 1325—under conditions not of their choosing. The negativity, abstraction, and insularity of academic feminism is then seen as failing feminist politics as such.

In a different context, Judith Jack Halberstam has pursued failure as a political art, a way to circumvent the disciplining force of academic tradition and slip the expectations of success and "toxic positivity."[26] Failure is a neglected utopian resource, a tactic of renegade feminists and pop cultural guerrillas. For WPS advocates, influence instead requires a pragmatic accommodation with reigning standards of seriousness and maturity.[27] Transposed to the circuit of advocacy and governance, failure is less of an aesthetic and more of a craft, both a motivating lack and a powerful rhetorical resource. Activists react to—*are energized by*—the failures of state response, the dissonance between promise and reality.[28] In this sense the endless deferral of full implementation is inextricably conjoined with the vitality of WPS. Frustration and resentment are part of the lived biography of the agenda, for those who have moved away from advocacy as much as for those who have persevered. In a different register, failure has its uses precisely as a rhetorical device in making feminist demands. In some sense, resolution 1325 is less remarkable for the change it effected than the discourse it enabled: the narrative of the failure of states (and others) to do what was required of them, a lack that cohered *as failure* because of all that the resolution and its successors demanded and implied. Failure has a temporal quality, marked in anniversary years and missed opportunities, recognition deferred and progress undone, incremental reform against the urgency of systematic change.

Failure, then, becomes the chronic generative condition of WPS. Rather than treating failure as a technical question—where acts of government are compared to grand promises, or policies scrutinized for their mechanisms of delivery and evaluation—we keep it in mind as an affective boundary: a sense of foreboding and disappointment pervading the WPS field. Against some critics, who regard WPS as a substitute for a real feminism that lies elsewhere, we look to follow the detour of failure, to map the dead ends and false starts.[29] Instead of asking after the practical barriers to implementation of the agenda, we interrogate the various practices enacted under the auspices of WPS. When viewed outside of the expectations of success—of "reproductive maturity"[30]—what is it that WPS labor does? How might thinking otherwise about the varieties of the feminist peace change how we view international policy and governance?

FEMINIST ENTANGLEMENTS

As we have sketched it, the vitality of the Women, Peace, and Security field subsists on feminist energies of various kinds. We refer to WPS as a feminist peace project in part to decenter the UN Security Council from our accounts and also to draw attention to its pre- and parallel histories, through which it is linked to a longer trajectory of peace activism and initiatives proximate to and far from the United Nations Headquarters in New York.[31] The immediate causes of WPS, emerging out of mobilizations in the 1990s, deserve dedicated comment (see chapter 4). These in turn have a complex genealogy, easily glossed in potted chronologies. For the discipline of International Relations, with its origin story of an interwar feud over world government, the prototype of WPS was present at the foundation as the 1915 International Congress of Women and its appeal to the warring parties.[32] Helena Swanwick, in what must count among the first feminist readings of modern warfare, argued then that "in militarist states, women must always, to a greater or lesser degree, be deprived of liberty, security, scope and initiative," seeing in the control of arms and international organizations a possible solution to the torment.[33]

In a different time and place, Claudia Jones situated the labor and welfare struggles of Black women in America alongside Cold War geopolitics and male supremacy within the same vision of "peace and security."[34]
For Jones, resistance took organizational form in groups like the antifas-
cist, pro-communist Women's International Democratic Federation
(WIDF), a solidarity circuit starting in the late 1940s where women from
colonizing and colonized nations forged a diagnosis of fascism's relationship to empire.[35] Of greater import for the history of WPS is the role of
the WIDF in spurring the Convention on the Elimination of All Forms
of Discrimination Against Women (CEDAW) and originating the International Women's Year in 1975, and hence the Decade for Women and
World Conferences on Women.[36] That the world conferences have more
recently been commemorated principally through then first lady Hillary
Clinton's rallying cry "women's rights are human rights"—itself a slogan
borrowed without credit from the Filipina women's movement[37]—is one
indication of how diverse feminist histories can be rendered monolithic
by the condescension of time. We could repeat the exercise for a variety
of other figures—Virginia Woolf, Eslanda Robeson, Rigoberta Menchú,
Chizuko Ueno—who understood the trajectories of equality, empire, militarism, justice, and freedom as inextricably entangled with women's
agency, individual and collective.

Alongside these histories may be placed other entanglements. Wom-
en's capacity for political violence—and the possible route from that violence to freedom—has been a recurrent fault line for feminisms, given
form in WPS debates over inclusive militaries, women insurgents, and the
politics of peacekeeping. Heavily criticized for assuming a generic feminine peaceableness, the connotations of "women" are far from settled in
the agenda, and practitioners have increasingly, if inconsistently, imported
antiessentialist perspectives (see the discussion on men and boys and sexual orientation in chapter 3). Though conventional accounts of the
agenda foreground the Security Council, even in this setting the agenda
serves multiple purposes, in crucial respects cutting against claims that
feminism has been militarized or securitized (as we explore in chapter 4).
National strategies are not simple echoes of what is negotiated in UN fora,
but themselves exemplify, revise, and at times resist contemporary forms
of femonationalism.[38] Though undoubtedly shaped by racial hierarchies
and colonial legacies, there is no single template of the agenda, and its

terms are today contested by forces beyond the Global North.[39] The clash of feminisms—liberal, social-reformist, state-nationalist, anticolonial, and communist—is articulated afresh, and sometimes leaves its trace in formal policy (as illustrated in chapter 5). The adoption of WPS by militaries enables a form of war-making, though the fracturing of feminist ideas has not gone unremarked.[40] Empowerment discourse—so contested within feminism—appears in WPS space in celebratory form along a continuum of civic and military virtue, ranging from UN Women's short-lived campaign featuring Wonder Woman as an honorary ambassador for the empowerment of women and girls to Girl Security's gender equality reformism in national security and defense (see figure 1.2).[41] Finally, new policy constructs extend and revitalize the feminist peace, in ways that offer opportunities to break with the conventions of the state system (for which see chapter 7). At each point, WPS may be understood as a scene

FIGURE 1.2 "To the Peace-Seekers," one of several materials offered by Girl Security, an advocacy group promoting women's participation in U.S. national security work.

Source: Girl Security.

in a wider series of feminist entanglements. Each of these moments or instances—instantiations—of entanglement reaffirms the agenda as a complex and relational system of governance, produced and reproduced across multiple locations and scales, in ways that make singular claims about the agenda's qualities impossible to sustain.

From the outset, the institutionalization of a feminist peace project in the working life of the UN Security Council caused some consternation; the scholars who documented and analyzed encounters in 1999–2000 expressed this concern explicitly in terms of "danger."[42] The adoption of resolution 1325 was a tremendous achievement of feminist activism, but the resolution was never intended to be an end in itself: feminist peace was a project, an ethos, resolution 1325 a tool. As Felicity Ruby asks, "If we cannot use this tool to participate in the 'big' security debates, and to challenge the 'inevitability' of the militarised framework of international peace and security, its foundation and structure, then what are we doing?"[43] And the danger was that the institutional context of the UN Security Council would blunt this tool, co-opting the feminist peace project and embedding in peace and security governance a narrow liberal concern for gender equality that Janet Halley describes as "governance feminism," and which in Carol Cohn's words "does not begin to get at the pernicious, pervasive complexities of the gender regimes that undergird not only individual wars themselves, but the entire war system."[44]

The wariness toward feminist rule, shared by some of the earliest advocates for resolution 1325, involved a form of WPS failure recognized and to some extent analyzed *preemptively*. For Halley, the danger lay in feminists wielding power uncritically; for others, it is to be found in feminist efforts being limited or routed by other forces. For feminists more broadly, WPS has been treated with skepticism, for reasons already mentioned. The actors and mechanisms of WPS often seem disconnected from—insufficiently entangled with—grassroots feminist mobilizations. The privileged role of international organizations and diplomacy, the technical language of national implementation, the frequent involvement of militaries and police forces, the place of gender mainstreaming within a larger discourse of liberal statecraft, and the advocacy of professionalized and multinational civil society organizations all contribute to a sense of WPS as distant from the front lines of contemporary feminist movements. Moreover, "an increasing number of states have adopted

National Action Plans that ostensibly incorporate WPS commitments into military policies and practices. These developments provide timely examples of anti-war feminism's institutional double serving imperialist agendas."[45] Thus, "security," too, is suspect, seeming to concede a radical antimilitarism to a compromised negotiation over which new and sanitized form violence will take.

Anticipating the defanging of critical politics through institutionalization, "feminist researchers have been particularly circumspect about allying themselves with military institutions implicated in martial violence and imperial incursions."[46] The relentless grinding of an institutional machine that is premised on the validity of both liberal values and militarized solutions to problems of peacelessness and exclusion can dull the edges of even the most pointed feminist critique. Careful attention should therefore be paid to "feminist 'victory' and 'danger' chronicles," which are "especially suited to masking the military logic of international security that generates and relies on women's inequality and marginalisation, in the west as well as outside it."[47] There is a both/and logic to the threads of entanglement: some, such as Halley, find sufficient reason to "take a break" from feminism given that feminists now "walk the halls of power" in the institutions of liberal governance and must therefore reflect on their complicity in the violences of those institutions—"any force as powerful as feminism must find itself occasionally looking down at its own bloody hands."[48] For others, the record of failure is a reason to redouble efforts in doing WPS differently.[49] We therefore tread carefully, preferring not to evaluate success or proclaim failure for *the* agenda at large, so much as to track the movement of hopes and myths, alterations and reversals, detours and paradoxes.

Scholar-practitioners are more conscious of these compromises than is sometimes appreciated by critics.[50] Engagement follows no single template. There are the accommodations made when working directly within the institutions of state; "critical friend" positions occupied by NGOs partly funded by and partly lobbying governments; even the "outsider" position of radical social movements that nevertheless entail demands on the powerful. From each of these vantage points the agenda takes on a different shape. The pressing questions relate less to the settled meaning and function of a set policy that is transferred across international space than to the contestation and fracture among the different visions and practices of gender enacted by and through governance actors and systems. More crucially for our purposes, when understood as encompassing a wider cast, the WPS field cannot reasonably be treated as only a state discourse or a technical apparatus. The contestations we trace are manifestations of many of the concerns that preoccupy feminists more generally.

GOVERNANCE AND *POLY-CY*

Although many researchers use (or casually reference) the concepts of policy and governance when discussing the WPS agenda,[51] there has been no systematic exploration of what this description entails theoretically, in terms of understanding the WPS agenda as a policy artifact or field of governance practice.[52] Research on the agenda more often engages questions of governance as the process of creating new norms and rules around gender, but the relationship between governance and policy is not well specified (nor is this the usual mode of encounter for WPS, as we explain in the following chapter). In this section, we relate our approach to broader disciplinary interrogations of governance, proposing that the WPS agenda is reproduced through governance mechanisms, entities, and initiatives enmeshed with diverse and divergent policy artifacts and practices in a dynamic array. To transcribe the cacophony, we are drawn away from macro-frameworks for theorizing governance as a particular logic of the international and eschew the choice between theories of governance organized around one principal mode or level of interaction (i.e., either discourse or practice, ideas or interests). Instead, we explore relational and reproductive effects in a less constrained vein, perhaps inevitably trading parsimony of explanation for situated promiscuity.

Despite the suggestion of "conceptual ambiguity" at the heart of debates about what governance *is*, the study of governance and the use of governance as a concept to leverage understanding of the events and phenomena of world politics has been a preoccupation of IR theory at least since the 1980s.[53] In its earliest form in IR discourse, governance was "associated with the concept of international regimes, occupying an ontological space somewhere between the level of formal institutions on the one hand

and systemic factors on the other."[54] By the early twenty-first century, the will to govern through institutions of global governance was identified as "one of the defining characteristics of the current international moment," with much intellectual attention paid to mapping out the actors and processes engaged in governance practice.[55]

The burgeoning field of critical research on governance sought to elaborate governance as a *process*, drawing on network theory and, later, practice theory to develop insights into the in-progress quality of governance arrangements.[56] Further, this literature challenges and extends the ontology of political action beyond the state, and beyond the recognition of international organizations as actors in international relations, to include non-state actors, including transnational advocacy networks, civil society organizations, and even individuals (e.g., state leaders, diplomats) in analysis of governance.[57] The vast expansion of corporate power and nonprofits generated "a newly emerging global public domain that is no longer coterminous with the system of states," indexed by "social capacity and agency that did not previously exist."[58] This insight necessarily decentered the state (or the intergovernmental organization) as the primary locus of political authority, and in parallel to the emphasis on process, governance arrangements and agents were rendered as vectors of power, using concepts and vocabulary drawn from critical and social theory to understand the "practice, mentality, [and] rationality" of governing within this decentralized system.[59]

Broadly speaking, we ally ourselves with others who critically scrutinize government processes and techniques in terms of their productive effects. The positivist epistemology adopted by most early governance scholars—preoccupied in IR in the 1980s with regimes—limited the study of governance mechanisms and arrangements, but there nonetheless managed to flourish a small scholarly community focused not only on the observable material conditions of governance but also its ideational components and the concept of values.[60] These researchers forwarded early expressions of governance as a relational activity, with James Rosenau, for example, proposing that "governance refers to activities backed by shared goals . . . [and] . . . is a system of rule that works only if it is accepted by the majority."[61] Developments in the study of governance in fields of policy analysis and public administration facilitated the forging of mutually enriching intellectual connections between the study of global governance and critical policy and governance literature, which in turn enabled the apprehension of governance as a composite practice of meaning-making with productive political effects.

As an anchoring point for a policy ecosystem model, we foreground the relationality of governance practices of all kinds (written, embodied, affectual, etc.) and at all levels. Theory in IR has recently experienced (not unironically, given the name of the discipline) a "relational turn,"[62] taking the insight that power is relational (which is, as noted by Marysia Zalewski, a rather familiar argument to feminist theorists)[63] and extending it to develop ontologies sometimes informed by Indigenous ways of apprehending the world of politics.[64] Relational thinking in the context of governance requires recognizing that governance entities (human and nonhuman) are activated by a web of mutual reference: "Things, persons, and events coexist in the complex relational context, without which none of them would exist at all."[65] These "things, persons, and events"—and policies, framework, statements, and protocols—are all and always *in process*, escaping attempts to define them outside the historical configurations that generate them. Their meanings, effects, and symbolic properties are always and necessarily tentative. What we study as global governance is the effect of this combined interaction.

"Relationality" can at the same time be a slippery term. In the name of an academic discipline, it connotes *polity difference*—IR is the study of the sum of the activity of bounded units (usually states) engaged in rivalry, alliance, trade, and domination. For a more recent generation, relationality means expanding the cast of protagonists, a way of recognizing the qualifies of other agencies beyond the state.[66] Contemporary global governance research is relational in the sense of seeing some domain of rules and regulation—such as international criminal justice, small arms control, electronic technology, development—as the product of a constellation of actors with diverse sources of authority.[67] But relationality is also an *ontological* perspective on how actors come to exist in the first place. Relational thinking focuses on the transaction, which, when "seen as a dynamic unfolding process, becomes the primary unit of analysis rather than the constituent elements themselves."[68] It entails a different view of entities from the macro- to the micro-level, from *societies* down to the psychic makeup of *individuals*.[69] Transactions are necessarily fluid, which precludes categorical stability.[70]

Despite the merits of thoroughgoing relationalism, our reading of the WPS agenda requires only a shallower version: that a diversity of agencies participate in distributed governance activities that constitute *the* agenda. What we call WPS is relational in that it has no pure prior, but rather emerges through encounters carried out in its name, a dynamism we capture in the concept of the ecosystem.[71] Though relationalism can entail "virtually microscopic analysis of how actors . . . co-produce institutional continuity and order,"[72] the chapters that follow are not exclusively about transactions at this level. We reconstruct specific moments in the production of WPS—for example, through negotiations over Security Council texts—which are microscopic in this sense, but also prize open the presumed macro-agencies of the agenda (the United Nations, national governments, regional security institutions, civil society organizations) to show the multiplicity of reproduction.

In this frame, "governing the feminist peace" acquires several valences: A first takes governing to mean *government*, a form of rule, where WPS is understood as already hegemonic, as already the operative form of the feminist peace, encompassing the logistics and technics of implementation. It is part of our argument that this powerful version of WPS does not exist, yet it exerts an imaginative pull for champions and critics alike. A second sense captures governing as an *attempt* at control, the effort taken to bridle something unwieldy, rebellious, wild. This feminist peace is always at risk of breaking free. A third resonance is with a kind of border work, disciplining *within* the feminist peace rather than as global feminist rule. This is closer to the idea of the feminist peace denied, confined, and subdivided, instrumentalized or defanged. We keep in mind all these senses of government in our encounter with the feminist peace, analyzing text, discourse, narrative, stories, artifacts, practice, and performance in relation to their circumstances of production, in relation to each other, and in relation to their reproductive effects to uncover relational vitality and failure.

Our approach conceives of governance as a complex and sprawling semi-systematicity of vital and relational connections across multiple scales, policy domains, and political formations, where agency is decentered, and where the multiplicity that is revealed requires rethinking questions of vitality and failure that otherwise presume a coherent and singular set of aims. We are attentive to the reproductive and generative effects

of governance arrangements and artifacts within the WPS agenda conceived as a complex governance system: policy and governance, then,
become visible as polycentric, polysemic, and polyvalent; hence, ours is a
relational theory of governance and "poly-cy," focused on reproductive
effects.

There are critical engagements with policy that move some way toward
the recognition of policy as generative, if not plural. Interpretative
approaches to policy explore not so much what a given policy means but
how it makes meaning and is, in turn, made meaningful: "Many public
policy issues have become so uncertain, complex, and polarized—their
empirical, political, legal, and bureaucratic merits unknown, not agreed
upon, or both—that the only things left to examine are the different stories policymakers and their critics use to articulate and make sense of that
uncertainty, complexity, and polarization."[73] These critical engagements
with policy architectures as symbolic frameworks, or stories of a kind,
offer a view of policy as being in flux. Such movement is indicated by
the vocabulary used to discuss "cycles" and "transfer" in the more conventional accounts of policy and governance, but the singularity and
coherence of policy is left largely undisturbed in even these critical
encounters.[74]

"Transfer" is, in fact, a revealing term of art for the replication or reformulation of a prescription from one governance system or institution
into another elsewhere. Two features of this language stand out for our
purposes. First, there is a movement implied in the metaphor of transfer,
with the policy artifact coming into contact with a secondary system or
institution beyond the environment in which it was initially formulated.
Second, the integrity of reproduction is presumed: policy is sufficiently
coherent to be copied, and in the transfer from one location to another
its nature, appearance, and meaning is normally unaffected. Even in interpretative accounts, which recognize that the policy itself may be interpreted differently in different contexts, narrated differently into different
storied configurations, the object of analysis remains the stable and immu-
table policy.

Stepping away from the conception of a singular and coherent policy
object that exists to be implemented in a one-to-one correspondence of
original and replica pushes us to think not about the *effectiveness* of implementation but rather about its *effects*, which may be diverse across

moments of nominal "transfer." The question becomes not "Why is the implementation of the Women, Peace, and Security agenda ineffective and/or limited?" but "What do implementation practices do?" Policymakers learn, mimic, compete, and coerce toward a horizon of success,[75] as policy is not made each time pristine and anew. The extent and content of a shared policy culture may profitably be studied against the benchmark of what the policy is understood to promise, its successes and its failures. We, however, seek a way of understanding the WPS field that is better attuned to the ongoing politics of plurality that constitute it and its generative effects.

To say that plurality is constitutive of WPS is to say more than that disagreements are common. Difference is inscribed in both the origins and logic of the ecosystem. The original achievement of resolution 1325 was to win great power support for a seemingly radical critique of great power politics. To the extent that feminist activists argued that the world remained so violent and unequal because so patriarchal, they appealed directly to the perpetrators, demands for equality enforced by the least democratic voting forum on earth, the UN Security Council.[76] They immediately faced the burden of success, "of using the strictures of [the council's] forms in order to undo it."[77] Since the apparent advance of National Action Plans, the mediating institutions of the agenda have become as diverse as the state system itself. The tension is somewhat lessened if WPS is regarded only as a tool deployed by some powerful states against others or lesser, though some inconvenient facts must be excised for this to be the only available story. Radical potentials and demands persist. Even for the sharpest critics, the only thing worse than security institutions having WPS plans would be for them to have none. Nor is the trouble only historical. WPS proves such a capacious domain that it sometimes feels as if it will never achieve stability or consensus. Differences of opinion occur elsewhere in global governance, but the fractures within WPS are constitutive—they are a part of how WPS comes to be visible *as* WPS, and how WPS actors come to be recognized as such. To pick up on the relational dimension (and foreshadowing chapter 6), there are WPS protagonists who gain traction precisely by having a rival vision of the feminist peace than others also claiming the WPS mantle. States do not operate as peers seeking technical solutions, but more often as the unlikely and unreliable allies of feminist movements. WPS advocates still bemoan their lack of influence precisely because many strands of the agenda remain so alien to diplomatic transactions and power-political considerations. The creatures of WPS depend on each other in relations that are sometimes symbiotic and sometimes predatory.

Our approach entails asking how events, entities, and experiences are positioned, made meaningful, and reproduce the agenda in and through the relational connections that sustain it and through which it is sustained. Each arrangement or artifact of governance simultaneously contains, reproduces, and exceeds the system of which it is also a part: we approach each aspect of the WPS agenda as both world and grain of sand, to borrow inspiration from William Blake. We explore the policy ecosystem of the WPS agenda in microcosm and macrocosm, examining the ecosystem as a manifestation of relational governance. In the process we encounter significant political questions about what and how we measure, and how we conceive of existence and effect, against which evaluations of "success" and "failure" seem meager or mean (and certainly partial). Next, we outline a method for such inquiry.

MESS AND METHOD

The profusion of WPS policy texts provides a rich archive for tracing the production and reproduction of governance. But the ecosystem model also opens other avenues of inquiry, which require alternative methodological approaches. John Law's work on how social science research reproduces the Euro-American fetishization of an already existing social world that is "independent and prior to an observer; definite in shape and form; and also singular (there is only one reality)" is instructive here.[78] Much work on governance systems, whether they are taken to be simple or complex, assumes the ability to isolate, monitor, evaluate—in fact, to know—the object of analysis in discrete terms and thus to explain cause and effect within that bounded context. It is hard to think of knowing otherwise. But the thing (or things) we try to know, and endeavor to explain, are plural, fragmented, and contested. What might it mean to approach the "policy itself along with all of the texts, histories, people, places, groups, traditions, economic and political conditions, institutions, and relationships that affect it or that it affects?"[79] Our perspective on this vertiginous web is driven in part by the instability of WPS itself, but also by the conditions of coauthorship (and our own separate methodological inclinations), and our ill-disciplined interest in feminist peace (and the traces of disciplinary training that follow us despite our disorderliness).

There is a deep-seated desire to master complexity embedded in the conventional modes of enquiry of International Relations as a discipline. The mythology and institutional positioning of IR as a social science reproduce the fetishization of positivism and render much of the discipline's methodological musings unsuitable for the kind of investigations we present here, or at least make us somewhat uneasy with their use.[80] One dimension of this unease, for want of a better word, is the presumed separation of researcher and the worlds we encounter inherent in much conventional social science methodology. Another is the assumption that "methods" themselves exist separate from the world to which they are "applied," waiting to be used to extract information in the form of data to be analyzed and made meaningful. A third and final dimension relates to the neat and singular linearity that is assumed to characterize the research process, which denies the messy realities of actually existing method: the iterations of research design; the back-and-forth between theory and empirics; the sanitization of the way that our theorizations constitute the empirical worlds we presume to "encounter" but actually "enact."[81]

We therefore follow Haraway in "arguing for politics and epistemologies of location, positioning, and situating, where partiality and not universality is the condition of being heard to make rational knowledge claims."[82] We are *necessarily* situated in our research, and the impossibility of separating our research and professional worlds from our research, professional, and other selves is a condition of our own research process. Our practices of collaboration make this imbrication more evident, as we enact a "we-self" through our writing such that we are not only held in the relational webs of attachment in and to the terrain in/on which we work, but also blur the boundaries between our authorial selves through our written account of the research process.[83] We write over each other, we write to each other in emails and marginal comments, and we thus write a coupled author into being. We find resonance with other accounts of collaborative writing and the constitution of a "writing we" through dissolution first of objectivity then of integrated subjectivity: "our senses of self have become fluid: stutterings, movements, verbs, becomings through writing. Even when one of us is writing we both are writing."[84]

Our writing self is not the only "thing" that is constituted through the research we undertake. Law argues persuasively that method is not "a more or less successful set of procedures for reporting on a given reality. Rather it is performative. *It helps to produce realities*."[85] This runs counter to the wisdom conveyed in hundreds of social science research methods programs, as according to this perspective, methods do not—cannot, in fact—exist independently of the world to which researchers purport to "apply" them. "Methods are instead performative practices experimentally connecting and assembling fragments of ontology, epistemology, theories, techniques and data through which substantive effects are obtained."[86] Recognizing the performativity of methods further connects researchers and their research worlds, as we enact the research world as we encounter it. In this project, this is particularly true, as the process of "connecting and assembling fragments" is how we have moved through the WPS world, necessarily finding ourselves on odd journeys and at a sequence of dead ends.

Our method centers the mess and complexity not only of the "thing" that we study but of the process of studying it. The admission that research *does not* proceed in accordance with neat and linear step-by-step methodologies is usually buried in footnotes or bracketed asides within monographs, if it is revealed at all. By contrast, our thought reversals, our practices of revisiting and revisioning, are (an irreplicable) part of our method. In resonance with "low theory," we seek "theoretical knowledge that works at many levels at once, as precisely one of the modes of transmission that revels in the detours, twists, and turns through knowing and confusion, and that seeks *not to explain but to involve*."[87] We move between knowing and not knowing, planning and enacting, devising and instantiating our WPS ecosystem even now, as we engage in the practice of trying to render the apprehension and actualization of its complexity. This is not (only) the process of producing iterative drafts of a piece of writing (though we do that too), but the method of thinking together, thinking through, and thinking otherwise over time about ourselves, our worlds, and our WPS knowledge. A critical aspect of this back-and-forth, the centering of complexity and the associated recognition that this focus means consistently reevaluating what can be known and how we can know it, is an underlying commitment to the unknowability of the social world in its entirety. We operate in accordance with the belief that "events and processes are not simply complex in the sense that they are technically difficult to grasp (though this is certainly often the case). Rather, they are also complex because they *necessarily exceed our capacity to know them.*"[88]

From the above discussion, we derive two significant commitments. First is a commitment to elaborate method, and to elaborate what we are doing as much as possible. Second is the commitment to center complexity, a commitment that is not borne of a desire to systematize or totalize but rather differently of a political impetus to surface and hold it fast as both object and practice of research. As Law explains,

> Parts of the world are caught in our ethnographies, our histories and our statistics. But other parts are not, or if they are then this is because they have been distorted into clarity. This is the problem I try to tackle. If much of the world is vague, diffuse or unspecific, slippery, emotional, ephemeral, elusive or indistinct, changes like a kaleidoscope, or doesn't really have much of a pattern at all, then where does this leave social science? How might we catch some of the realities we are currently missing?[89]

Like Law, we offer this not in a redemptive sense, or to assert that our partial, situated, and messy undertaking of knowledge production is "better" than any other, but to excavate complexity "all the way down," from concept (of WPS ecosystem) to method (of WPS enactment). Sharing an aesthetic sensibility with Michael Shapiro's transdisciplinary method, for example,[90] Saara Särmä develops a new way of knowing through her work with collage as an "art-inspired methodology."[91] Drawing inspiration from Särmä, we offer not collage as such, but *bricolage*: the construction of an artifact (this book, and the formations of knowledge we present) through the assembly or arrangement of already existing and new descriptions, insights, and practices, often entailing different disciplinary or methodological techniques.[92]

The bricolage method, with its connotations of modeling and materiality, unfolds with diverse tools and modes of encounter, encompassing textual, interpersonal, affective, and aesthetic relations. In resonance with its original appearance in the work of anthropologist Claude Lévi-Strauss, bricoleurs are those who "pick up the pieces of what's left and paste them together as best they can."[93] Similarly, Särmä explains that her collage methodology "works as an engagement with fragmented ways of knowing and scrappy research material."[94] The collage *as process* and the collage *as product* is in keeping with the research mentality we bring to bear on our WPS ecosystem, which is also characterized by "fragmented ways of knowing" and an almost overwhelming array of research material.

Through bricolage we spin an interpretive web. This is not just to say that there is an irreducible quality of judgment and positionality in our argument. Rather, the act of moving across sites of WPS usually treated separately, of juxtaposing the said with the unsaid in official texts, of identifying affinities beyond the agenda and fractures within it, is a conscious step beyond the usual alignment of a research question with a carefully elaborated theory. Though the web is a lattice of connection and relations, it is in one sense *flat*: our initial material is the surface promise and instruction of the resolution and policy document, easily dismissed as a mere veneer on true politics. We work outward from these texts along a relational plane, cataloging the narratives of production, the generative and reductive partiality of policy, the juxtaposition with parallel plans and movements. Commonly, scholars develop a theoretical insight into one possible explanatory mechanism and demonstrate its ramifications in a surprising context: how a new prohibition was created, or a hegemonic logic overcome. Students are encouraged to identify such puzzles and dwell on their significance. Against this background our interest in the WPS agenda is unseemly. We address a domain that cannot yet claim a great transformation of world politics; but neither is it a tentative dream-wish. Our method is so appropriate precisely because WPS is both voluminous and hollow, suspended between irrelevance and accomplishment. We do not excavate the underlying causes of this or that feature of the agenda, as might be done in determining which coalitions are most likely to make progress on a given theme or correlating failures in implementation to resilient institutional dynamics. To do so would be to treat the WPS agenda as the effect of something else. Policy and practice rendered thin and brittle. We are instead infatuated with the dappled, glittering surface of the agenda in its circulation and reinvention. We follow the representational face of WPS; in the process we dissolve the appearance.

Aside from the formal acts of collaboration by which we have, for example, built the datasets of texts we outline below, we have, individually and together, built and consolidated relationships with people, institutions, and archives that enable our research in ways that are particular to us. In one sense, this means that our research is inevitably, even intrinsically, irreplicable: no one can repeat the same conversations that we had in corridors at conferences, sparking ideas about a particular aspect of WPS work to explore; and no research team can reproduce the experience of thinking through the thesis of this book fueled by jet lag and espresso in a cramped London café. But these are strengths, not limitations, of our method and our contribution. Practice theory exhorts the benefits of interwoven and plural ties that form relationships across epistemic communities that transcend boundaries: "the multiple connections of academic research to actors, fields and practice are actually its strength and not a distortion that requires correction."[95] Likewise, we see our multiple personal/professional, and individual/collaborative, connections across our research field as its condition of possibility and its touchstone: we write about a community that is in many senses our own community, which keeps us honest (or so we hope).

In terms of data, we are eclectic, as befits our "radical openness." We have also engaged in interviews and informal conversations about WPS activities and experiences. Our interviews and conversations have explored aspects of WPS practice at different tempos and in earlier studies that did not always take the WPS ecosystem as its ultimate object, going back over a decade. Some of these interviews and conversations are attributed throughout the rest of the book, with the year of recording noted (fourteen interlocutors agreed to be cited in the following chapters, on condition of anonymity). Some of these conversations prepared the way for formal interviews, some inspired new ways of thinking about existing provocations, and some posed new provocations as our inquiry unfolded. These are not formally attributed, nor are they used as the source or credibility backstop for argumentation, but they inform us nonetheless. Further, we have had our own WPS experiences and engaged in our own WPS activities: attending the annual open debates, for example, or offering advice to government on WPS-related programs and policies. We have attended hundreds of discussions of WPS, as the invited "experts" at regional organizations, as observers of civil society initiatives and shapers of practitioner-academic networks, among women's activist circles, in hospitals and police stations, the grand halls of foreign ministries and think-tank drinks receptions, and in a steady stream of research seminars and workshops. These interview and experiential data also form part of the stuff of our analysis, an integral part of the bricolage we construct. We are *doing*, and *undoing*, WPS through our interrogation, excavating its logics and vectors of power, not in an effort to remake or make better, but to show how research practices—as well as the knowledge claims that research generates—are not only premised on, but are productive of, the stability of the "object of analysis."

THE STRUCTURE OF THE BOOK

Following on from this introductory chapter, in chapter 2 we put the WPS agenda into question, beginning the work of conceptualizing the agenda as a policy ecosystem. The primary contribution of this chapter is to distinguish the treatment of the WPS agenda as a policy ecosystem from its treatment as a norm, or normative framework, and as a regime. We explain the advantages of the concept of ecosystem, laying the foundation for the work we undertake in chapter 3, in which we map the ecosystem. As we explain there, our formal delineation of the ecosystem contains 237 documents: 33 from the United Nations; 161 National Action Plans (NAPs); and 43 articulations of international and regional organization policy on WPS (this category also includes a few instances of national WPS policy that are not comfortably categorized as NAPs). We explore many dimensions of this textual surface of the agenda before illustrating the relationship of the WPS ecosystem to adjacent others. Together, chapters 1–3 comprise our theoretical complaint and empirical starting point for the investigations that we present in subsequent chapters.

In each of these remaining chapters (4–7) we focus on elements of the ecosystem. As befits our relational approach, we treat each not as a fixed category of actor, as if the UN contribution plus the national government

contribution plus civil society equals WPS; rather, we show that each combines with others to generate the agenda. Indeed, the sites and fracture
points indicate crucial nodes in the ecosystem, points of transaction and
reproduction, marked as often by fracture as by a successful governance
outcome. Chapter 4 takes as its analytical focus the actors, institutions,
networks, and artifacts that represent the institutional home of the WPS
agenda: the United Nations. This chapter explores the reproductive
dynamics and relational connections that constitute the agenda in this
context; we explore the negotiation and content of the adopted WPS resolutions as a way of elaborating the complexity of feminist peace principles, and engage with other thematic agendas at the Security Council,
including the emergent sexual violence regime, and the Children and
Armed Conflict agenda, as a way of delineating the specific effects of WPS
policy and practice. We also show the ways that WPS moves in the other
UNs—political, bureaucratic, epistemic. Chapter 5 explores the "domestication" of the WPS agenda. The formation and adoption of NAPs for
the implementation of the WPS agenda is a core process within the WPS
ecosystem, and the NAPs themselves core—and generative—products. We
tease out some divisions and distinctions within the NAP population, and
also the embedded tensions within the agenda that emerge through NAP
politics, related to the applicability of the agenda to domestic politics in
general, but especially to the differential recognition of "conflict," the variations of militarism, and the politics of Indigeneity.

The theme of tensions carries over to chapter 6, which investigates fractures in feminist peace politics and practices. We explore significant
points of contestation, including the presumed homogeneity of "civil society," the endorsement by NATO—a military alliance—of what is deemed
to be (by some of its proponents) an antimilitarist agenda, and the erasure of southern agency in representations of WPS expertise. The final
substantive analytical chapter navigates the borderlands of the WPS ecosystem, exploring areas of hybridity and mutation. We focus on just three
examples: the proximity with women's human rights governance through
CEDAW, and in particular General Recommendation 30; the expansion
of rights discourse into other spaces, notably sexual and reproductive
health rights, and rights protections for sexual and gender minority communities; and arms control, the chronic trouble at the heart of feminist
peace activism.

In the concluding chapter, we reinforce the argument we develop throughout regarding the pressing need to forget "the WPS agenda" as such. The ecosystem defies prescriptions of neatness and confounds neat prescriptions. The WPS agenda is a product of feminist peace politics that has been born into an architecture of global governance within which it cannot be contained, and it contains a multitude that cannot be decisively known. "Since many systemic properties are emergent, arising from the relationships and interaction of the parts over time, the whole can be said to be 'greater than the sum of its parts' and thus the dissection of a system into its components, either physically or theoretically, destroys that system and precludes a full understanding of its dynamics and properties."[96] But dynamics and properties can be apprehended, the generative effects of processes can be traced and elaborated, the connections and conduits of knowledge and meaning can be mapped using an approach that is attentive to relationality and reproduction. This is the project we undertake in the pages that follow.

2

BECOMING POLICY ECOLOGISTS

In late April 2019, Nadia Murad addressed the United Nations Security Council during its annual open debate on sexual violence in conflict.[1] Murad had gained an international profile as a courageous and articulate survivor of atrocities carried out by Daesh—the so-called Islamic State—against the Yazidi ethno-religious community during its conquest of northern Iraq five years earlier. In her short speech, she urged the council to end its reliance on slogans and finally prosecute sexual violence and other grave crimes. Accompanying Murad was her lawyer, Amal Clooney, who challenged the council to rise to this, its "Nuremberg moment, its chance to stand on the right side of history,"[2] by finally referring the "situation," as it is known in legal terminology, to the International Criminal Court, or, alternatively, for some council members to circumvent the recalcitrant great powers and set up a hybrid court by other means. The meeting culminated in a new resolution, the ninth in the Women, Peace, and Security series, though the council ignored Murad and Clooney's proposal, opting instead to buttress its previous resolutions with calls to strengthen documentation, training, accountability, and survivor care.

In the year before she delivered her plea in New York, Murad had jointly been awarded the Nobel Peace Prize with the Congolese gynecologist Denis Mukwege for their activism on rape as a weapon of war. The prize—the greatest single totem of moral standing in global politics—is awarded each year by a committee of the Norwegian parliament from funds bequeathed by arms dealer turned humanitarian Alfred Nobel at the end of the nineteenth century. Murad has since lent her name to a set of international standards on documenting sexual violence in conflict, developed in collaboration with a criminal investigation training institute based in the Netherlands and the UK government's Preventing Sexual Violence Initiative (PSVI). The resulting Murad Code was one of several projects funded by PSVI, alongside training for the Malian Armed Forces, resourcing a United Nations team of experts on sexual violence, and grants to civil society programs. Mukwege's foundation subsequently advocated for a new international treaty prohibiting sexual violence along similar lines those concerning the use of chemical and biological weapons, a call taken up then British foreign secretary and subsequently short-lived prime minister Liz Truss during the writing of this book. The PSVI was most famous for its cochairs, former British foreign secretary William Hague and actor, director, and UN special envoy Angelina Jolie, whose films *In the Land of Blood and Honey*, *The Breadwinner*, and *First They Killed My Father* have fed global consciousness of war's gendered burden. Both Hague and Jolie also held roles as visiting "professors in practice" at the London School of Economics, where a Centre for Women, Peace and Security had been partly financed with fines levied on banks for interest rate fraud.[3] A new generation of practitioners and activists received training in WPS there, graduating from one "sister" in an international sorority of such research centers.[4]

Murad's six-minute speech was but one instance in a mosaic of events and relations, institutions and movements, talk and text, united by reference to a form of violence—that which is in some sense *sexual*—occurring in situations categorized as *wartime* or *conflict-related*. The emergence of a global coalition to prevent and punish sexual violence is by now inextricably linked with WPS. Though the attempt to secure accountability for Daesh atrocities through the Security Council deserves close attention in its own right, similar constellations of actors may be found throughout the agenda, working across boundaries of domestic and international, formal and informal, state and society, military and civil, lay and expert, public and private. As well as the national governments that are invariably the target of appeals for resources and action, the WPS circuit runs on an expansive cast of women's groups, humanitarian agencies, freelance consultants, celebrity activists, academics, private philanthropic foundations, lawyers, investigative journalists, religious authorities, intergovernmental agencies, international courts, treaty bodies, think tanks, and military alliances.

Scholars are prone to sorting this variety into categories: some of those engaged with the agenda belong to "epistemic communities," a strata of experts producing influential ideas and information; others are activist members of "transnational advocacy networks" adopting common strategies to agitate for change; there are "norm entrepreneurs" propagating new standards of justice and "antipreneurs" looking to undermine them; rival bureaucracies competing for influence, whether to own or disavow a policy agenda; powerful individuals who seize opportunities to generate new initiatives and funding streams; the "philanthropic power" and "knowledge networks" represented by foundations and think tanks; the "thought collectives" that develop new paradigms of rule; and of course "the state" itself, both as a sovereign entity and as a short-hand for the diverse activities carried out under its cover or in its name.[5] Each of these collectives draws on different sources of authority: an institution they represent, powers delegated to them by states, professional expertise, moral credibility, or their miscellaneous powers of finance and influence.[6]

Further, the various participants act out their roles, constrained by peculiar institutional habits and rules. Diplomats are not (necessarily) professing their inner beliefs but putting into action the formal doctrine of the government of the day; activists are always to some extent accountable to a movement; criminal prosecutors are bound to translate injunctions against gender violence into the protocols of law, however alive they may themselves be to the rival interests of the great powers. These agents do not operate in isolation, but move in relation to each other, to many others: states increasingly fund civil society groups, local and global, sometimes in alliance and sometimes in competition; groups buttress their advocacy with academic research commissioned by foundations and funds; the contributing scholars on occasion become celebrated experts in their own right, with the opportunity to shape strategy or public debate; foundations thereby cultivate the expert communities that develop new policies; social movements make demands for reform, embraced by some governments and denounced by others; taking up the call of justice, international courts operate within the bounds, formal and informal, set by state power.

Importantly, however, "WPS" is less a single mission to which all contribute than a label that obscures significant divisions over the feminist peace. In this chapter, we begin the work of revealing this web of contention through an exploration of the concepts that shape our study of policy and governance. The first section explores the prevailing view of WPS as a norm or normative framework, reviewing the constitutive rules of the agenda as enshrined in resolutions of the United Nations Security Council. These canonical iterations of WPS normativity are the most celebrated proof of the vitality of the agenda, its ability to generate movement and change across the tiers of international politics. WPS protagonists are frequently analyzed in relation to this normative architecture, the interest being how this complex of state and non-state actors strives and stumbles in the course of implementation. A second section sets out the limits of norms as a framework for understanding the multiple practices of WPS. At issue is the tendency of norm scholarship to produce a certain image of progressive change, but also the fissure between the norm as an imagined contract of international society, broadly endorsed and upheld, and the everyday violation of its terms. Generalized critique gains greater purchase in the WPS field, where norms do not cohere in the way they are expected to, and currently do not weigh heavily on state behavior. The diagnosis of a chronic implementation gap is repeated from practically every quarter. In short, nowhere is the motif of failure so evident as in the claims made for the normative achievements of the feminist peace. A final section then previews the alternative concept of the policy ecosystem that is taken up in the next chapter, encouraging us to think otherwise about the agenda itself, and forming the basis for the studies in the remainder of the book.

NORMATIVE HORIZONS

Whether in relation to sexual violence, peace accords, conflict prevention, or disarmament, advocates of the agenda have always understood it as a "conduit for feminist ideas."[7] Though the particulars differ in each case, every WPS specimen may be viewed against this speculative horizon, a near future defined by feminist principles and governed by feminist rules. In the language of IR scholarship, these are *norms*: "standard[s] of appropriate behaviour for actors with a given identity."[8] The language of norms has become both ubiquitous and indispensable. To analyze the emergence

TABLE 2.1 Constituent norms of the WPS agenda

Norm	Standard of behavior	Textual basis*	Mechanism/enforcement	Norm effects
Participation in conflict resolution and peace processes	Women affected by conflict should be represented in the negotiation of peace accords, and in conflict-prevention and -resolution measures. It is increasingly emphasized that representation must be "meaningful."	1325, 1, 8b; 1820, 3, 12; 1888, 16; 1889, 1, 15; 2106, 5, 11; 2122, 1, 7b, 8; 2467, 16d, 20; 2493, 2, 3, 4, 9a	Formal inclusion within negotiating delegations; women's delegations; women mediator networks	Regulative (prescriptive) + constitutive
Women's leadership	Women should be represented in the highest levels of decision making and leadership in the United Nations and intergovernmental processes—for example, as special representatives and envoys.	1325, 2, 3; 1889, 1, 4; 2122, 1; 2242, 8; 2493, 9c	Special envoys	Regulative (prescriptive) + constitutive
Participation in peacekeeping	Women should be actively recruited into and involved in all peacekeeping and peace-building measures. Women's groups should be consulted by UN missions (see also "Protection dialogue").	1325, 4, 15; 1888, 19; 1960, 15; 2106, 14; 2122, 9; 2242, 8; 2467, 23,	Quotas/targets; mission mandates	Regulative (prescriptive)
Women's human rights	Post-conflict institutions must protect and respect the political and civil rights of women and girls.	1325, 8c; 1889, 2, 7, 11, 14; 2493, 5, 6	Women's empowerment programs; anti-harassment measures; Convention on the Elimination of All Forms of Discrimination Against Women	Regulative (prescriptive)

(continued)

TABLE 2.1 Constituent norms of the WPS agenda (*continued*)

Norm	Standard of behavior	Textual basis*	Mechanism/enforcement	Norm effects
Gendered protection	All actors must take measures to protect women and girls from gendered harms and address the particular needs of women; for example, in refugee camps, during resettlement, and in disarmament, demobilization and reintegration programs.	1325, 8a, 9, 12, 13, 14, 10; 1820, 9; 1889, 12, 13; 2016, 16a, 17; 2122, 5, 10; 2467, 13; 16b, 18, 27, 31	National legislation; Convention on the Elimination of All Forms of Discrimination Against Women; Office of the Special Representative of the Secretary-General on Children and Armed Conflict	Regulative (prescriptive)
Protection dialogue	Protection measures should be designed in collaboration with women's groups and affected women. More recently, the United Nations Security Council should be briefed directly by women's groups.	1820, 3, 10, 11; 1888, 14; 1889, 10; 1960, 12; 2106, 21; 2122, 6, 7a; 2242, 1, 5b, 5c; 2467, 19, 21	Consultations; Security Council briefings	Regulative (prescriptive)
Prohibition on wartime sexual violence	All parties to armed conflict must desist from perpetrating sexual violence, and especially take measures to protect women and girls from such violence. Recently, the prohibition has more explicitly recognized men and boys as potential victims of sexual violence.	1325, 10; 1820, 2, 3; 1888, 1, 2, 4, 18; 1889, 3; 1960, 2; 2106, 1, 2, 10; 2467, 1, 5	Military discipline; training in gender and international humanitarian law	Regulative (proscriptive) + regulative (prescriptive) + in parts constitutive
Anti-impunity	Sexual and gender-based violence, as elements of war crimes, crimes against humanity, or genocide, must be prosecuted in national and international courts, addressed in mediations, cease-fires, and peace accords, wherever possible excluded from amnesties, and increasingly result in sanctions against perpetrators.	1325, 1; 1820, 4, 5; 1888, 7, 8a 9, 10, 11, 17; 1889, 3; 1960, 1, 3, 5, 7; 2106, 2, 3, 12, 13; 2122, 12; 2242, 6; 2467, 3, 10, 11, 14, 15, 16c, 25, 26, 30, 33	National and international courts; peace accord provisions; sanctions committees; Office of the Special Representative of the Secretary-General on Sexual Violence Conflict	Regulative (proscriptive) + regulative (prescriptive)

Justice for sexual violence survivors	Holistic justice, responsiveness, assistance, accountability response, latterly reparations.	1820, 13, 14; 1888, 6, 8b, 8c, 13, 15; 2106, 4, 16c, 19, 20; 2122, 10, 11, 13; 2242, 14, 16; 2467, 14, 15, 17, 18	Legal aid; judicial reform; reparations; sexual and reproductive health and rights guarantees	Regulative (prescriptive)
Prohibition on sexual exploitation and abuse	Zero tolerance for sexual exploitation and abuse (SEA) in UN peacekeeping missions. SEA is defined more broadly than sexual violence to include, for example, transactional sex.	1820, 7; 1888, 21; 1960, 16; 2106, 15; 2242, 9, 10. See also separate peacekeeping resolutions (2436 and 2272)	Awareness training; mission accountability mechanisms; UN Office of the Victims' Rights Advocate; withdrawal of troop divisions	Regulative (proscriptive)
Gender perspective	All conflict analysis should be gendered; training and awareness raising for relevant institutions; gender mainstreaming in missions, debunking of myths on gender and sexual violence; appointment of gender advisers.	1325, 5, 6, 7, 17; 1820, 6, 8; 1888, 3, 12, 20, 22; 1889, 7, 8; 1960, 10, 11, 13; 2106, 7, 8, 14, 16b, 18; 2122, 3, 4, 7c; 2242, 4, 5a, 7; 2467, 3, 22, 24; 2493, 9b	Training; gender and women protection advisers; national government initiatives	Regulative (prescriptive) + partly constitutive
Scrutiny	Regular reporting to Security Council, information sharing within UN system; investigating and documenting, especially of sexual and gender-based violence (United Nations and national governments)	1820, 15; 1888, 5, 8, 23, 24, 25, 26, 27; 1889, 5, 6, 17, 18, 19; 1960, 3, 4, 6, 8, 14, 17, 18; 2106, 6, 9, 22; 2122, 2, 15, 16, 18; 2242, 2, 17; 2467, 2, 4, 6, 8, 9, 36; 2493, 7, 8, 10	Secretary-general reports; offices of special representatives	Regulative (prescriptive); coordination norm

(continued)

TABLE 2.1 Constituent norms of the WPS agenda (*continued*)

Norm	Standard of behavior	Textual basis*	Mechanism/enforcement	Norm effects
Sexual and reproductive health and rights	States should provide services to survivors of sexual and gender-based violence without discrimination, maintaining "comprehensive health services."	1889, 10; 2106, 19; 2242, 16; 2467, 16a	Sexual and reproductive health and rights services	Regulative (prescriptive)
Preventing and countering violent extremism	Women's participation, leadership, and empowerment to be integrated into United Nations and member state strategies on countering terrorism and violent extremism. Integrating links with violent extremism into gender perspective.	2242, 11, 12, 13; 2467, 28, 29	UN counterterrorism bodies; National Action Plans on violent extremism and terrorism	Regulative (prescriptive)
Funding	Member states should fully fund all WPS activities.	1889, 9; 2242, 3; 2467, 35	National Action Plans; aid and development instruments	Regulative (prescriptive)
Small arms control	Member states and United Nations entities should ensure women's participation in preventing "the illicit transfer and misuse of small arms and light weapons" (2122, 14).	2122, 14; 2242, 15	Disarmament, demobilization, and reintegration programming; security sector reform initiatives	Regulative (prescriptive)

* Numbers refer to operative paragraphs in UN Security Council resolutions. Each o.p. is only cited once, except in a few cases (e.g., where both prohibition and impunity are mentioned, or where reproductive and sexual health overlaps with other support for survivors).

Source: Compiled by the authors.

of a new standard, or to be surprised at a break from common procedure, is invariably to invoke the existence of a norm. Norms have emerged as "distinct social objects" or "independent quasi-objects" to be categorized and measured, their relative impact evaluated against other pressures like coercion or self-interest.[9] WPS is most commonly seen as a norm or normative framework on these terms, announced to the world in October 2000 and implemented unevenly since.[10] The origin, scope, and status attributed to one or many WPS norms varies: resolution 1325 itself has been described as "a global norm," implying an authoritative legal status, and as "an international norm" for some of its state advocates; but also as just one "expression" of a larger gender-mainstreaming norm, or in its early days as contributing to a "a new normative framework for peacekeeping."[11] The sense of WPS as instead containing multiple sub-elements is signaled in references to it as a "normative framework" or a "norm bundle."[12] Its purchase is both questionable—a "work in progress"—and also settled.[13] In whatever case, the unanimity of the Security Council in passing that first resolution was read as a decisive affirmation of gender equality, demonstrated in the much-cited description of the resolution's passage as a "watershed" moment, the resolution itself "unprecedented."[14]

By a common metric, adoption by more than a third of states indicates that a norm has reached a critical mass, soon to be internalized across the state system.[15] As of early 2023, 107 (or 55 percent) of the 193 UN member states had adopted at least one National Action Plan;[16] WPS may thus be considered a definitive standard of peace and security governance, alive with promise.[17] Radhika Coomaraswamy has recalled, for example, that "resolution 1325 was a big breakthrough in introducing new norms on women, peace and security to an arena that which was a hundred per cent male."[18] For some advocates, the standards of behavior associated with WPS quite simply *are* international law, becoming more authoritative with each subsequent resolution.[19] The vitality proliferates: 2,500 specific commitments have been counted in the first ten *thematic* WPS resolutions alone, implicating more than twenty distinct actors.[20] The ramifications for "country situations" on the council agenda are greater still (see chapter 4). Policymakers celebrate their contribution to a new norm, or its transmission to military settings.[21] UN Women understands itself as preoccupied with a "robust set of internationally agreed norms and standards."[22] Others present from the beginning have viewed resolution 1325 more modestly as one tool among others, if one with an "enthusiastic constituency of women's and peace groups throughout the world."[23]

Despite much-noted failures of implementation, the normative promise persists: the 2015 Global Study—a high-level review commissioned by the UN secretary-general to examine the health of WPS—proclaimed movement toward a normative framework as the agenda's "greatest success."[24] As we were finalizing this text, eight governments due to hold the Security Council presidency in 2021–2022 declared an initiative to "drive forward implementation of the WPS normative framework" in the face of inertia.[25] The language of "framework," moreover, suggests that norms are complementary—the foundations, floor plan, and facade of a single architectural project, or perhaps different outposts rendered in a common style. Though WPS has sometimes been described as a single norm that is either authoritative or in the process of gaining acceptance, it is instead closer to a "bundle" of norms, whose logical and practical relations are subject to considerable dispute.[26] At a different level of abstraction, the agenda might be viewed as one of the largest contributing elements to the "supernorm" of gender equality, a cluster of norms with family resemblances aspiring to "a unified and coherent framework."[27]

Early studies in IR sought to show that norms shaped the instrumental level of policymaking, the foreign policy "interests" of protagonists, and the unquestioned "identities" that established international personhood.[28] *Regulative* norms constrain behavior by defining the limits of the acceptable. They imply rules, and a system of reward and punishment for conformity or violation. The nuclear weapons taboo gives rise to a rule— "do not use nuclear weapons first"—that constrains states even where there are apparently self-interested reasons to ignore it.[29] The prohibition on the use of sexual violence by armed groups is a norm of this sort. Regulative norms are often proscriptive, forbidding or restricting behavior, but may also be *prescriptive* in requiring that states carry out certain actions. By contrast, *constitutive* norms are concerned with fundamental identities, which they confer and express. Where regulative norms govern what may be done, constitutive norms dictate who or what counts in the calculus of action, and why. The classic example is sovereignty, a criterion for whether some assemblage of people, space, and capacity counts as a "state."[30] The constitution of sovereignty involves recognition—in the most practical terms, a formal diplomatic recognition of states by other states—the terms of which are historically specific.

Yet the simplified distinction between regulative and constitutive effects soon runs into difficulty. "Identity" carries many resonances, is inevitably multiple when applied to a nation-state or recognized power, but when understood as a set of characteristics or capacities is at least in part shaped by the pattern of acts carried out in its name. The constitutive threshold implies an accounting of adherence to relevant regulative norms. The diagnosis of a state as "rogue," for example, is determined by reference to more than a scorecard outlining some set of rules, but alludes, rather, to a possible change in ontology: a state that ceases to be a state because of its actions. As Nina Tannenwald argued in the first wave of norms research, it is therefore more helpful to think of the different *effects* that flow from the same standard of conduct.[31] Regulative and constitutive effects combine in policy artifacts, and others have already noted that resolution 1325 contained aspirations at both levels.[32] The expectation of gender-balanced decision making within states can be read as "constitutive" insofar as it sets the parameters of legitimacy and recognition between states.[33] The goal of "participation" is likewise at least partly constitutive, a "metagovernance" norm that instructs on the legitimacy of a process of decision, rather than stipulating a particular outcome.[34] The prohibition on the use of sexual violence by armed groups appears straightforwardly regulative, but also exerts a constitutive effect in underscoring that sexual violence *is* an "international peace and security" issue (e.g., S/RES/1960 2010, o.p. 1; S/RES/2106 2013, o.p. 1), a proposition by no means widely accepted before the passage of resolution 1325.

Table 2.1 sets out our diagnosis of the constituent norms of the agenda as they have been developed in the thematic resolutions of the Security Council. (The council is not the sole source of WPS norms, though it is the most authoritative.) The order in which they are listed indicates their relative importance in WPS discourse, though this should not be taken to mean that their status is settled. The coherence is in important respects an unstable construct, produced through claims and counterclaims, rather than existing as a logical and necessary interrelation of parts.[35] As we will explore in more detail shortly, few if any WPS norms are either universally endorsed or robustly enforced. Our list is unlike others, which emphasize running themes like "participation" and "protection," tending thereby to treat specific new claims for a prohibition or promise as organically foretold by what had come before, a natural evolution where we emphasize moments of disjuncture.

In providing an anatomical chart, we describe standards of conduct expressed through the canonical texts of the agenda and action (how the norm is *expected* to work). For instance, the general principle that women should "participate" has been articulated variously as a standard for high-level decision making within the United Nations, for the recruitment practices of militaries and police forces contributing to peacekeeping, for delegations to peace processes, and for dialogues with local civil society groups in conflict sites. These demands are not equivalent or interchangeable, as is underscored by long-running disputes among states over the reach and content of the principle. As proclamations in favor of gender equality have increased, the question of who is permitted to benefit—the identity politics of "women's leadership"—has become more contentious. Other standards that may appear to naturally cohere—such as the package of proscriptions and prescriptions around sexual violence—generate tensions in practice, where holistic or community articulations of justice may differ from the international criminal prosecution preference of much anti-impunity work. Still others appear marginal in council-approved texts but enjoy attention elsewhere: the funding norm is relatively weak, receiving only a handful of direct references, but is a prominent demand of the WPS circuit in its civil society and academic manifestations, where financing cycles and reporting burdens on the transnational women's movement are as much political as technical complaints. Likewise the scrutiny norm, apparently less fundamental than others but credited with driving changes to a culture of impunity.[36] In short, this list of norms is the aspirational agenda as iterated by coalitions through the council, not to be confused with a systematic architecture, a behavioral commonplace, or a universal ethic.

NORM TROUBLE

When WPS is understood primarily as a bundle of clear regulative norms united by the promise of gender equality, it becomes possible to trace its growth and acceptance among the society of states, and to track the gap between its promise and contemporary reality. The norm object corresponds to a worldview emphasizing the importance of intersubjective expectations, ideas, and beliefs, a "social" fabric of international life. The

perspective is a natural ally of WPS scholars, many of whom readily con-
fess political and practical investments in the feminist project. The language of the norm also helps *produce* the agenda, in that accounts of conduct are never only descriptive but contribute to the sense of its demands
as enduring, legitimate, and in need of an answer. When related as a progress story, the vitality of WPS lies in the struggle for these new standards
of conduct, the transformation of patriarchal rule(s). Yet the norm perspective has a number of limits. Most obviously, given the defining motif
of failure, the aggregated WPS norms simply do not operate as the ideal-
ized image of constraint predicts. The analytical promise of norms is in
parallel marred by the teleological and Eurocentric tendencies of the literature, and by the capaciousness of the norms perspective.

The first troubling of the agenda arises from the relation of its parts,
which are neither as coherent, integrated, or efficacious as talk of *a* global
WPS norm (or normative framework) would suggest. When traced across
two decades of Security Council resolutions, national plans, and reports
on implementation, the core WPS norms may appear robust, reaffirmed
in each iteration and invocation. Repetition is a key resource for advocates
of the agenda, demonstrating the customary legal basis for the agenda and
providing a textual basis for accountability.[37] Diplomats and activists will
comment on how a fragment of language, an invested frame or term, had
been imperiled or rescued in the drafting process (see chapter 4). Participants in the WPS circuit thus articulate an implicit causal pathway from
resolution text to standard of conduct to global internalization or enforcement. But norms that appear settled on paper are deeply insecure, often
ambiguous in their reach and lacking in force. The trouble is not incidental but endemic and reflects the abiding structural paradox of the agenda
as a feminist project operating in conventionally patriarchal spaces.[38] We
will have reason to return to the ambivalence of WPS principles and rules
later on, but here we highlight a handful of normative agenda items where
the gap between norm promise and governance practice is most evident.

Practically every introduction to WPS (including ours) describes four
pillars subtending it: participation, protection, prevention, and post-
conflict relief and recovery.[39] Prevention in the sense of preventing conflict was always a central demand of feminist peace activism, and the link
to gender equality was "one of the most radical components of 1325."[40] Yet
in the text of the resolutions themselves, the prevention "norm" appears
only in constrained forms—in the participation of women in existing

conflict-prevention mechanisms, the prevention of sexual violence implied by the prohibition norm, women's contribution to controlling the spread of *small arms and light weapons only*, and latterly the role of women in preventing "violent extremism"—rather than as a substantive goal on its own terms. Though fundamental to visions of an original or unadulterated peace vision, the prevention of war is barely visible in the policy field.[41]

The initial scope of resolution 1325—covering "all decision-making levels in national, regional and international institutions and mechanisms for the prevention, management, and resolution of conflict" (S/RES/1325 2000, o.p. 1)—encompasses a vast domain of policy and practice. Yet there are instances of participation—such as the number of female parliamentarians in any given country—that are not registered in formal WPS monitoring.[42] More, renewals of the agenda have become increasingly specific about the offices in question—for example, in election preparation and pre-negotiation processes, in donor conferences and demobilization programs, underscoring the lack of consensus over what it means for women to "participate" (S/RES/2242 2015, o.p. 1; S/RES/2467 2019, o.p. 23; S/RES/2493 2019 o.p. 10(b)). That lynchpin of WPS has proven mercurial not just because it instructs in the *process* of decision making, but because its prescriptive regulative effects are only the surface of rival visions of constitutive change. An increase in the recruitment of women to militaries and an increase in women's assignment to diplomatic missions may both qualify as evidence of the participation norm in action, even if the first is correlated with higher levels of conflict and the latter with greater success in negotiating peace. Additional norms plausibly present in the agenda—such as the inclusion of a "gender perspective" in military planning—are more ambiguous still (a point to which we return in chapter 6).

The aspiration to WPS norms—a feminist world order to come—is also at odds with the characteristic of norms that usually captures the interest of IR scholars: their effect in *meaningfully constraining* the behavior of international actors.[43] For many of the canonical international norms—the nuclear and chemical weapons taboos, the global land mine ban, prohibitions against slavery and colonialism—adherence is substantive and widespread, with violations prompting significant response. Other aspiring rules in the realms of human rights, environmental regulation, and aspects of sovereignty are less universal, but deeply ingrained where they are accepted. Some of these nonuniversal norms are sisters to the WPS agenda, such as the norm of female suffrage.[44] But the feminist peace lacks both breadth and depth. There is at best patchy evidence that new standards of conduct have taken hold, and then only in relatively isolated areas of policy. The partiality and failure of norms is a regular refrain for WPS practitioners and observers alike. In the first decade of the agenda, there were only three peace processes where women were signatories and the overall number of women signatories actually decreased.[45] Since 2015, only 6 percent of the signatories to peace agreements have been women, compared to just 11 percent of mediators and 14 percent of negotiators.[46] The number of agreements with explicit provisions relating to gender equality rose in the early stages of the agenda, but have since fallen to the same level as in the 2000–2004 period.[47] Even for women's participation in the armed forces, often cited by critics as the agenda's quintessential subordination of feminism to militarism, there is no general "standard of appropriate behavior" in evidence. In the fifteen years since the United Nations began reporting, the percentage of women deployed on peacekeeping missions as troops, officers, or military experts has barely risen from 1.6 percent to just 6.3 percent.[48] And as several waves of scholars have reminded us, such simple quantitative measures are unlikely to capture the impact, in multiple plausible directions, of women's contributions.[49]

The faltering of actually existing participation has occurred at the same time that diplomatic language has been strengthened by reference to "full" and "meaningful" participation. Clearly, there is not widespread adherence to this norm: women are still excluded from peace dialogues more often than they are included, and they continue to face stubborn barriers in militaries.[50] While many WPS norms are frequently referred to by relevant actors like diplomats, and while the spread of the agenda appears to testify to a broad consensus, these expressions of support do not in themselves indicate deep or lasting changes in behavior. They are prominent discourses of the WPS field, but this is no guarantee of effect. A possible exception may be the anti–sexual violence norm, widely regarded as the area of "prevention" and "protection" where states have expended the most energy, and where norm violations by at least some parties can be met with sanctions.[51]

One way to describe this mix of vitality and failure is to say that agenda norms have significant *validity*—in that they are widely affirmed and circulated—but lack *facticity*—seldom guiding the actions of agents to any meaningful extent.[52] Standards may be institutionalized without being implemented.[53] The language of the norm tends then to mislead, encompassing both those rules that are nearly always followed and those that exist primarily as aspirations; both the normal *and* the exceptional. That some principles are consistently "validated" without becoming embedded in "factual" practice indicates the limits of measuring international social progress primarily by reference to declarations in its favor. The problem is compounded by the inverse phenomenon of standards of conduct that are widely obeyed in practice, but which are not championed as such, what have otherwise been called "hidden" norms.[54] Of special relevance to WPS is the norm against female combat, which is currently more robust than the counter-norm of the full and meaningful participation of women in militaries.[55] Though opponents publicly argue against integration (e.g., on grounds of efficacy, discipline, and/or tradition), these shared expectations are rarely if ever raised to the level of normative declarations of the kind included in Security Council resolutions or issues at intergovernmental summits: the anti–female combat norm "has not been translated into written form and did not engender any kind of legal framework until after World War II. Even then, legalizing the norm has not been widespread."[56]

Though there is likely no truly uncontested norm in world politics, the WPS field is unusually lacking in facticity. Consider a policy norm from a quite different domain: economic governance. A feature of the global trade liberalization program spearheaded by the International Monetary Fund and operating under a universal horizon of conformity to the rule, the currency convertibility norm has been a major plank of the global economic order since the middle of the twentieth century. The norm had to be invented, and it emerged from the failure of quite different systems such as the gold standard and currency sovereignty.[57] Membership in the Bretton Woods order generated legal obligations, codified in formal articles of agreement. Though there may be ambiguities over specific transactions, and while it is possible to distinguish between *degrees* of convertibility, there is no confusion over what the norm requires: the abolition of pre-existing legal barriers and controls on the free exchange of a currency into another currency.[58] That acceptance of the norm grew over a period of decades has stimulated interest in the preparation, sequencing, and legitimacy of norm change.[59]

As with WPS standards, the current account convertibility norm involves subordination of national, even democratic, preferences to a permanent regime empowering international policy experts and supranational organizations. But unlike WPS, the norm is well-demarcated from related others in the same space, is accepted by states on a widespread basis, and is consistently implemented. For *capital* account convertibility, the convergence of national policies around the norm in the late 1980s and 1990s followed a similar pattern. The norm became contested once blamed for the late 1990s Asian financial crisis, while for academic observers its sources functioned as a test case for a constructivism of epistemic communities.[60] But there was, again, no debate about what the norm entailed, with its advocates split only over whether to be gradualist or revolutionary.[61] The puzzling feature of the norm was that it became hegemonic institutionally despite not being strongly advocated by hegemonic nation-states. Viewed alongside other standards of appropriate behavior, WPS norms are therefore unusually weak, and invite different questions: not how they became successful, but rather why they remain so contested; not whether states adopted them from coercion or socialization, but why state adoption is so shallow; and not how they relate to a seismic shift in cultures of security, but why the change they promise is so chronically deferred.

A second source of trouble is the teleological and Eurocentric baggage of norms discourse, and the implications of postcolonial and decolonial criticism for stories of the agenda's progress.[62] Norms research conventionally posits a sequence by which norms take hold among a distinctive class of international actors. In Finnemore and Sikkink's original life cycle model, norm entrepreneurs focused their efforts on states, and it was states as discrete units that were socialized and formed the population in which norms were eventually internalized, generating significant critique of the "whitewashed treatment" of international norm diffusion that most models offer.[63] Given the importance afforded to states in IR scholarship, subsequent research has largely retained an orientating state-centrism, with the extent of WPS diffusion established by reference to the adoption of NAPs.[64] The movement is from the Global North to the Global South (but see chapter 3). At the same time, the agenda is frequently identified with the United Nations as an entity not reducible to its member states, by reference to the decisions of the Security Council as determining what states then implement, but also in detailing the disproportionate involvement of UN agencies and offices in taking up aspects of the agenda, from responses to sexual violence to brokering peace agreements to implementing peacekeeping mandates (see chapter 4).

In both cases, WPS norms are expected to "move" at varying speeds across global space. The image of an ethical injunction or habit of behavior in transit—jumping from one mind to another, transplanted into an institution, imported from a model society elsewhere—is a defining motif of norms discourse. In early iterations, the "cascade" of norms implied imitation of leading states by the broader population of others.[65] Later ideas of "diffusion" and "localization" placed more of an emphasis on horizontal transmission or the reconstruction of norms through situated interests and identities.[66] On occasion the norm cycle can be interrupted by events, drawing scholarly curiosity to the unnatural conditions that prevent stabilization.[67] Especially where norms are associated with progressive or benevolent outcomes, the tendency is to cast them in a developmentalist light, with postcolonial states gradually brought within the orbit of a "world" culture that is always already Western. Today "contestation" opens the field to a multidirectional political process, though often with regard to the same norms as before.

The standard norm travelogue need not venerate hegemonic powers. For example, in Keck and Sikkink's story of suffrage and antislavery movements, dissidents rather than governments are the instigators of radical change. Yet White and Western sources occupy a privileged space in the transnational circulation of standards—for example, "as ideas originating with feminists in the United States and Europe sparked global debate."[68] Invocations of "international society" too often lend themselves to an obscuring of colonial history and colonial difference, mistaking a violent and contested hegemony for the consensual expansion of liberal rule.[69] The legacies of colonial knowledge may indeed obstruct the acceptance or "internalization" of norms propounded by dominant states, even where these appear congruent with the struggles of movements within the Global South.[70] The lens of "localization" can allow agency for a larger number of actors, but continues to presume a settled end state, and does little to trouble assumptions about who generates norms or how change occurs. The "gap" within WPS is not only that between declaration and delivery; WPS narratives are also implicated by how they locate failure, and the origin stories they tell about vitality.

The image of civilization is a feature of both practice and analysis. States in the Global North treat their NAPs on WPS as external facing, matters of defense, security, and aid, while the Global South becomes the laboratory or implementation site of the agenda, necessitating various internal reforms (see chapter 5).[71] At the same time, scholars can take the appearance of detailed policy texts as proof of a deep dedication to gender equality projects, tracking the diffusion of WPS over time from a European core centered on Scandinavia and western Europe outward to lagging adoptees. Where the agenda is figured as a product of international organizations, the direction of movement remains, with the wellspring of "the international" (here, the United Nations Security Council, and particularly the Western powers within it) feeding "the national" (government plans and strategies) and finally reaching "the local" (commonly conflict-affected spaces but also specific institutions like national militaries). Experts and epistemic communities overwhelmingly based in the Global North then act as necessary facilitators of diffusion and adoption.[72] The common vocabulary for WPS as an interstate process bolsters this anthropomorphization or personification of the state, as if there are homogenous and distinct actors who "champion" the agenda or resist it, who are "friends" or "enemies" of the feminist peace (language we mimic at points in what follows). Where the expected sequence is not observed, it becomes all too easy for scholars to impute either a "failure" of socialization or the presence of some obtuse local proto-norm, rather than figuring with the autonomous values and reasoning of others.[73]

Postcolonial critiques of the reigning constructivist paradigm do not on the whole dispute that norms exist in the shape of intersubjective ideas of proper conduct or beliefs about what it is right to do in international politics. Nor need they imply that norms are always artifacts of hegemonic power. Norms may be radical and revolutionary as well as narrow and technical. There are norms against colonization and slavery, and in favor of national self-determination. Though whiggish histories of gender equality are arguably most common, the emergence of a norm like suffrage may be examined as the combined effect of distinct struggles animated not by imitation but by political sources specific to their time and place.[74] The expansion of the self-determination norm in the age of decolonization (or, put otherwise, the growth of a new and robust anticolonial norm) has been attributed to the interaction of anticolonial resistance movements, the delegitimization of racism, changing domestic opinion, and the advent of "trusteeship."[75] Though some of these factors were liberal in character, or took effect primarily in the imperial metropole, the emergence of the norm cannot be explained without attributing significant agency to insurgents, dissidents, and rebels.

As we show in the coming chapters, the prevailing idea of gender equality norms as diffusing uniformly from the West is complicated by the sequence of policy adoption, the role of feminist movements in the Global South in the prehistory of resolution 1325 and in the development of the agenda, and by resistance to key elements of the feminist peace at its supposed origin points. WPS norms are met with resistance, but are also repurposed and reinvented in ways that reflect specific feminist mobilizations and variants of feminism.[76] The point, then, is not to reject WPS as a neocolonial imposition, or as simply functional for great power interests, as is sometimes proposed.[77] Rather, the agenda in its multiplicity is embroiled in the same tensions and legacies as other forms of governing, whether or not these are strictly regarded as norms. Transnational campaigns to end violence against women; explanations for violent conflict; the construction of international law; military and police interventions; standard-setting for domestic institutions; the very idea of a global feminist movement—all have been implicated in reproducing the discourses and practices of imperial and colonial order.[78] Removing the "epistemological blinkers" of much norm research therefore allows for greater recognition of hybridity and entanglement, an agency and presence beyond the "localization" of standards forged in the metropole.[79]

Both the accumulated ambiguities of the agenda and the broadly liberal style of much norm argumentation relate to a third limiting feature: the capaciousness of norm discourse. It has long been an issue that "norm" has conflicting meanings, variously denoting dominant practices (a "behavioral norm"), expectations shared among participants, even if these are not justified in ethical terms and not consistently observed (a "standard of behavior"), and a kind of ethical proposition that may or may not be widely shared by others (a "normative belief").[80] These ambiguities—which persist in the framing of WPS norms—produce a sense of "working in a conceptual cloud."[81] In response to criticisms of the norm concept as reified or static, an increasingly specific scholarly vocabulary classifies rules according to those that are "robust," "degenerating," "contested" (discursively or behaviorally), "localized," "dynamic," "static," and so on. In one sense, the all-encompassing norm perspective prompts a recognition of world politics as thoroughly *social*, constituted at every point by intersubjective expectations and judgments, a world of ethical choice and collective identities rather than a stark theater of brutal calculation. But capaciousness is also overdetermination: a flattening of world politics into endless variations on a theme.

The recent spate of writing on norm contestation foregrounds the flux of activity around norms: standards are not settled, but debated, extended, undermined, and revised in an ongoing process that unfolds across multiple sites. Yet it is no longer clear whether it is always "norms" in the same sense that are being studied. Where norms once entailed fundamental agreed rules, ideational and cognitive, they now also subsume practices, even if "practice" is often analyzed only as a style of enunciation. As well as socialized or internalized rules, interest-based calculations by states have been described as a form of "contestation" rather than as violation or evidence of noncompliance.[82] "Contest" here means to bring a different ethical argument or experience to bear so that a norm's ultimate shape is the product of the negotiation of these rival versions of the same idea; but to "contest" is also to break away from, instrumentalize, or violate in ways much closer to the sort of "rational actor" explanation that preceded the turn toward norms. It thereby becomes possible to triangulate any given event or utterance in normative space, to include every idea about conduct that might generate argument, but also to refer to all those standards of behavior that are taken for granted, every act understood as conformity to or rebellion against a norm.

Consider a recent work on WPS norms. Beginning with the norm not as a distinct social object but as the locus of a political struggle for recognition, where the goal is to show how agents with differing opportunities react to pressures or fight for new values, Antje Wiener consciously offers a "global" alternative to norm parochialism. Like ours, the project is attentive to the reproduction of meaning in iteration and to a shifting cast of characters.[83] WPS—read as effectively identical to the prohibition on wartime sexual violence—is examined as a new fundamental norm, a core constitutional rule of global order. Norms can have a formal character (as officially declared) but are also validated by stakeholders in social form (through habits in a group) and culturally (once part of individual background practice).[84] An intricate typology distinguishes by level, scale, moral reach, and impetus, illustrated by the development of the agenda in the Security Council and the visibility offered by William Hague as the first head of the United Kingdom's Preventing Sexual Violence Initiative. It thus becomes possible to study the "normative opportunity structure" and "normative meaning-in-use" purely at the level of diplomatic practice and official semantics—that is, without reference to whether shifts in the discursive terrain of summits and speeches correspond to effects elsewhere—even as the framework recognizes that unequal access to deliberative space confounds both the global "multilogue" and local ownership. And because all utterances—and even all practices—contain an inescapable normative dimension, the politics of WPS becomes synonymous with the diplomacy of WPS.[85]

In short, norms have become a meta-frame that crowds out other interpretations and questions. Newly attuned to the instability of norms, our fellow researchers may see no contradiction in studying WPS as *both* a sufficiently coherent architecture of shared standards of behavior and an internally differentiated and contested field. For example, in their model of a norm *circle* of emergence, stabilization, and contestation, Park and Vetterlein sketch an endless unfolding, where contestation precedes emergence rather than just punctuating stability.[86] Apparently established norms can in turn be shaken by failure, uncertainty generated by some external shock, or changing public sentiment.[87] While such dynamism will doubtless shed light on sub-stations of the WPS circuit, it confronts in our case the pluralism of normative structure. The constitutive norms of the agenda derived from the Security Council resolutions do not progress at the same pace and are crowded in by the addition of new topics and demands, from climate change to cybersecurity.

The pluralism of the agenda is matched by its instability. A normative field may be characterized by contestation over the specificity of the rule(s); the appropriate authority to enact them; the means of implementation; the mechanism of enforcement; the extent of state adherence; dissent and revision of the norm following some inflection point; or its interaction with other norms and embedded practices. Scholars focus on one or other point in this arc. Often this means attending to the "how" over the "what" of norms, a decree of efficacy and success being the starting point.[88] Yet for WPS, the volatility is especially deep-seated, with the agenda characterized by contestation across all of these dimensions at once. The agenda is an archipelago in the midst of a constant tempest. Even where the thicket of rules is densest—where a country has entrenched special offices, departmental protocols, dedicated funding streams, gender committees, and civil society liaison groups—it is nevertheless precarious. Past adherence is no necessary guide to future practice, and no guarantee that the same topics and priorities will persist. Only where WPS is codified in domestic legislation is there any binding commitment, and even here it is only required that a national plan is generated, not that it enforces certain standards.[89]

Though WPS scholars and practitioners are keenly aware of the differing ways in which the agenda may be mobilized, the implications of tensions in meaning and use have generally not led to a reconsideration of norms as the ultimate horizon of WPS practice. We, too, are led to refer to norms, for the pragmatic reason that many advocates speak of WPS as a program of standards and rules of conduct, and because of the term of art's embeddedness in a scholarly conversation about change in international politics. There remain, however, compelling and mutually reinforcing reasons to think *beyond* the norm framework, with its chronic ambiguities over content and practice and its tendency to a reified and singular view of agreed standards diffusing from a liberal center. As we will have occasion to stress again, WPS is *not* an agenda defined by strong rules, broad socialization, or robust enforcement. To grasp this field of contention, we propose not a successor theory, but an alternative model that opens a broader horizon of production, reproduction, disruption, and contestation.

TOWARD THE POLICY ECOSYSTEM

To sidestep the accumulated tensions of the norm perspectives, we approach the agenda otherwise and draw from ecology to theorize the contested field of policy. Instead of evaluating WPS as a consolidated norm architecture or framework, or mapping the agenda in terms of the scale and location of its failure, we define the WPS *policy ecosystem* as the field of activities, actors, and artifacts interacting in the name of "Women, Peace, and Security."[90] The criterion for inclusion in the ecosystem is performative: WPS agents are those agents that say they are doing WPS. In our conception, an ecosystem always involves this referential quality, *an acting in the name of.*[91] We are not decisively or monolithically naming a sphere of activity but seeking to capture a relation. The WPS policy ecosystem is moreover not synonymous with "feminist international politics" or "gendered security practice." It is one field within that wider landscape, or a practical manifestation to be analyzed with those theoretical frames. The borders of the ecosystem are porous: agents enter and exit as they mobilize the language of the agenda. This carries the implication that there are actors addressed by WPS policy—because they are mentioned in the resolutions, named by the secretary-general, investigated by commissions and researchers, or targeted by activists—who are nevertheless not members of the WPS circuit or inside the WPS ecosystem when they deny or ignore the agenda.

The ecosystem is a complex intersection of circuit and field containing a multitude, akin to the "bestiary" of entities that set the parameters of scholarly inquiry.[92] Given the porosity and fluidity of the ecosystem model, these activities, actors, and artifacts include, but are not necessarily limited to, diplomats, celebrity humanitarians, protocols, policies, guidelines, advocacy campaigns, manifestos, the offices of special representatives, bureaucrats, activist networks, social movements, institutions, training manuals, government ministries, journalistic dispatches, communities, and individual citizens and subjects.[93] The ecosystem is not the terrain only of states, or the operating space of international organizations, but remains constitutively open.[94] The field confers purpose, the sense of some agent acting for or against a tendency of the feminist peace. But as a reservoir of discourse and sedimented memory, the field of the agenda—its pillars and themes, emerging concerns and forgotten arguments, jargon and manifestos—is more than a permission slip for action by its inhabitants. In eschewing the norms perspective, we do not substitute an instrumental sense of WPS as an excuse for self-interest or a mere ideological cover. Referentiality weighs heavily and uneasily. The ecological perspective is expansive, and locates the discrete object of "policy" (a given text issues by some recognized authority) in a relational web, taking in "the policy itself along with all of the texts, histories, people, places, groups, traditions, economic and political conditions, institutions, and relationships that affect it or that it affects."[95]

There are four advantages to the ecosystem model. First, there is the recognition of a potentially confounding diversity: an ecosystem consists of multiple organisms and features of various types coexisting in different and relational connection to one another.[96] The plurality of policy as ecosystem is inherent and not reducible to success or failure against any one metric. There are multiple agents within the circuit, all of which have different and even competing needs and interests, and which make different and sometimes conflicting contributions. The relationship between the agents and the environment (or "structure," for the more traditionally minded) is one of mutual constitution, reaffirmed and re-visioned through the dynamism of the ecosystem. More specifically, these processes reproduce not only the system as a whole but also the elements or components within it, in and through iterative repetitions that mutate, gently shift, deliberately revise, subvert, or faithfully render the assumed "original" that was always multiple. Reproduction has a number of cognitive affinities or associations for our purposes: there is mimesis, the attempted replication of a particular object or set of practices (although some slippage always occurs between the original and the replication); recombination, the intergenerational transference of characteristics and qualities (temporal transformation, genetic markers/memories, heritage, and antecedents); labor, the processes through which political artifacts are maintained and nourished; and discursive practice, the textual dimensions of meaning-making and fixity/stabilization. This list is, of course, neither exhaustive nor exclusive: there is overlap between the different registers of reproduction. Reproduction indicates not just a map but a family tree, a genealogy and history.

Second, interpreting policy ecologically encourages us to think holistically. Scholars might focus on any one component at a given moment, but conceptualizing policy as ecosystem encourages us to keep the emergent whole in mind even as we engage closely with its parts. Again, the whole casts a shadow: claims are continually being for and against "WPS" and "the agenda." The "field" of the ecosystem always implies interaction in space (an office, on either end of a fiber-optic cable, on a military exercise, in a brief and hushed conversation behind the main stage), but not therefore a strictly designated location like the UN, nor one side of a dichotomous pair, as happens in the idea of the authentic and immediate knowledge that comes from the "field" in research. The term resonates with the arenas in which WPS happens: a field of action; a field of play; a training field; the organizational field;[97] fieldwork; and the field of power relations.

Third, conceptualizing policy through ecology also keeps us attentive to the borderlines and boundaries between different policy ecosystems and non-policy domains. By delimiting the ecosystem in terms of those actors that explicitly name their work as WPS, or are invoked by others as doing WPS, we exclude mobilizations for gender equality or otherwise derived from feminist principles that do not take up the agenda's terminology, even though they are evidently related to the WPS ecosystem, caught in the same entanglements (see chapter 1). Ecosystems overlap. As we explain in the next chapter, we can relate the more open form of the ecosystem to other governance structures like regimes, and to other cognate ecosystems. In some cases, the links between ecosystems are obvious, and are the topic of commentary, as with the concentration on women's rights as a focus of the human rights ecosystem. In others, such as the climate change regime, the mutual implications are underexplored. We explore these boundaries not to deny the specificity of WPS—a specificity that obtains as much in the claiming of a common mission than in any provable reality of one—but to show how the specificity is produced, how it is governed.

Acknowledging this topography also illustrates the potential utility of the ecosystem model beyond WPS. The "Responsibility to Protect" field of practice, or R2P, as it is widely known, is an example of a proximate ecosystem in contact with WPS that might fruitfully be subjected to ecological analysis. R2P emerged in the early 2000s in response to the inability of the international community to prevent and respond to genocide and mass killings in Rwanda and Bosnia, which were perceived as failings of the United Nations system of security governance.[98] The concept was formulated in the report of the International Commission on Intervention and State Sovereignty and embedded in UN architecture through the adoption of the outcome document of the 2005 World Summit by the General Assembly, in which R2P was expressed in the "4 crimes, 3 pillar" configuration that has somewhat come to dominate, though important elements of contestation over this structure remain.[99] Like WPS, R2P has been debated in terms of whether and how it functions as a norm in world politics,[100] whether and how it is or should be enacted by the UN Security Council,[101] and whether it reflects or reproduces hierarchical power arrangements within and between states.[102] Also like WPS, R2P is sustained and reproduced by an extensive and diverse array of advocates, research centers, committed diplomats, state leaders, think tanks, policy documents, and UN entities, and yet—still more like WPS—R2P's limited traction and implementation shortfalls are often lamented.[103] Despite these superficial similarities, the dynamics of the R2P ecosystem, if it is to be conceptualized in those terms, would require more detailed examination. We gesture to R2P only as an example of another complex governance system that can be traced in terms of its linkages with other policy domains and delineated as a porous yet bounded entity that it (re)produced through its enactment and documentation.

The fourth and final advantage is that the broadened horizon, taking in features beyond the policy artifact itself, allows for an examination of less obvious or hidden aspects of the agenda. For understandable reasons, the analysis of the agenda to date has focused heavily on policy texts, assessing fidelity to the agenda by the presence or lack of pillar language, and the degree to which drafters meet the original radical promise of feminist peace. We, too, deal in this explicit surface of policy—its lexicon and matrixes—in the next chapter, which also serves as our introduction to the products of the Security Council, national governments, and other agents of the agenda. But by considering what is around and behind policy texts—their environment—we are able to critically interrogate the conditions of their production, the constituencies co-opted and excluded, the opportunities not taken, the fracturing sense of what WPS is and could be. Ironically, given our interest in text and discourse, we sidestep the norm perspective partly because it leaves so little space for an examination of what happens in and beyond policy except as an index of failure.

There are potential pitfalls in using a naturalist metaphor.[104] Our understanding of ecology is not evolutionary or teleological. While we seize on reproduction as a lens through which to study the politics of difference and the labor that is expended in perpetuating WPS, we do not argue that WPS is organically improved over time, nor that it automatically becomes more complex or sophisticated. The parameters of the ecosystem are not set in advance by inherent features but arise out of the relational interaction of the actors and entities within it, who are included by virtue of their own claims for themselves as advocates, implementers and critics of WPS, or by the status in the WPS ecosystem that they are ascribed by others. The ecosystem concept offers an exploratory frame; we develop the concept to include relations and reproductive effects otherwise commented on in isolation, permitting a close reading of WPS sites both familiar and strange that does not decide in advance the ultimate horizon of WPS practice.

The risk is that what we gain in comprehensiveness we lose in explanatory specificity. For each creature in the ecosystem there is a niche, and a possible investigation of causes and dynamics: Why did this government adopt the agenda at a given time and in a given way? What explains the emergence of novel themes and the refusal of others? How might we track who is being marginalized and who is ascendant? The rationale for a sustained examination of one part or other of WPS is that specificity permits detailed analysis and potentially the development of general causal claims: looking only at advocacy networks, or courts, or states, it is possible to comment on their particularity and to challenge settled ideas of cause. The turn to ecology does not refute such studies—it is instead an awkward cradle in which more granular explanations may coexist, and we draw eclectically on these perspectives. Our studies in the coming chapters take in too many corners of the ecosystem to sustain any one such focus, even as the ecosystem concept encourages them. While we engage some of the key debates in the field—over securitization, co-optation, hybridity, and hierarchy—we do not develop parsimonious accounts at the length some may wish. Our wager is that we are able to say enough of interest about the ecosystem at large to make up for it. Our elaboration begins in the following chapter.

3

MAP, TERRITORY, TEXT

T he vitality of "Women, Peace, and Security" as a political agenda, its global circulation and articulation, reflects the breadth of its scope and the ambition of its elements. As the last chapter set out, the agenda is much more than a set of technical provisions. The common sense of WPS as a package of norms is undermined by the degree of contention around fundamental principles and their operationalization across different sites (sites to which we turn in the chapters to come). In approaching WPS as an ecosystem, we have also drawn attention to a universe of practice and relational connections behind and beyond the canonical international and national pledges. These are topics for dedicated chapters to come. In this chapter, we lay out our map of the policy surface of the agenda, the critical coordinates for who and what WPS is.

An ecosystem is necessarily spatial: an area within which the elements of the ecosystem are contained, and which borders/is bounded by other governance domains. Global governance at large has been described as "the sum of myriads of configurations of shifting actors engaging and disengaging in different issues," and multiplicity is today widely accepted as a condition of possibility for agendas from sustainable development to criminal justice.[1] In the two previous chapters we gave reasons for going further still, to explore the relationality behind institutionalization, and to do so with a sensibility attuned to the necessary mess of the WPS world. In speaking of a policy ecosystem, we indicate both a literal and figurative distribution. As a matter of location, the agenda is negotiated, resisted, propagated, and made operational in spaces—most obviously the chamber of the United Nations Security Council in New York (though the fundamentals are agreed long before the "debates" happen), but also foreign ministries, peacekeeping headquarters, community consultations, international tribunals, military think tanks, and so on—each of which is organized according to different protocols and cultures.[2] The space between agents of the feminist peace—their positionality, perspective, senses of mutual understanding or alienation—is also relational, given by the rival conditions of their formation, even if collaborations take place in the same building. With the ecosystem model comes the idea of WPS as having territories and an exteriority, both contoured by the twin dynamics of vitality and failure.

This is the terrain that animates this chapter: we chart the WPS ecosystem by mapping out actors, policies, and relational connections to show how the agenda is reproduced, alongside those proximate systems that nourish and are nourished by it. As noted in the previous chapter, the ecosystem comprises the circuit—the agents of the agenda, nodes both governmental and not, creating energy when connected—and the field in which it is cradled—a flow of discourse and practice, the emergent tendencies of contention and assembly. The circuit involves transactions among what have been called "global governors": "authorities who exercise power across borders for purposes of affecting policy. Governors thus create issues, set agendas, establish and implement rules or programmes, and evaluate and/or adjudicate outcomes," with two provisos: that the division between external and internal rule is unstable, and that our initial *policy* map in this chapter does not include *all* such governors (civil society and to some extent academic governors are discussed in later chapters).[3] The field is more than what the governors say about WPS. In line with theorizations of productive power, discourses are both diffuse and constitutive, obeying no single authority and helping to establish the identities of agents.[4] For this map we are again concerned with formal properties of the field, meaning those rhetorical nodes that cross the threshold of codification as policy. The circuit is the "who" of WPS policy, the field the "what."

This mapping is an important first offering in laying out the processes of reproduction and relational constitution, complemented by an

elaboration of proximate and overlapping ecosystems in the second section of this chapter. In subsequent chapters, we take up some of these
generative, germinal moments of constitution and connection to identify
the emotional and care labor of civil society, the conscious crafting of
national projects, the mobilization of machineries of government and
governance organizations—different vectors and valences of embedding or attachment, degrees of failure. These WPS practices shape and
form the agenda in plural and disruptive ways; the production of a co-
opted or instrumentalized or bastardized version of WPS is a face of failure, as is the reproduction of a narrow, limited, static WPS. Contestation
that might seem to signal the "failure" of WPS as it is constricted, manip-
ulated, or reneged on can also represent a moment for the introduction
of new life, new "issues," the energy of a counter-hegemony on the terrain created in earlier moments. We use the map as a starting point for
inquiry into what lies behind policy, as it guides us through and around
the field of practice that we interrogate throughout the book, serving as
an outline for an extended investigation that is both archaeology and
assemblage, or bricolage.

MAPPING WPS

The Women, Peace, and Security agenda contains a multitude. Even before
considering the range of actors now engaged with it in some way, there
are numerous documentary artifacts that lend themselves to interrogation as part of an investigation into WPS (re)production. As an opening
move, we examine the totality of *policy texts* as the canopy of the agenda—
the nodes of governmental authority and discourse that represent the
official face of WPS, and which are sometimes mistaken for it. An aerial
view allows us to identify the major flora and fauna of the ecosystem, and
to track changes in their vibrancy over time, though we are also liable to
miss the diversity of the undergrowth, the liveliness on and below the surface. The agenda *as policy* is situated in a dense and contested web of
global gender politics that finds expression in innumerable other forms,
as the circuit includes experts, movements, civil society groups, and nongovernmental agents who power the agenda without the protocols of

sovereignty. Nongovernmental WPS is as populous as its official counterpart. Consider a text beyond our policy map: an open letter on the twentieth anniversary of resolution 1325, submitted to all ambassadors to the UN by 558 separate activist groups, ranging from such recognizable names as Oxfam and Amnesty International to diverse local groups with a minimal online footprint. Such landscapes of WPS practice cannot be captured in strategic documents; many manifestos for a feminist peace will not bear codification as distinct policy. We track the impact of some of these practices in later chapters. Nor does the canopy map include every governance mechanism implied by policy: we exclude the technical quotas, specialized funds, implementing offices, or evaluative reports that follow, each of which might exhibit its own governance logic. The map we present here is only of the most obvious and explicit level of the WPS ecosystem, one of many imaginable and not the last that we will explore.

WHO DOES WPS

Our map surveys the major attempts to implement the agenda between 2000 and 2020, with the body of WPS documents organized into three categories.[5] The first category covers 33 documents from the United Nations system, comprising the Security Council's WPS resolutions, statements by the presidents of the council, and key initiatives from outside the council, such as General Recommendation 30, issued by the Committee on the Elimination of all forms of Discrimination Against Women (the "UN system" subset).[6] Second, we include every available National Action Plan released until 2020, representing the fullest survey yet assembled, and including some plans translated into English from their language of origin for our analysis (the 161-strong "National Action Plan" subset).[7] Third, we take what we believe to be the most comprehensive collection of international and regional organization policy on WPS, as well as those few cases where national policy has been made outside of the context of a NAP, such as the U.S. Congress's Women, Peace and Security Act of 2017 and Canada's "Feminist International Assistance Policy" (the "regional and other WPS" subset).[8] There are 43 such documents in this first iteration of our dataset, for a combined total of 237 WPS policy documents across the three categories. We filtered documents on the basis of four criteria: (1) explicit reference to WPS (as a term or via thematic Security Council resolutions); (2) the inclusion of policy language declaring or mandating action with some specificity; (3) issued by a national, regional, or international government entity; and (4) falling within our 2000–2020 time frame (for details, see appendix 2).

Apprehending the governmental circuit in this way immediately reveals several features of note. First, the sheer volume of WPS policy underscores its success as a technical language of governance. To the extent that policy documents give expression to the norms we outlined in the last chapter, the weight of WPS policy demonstrates the *validity*—that is, the public affirmation, regardless of enforcement—of at least some feminist rules among a significant and growing number of actors in the formal international system. This point is well-known to WPS scholars but is underappreciated in the wider literature on global governance. Documenting the volume of WPS policy also reveals that "WPS" resides in and is determined by no single document, even a document with the authority provided by the imprimatur of the UN secretary-general or Security Council. Our map establishes that states are complemented by a diverse collection of institutions—some domestic, some supranational—that implement the agenda in ways that may involve symmetry or divergence, and where the identity and motives of contributing parties are not always evident. For example, the United Kingdom, under its last five governments (involving all three of the country's main political parties), has been engaged with the agenda through a permanent seat on the UN Security Council (where the United Kingdom is the "penholder," or the state that leads negotiations and drafting, on the agenda at large); as a producer of the United Kingdom's NAPs on WPS (of which there have now been five); as a major power in the North Atlantic Treaty Organization (NATO) and member of its Euro-Atlantic Partnership Council, which agrees the NATO WPS policy; until 2019 as a member of the European Union, where overarching WPS strategies are passed by the Council of Ministers; and since 2012 through the Preventing Sexual Violence Initiative, which contributes to national WPS objectives, but also sits somewhat apart—not to mention the input of officials in influencing other governments' WPS strategies, the contribution of UK finances to WPS initiatives, or the role of nonstate WPS experts to some extent supported by British funds or patronage in the global policy circuit.

Second, we are able to track *when* WPS gained traction across various levels and domains. The number of policy artifacts of all kinds produced each year steadily rose between 2000 and 2010, followed by years of stability at a reduced level before another uptick and plateau from 2017 onward (see figure 3.1).[9] The end of the first decade of WPS appears to mark a shift, but in the formal terms of norm diffusion, the "tipping point" of a third of states adopting WPS policy comes in October 2016, with

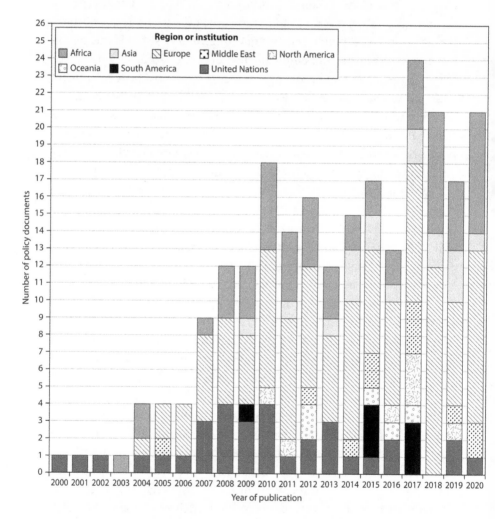

FIGURE 3.1 Number of WPS policy documents produced by year (*n* = 237).

Source: Graph by the authors.

Timor-Leste's first NAP.[10] Though establishing the sequence in which plans were released does not in itself explain how and why WPS took hold, the trajectory for each category of documents confirms the broad consensus view of when the agenda consolidated and the importance of anniversary dates in stimulating policy announcements (see figure 3.2).[11] But it also reveals the early role of some states that have subsequently been less visible in WPS discourse, and demonstrates that regional and non-NAP national initiatives have become more common in several regions outside the Global North or West.

Third, by subdividing the documents produced each year by the type of entity that produced them, we confirm that it was *states* in particular that proliferated WPS policy artifacts after 2010; the activity of member states (including "national government" and "national government non-NAP" in figure 3.2) accounts for the greatest increase in WPS policy documents. More recently, states have implemented WPS outside the context of NAPs, through bespoke government initiatives and occasionally legislative action, which create parallel mandates for the agenda. The "domestication" of WPS is thus confirmed as a key feature of the ecosystem (see chapter 5).[12]

Fourth, we note that the geography of WPS is more complex than is often appreciated. While the first NAPs were issued by European governments (and specifically "good citizen" states like Denmark, Norway, and Sweden),[13] the earliest policy document to take up the mission of resolution 1325 outside the UN was the Maputo Protocol to the African Charter on Human and Peoples' Rights on the Rights of Women in Africa, agreed by the African Union in 2003, followed by the Solemn Declaration on Gender Equality in Africa and the Dar-es-Salaam Declaration on Peace, Security, Democracy and Development in the Great Lakes, both in 2004. Although in all three cases references to WPS are fleeting in comparison to what followed, they point to a larger pattern of early adoption. Between 2000 and 2010 (the first half of our period of analysis), African regional organizations account for seven of the fifteen policy documents issued beyond member states and the UN.[14] The first brace of NAPs outside of Europe was also located in Africa (Côte d'Ivoire and Uganda in 2008, Guinea and Liberia in 2009). Again, this chronology alone does not answer the critique of WPS as a project of White feminism or as implicated in neocolonial hierarchies (see our discussion in the previous chapter, and

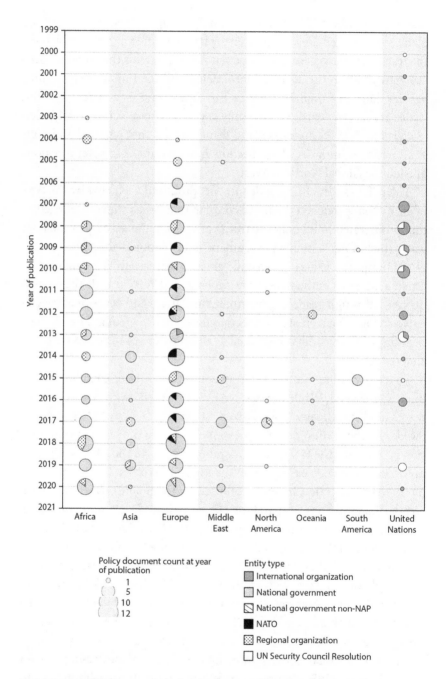

FIGURE 3.2 WPS documents, by issuing entity and location (2000–2020).
Source: Graph by the authors.

also the analysis in chapter 5, pp. 137–148, and chapter 6, pp. 153–154 and 166–175). Instead, it establishes coordinates for the agenda outside of the narrow diffusionist model, opening up questions about the terrain of reproduction and contestation.[15]

The African sources of WPS also left their trace in the content of early policy. As well as the foundational role of Namibia in the first Security Council resolution (discussed in chapter 4), groups like the Mano River Women's Peace Network served as exemplary cases in the power of feminist mobilization against war (Liberia NAP I 2009, 31; Sierra Leone NAP I 2010, 6, 10; ECOWAS Plan 2010, 3, 12). Operating across Guinea, Liberia, Sierra Leone, and Côte d'Ivoire from early 2000, the network pursued disarmament and mediation in the conjoined Liberian civil wars, succeeding in convening parties outside of the UN umbrella.[16] Along with other women's groups like the Women in Peacebuilding Network, it was one initiator of mass action commemorated in the internationally acclaimed documentary *Pray the Devil Back to Hell*, becoming an observer to negotiations, a signatory witness to the Liberian peace accord, and in 2003 a winner of the United Nations Human Rights Prize.[17] As well as its appearance in West African national and regional WPS plans, the Mano River women have been cited as a precursor of resolution 1325 (S/PRST/2001/31, 1; S/2004/814 2004, 6; Sierra Leone NAP I 2010, 7), and as perhaps the leading early example of the transformative power of women's activism.[18]

In the first years of the agenda, the network was repeatedly named in open debates on WPS at the Security Council, at once a reminder of why 1325 existed and a proof of what it could achieve.[19] As a peace movement formally linked to the regional organization ECOWAS (the Economic Community of West African States), the network hints at an alternative history of the WPS circuit and peace governance, one that did not spring from either "the" United Nations as expert secretariat or European liberal feminism.[20] Not coincidentally, the four state members of the Mano River Union were also the first four states in Africa to adopt NAPs.[21] The women's network remains engaged in the feminist peace project as a member of the Global Network of Women Peacebuilders (see also chapter 6, pp. 172–175). Yet the sense of the African women's movement as a powerful agent of the WPS circuit would soon evaporate, returning only occasionally and in less emblematic fashion.[22]

From this mapping, we are able to make visible areas of contestation that would otherwise remain obscured. For example, one underappreciated early "diffusion" of the WPS agenda occurred in 2005, when a Palestinian presidential decree endorsed resolution 1325. The decree did not bloom into a NAP-like form for another decade, but may be read in conjunction with an amendment to Israeli national law providing for women's political participation passed in the same year, though not framed in the explicit language of WPS (and therefore excluded even from our set).[23] Neither document is captured by the conventional NAP-centric or UN-centric approach to the agenda. The then novel WPS frame was expected to yield new forms of peace building through women's participation, such as when Jerusalem Link (an organization of Israeli and Palestinian women) participated in an Arria formula meeting in 2002, an event subsequently celebrated as a promising example in an early UN study of WPS.[24] The parallel developments also fed the International Women's Commission for a Just and Lasting Peace, supported by UNIFEM (the United Nations Development Fund for Women) and based on resolution 1325, where Israeli, Palestinian, and international women's delegations met on a conflict-resolution platform (we return to this fracture in chapter 5, pp. 125–126).[25]

WHAT WPS DOES

To yield quantitative data about the constitutive issues of the WPS field, we used content analysis software (NVivo 12) to run frequency searches of key terms expressing differing—and often contentious—elements of the feminist peace. The searches were run across the full policy set (237 documents) and also for each of our three subsets. Our nodes of key terms are divided into "pillar" and "non-pillar" issues. For the former we cleave as closely as possible to the accepted core terms for each of the four pillars—"participation," "protection," "prevention," and the combination of "relief and recovery" and "humanitarian"—allowing also for variations such as "participating" and "protected."[26] For new issues, we combine a strategy of coding while browsing—documenting which words were appearing with relative frequency to generate our list of terms—with a review of the scholarly literature on WPS for clues as to what is perceived as animating the agenda at any given point.

The result is a cluster of terms for each "non-pillar" issue, from which we highlight eleven: refugees; LGBTQIA+; sexual and reproductive health;

climate change; transitional justice; men and boys; human rights defend-ers; arms; terrorism and extremism; sexual exploitation and abuse; and race and coloniality.[27] We have also tracked the prevalence of sexual vio-lence over time. Each issue's count combines the counts for a set of cog-nate terms, for example, "sexual and reproductive health" by references to "reproductive," "family planning," "abortion," "contraception," or "sex-ual health." Full details of search terms are available in our codebook as appendix 3. Search results were transcribed into Excel and tabulated by frequency over time to show how the agenda is reproduced. We document the relative influence of differing conceptions and elements of the WPS ecology below, using the total issue count weighted by the number of WPS documents published in that year as our indicator. This measure allows us to control for fluctuations in the number of WPS actors publishing plans in any given year, while nevertheless tracking increases in the sheer quantity of discourse as documents get longer and the ecosystem canopy denser as trigger terms are mentioned more often.[28]

In selecting these terms, we have attended to existing WPS terms of art. The prevalence of the four "pillars" as a shorthand in policy and prac-tice allows for strong inferences about the meaning of root terms. A NAP that includes no language on women's participation is positioned relative to the wider field by a quite specific and nontrivial difference. It is not sur-prising, then, that only 2 NAPs out of the 161 we studied made no mention of participation: the 2006 UK and 2009 Guinea NAPs.[29] The non-pillar issues we track do not command the same consensus, but here, too, the significance of language is well-demarcated by larger patterns of institu-tionalization. We are thus able to bracket long-running theoretical and meta-theoretical debates about discourse and signification.[30]

Figure 3.3 provides an overview of the attention given to the four pil-lars from the start of the agenda until the end of 2020, covering all the documents in our dataset ($n = 237$). Each "ribbon" represents the weighted number of mentions of the relevant search term.[31] The growth in men-tions of pillar terms, even correcting for the increase in the overall num-ber of WPS documents, is indicative of a consolidation of the agenda around these principles. This accords with the scholarly literature on WPS, where the pillars are increasingly invoked as the constitutive ele-ments of the agenda, raising questions about the balance to be struck between them, and the differing meanings that may be invested in the same word.[32] The role of the pillars in WPS discourse is much discussed,[33]

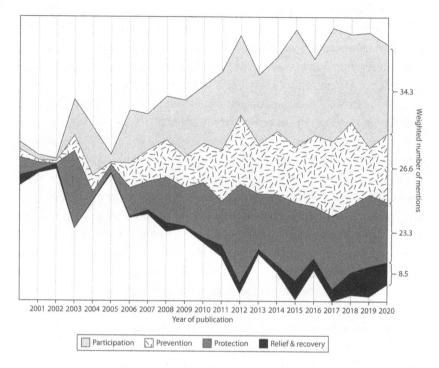

FIGURE 3.3 Mention of the four pillars in all ecosystem documents over time (2000–2020, *n* = 237, weighted by number of documents published each year).

Source: Graph by the authors.

and our mapping broadly confirms the consensus view that the wider grounding of the agenda in participation in all its senses has increasingly come under pressure from a fixation on sexual violence as an exemplary form of atrocity, activating the "protection" side of the agenda to the detriment of the deep social, political, and economic transformations implied by alternative articulations of WPS.[34] "Participation" and "protection" are the most widely invoked of the pillars, and post-conflict relief, reconstruction, and recovery consistently the least mentioned from the start.

While "participation" is still the weightiest concept in practically every year of policy, its relative domination slips, especially once hemmed in not just by "protection," but by the take-up of "prevention" aimed at terrorism and violent extremism. This trend is by no means invisible. Practitioners and activists have been keenly aware of it, and different resolutions

issued by the Security Council may be read as signs of an ongoing struggle over the parameters of canonical WPS (see chapter 4). In the UN system documents, the fortunes of "participation," "prevention," and "protection" have been closely intertwined since 2006, with "prevention" the most
dominant. By contrast, the hierarchy of pillars is less ambiguous in the
set of NAPs, with "participation" invoked most by some distance, and
"protection" in second place in nearly every year until 2016, when mentions of "prevention" overtake it, reflecting the grammar of antiterrorism
measures rather than the prevention of conflict at large. "Sexual violence,"
whether treated as a synonym for protection or not, clearly predominates
(see also figure 3.8 below). But even here, the internal distribution of the
field is not as sometimes supposed: of the ten documents with the most
mentions of "sexual violence," eight are from Africa and two from
Europe.[35]

As the agenda has grown, so, too, have new issues been added to its
remit, in some instances through the canonical texts of the Security Council, in others through innovations by other WPS actors. In themselves,
these moves constitute an important archive for studies of agenda setting
and the salience of advocacy frames. Mapping the frequency of non-pillar
issues across our three categories of documents advances two further
aims. First, by looking to the emergence of more discrete terms, we can
sharpen our analysis of the pillars themselves. "New" issue areas do not
arise in splendid isolation from previous debates, but instead often represent a particular interpretation of the WPS mandate. This is the case
for references to terrorism and extremism as a variety of "protection" and
"prevention," for transitional justice as a tool of "participation," and for
references to sexual and gender identity or men and boys as signals of the
agenda shifting away from general categorizations of "women." Second,
we are able to more concretely establish whether and how the agenda is
being recalibrated. Is the agenda pluralizing, as many observers suspect?
If so, what does the take-up of new terms tell us about the actors that constitute the ecosystem of WPS? What tensions and conflictual relations
enter the ecosystem through its growth? There are inevitably alternative
candidates and subdivisions for the expanding menu of WPS issues. Here
we present broad trends, and in the chapters to come offer more nuance
within some issues, such as "arms" and "race and coloniality" (see chapters 7 and 5, respectively).

As noted above, it is possible to identify 2010 as a major point of consolidation, and it is evident from our mapping that issue areas proliferate after that point. The expansion reflects pluralization: the production and commonly the reproduction of new issues, which, in turn, constitutes what "the WPS agenda" *is*—and what it is not. The increased diversity of WPS is shown most clearly in figure 3.4, which shows marked increases, across the totality of WPS documents in the ecosystem, in references to asylum seekers, refugees, or displaced persons (after an outlier peak in 2002); terrorism or extremism (especially from 2012); transitional justice; and race and coloniality. Engagement with issues like climate change and arms control fluctuates. Sexual and reproductive health becomes more prominent as a concern, driven heavily by a sliver of governments, especially Canada, Tajikistan, and through the Council of the European Union. It also features significantly in plans from Senegal, Indonesia, Italy, the United Kingdom, South Sudan, and Liberia, cutting against assumptions of a generic resistance emanating from the Global South. We are also able to discern a recent uptick in attention to LGBTQIA+ issues, although the incorporation of sexual orientation and gender identity remains extremely limited.[36]

For an effort to end the global marginalization and harming of women, WPS policy has been surprisingly circumspect about the perpetrators, beneficiaries, bystanders, sometime victims of, and prospective allies against, patriarchy: men. WPS documents are replete with references to men as the metric for gender equality, as in statements of the form "the importance of equal participation of men and women in preventing and resolving conflict" (Serbia NAP II 2017, 7). In such formulations, men are not the targets of policy (as might be the case in "positive masculinity" projects), but a standard against which the implementation of the agenda is measured. The combined phrase "men and boys"—which we use in our coding alongside mentions of masculinity and the masculine—better captures attempts to recognize, in the words of one recent example, that "men and boys . . . may be opponents of or advocates for gender equality, as well as survivors of gender-based violence" (United Kingdom NAP IV 2018, 6). In a slowly emerging seam of WPS, men and boys are identified as in need of mentoring to renounce discriminatory attitudes, or as partners to implement gender equality measures (e.g., United States NAP I 2011, 7, 19; Solomon Islands NAP I 2017, 27, 37; SADC Plan I 2007, 10; Netherlands NAP III 2016, 35).

By some margin, the policy document with the most references to men and boys in the first twenty years of WPS is the UK government's third action plan, released just after the founding of the PSVI and the passage of resolution 2106 in the Security Council under British stewardship, an organized symmetry intended to decisively recognize men and boys as sexual violence survivors.[37] Masculinity floats through the ecosystem as a stimulus to conflict, largely confined to the behavior of others: "the problem that exists in *some areas of the world* stemming from predominant notions of masculinity" (German NAP I 2013, 4, emphasis added; see also Switzerland NAP II 2010, 10; Norway NAP II 2011, 18; South Sudan NAP I 2015, 17; Uganda NAP II 2011, 10). At points, masculinity acquires enough force to be linked to a specific harm, such as genital cutting (EU

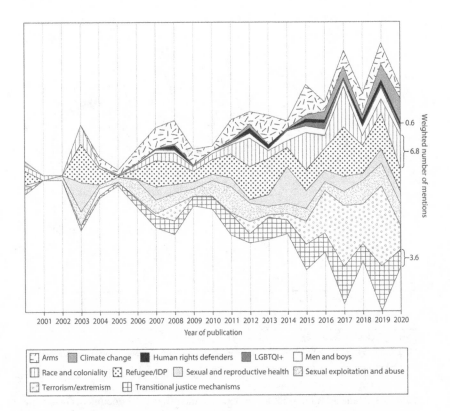

FIGURE 3.4 Mentions of new issues in all ecosystem documents over time (2000–2020, *n* = 237, weighted by number of documents published each year).

Source: Graph by the authors.

Plan II 2015, 28). In a handful of cases the gender perspective is applied internally, to the culture of military institutions (e.g., Ireland NAP III 2019, 30; NATO Directive I 2017, 3). In its grappling with the domestic legacies of conflict, Guatemala strives for nothing less than the "construction of a new masculinity" (Guatemala NAP I 2017, 48, 72; see also chapter 5, pp. 143–147). Just beyond our time frame, a more expansive unsettling of gender binaries in policy is discernable (e.g., Australian Government 2021, 17, 30). But these rare cases apart, at the level of formal policy, the circuit has only just begun to reckon with the plurality of gender.[38]

Examining the constituent parts of the agenda reveals different emphases on these "new issues," which reinforces the extent to which (re)production varies by/in different entities. Figure 3.5, for example, shows that

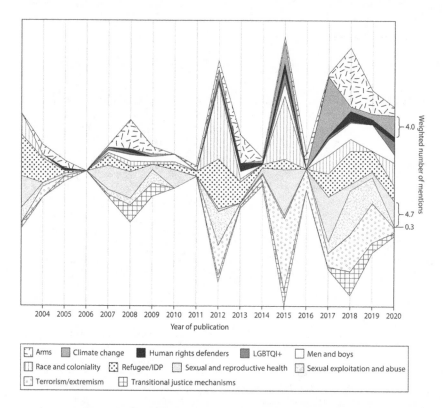

FIGURE 3.5 Mentions of new issues in regional and other WPS documents over time (2003–2020, $n = 43$, weighted by number of documents published each year).

Source: Graph by the authors.

references to extremism/terrorism are almost entirely absent from regional organization and related WPS documents, appearing only fleetingly in 2004 and then disappearing until 2012. The same issue was included at a lower level in NAPs, starting in 2007 with the first Austrian NAP, with attention spiking after 2016 (see figure 3.6). Terrorism and violent extremism have now become a major WPS issue across all three document categories, underlining the highly contentious grafting of contemporary security practices onto feminist attempts to stymie militarism through the agenda.[39] Importantly, the arrival of "terrorism" and "violent extremism" across the three documentary sets predates their appearance in the WPS resolutions themselves, again upending the conventional logic of policy transfer and norm diffusion.

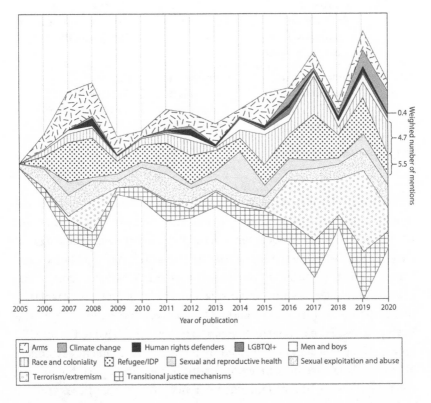

FIGURE 3.6 Mentions of new issues in NAPs over time (2005–2020, $n = 161$, weighted by number of documents published each year).

Source: Graph by the authors.

TABLE 3.1 Top three non-pillar issues in each document category
by five-year period

Period	UN system	NAPs	Other WPS
2000–2005	Sexual exploitation and abuse Transitional justice Refugees/IDPs	n/a	Refugees/IDPs Human trafficking Arms
2006–2010	Refugees/IDPs Race and coloniality + Transitional justice Sexual exploitation and abuse	Human trafficking Refugees/IDPs Arms	Sexual and reproductive health Human trafficking Arms
2011–2015	Refugees/IDPs Terrorism and extremism Transitional justice	Human trafficking Refugees/IDPs Arms	Race and coloniality Terrorism and extremism Refugees/IDPs
2016–2020	Terrorism and extremism Arms Transitional justice	Terrorism and extremism Refugees/IDPs Transitional justice	Arms Refugees/IDP Terrorism and extremism

Source: Compiled by the authors.

Table 3.1 summarizes the top three non-pillar issues in our three categories of WPS document over time, as measured by number of mentions weighted by number of documents in rough five-year blocs (running from October 2000 through the end of 2005 for the first).[40] As might be expected from its sometime humanitarian role, the focus in UN documents is more heavily on refugee, asylum, and displacement issues, and it is notable that this emphasis is mirrored in national initiatives and regional and other WPS policies. Transitional justice concerns have also been to the fore. But both have been gradually replaced by terrorism and violent extremism. NAPs have likewise prioritized terrorism in the recent past, but are also consistently more likely to include references to human and sex trafficking, indicating the role of states' police function on the more coercive end of WPS practice.[41]

Among regional and other national bodies, applications of WPS are evident that cut against hegemonic grain of the agenda, such as the appearance of "reproductive rights" in the 2006–2010 period, driven by several documents that made links between WPS and development priorities, such as the Southern African Development Community (SADC) Gender Policy, the SADC Protocol on Gender and Development, and to a lesser extent the European Union's Comprehensive Approach to the Implementation of 1325 and 1820. Though regional organizations have contributed to the dominance of terrorism, trafficking, and refugee concerns, they have also at points foregrounded race and coloniality. The appearance of colonialism—usually taken as incidental or actively suppressed in the agenda (see chapter 5 especially)—is less surprising on closer scrutiny, as it is almost entirely driven by references to the Israeli occupation of the Palestinian territories in two documents of the League

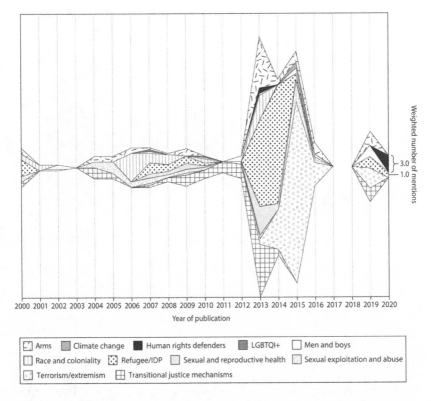

FIGURE 3.7 Mentions of new issues in UN WPS documents over time (2000–2020, $n = 33$, weighted by number of documents published each year).

Source: Graph by the authors.

of Arab States (Plan I 2012 and Plan II 2015). It should, however, be stressed that the uptake of these more diverse domains of WPS are outstripped for every set of actors in almost every time period by the domination of sexual violence (see figure 3.8).

To take a quite different area, there is limited but growing energy in the WPS ecosystem around LGBTQIA+ experiences of war and peace. This has been generated not by council resolutions, but by other WPS actors. By our count, there are no clear mentions of the applicability of the agenda to LGBTQIA+ people before 2007, whereas General Assembly documents on violence against women (overlapping with, but not dedicated exclusively to, WPS) reference sexuality in connection with protection from HIV/AIDS (A/RES/61/143, 4; also A/HRC/RES/14/12, 4).[42] It is not until 2011 that the first mention is made in the NAPs of Nepal and the United States, and only expansively in the latter.[43] More recently, recognition can be found in the European Union's Gender Action Plan and

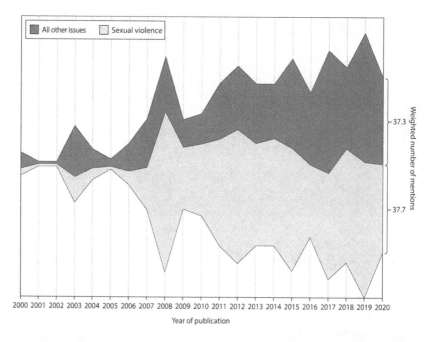

FIGURE 3.8 Mentions of sexual violence relative to all new issues in all ecosystem documents over time (2000–2020, $n = 237$, weighted by number of documents published each year).

Source: Graph by the authors.

South Africa's long-awaited NAP, speaking to an unstable and disparate coalition. As others have observed, neither the WPS discourse on women nor that concerning the inclusion of men has made much space for queer critique, and human rights fora may offer more promise than security spaces, including in the genre of the resolutions themselves.[44]

As these moments of policy productivity indicate, the vitality of the agenda is not driven by any one source or actor. Different entities and coalitions represent and therefore reproduce the agenda in diverging ways over time. It is not just that the various elements of the agenda are "contested," as this formulation suggests a core around which contention occurs. Nor is plurality merely the effect of an implementation gap, where some actors deliver on all aspects of the agenda while others only engage with some, if they engage at all. Rather, the very meaning of WPS is mutable, even in its surface text gesturing to rivalrous versions that lie beneath.

THE ECOSYSTEM AND ITS RELATIONS

So far, we have mapped the canopy of the WPS ecosystem, the policy relations that constitute one strata of the agenda. To provide a way of encountering the depths of the agenda into which we descend in the following chapters, we presented a surface elaboration through a quantitative analysis of some of its characteristics. The life of WPS, according to this perspective, is varied, but it is most certainly a life, with a rhythm, temporality, organisms, and reproductive elements. We have offered a preliminary excavation of WPS, outlining both the circuit of WPS actors—asking "Who does WPS?"—and the field of WPS activity—asking "What is WPS?"—capturing our broader investigation in microcosm. Through our analysis, we have illustrated the plurality and fractured nature of the ecosystem, revealing the surprising multiplicity of those bringing WPS to life in various guises across time and continents and the fissures and fractures in the edifice of an agenda that is frequently presumed to be holistic and even seamless.

In closing, we briefly foreshadow the borderlands of WPS, the proximate ecosystems that we engage in depth and detail in chapter 7 and throughout the chapters that follow this one. The plurality of WPS, what we have referred to as its chimeric quality, is also a feature of the connections radiating out from the agenda into wider governance domains. When considered as one expression of a supernorm of gender equality, WPS might be functionally distinguished as that community of policy and practice that addresses the battlefield and its aftermath, while others look to the "economic" or "social" sphere, intervening on the gendered aspect of poverty or trade, peacetime rights, or the participation of women in combatting environmental degradation. Following the prompt of an ecological perspective, we identify several proximate ecosystems, each with their own named area of competence, their own assembly of authoritative texts, standards of conduct, and guides to implementation, their own constitutive tensions and internal variants.

Our interest lies primarily in the borders of these ecosystems, the areas where policies relate and translate, but also where acts of differentiation take place, where an event or problem is decisively claimed as belonging to one or other. The act of positioning is necessarily organic, as it is assumed in each case that there is cross-pollination between the governance systems across the boundaries with WPS. As with our own ecosystem of interest, each may be categorized in a range of ways, subdivided into a narrower domain of technical expertise or subsumed in a larger concern, like the English school concept of an "institution" of international society such as diplomacy. The relations between several (inter)related ecosystems are shown in figure 3.9, though we note that the diagram presents an illusion of stability and fixity. We include the diagram and brief discussion here only to gesture at the existence of the policy world beyond WPS.

By way of a brief example: the association between human rights and security has a peace dimension that infused and informed the development of the peace governance ecosystem. Peace work at the United Nations, and by states and other actors, gradually began to be oriented over decades from the 1980s toward the attainment of sustainable and positive peace, in line with the concept of human security (as articulated in the 1994 *Human Development Report*).[45] Ideas about positive peace, defined by Johan Galtung as "the integration of human society,"[46] percolated through the UN and more broadly, with some states—such as Canada—operationalizing a commitment to positive peace in foreign and security policy.[47] Contrary to the assumption that conflict was inevitable and peace merely its absence, endeavors were focused on preventing conflict and creating the conditions for peace. This included recognition not

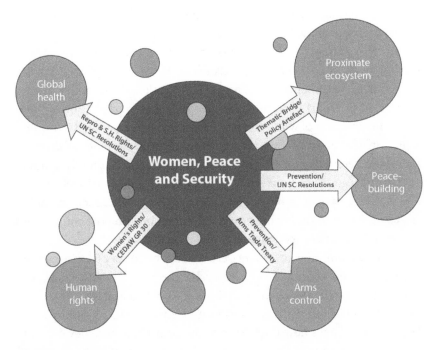

FIGURE 3.9 Proximate ecosystems.

Source: Graph by the authors.

only of the ways in which violence and insecurity undermines human rights and affects specific constituencies differently (giving rise to the Children and Armed Conflict agenda and the WPS agenda at the UN Security Council), but also of the need to provide institutional support to peace: to invest in peace governance and peace infrastructure. Thus, in the late 1990s and early 2000s, the UN undertook to establish the contemporary peace-building architecture, commencing with the United Nations Peacebuilding Commission (UN PBC), which was founded by the adoption of UN Security Council resolution 1645 in December 2005 (S/RES/1645 2005). Resolution 1645 affirms a commitment to the principles of the WPS agenda, forging a strong connection between this emergent area of the peace governance ecosystem and the WPS ecosystem.

In turn, there has always been vibrant WPS activity in the sphere of peace work, with nine of the ten resolutions emphasizing women's contributions to peace building and conflict prevention (the exception being resolution 1960, which is an interesting resolution in several ways, as we discuss in the following chapter). Resolution 1889 elaborates in some detail on the mandate of the PBC to "ensure systematic attention to and mobilisation of resources for advancing gender equality and women's empowerment as an integral part of postconflict peacebuilding" (S/RES/1889 2009, o.p. 14). In paragraph 19 of the same resolution, the secretary-general is directed to report back to the Security Council in the following year on the involvement of women in peace building, which resulted in the presentation of a report of the secretary-general entitled *Women's Participation in Peacebuilding* to the council and the General Assembly simultaneously in 2010.[48] The 2010 report concludes that the security of women, and women's agency in peace and security governance processes, act as "force multipliers" for lasting peace, further embedding the connections between the peace ecosystem and the WPS ecosystem.[49]

The peace-building governance ecosystem's proximity to, and increasing imbrication with, the WPS ecosystem reproduces both systems of governance *in relation*; opening up both the content and the contours of the peace-building governance system and exploring its proximity to the WPS agenda shows how the two governance systems have developed in and through connections and ruptures both among and between them. In the following chapters, we trace many other borderlines and interconnections, navigating proximity to, and interrelation with, among others, human rights governance, the governance of sexual and reproductive health, and the governance of sexual violence. These additional or emergent ecosystems interact with WPS in generative and also disruptive ways, which is part of the thread of failure that we examine through our account of WPS. Together with the two previous chapters, the analysis presented here forms the foundation of the investigations we undertake in the next four chapters. In this chapter, we have conducted an initial mapping of the WPS ecosystem, and reflected on connected and proximate ecosystems, to think beyond the agenda and consider how it is always a thing in flux, held in multiple relations and exceeding attempts to shrink it down to something more singular and manageable. In the remainder of the book, we momentarily hold steady elements of the ecosystem for analysis of various dynamics that reveal, through excavation, the reproduction and relational constitution of WPS in all its messiness. We begin in the following chapter with our analysis of the WPS resolutions and the stories of their becoming.

4

PRODUCING AN AGENDA AT
THE UNITED NATIONS

I f the Women, Peace, and Security agenda has an official date of birth,
it is Tuesday, October 31, 2000, just after 12.15 p.m. eastern standard
time. More important than the hour was the place: the chamber of the
United Nations Security Council. Registration took the form of a unanimous resolution passed by the fifteen states then constituting the council, a deliberation that took about a minute. The birth was also an inauguration, a founding event, the beginning of a family to which would be
added nine further resolutions over the next two decades.[1] In that time,
"WPS" would be the cue for other events in the same chamber—presidential
statements, reports of the secretary-general, briefings and letters from
expert and advocacy groups, and two dedicated "open debates" each
year—and throughout the United Nations, in its offices and corridors.
There, in Turtle Bay, New York City, the Security Council, UN Women,
and the NGO Working Group on Women, Peace and Security sit within
some three hundred meters of each other, the most concentrated physical
manifestation of the sprawling "policy architecture" of WPS.

The Security Council looms larger than any other site in the WPS ecosystem, and its resolutions captivate analysts more than any other genre
of WPS text. Scholars track vocabulary from one resolution to another;
activist coalitions provide blueprints for innovation and implementation;
a small industry monitors and rates the council's transactions for inclusivity.[2] This privileged location is signaled by a prevalent shorthand: "the

United Nations' Women, Peace, and Security agenda," a possession and a gift.[3] The UN appears in such a phrase as an impetus from beyond or above, a moral conscience or expert counsel. The content of WPS, the wellsprings of its vitality and/or failure, might therefore seem to reflect "the UN's aspirations,"[4] its different branches and committees pursuing a joint project.

The shorthand captures an ideal of the United Nations, free from the base traffic of power politics, or perhaps takes the actions of one of its parts for the whole. *The* United Nations is in truth a governance machinery of many bodies and functions, arranged above, alongside, and against the states that are formally its constituent members, and at the same time engages with other networks, agencies, and organizations beyond the state. Sovereignty and supranationality are in tension, in what has been identified as the paradox of the UN.[5] Moreover, there is not one but (at least) three UNs: an intergovernmental arena; a secretariat; and an informal public policy network.[6] WPS plays out across all three, drawing vitality and inspiration from civil society actors heavily represented in the third UN, gaining institutional power in the gender expertise of the second, and chronically ambivalent with regard to the first. As a relational perspective might predict, WPS emerges from transactions within and beyond this multiplicity.

As an intergovernmental authority, the first UN is itself split, some of its congresses operating on a nominally democratic basis—the General Assembly, for example—while others entrench the power coordinates of 1945.[7] The presumption of equality that underpins the General Assembly as an intergovernmental authority affords legitimacy to "the UN" as a singular political actor; as Inis Claude famously commented, "while the voice of the United Nations may not be the authentic voice of mankind [*sic*], it is clearly the best available facsimile thereof."[8] This presumption notwithstanding, it is the Security Council—rather than the General Assembly—that has disproportionate influence over the affairs of the organization (including through the election of each successive secretary-general, who is often presumed to be a synecdoche for the UN and who is elected by the General Assembly *on recommendation from the council*). Popular expressions of the need for "the UN" to take action in the face of horror or disaster are, indeed, often appeals to the powers of the council specifically, to intervene, prevent, cajole, limit, and dictate, its ultimate authority being that of force.

The Security Council speaks with an uncanny voice, fifteen states often unanimously issuing pleas for action to a club of nations of which they are also members, a court and parliament where five states reserve exceptional rights.[9] Resolutions are its "most tangible products,"[10] the nearest thing to a diktat of world government. Though there is no agreement on the status to be afforded intergovernmental organizations, the council is at the very least a highly privileged space for justificatory discourse, a "Parliament of Man" where delegates labor to articulate, defend, and coalesce around arguments that must be, or seem to be, legally binding.[11] Feminist peace politics has been compared to a search for code words granting access to the council,[12] the right metaphors tapping a utopian potentiality.[13] Once states had admitted the relevance of gender in open session, it was hoped that their own speech would bind them, an indelible confession and promise.[14] As one member of the UNIFEM team charged with refining the WPS agenda noted, resolution 1325 was treated in these early days as "almost a talisman,"[15] and the council chamber acquires a nearly magical quality in such accounts—a source of vitality and only latterly a site of failure.

The resolutions themselves—primary texts within the WPS policy ecosystem—are similarly emblematic of vitality and failure. In this chapter, we chronicle the development, context, and contestation of each resolution, including engagement with some resolutions that were drafted and ultimately neither debated nor adopted. The energy devoted to making resolutions possible, agreeing language, and tracking implementation is a form of vitality, to be acknowledged and analyzed alongside failures of the resolutions and the mechanisms that generate and propagate them: the chronic sense that resolutions are not "working" properly or as intended, for example, and the periodic realization that thematic resolutions in particular—and the collective decisions of the Security Council in general—do not have the effect with which they are sometimes credited, as a final arbiter or supreme decision-making entity. Our microscopic investigation of how WPS is produced and reproduced at the UN also highlights the emerging multiplicity of WPS, with different countries vying for their versions, and differing coalitions across civil society, bureaucracy, and states (the three UNs again).[16] These dynamics of contention can be tracked in and through the resolutions and related UN products (the WPS presidential statements, for example, testimony at open debates, and the secretary-general's annual reports). These practices are interpreted as manifestations of both vitality and failure: a signal of the growing prominence of WPS (where previously it was not recognized as significant enough to fight over); and a marker of the inability of supporters and detractors alike to agree on what the essence of the agenda *is* (could be/should be).

The literature on WPS evinces an easy slippage from resolution 1325 to the agenda as such, and from the Security Council to "the United Nations." As our ecosystem framing indicates, no such synergy exists. Studies of final resolution text, even those that consider other documents in the WPS ecosystem at the UN, are inevitably partial. They can elide the particular conditions of conception and birth for each resolution, the way that each is vital—and failing—in its own way, even as it mimics, reflects, and mutates what has come before (this acknowledgment draws into question especially the view of resolutions unfolding as a single colonial nexus, discussed below). Foregrounding the role of contingency, of move and countermove, we explore the iterative process of agents mutually shaping the field of production and reproduction, with participants often commenting on the difficulty of identifying the initial source of an idea or phrasing. We draw on interviews with policymakers and practitioners and analysis of how resolutions changed across drafts to excavate the political meaning of the resolutions at the time, and how they are now remembered in the WPS sequence.[17] (To our knowledge, this is also the first work to analyze WPS resolutions that were drafted but never passed.)

Following on from our new history of the resolutions, we examine the emergence of parallel and overlapping policy work within the UN system, such as in the splitting off of peacekeeper "sexual exploitation and abuse" into a human resources issue. Apparently central WPS themes travel under different governance rubrics. We also explore the development of an anti–sexual violence regime based in the UN system as the aspect of the WPS agenda that has most closely followed standard models of global governance, with the creation of dedicated offices, a consolidating mechanism for sanctioning perpetrators, and a collaborative exercise across UN entities and member states in developing standards and conducting investigations. These moments of elaboration and division give substance to the discursive ebbing and flowing we documented in the last chapter: we now track the circuit of agents who have contingently produced what becomes reified as WPS from on high. Against views of the UN as the owner of the agenda, or accounts of the Security Council as primary, we show how the agenda manifests differently across the layers of international institutions.

SERIES, DUEL, THEATER

Within the policy ecosystem of WPS, the resolutions occupy the most prestigious perch, a result of their status *as* resolutions of the UN Security Council, the international body charged with the maintenance of "international peace and security" in accordance with the Charter of the United Nations. With rare exceptions, however, thematic resolutions invoke powers associated with chapter VI of the United Nations Charter, intended as "recommendations" toward the settlement of disputes. Unlike chapter VII "enforcement" measures, they do not authorize the UN or member states to employ force in the shape of a peacekeeping mission or military coalition. The vocabulary of authority differs: chapter VI is indicated by operative paragraphs in which the council "urges," "encourages," "calls," and "invites"; the text of chapter VII is more assertive, a succession of "decides," "resolves," "authorizes" and "demands."[18] The category of "thematic resolution" is symptomatic: celebrated for their capacity to diagnose structural harms and redefine the terms of security, they are also commonly dismissed as the least significant genre in the council library.[19] The general distinction between chapters VI and VII, and the indifference of conservative security theory, can give the impression that thematic resolutions are futile, and yet they exercise influence by other means. At the level of customary international law, the accumulation of "nonbinding" resolutions nevertheless consolidates a paradigm that draws on other sources, such as treaties and consistent state behavior.[20] When it echoes settled international law, the council acts as "an institutional enforcer"; where there is dispute, its resolutions bolster the arguments of one side.[21]

WPS resolutions are a touchstone of the agenda, even as they do not—cannot—contain the agenda's multitudes. Despite references over the years to "resolution fatigue,"[22] the agenda has proliferated through resolutions because the formal text *matters*; the resolutions affect not only the direction and growth of the agenda, but also chart its discontents and ruptures. Various resolutions (and non-resolutions, resolutions that never saw the floor of the council for deliberation) have been hotly contested for one reason or another. One of our research participants, for example, commenting on the resolutions of 2013, said that there were "concerns about an additional resolution on participation. . . . We said this to the P3 [the United States, United Kingdom, and France]—that if you do a resolution on sexual violence and conflict you're going to imbalance the agenda, and you have to do resolutions on the other elements of the agenda . . . you can't do one only on sexual violence and conflict and leave it at that."[23]

As another informant explained, "the smallest looking edit can contain a whole world of stuff."[24] Deliberation is a high form of diplomatic practice; one member of the council, we were told, is renowned for compressing the timeline for negotiations "as much as possible, to squeeze everyone to the point of exhaustion so that they just give up,"[25] *because* the assistance or obstruction rendered to the agenda at large is significant. Though writing of a different context entirely, Edward Luck affirms the significance of the council's words, noting that, throughout the bloody history of Israel's occupation of the Palestinian territories, "the wording of resolution 242 of 1967—and differing interpretations of it—still is cited by the parties as a critical plank in any formula for a durable peace."[26]

Measured by weight of resolutions, WPS is the largest of the Security Council's thematic domains, those concerns that transcend the detail of any particular conflict, and which have flourished in the era of human security, among them "Protection of Civilians," "Children and Armed Conflict," "Health Crises," and, most recently, "Youth, Peace, and Security." The volume of WPS resolutions is itself held up as evidence of vitality and failure: on the one hand, the sustained life given by the actors who nurture and challenge it; on the other, the need for continued adoption of resolution after resolution, when the proper emphasis—so it is said—should be on implementation. The resolutions are attributed shifting meanings in rival approaches to the agenda. In ecosystem terms, the resolutions are a fundamental reference point: when there is action *in the name of* WPS, an interpretation of the resolutions is often explicit, and otherwise implicit—as instructions being dutifully followed, as a license for new efforts, as a partial security discourse to be supplemented or improved, as a barometer of great power commitment to gender equality, even as inconsequential words irrelevant to real peace work. The Security Council is a node of differentiation within the field, a body generating affect, with the resolutions the material for arguing over. Perhaps no other type of policy artifact better showcases our argument that texts are mutable and transfer unstable.

Within the circuit of WPS practice, the resolutions are granted different meanings. We identify three. The accumulation of canonical text has been interpreted as a *series*, with each resolution deepening the rule and rules of the feminist peace; as a running *duel*, council votes bolstering one or other side of the contest(s); or as *theater*, an alibi for the endless deferral of practical action. In the coming pages, we report on the treatment of the resolutions and associated artifacts through each of these lenses. Vitality and failure are evident across all three, and all three are both possible (in the sense of empirically verifiable interpretations of the production of WPS at the United Nations) *and* provide conditions of possibility for the WPS ecosystem (in the sense that at any given time the ecosystem's development or diminution may be described as having one or more of these qualities). In their interpretations of the resolutions as series, duel, or theater, agents emplot the agenda, their rhetoric shaping and contesting the past and future of feminist peace.

In the serial model, the foundation of 1325 is extended by the creation of new offices and techniques (evidence-gathering bodies, peacekeeping mandates, sanctions instruments) and consolidated as legal obligation, crystallizing as custom through repetition. Council themes in principle follow a developmental path, new text supported by citation to resolutions past, adapting with each iteration to a growing body of knowledge and unanticipated operational challenges. Though it is sometimes intimated that 1325 already contains the whole of feminist peace in miniature, practitioners frequently explain the passage of resolutions as evolutionary, perpetually in need of renewal and elaboration. Serial discourse is ubiquitous at the annual open debates on the topics of WPS (conventionally in October) and sexual violence in conflict (conventionally in April) as member state representatives reinforce the unidirectionality of WPS.[27] The WPS series is an *inheritance*, a responsibility and sometime burden, a referential chain. The next resolution offers a ready horizon for progress, and there is always another resolution coming.

If in the first conception WPS is distinguished from the traditional security paradigm that it challenges, in a second the more consequential split is among the resolutions themselves, arranged in the posture of a duel. As discussed for the agenda at large in chapter 3, it is common for activists and observers to distinguish between two versions of the agenda, one that prioritizes the "participation" of women, the other their "protection," through the prevention of and response to sexual violence in conflict.[28] The split maps almost exactly onto the distinction between resolutions promoting various rights and those that focus on conflict-related sexual violence. In the duel, council texts are read as bolstering one side or other, signaling power or vulnerability, each negotiation undertaken under the threat of co-optation, the risk of "setting back this agenda by twenty years. . . . We fought very hard for recognition of autonomy, agency, human rights . . . gender equality," in the words of one interlocutor.[29] The duel has institutional correlates: participation resolutions are more closely linked to the demands of civil society, sexual violence resolutions to national preferences or specialized UN offices; the former are more openly debated, the latter more narrowly technocratic.[30] Viewed from another quarter, it is the prevention (narrowly, of sexual violence) lineage that has achieved most in the way of accountability and the transformation of security institutions. Vitality and failure may be claimed for either side, and haunt both.

Finally, the council politics of WPS may be seen as a kind of theater, connoting superficiality and distraction. Many activists bemoan the energy devoted to resolution making when so much of what has already been promised lies unimplemented, an exasperation expressed as resolution fatigue, a characteristic form of the WPS failure narrative.[31] Failure in the wake of success: in the second decade of the agenda, as it reached critical mass, states became more eager to claim WPS for themselves, the prize being the shepherding of a new resolution, simply "because that's the thing you do. You adopt a resolution at the open debate."[32] In this vein, the student of WPS at the UN becomes a dramaturge, sketching the performances and soliloquys of "actors." The intensity of activity around resolutions indicates less that the precise text is of material consequence than that a ritual is underway, the labor of effective policy happening elsewhere, offstage, if at all.

ORIGIN STORIES

As has been much rehearsed, the WPS agenda was built on a history of feminist theory and practice stretching back at least a century in international organizations, gestated in a range of sites, from The Hague in 1915 to Beijing in 1995 (but see chapter 7).[33] The design of the first WPS resolution grew from gatherings spurred by the Beijing Platform and UN operational reviews. In May 2000, at Windhoek, Namibia, a declaration and plan of action were agreed by delegates from the worlds of peacekeeping, diplomacy, and academia. Netumbo Nandi-Ndaitwah, then Namibia's minister for women's affairs and child welfare, was the seminar's host, and had previously been rapporteur general at the Beijing World Conference on Women.[34] On its face an attempt to induct more women into multidimensional peacekeeping missions, the seminar dealt with technical questions of interview protocols, budgetary provisions, terms of reference, and training curricula.[35] Yet its coalition seeded language that would flourish a few months later in 1325, with effects far beyond UN operations. This transformation had always been the larger objective for some, energized by "savvy strategic visions [and] laser-focused calculations."[36]

The seminar's location in Windhoek was itself significant: Namibia had won independence from apartheid South Africa—and joined the United Nations—just a decade earlier, an achievement linked by participants to the benefits of peacekeeping (the Transition Assistance Group mission having recently overseen the first elections of a free Namibia).[37] In 2000, Namibia was simultaneously an elected member of the Security Council, president of the UN General Assembly, and chair of the Beijing+5 summit, which began almost as soon as the ink on the Windhoek Declaration was dry.[38] Namibia was due to take presidency of the council for the month of October, and with other supportive governments of the time—including Bangladesh, Canada, Jamaica, and Mali—worked to translate the spirit of Windhoek into a resolution.[39] Several of the driving participants were veterans of the liberation movement, and Nandi-Ndaitwah has been credited with the first suggestion of a resolution, mirroring Namibia's innovation of children and armed conflict the year before.[40] The United Kingdom and the United States, later to take up "penholder" roles on

WPS and sexual violence, respectively, as permanent members of the council, did not obstruct the campaign, but neither were they its origina- tors. The timing was savvy: "in 2000, the doors were open just wide enough for women to squeeze into a Security Council debate for the first time," as three WILPF activists put it in an early memoir.[41]

Beijing was to become the indispensable reference point, Windhoek the neglected source. Yet both were also culminations of wider trends not marked in resolution preambles. Outcome documents from the 1985 Nai- robi World Conference on Women had put women's participation in direct conversation with barriers to wider human progress encompass- ing the arms race, occupation, apartheid, land seizures, sex discrimina- tion, and imperialism; the two explicit causes were an end to apartheid in South Africa and Palestinian self-determination.[42] Entirely unacknowl- edged in agenda histories are antecedents such as the 1993 Kampala Action Plan on Women and Peace, congregating under the auspices of the United Nations Economic Commission for Africa and the Organisation of African Unity (later to become the African Union). At Kampala, del- egates agreed an action plan for the "full involvement of women in polit- ical and economic issues," encompassing a continuum of violence from household to armed conflict (though not mentioning sexual violence explicitly), and alongside demands for empowerment and peace educa- tion.[43] Its closing paragraphs recommended that the United Nations do better on inclusion, including on military and peacekeeping missions, and that "the interests of women [be] adequately represented in the Security Council."[44] The ecosystem has a hinterland (see also chapter 7, pp. 179–185 on CEDAW and pp. 192–199 on prevention precursors).

Advocacy around 1325 coupled a process unfolding within the second UN (principally in peacekeeping roles and at UNIFEM) with the efforts of a transnational advocacy network intersecting with the third UN of policy networks.[45] The NGO Working Group on WPS was founded in 2000, between the annual summit of the Commission on the Status of Women and the Windhoek Seminar, representing a coalition initially numbering five organizations (Amnesty International, the Hague Appeal for Peace, International Alert, the Women's Commission for Refugee Women and Children, and the Women's International League for Peace and Freedom).[46] International Alert's "Women Building Peace" initia- tive received $180,000 from the Ford Foundation, recalled as always intended to produce a resolution.[47] Working from the space afforded by annual gatherings of the Commission on the Status of Women, the coalition split the difference between radical antimilitarism and a more liberal prospectus for rights and inclusion.[48] The role of advocacy across civil society and practitioner roles was undoubtedly generative, "*necessary* to transform a concept, or new discourse, into an institutional force."[49]

The energy for resolution 1325 was produced across emerging ecosystem niches—governmental, activist, bureaucratic, and philanthropic. The emerging WPS coalition was forged through reciprocity and relational connection: Namibia hosted the Windhoek seminar, the outcomes of which informed the documents collated by the NGO Working Group, which lobbied Namibia in its role as Security Council president to schedule a special open session for October, and simultaneously coauthored the text that became 1325.[50] Reports and evidence were assembled in haste by academics and civil society researchers to satisfy delegation demands for "research on the ground" before a resolution could be considered.[51] At the Arria formula meeting in late October, the Jamaican ambassador, Patricia Durrant (who was also chair of a UNIFEM committee), convened representatives from NGOs and one regional organization—the African Women's Committee on Peace and Democracy of the Organisation of African Unity—who presented arguments to council members.[52] The language of the draft consciously borrowed from the precursor UN canon, rearticulating the council's well-established remit in gender egalitarian terms.[53] UNIFEM provided advice while negotiating the politics of the UN, multiple, "visible and invisible at the same time."[54] This—and not a Western power stratagem to appropriate feminism—was the first WPS circuit.

Elisabeth Rehn (the first female defense minister of Finland) and Ellen Johnson Sirleaf (Liberian minister of finance, later president and Nobel Peace Prize winner) are often quoted for their characterization of 1325 as a "watershed political framework." They also saw that the symbolic power of the council operated in retrospect: it had "given political legitimacy to a long history of women's peace activity."[55] In the nearly synonymous phrase of one participant, women's issues had thereby gained "*security* legitimacy."[56] The unanimity of passage has subsequently been viewed as "formal validation at the macro-scale" of a new fundamental norm making sexual violence a matter of security proper.[57] Despite the solemn reverence with which the first resolution is remembered, the mood at the time was somewhat different. Participants recall "a mix of laughter, plain astonishment accompanied by sophisticated ridicule" in the chamber.[58] Largely lost is the question of what the state representatives not already part of the coalition understood themselves to be voting for.[59] Despite the precarious acceptance of feminist arguments, for many activists the passage of the resolution *was* the achievement, often described as a "tool" for empowering local women's movements, and not yet the first of a series unfolding without determinate end. In contrast to the flurry of resolutions that followed toward the end of the first WPS decade, the period immediately after October 2000 was quiet. The event was singular: "No one in the Security Council thought it would go beyond that one day."[60] For eight years, "1325" simply *was* the agenda, and energies across the UN were concentrated on establishing the architecture of monitoring and protocol, on turning a resolution into a running agenda item, and on translating and popularizing the resolution text beyond it.[61]

These efforts were supported, in normative terms, by the release not of more resolutions but of statements from the holders of the office of the Security Council presidency each October marking the anniversary of 1325's adoption. Presently, there are fifteen presidential statements related to the "item entitled 'women and peace and security,'" the language used to indicate their thematic relevance. Seven of these statements were released in the "quiet" period between the adoption of 1325 and the adoption in June 2008 of resolution 1820. The vitality of the agenda is evident in these statements, though the absence of further resolutions may be considered a marker of failure. "Unlike resolutions Presidential statements require consensus: somewhat paradoxically, it may therefore be easier to secure the adoption of a resolution than a statement."[62] The WPS presidential statements, particularly the 2004 statement (S/PRST/2004/40) and the October 2007 statement (S/PRST/2007/40; there was another in March of that same year, but it was rather uninspiring), have been influential in the reproduction of the agenda across the UN system and beyond. The former "encourages" member states to develop National Action Plans to guide the implementation of resolution 1325 (S/PRST/2004/40; see also chapter 5); the latter laid the groundwork for the 2010 "system-wide evaluation" of progress in implementing 1325 across the UN, governed by the

United Nations System-Wide Action Plan. The statements now coexist with resolutions as spurs to policy, but in the period 2000–2008 they were the primary acts of nourishment for the nascent agenda.

THE RESOLUTION THAT WASN'T

The text of the first resolution, since repeatedly parsed and scrutinized, embeds some of the tensions of its genesis, the seeds of both vitality and failure, as well as the conditions of both duel and theater, beyond the superficial appearance of a series represented in table 4.1. Though the series would subsist on presidential statements for nearly a decade, there was an early effort in 2006 to consolidate WPS in the first of two resolutions that never were, notable for the conditions of their failure. Motivated in part by reflections at the fifth anniversary of 1325, elements of the civil society coalition began to build a case for a second resolution, one that would address "gender-based violence," or GBV, a crucially different formulation than the focus on sexual violence that would follow. Of the five types of violence listed in an early draft, only rape would be explicitly cited in the canonical sexual violence resolution successfully passed two years later. Instead the 2006 preambles and operative paragraphs identified sexual violence as but one type of gender violence, demanding "the immediate and complete cessation by all parties to armed conflict of all acts of gender-based violence with immediate effect" and an "end [to] impunity for all acts of gender-based violence as part of a comprehensive approach to seeking sustainable peace, justice, truth and national reconciliation."[63]

Though drafts of "the GBV resolution" (as we think of it) focused exclusively on women and girls as targets of violence, each iteration also took an expansive view, stressing the impact of all violence against women on rights, development, and peace objectives. Advocates for a resolution argued that it would "deepen the discourse" at the Security Council, drawing parallels with the success of the Children and Armed Conflict resolution series. Viewed in light of the duel narrative that was to develop, the 2006 drafts offer an alternative history, where WPS discourse was less fractured by arguments over the outsized attention given to sexual

TABLE 4.1 The thematic series, origins, and contestations

Resolution (date)	Council president	Origin/coalition	Contested language	Operative effects
1325 (Oct. 2000)	Namibia	Windhoek, Beijing+5, NGO Working Group on WPS, Namibia, Bangladesh, Jamaica, Canada, Mali	"Gender issues" Women as subjects in need of protection	Increased women's participation in leadership and field operations Gender perspective for peacekeeping Gender perspective for peace agreements Special measures on gender-based violence WPS guidelines for member states Study on impact of armed conflict on women and girls
The GBV resolution (2006)		Parts of civil society, United Kingdom	"Gender-based violence" Hierarchy of violence	Data mechanism on GBV in conflict List of parties to conflict using GBV GBV training for UN personnel Gender perspective and advisers in regional and subregional bodies
1820 (June 2008)	United States	UNIFEM + WPS civil society, United States, United Kingdom as coordinators	Sexual violence as "tactic of war" Sexual exploitation and abuse	Demands end to all sexual violence against civilians in conflict Demands military protection and disciplinary measures Affirms zero-tolerance policy on SEA Protection guidelines to UN peacekeeping missions Intent to sanction parties committing sexual violence
1888 (Sept. 2009)	United States	United States, United Kingdom	Participation-protection duel	Creates Office of the Special Representative of the Secretary-General on Sexual Violence in Conflict Strengthens UN Action Creates team of experts on sexual violence Women protection advisers to UN peacekeeping missions

Resolution	Sponsor	Theme	Provisions
1889 (Oct. 2009)	Vietnam	Reporting mechanisms Development language	Global indicators on 1325 Provisions on gender equality in UN mission mandates Attention to education, refugee camps, disarmament, and empowerment aspects
1960 (Dec. 2010)	United States	State Department	Working group equivalent to Children and Armed Conflict Sanctions	Annual reports on sexual violence Monitoring conflict parties' commitments on sexual violence Cooperation between SRSG on children and armed conflict and SRSG on sexual violence in conflict Sexual violence to be considered in mandate authorizations and renewals
2106 (June 2013)	United Kingdom	UK PSVI	Sexual violence (Penholder procedure)	Explicit recognition of men and boys as victims of sexual violence Exclusion of sexual violence from amnesties in conflict resolution Urges targeted sanctions for parties committing sexual violence UN support to integrate sexual violence measures in national disarmament, security sector, and justice reform Further deployment of women protection advisers and gender advisers
2122 (Oct. 2013)	Azerbaijan	Azerbaijan, UN Women, WPS civil society	Participation-protection duel	Strengthens UN Women's role High-level review of WPS

(continued)

TABLE 4.1 The thematic series, origins, and contestations (*continued*)

Resolution (date)	Council president	Origin/coalition	Contested language	Operative effects
2242 (Oct. 2015)	Spain	Spain, United Kingdom	Countering violent extremism Abortion in humanitarian settings	Applies WPS across all Security Council "situations" Greater integration of WPS and counterterrorism in NAPs UN Counter-Terrorism Committee integrates gender Informal Experts Group on WPS Gender and sexual violence expertise for sanctions committees Women's civil society to brief Security Council
2467 (Apr. 2019)	Germany	SRSG, Germany	Sexual and reproductive health and rights International Criminal Court	Strengthen 1888 and 1960 monitoring Commission of inquiry to include sexual violence in mandates Encourages informal community-protection mechanisms
2493 (Oct. 2019)	South Africa	South African, council consensus	—	Restates previous resolutions
The twentieth-anniversary resolution (Oct. 2020)	Russia	Russia	Participation Prevention of conflict-related sexual violence Civil society support	Commemoration of 1325 Calls for more women in peacekeeping Encouraging regional WPS

Source: Compiled by the authors.

violence, and better integrated with other feminist and humanitarian instruments (the Convention on the Elimination of All Forms of Discrimination Against Women, the Refugee and Geneva Conventions). Discussing this period, Sam Cook explain that several of those involved at the time

> argued that Resolution 1325 provided a broad and fairly comprehensive framework for a range of issues and singling out one issue was both arbitrary and perhaps even dangerous. Some believed that this focus would take away from the powerful breadth and depth of Resolution 1325. They argued that it would diminish the importance of Resolution 1325 by reducing the women, peace, and security agenda to issues of sexual violence and victimhood again. . . . *This argument had been successfully used by a small group of NGOs in 2006 to block an earlier attempt to adopt a similar resolution.*[64]

The 2006 proto-resolution thus failed for reasons that would become a motif of the WPS field: though most NGOs were in favor, a handful feared creating a "hierarchy of violence" through the gender focus, and maintained that 1325 was a holistic "brand" to be preserved against new texts that might subdivide it.[65]

The second resolution proper arrived in 2008, bringing with it the conception of WPS as a duel. Resolution 1820 identified sexual violence as a "tactic of war," advocated targeted sanctions and amnesty exclusions in response, expanded the range of peacekeeper training and protection measures, and at the same time affirmed "zero tolerance" policies on sexual exploitation and abuse (SEA) perpetrated by peacekeepers themselves.[66] The resolution had its basis in discussions among a group of self-described "feminist humanitarians" working across the third and second UNs, from civil society, and from the emergent bureaucracy of UN Action Against Sexual Violence in Conflict (also known as "Stop Rape Now"), a network of UN entities established the previous year.[67] Practitioners recall a series of "very tense tea parties" convened by the wife of the US ambassador to the UN at the Waldorf Astoria in New York, part coalition building, part interrogations on how women leaders from across the UN intended to stop sexual violence crimes.[68] In the same period, a "like-minded group" of officials began to meet regularly, less on the directions of their respective capitals than from personal commitment to gender issues in their portfolios.[69]

Animated by the lack of redress for unfolding atrocities in Darfur and eastern Congo, a relatively small circuit collaborated in New York but also at Wilton Park, a retreat in West Sussex, England, where the idea for a resolution appears to have been first suggested, and where the initial text was drafted by a British diplomat, an American State Department official, and a UNIFEM official.[70] Plans came together at pace and development of the resolution was "amazingly swift";[71] 1820 was passed by the council three weeks after first drafting. Its authors had avoided drawing too strong a link between peacekeeper behavior and "conflict-related sexual violence" as a category, conscious that it would cost support within the UN,[72] although a single reference to peacekeeper sexual exploitation and abuse remained in the finalized text (S/RES/1820 2008, o.p. 7).[73] Initially conjoined in 1325, "weapon of war" and "SEA" trajectories were to continue to diverge, culminating in a formal split in which resolutions explicitly addressing SEA are today not counted as belonging to the thematic WPS canon at all (we return to this briefly below).

Though state representatives credited much of the language in 1820 to UNIFEM and allied NGOs,[74] the most significant split lay within civil society, where some resisted the "tactic of war" framing.[75] This division is glossed over, with the fissures and fraying edges concealed by the telling and retelling of the institutional embedding of the agenda: "In the face of later things, it [1325] suddenly becomes this perfect object of civil society engagement. And then nobody was corrupted and nobody gave up on their principles and everybody was pure. And that happens similarly with 1820. And some of it is because NGOs want to appear as a unit and as a force."[76] The idea that NGOs would not act in concert but rather participate in contestation over the agenda is anathema to the production of WPS, which conventionally sees the homogeneity of civil society as key to its legitimacy and to the established scripts of the circuit.

Visible as, by turns, series, duel, and theater, in the years either side of the tenth anniversary of 1325 the contest between "prevention" and "participation" intensified, as did the desire of states to claim the agenda (or some part of it) for themselves. The next resolution in the canon—1888— institutionalized the UN's anti–sexual violence work through the office of the special representative of the secretary-general (SRSG) on sexual violence in conflict, also expanding the role of gender advisers in peace-keeping.[77] Resolution 1888 was largely a U.S. initiative, timed to coincide with its diplomatic reengagement in the wake of the Bush administration.[78] The rotating-chair protocol in the council allowed Hillary Clinton, long a WPS figurehead and at the time U.S. secretary of state, to preside over the session, just a week after Barack Obama became the first U.S. president to chair a meeting of the council.[79] The confluence of personal conviction and foreign policy left little space for input from the wider coalition, and the purpose of the resolution was in any case tightly focused, putting sexual violence on the same footing as other thematic areas like children in armed conflict, which already had its own SRSG. Negotiations were largely led by the UK officials who had taken a prominent role in 1820 and who were given significant latitude, "provided Hillary got to raise her hand in the room and do all of that kind of stuff."[80]

Just five days later, the council passed another WPS resolution, the timing alone indicative of a split, resolutions being precious enough commodities. Resolution 1889 reaffirmed participation and rights as the essence of WPS, urging the appointment of more women envoys and advisers, and requiring reporting on implementation. Formally introduced by Vietnam, it was the first example of states outside the Global North taking ownership of the agenda in the UN since the Windhoek coalition of 1325. A first draft drew heavily on the language of development and peacekeeping, a position associated with the less interventionist wing of WPS politics, tracking the general concern that maximalist Security Council declarations would be used to invalidate sovereign authority.[81] To policymakers who had been involved in 1820 and 1888, Vietnam's draft lacked substance, and a coalition of UNIFEM officials and diplomats pressed for more concrete measures, proposing alternative operative paragraphs on indicators, though with no great confidence of support in the council.[82] Though some took Vietnam as a proxy for Beijing's interests, it is notable that the resulting text strengthened the reporting mechanisms of WPS, a development resisted by both Chinese and Russian ambassadors to that point.[83]

As the first decade of WPS came to a close, more states were laying claims to some part of the WPS field, articulating rival investments and interests.[84] Within the P5, there had emerged a clear split between Russia and China on the one hand and the P3 on the other, ranged in opposition along either side of a duel over the proper placement of WPS at the UN. Russian representatives are known for objecting to any perceived proliferation or overgrowth of the agenda: on the topic of sexual violence in conflict, we were told that "Russia will speak up and say, 'Sexual violence is no worse than many other violations. Certainly, it's better than murder. Why are we making such a big deal out of it?' They still say that they think it belongs in the General Assembly, not as a peace and security issue. They are not likely to change their mind on this."[85]

State politics plays out in the WPS negotiations and open debates as well, with member states' interest following allegiance in many cases. The uptake of the agenda by non-permanent members was not always welcomed by practitioners, who often feared stagnation of the agenda, or attributed personal or national vanity as a motive: the impetus of *being seen* to bring a resolution.[86] Developing and shepherding a resolution through to adoption is seen as "a badge of pride to have for many of the non-permanent members,"[87] though this can cause issues when, for example, a non-permanent member holds the presidency, particularly in the anniversary month, and decides that a resolution product is essential to their success in that role (as was the case for resolution 2467, as elaborated below). More, the role of "penholder" states—the United Kingdom, the United States—is not uncomplicated, as these states have leveraged their institutional privilege to seed and prune the agenda in line with the directions they receive from their capitals. This is initially particularly evident in the development of resolution 1960.

ANNIVERSARY AND BACKLASH

Given the emerging plurality of state investments in WPS, it is perhaps surprising that 1960, adopted a matter of months after the tenth anniversary of 1325, would be so much the product of one state, and with such a specific purpose. In further specifying the potential for sanctions and elaborating protocols for monitoring, information sharing, and designating armed group perpetrators of sexual violence, drafters from the U.S. State Department sought once again to give sexual violence the same institutional status as children and armed conflict.[88] In this it was the natural extension of 1820 and 1888. Where 1889 had sought annual reports on WPS progress, 1960 now added annual reports on sexual violence, underlining the bifurcation into distinct streams. The negotiations are as notable for what did not survive to the final vote: an attempt to set up a working group as a formal subsidiary body of the council, as existed for children and armed conflict, which would have formal powers to investigate armed groups and recommend sanctions and other measures for crimes of sexual violence (S/RES/1612 2005).[89] The proposal was quickly quashed given the objection of Russia and China to the expansion of substantive council powers, but would linger, reemerging later as the Informal Experts Group in resolution 2242.

The agenda continued to proliferate beyond the council after 2010, internalized in individual government projects. One specimen was the UK's Preventing Sexual Violence Initiative, cochaired by Foreign Secretary William Hague and Angelina Jolie (see chapter 2, pp. 34). Hague's abolitionist vision entailed a new council resolution to accompany declarations by the G8, the development of an international protocol on investigating crimes of sexual violence, and a major summit in London. Hague's eagerness overturned standard diplomatic protocol, the United States being the formal penholder for sexual violence resolutions, manifest in the role of the State Department in arranging the 1820–1888–1960 sequence. Consultation was minimal, any input from the second or third UNs eschewed in favor of an assertive anti-impunity message.[90] In its substance, 2106 added little, identifying an expanded role for gender advisers and investigations, and reiterating the role of tribunals and training.[91] It was celebrated most for the named inclusion of men and boys as potential survivors of sexual violence, a signal of greater subtlety in thinking about gender violence, though an overstated achievement in textual terms.[92] The recognition was interpreted by different parts of the WPS circuit as a much-needed advance, as another example of the sexual violence fixation, and also as a variety of theater.

Just as 1888 had its reply in 1889, so, too, did the UK resolution produce a backlash, in this case passed a few months later under the presidency of Azerbaijan.[93] In contrast to 2106, resolution 2122 was in large part the product of drafting from UN Women,[94] again stressing the rights language of women's leadership, women's participation as military and police personnel, its main substantive points being the identification of women's groups as experts in armed conflict, to be consulted as much as saved, and the creation of a high-level review of WPS. Civil society advocates were also "extensively involved in the preparation for 2122 . . . [and] very involved in the discussions leading up to whether or not there should be another resolution and also what that would look like."[95] Where the UK resolution had included fifty-six references to sexual violence, there were just eight in the rejoinder text.[96] The British government was unsurprisingly resistant given its own claim on WPS earlier in the year, requiring advocacy from within the second UN on the utility of a "rebalancing" resolution, and the need to cater to Azerbaijan's initiative. The result was arguably more influential, seeding the infrastructure of monitoring and implementation later to be applied across the suite of council business.[97] As the dialogue between the British and Azerbaijani resolutions indicated, diplomatic prestige was increasingly at stake, implying a less monolithic coalition: "back to the multiplicity of voices, now you have in the council eight countries that say WPS is a priority, whereas before it was two or three. . . . It makes it harder to control, like every member state can have their own [resolution]."[98]

By this stage in WPS history, an anniversary event was inevitable, though, in "integrating" WPS and counterterrorism, resolution 2242 was to prove one of the most controversial of the series, dividing activists and practitioners even more starkly than the sexual violence resolutions before it.[99] The language of "violent extremism" exposed fractures over the representation of "local women" (a major figure of WPS discourse) and the question of who could speak on their behalf. While some civil society groups maintained that women were already active in countering extremist movements and would benefit from the support of the council, others saw in "P/CVE" (preventing/countering violent extremism) policy a repeat of the co-optation of feminist arguments in militarist and carceral projects. This version of the WPS duel pitted "inclusive security" against "antimilitarism," rival political theories identifiable throughout the ecosystem (see also chapters 1 and 6). Less noted was the impact of 2242 in drawing the first and second UNs closer, mandating a WPS focus across all country situations on the council's docket, and creating an Informal Experts Group (IEG), a less powerful entity than the working group considered five years earlier, though no less hard fought for that. Co-drafted by the United Kingdom and Spain, and introduced by the latter as a

crowning achievement of its presidency,[100] the controversy of the IEG generated tense negotiations, with UN Women providing an "encyclopedia
of justifications" for friendly diplomats and state councilors to draw on.[101]
By the morning of the open debate Russian intentions remained unclear,
with the possibility that their representative would abstain, though ultimately their objection was made only in spoken remarks.[102] Another dispute related to a late operative paragraph referencing "the full range of
medical, legal and psychosocial services" for women, code language for
abortion rights, softened from the original in response to Russian and
Chinese pressure.[103]

As the twentieth anniversary of 1325 loomed, the WPS field was marked
by a number of disputes, hardening into well-established camps across the
three UNs. Two resolutions were passed in 2019, resulting in a crisis that
would reverberate into the anniversary year and beyond. The presidency
of Donald Trump had jeopardized the alliance structure that WPS advocates had relied on since the late 2000s, and the influence of evangelical
ideology was at its zenith. Though the timing was clearly inhospitable to
progressing the agenda, Germany had, like others, declared its overwhelming commitment to the agenda, with resolutions by now the settled signal of such commitment.[104] For the first time, the United States
took the role of antagonist, shedding its penholder role and resisting language on sexual health and reproductive rights that had appeared in previous resolutions, and that was initially reiterated in the German draft,
intended as the next in the developmental series on sexual violence.[105] Also
contested was a passing reference to discrimination and persecution on
the basis of sexual orientation,[106] again antithetical to the Trumpian blend
of fundamentalism and machismo. In the midst of a split in the historical
WPS alliance, a proposal for a stronger "mechanism" of the council initiated by the SRSG's office also faltered.[107] Despite last-minute concessions
from the German delegation, resolution 2467 passed with the language
on reproductive rights and the International Criminal Court compromised at U.S. insistence, *and also* with Russia and China abstaining, the
first and so far only WPS resolution not to secure unanimous support.[108]
It was received almost universally as a failure, the agenda undercut by
omission.

Six months later South Africa tabled a reparative text, praising
progress to date while repeatedly urging full implementation of existing

promises. Sexual violence again offers a point of stark contrast: whereas the April resolution contained over a hundred references to sexual violence, the October resolution featured none. Resolution 2493 won the votes of all fifteen council members, a ritualistic reassertion that came with a price: "the resolution itself, it was very thin, it had nothing";[109] "apparently the sole wish of the South Africans was to bring the Security Council back to unanimity on WPS."[110] The consensus was to be relatively short-lived. The following year the twentieth anniversary of resolution 1325 passed unmarked by the council, despite negotiations progressing far enough for formal publication. This Russian draft—widely taken as a wrecking text—broke from prior practice in not drawing on the expertise of the second UN (in the form of UN Women) or consulting with the third (as represented by the NGO Working Group).[111] Deploying language from the early years of WPS, the Russian draft was widely understood as a sign of failure in the guise of progress, exploiting the momentum for an anniversary resolution at all costs to blunt the progress of implementation proper. For the "like-minded" states, the move was only the latest intervention against "liberal world order," the Russian legation seeking to "bait" others into a veto.[112] Part duel, part theater, the failed effort to add an eleventh resolution to the series might paradoxically become the source of its vitality into the third decade.

DISTRIBUTION AND DIVISION AT THE UN, MULTIPLE

Beyond the Security Council, the WPS ecosystem has grown somewhat rhizomatically, haphazardly, across the UN system. Space constraints prevent us here from mapping the spread comprehensively, so in this section we trace some significant ripples outward from the resolutions and presidential statements. We first briefly explore system-wide implementation of WPS at the UN, before discussing the development of governance mechanisms and apparatus relating to SEA and sexual violence in conflict.

System-wide responsibilities have been part of the agenda since the 2004 presidential statement, which—in addition to lauding the production of National Action Plans by member states—requested the development of an action plan to guide implementation at UN Headquarters. Following five years of negotiation and contestation, by 2010 the secretary-general was reporting on twenty-six separate indicators to track implementation, twenty of which are the primary responsibility of various UN entities (see table 4.2). Tendrils of prevention, protection, and participation are thus evident across the system, directly under the rubric of WPS resolutions in some cases, and visible even when bureaucratically demarcated from formal WPS in others. An example of the former is the sexual violence regime, a cutting from the WPS agenda that is now a symbiote, neither truly independent from nor the same as WPS, while the latter is exemplified by the UN system's treatment of the issue of SEA. Briefly, we address each in turn.

The "prevention" pillar was intended to have a much broader remit than solely sexual violence, as captured in the 2007 secretary-general's report in which practices under that theme aim to "mainstream a gender perspective into all conflict prevention activities and strategies, develop effective gender-sensitive early warning mechanisms and institutions, and strengthen efforts to prevent violence against women, including various forms of gender-based violence."[113] In 2009, however, with the creation of the SRSG on Sexual Violence in Conflict, there was a perceptible narrowing and focus provided for efforts toward that remit, through the creation of a micro-system that draws nourishment from the WPS ecosystem while exercising relative autonomy within it and beyond it. As we were told a few years later, "when this mandate was created . . . there was all of a sudden a strong focus on conflict-related sexual violence, a lot of visibility. When you have a special office for that, it's like the children in armed conflict: all of a sudden you have resources, you have an open debate every year, so it's like, oh, we have an open debate on children in armed conflict, we have an open debate on conflict-related sexual violence, and then we have the usual open debate on 1325," the implication being that this targeted focus area diverts resources and attention from other aspects of the agenda.[114]

The weight given to sexual violence in the evolution of WPS ties the SRSG and resolution provisions to an emerging regime: a supranational assembly of rules and institutional protocols. Individual elements predate WPS but have been given new force by its political status. Among them

TABLE 4.2 Changing mechanisms of monitoring and evaluation, 2004–2010

2004	2005	2007	2009	2010
S/PRST/2004/40	S/2005/636	S/2007/567	S/RES/1889	S/2010/173
Requests System-Wide Action Plan (SysAP) on the full implementation of UNSCR 1325	First SysAP (2007–2009) organized around 12 areas: A. Conflict prevention and early warning; B. Peacemaking and peace building; C. Peacekeeping operations; D. Humanitarian response; E. Post-conflict reconstruction and rehabilitation; F. Disarmament, demobilization, and reintegration; G. Preventing and responding to gender-based violence in armed conflict; H. Preventing and responding to sexual exploitation and abuse by United Nations staff, related personnel, and United Nations partners; I. Gender balance; J. Coordination and partnership; K. Monitoring and reporting; L. Financial resources.	Second SysAP (2008–2009). Consolidates 12 areas for action into five thematic areas: 1. Prevention; 2. Participation; 3. Protection; 4. Relief and recovery; 5. Normative.	Calls for indicators to track implementation of UNSCR 1325	Reported on 4 of 5 thematic areas identified in SysAP (2008–2009). "Normative" dimension deemed to "cut across" the remaining 4 thematic areas. Develops 26 indicators to track implementation, categorized using the 4 thematic areas. Each indicator is clearly linked to a goal. 20/26 indicators are primary responsibility of various UN entities; 6/26 indicators are primary responsibility of member states.

Source: Reproduced from Laura J. Shepherd, "Advancing the Women, Peace and Security Agenda: 2015 and Beyond," NOREF: The Norwegian Peacebuilding Resource Centre, August 28, 2014, https://noref.no/insights/publications/themes/gender-and-inclusivity/Advancing-the-Women-Peace-and-Security-agenda-2015-and-beyond.

are the categories of international humanitarian law—war crimes, crimes against humanity, and genocide—under which sexual violence may be prosecuted in tribunals. The International Criminal Court and an overlapping patchwork of ad hoc and hybrid courts are bound to WPS through resolution text, where the international court is the preferred vehicle for justice and accountability (e.g., S/RES/1325 2000, o.p. 9; S/RES/2122 2013, o.p. 12; S/RES/2242 2015, o.p. 14; S/RES/2467 2019, o.p. 15). International criminal law is in turn supported by commissions of inquiry and a sanctions mechanism operated from different parts of the UN. The former is authorized by the Human Rights Council and frequently include sexual violence in their mandates—for example, in Myanmar and Libya (A/HRC/42/66 2019, 3; A/HRC/RES/43/39 2020, o.p. 31). The latter operate through the Security Council's sanctions committee and have been slowly but progressively strengthened, with "stand-alone" sexual violence criteria applied to the Central African Republic and South Sudan "situations."[115] This work is supported in turn by international standards growing out of WPS initiatives, such as the International Protocol on the Documentation and Investigation of Sexual Violence in Conflict and Murad Code, both sponsored by the UK's Preventing Sexual Violence Initiative. Though the labor has been long, and its results have hardly gone unchallenged, the contributing parts of the anti–sexual violence governance project are increasingly formalized and complementary.

The resources available for the issue of sexual violence in conflict—meager as they may be in the grander scheme—has led to a flourishing, and this success is seen by some to have been to the detriment of other mandates, or the more comprehensive agenda in its entirety. In an environment in which council members need constant reminding to integrate WPS work into other thematic areas and country-specific discussion, it is a significant advantage to have the backing of a special representative: "the SRSG office has someone who does it [advocacy] . . . and they have one issue, they do it on every single country [on the agenda of the council], and they're very effective at it; I don't begrudge them that because it's a very important issue, but the rest of the agenda needs to be discussed as well."[116] The issue of sexual violence in conflict is thus emblematic of both the failure and the vitality of the broader WPS project: at the level of international diplomacy, sexual and gender-based violence is visible as never before—even *hyper*visible[117]—while its recognition threatens to deny the broader feminist peace.

The issue of sexual exploitation and abuse by UN personnel specifically is another instructive case. Unlike the sexual violence regime, SEA has been largely cut off from the core business of WPS at UN Headquarters. The prevention of SEA has grown out of but developed separately from *thematic* council work; the issue of SEA by UN peacekeepers has been consistently and persistently raised across field mission sites since the 1990s, with the problem attracting significant institutional attention in the early 2000s, in part as a result of the adoption of 1325.[118] One of the earliest institutional moves to mitigate the ongoing harms of SEA by peacekeepers was a resolution adopted by the General Assembly in 2003 that related specifically to documented instances of sexual misconduct by various UN personnel in Guinea, Liberia, and Sierra Leone.[119] This resolution was quickly followed by the "zero tolerance bulletin" released by then UN secretary-general Kofi Annan, which outlined the standards of behavior expected from UN staff, and the adoption of reporting requirements to the General Assembly.[120] The bulletin "was a cornerstone of SEA policy development, and reinforced the mandate laid out in UN Security Council Resolution 1325 for interveners to protect women from post-conflict sexual and gender-based violence."[121]

Building on a history of policy actions designed to ensure good conduct from UN staff, the bulletin and accompanying initiatives galvanized the humanitarian community and SEA prevention protocols proliferated under the auspices of the newly formed Inter-Agency Standing Committee Taskforce on Protection from SEA in Humanitarian Crises.[122] These preventative measures were evaluated in an investigation led by Prince Zeid Ra'ad Zeid Al-Hussein, and described as "manifestly inadequate" by the secretary-general when he presented the resulting report to the General Assembly.[123] The recommendations from the Zeid report were taken up by the institution in an inconsistent and rather limited fashion; in 2013, a similar report "made almost identical recommendations, noting the need to considerably strengthen enforcement of SEA policy—such as providing missions with investigative capacities via a fully resourced independent investigative unit—and to provide assistance to victims of SEA."[124]

The issue was elevated to the Security Council in 2016, and resolution 2272 on SEA was adopted that March, under the rubric of "United Nations peacekeeping operations," rather than WPS. The resolution's preambular material cites resolution 2242 (S/RES/2242 2015) as part of its documentary heritage, but otherwise does not engage the agenda; the only mention in the resolution itself is an encouragement directed at WPS as a relevant "mechanism" "to continue to include allegations of sexual exploitation and abuse in their regular reporting to the Secretary-General."[125] Thus, despite what are in many ways common roots—traceable back to Windhoek and the focus on gender and peacekeeping—the SEA agenda has been bureaucratically severed from WPS, a de-linking that practitioners and scholars have problematized.[126] "The individualization of SEA and focus on conduct and disciplinary responses reflects a broader trend related to gender issues: technocratic 'fixes' have been prioritized over efforts that address the underlying causes of gendered inequality and violence."[127] WPS is seen to "succeed" here in responses to gendered inequality and harm, where institutional responses to SEA continue to fail, though in terms of prominence, resources, and political will, success and failure are not so easily divided.

In addition to specific issue areas and the ebb and flow of their connection, the creation and installation of UN architecture is another dimension of the rippling out of WPS from the resolutions across the UN system. The creation of UN Women in 2010 at the behest of the General Assembly consolidated the functions and mandates of the Office of the Special Adviser on Gender Issues and Advancement of Women and the Division for the Advancement of Women of the Secretariat, which, along with UNIFEM, had provided extensive institutional support and leadership, well prior to the adoption of 1325. As UN Women bedded into the shifting institutional framework at UN Headquarters in New York, WPS emerged as a key area of activity for the new entity, which was seen by some to counterbalance the creation of the dedicated SRSG on sexual violence in conflict. UN Women was to perform a similar role, advocating and undertaking administrative and logistical responsibilities to forward the implementation of the agenda. From 2015, this included acting as the secretariat of the IEG generated by the adoption of resolution 2242. Though not widely discussed, those within the WPS circuit at UN Headquarters claim the IEG as a major success of the agenda over the past decade; it brings council members—state representatives and their mission staff—into direct contact with those affected by the conflicts the council is deliberating, providing language and precedents on request from states. Simultaneously, UN Women's position within the institution is strengthened, and its function as a source of credible and legitimate WPS expertise reaffirmed. WPS thus not only influences the substance with which the UN is concerned—the stuff of international peace and security—but also the governance structures through which this work is executed.

POWER AND DANGER REVISITED

Analyzing just a fragment of the WPS ecosystem—those aspects of it located at and anchored in the work of UN Headquarters in New York—reveals its plurality. In part, this is a story of how human rights, protection of civilians, and gender equality themes have given way to feminist peace, or have been rearticulated as feminist peace, a story of feminist *progress* and its generative effects. Other ways of establishing the lineage of the agenda are possible: in the case of Namibia's role offering an almost complete inversion of whitewashed history, the version of what WPS is supposedly not (or is no longer): led by the Global South, imagined out of anticolonial struggle, and grounded in success. We have traced out not only the series of WPS resolutions but also the dynamics of contestation (the dueling claims about what motivates or lies at the heart of the agenda as well as attempts to contain difference through the assertion of a true canon) and institutional change that extend beyond the council. We have attempted to show through our discussion in this chapter that early feminist insights about the "power and danger" of institutional homing were prescient,[128] and the precarity of this positioning persists.

The networked relationality of WPS at UN Headquarters is also apparent in our exploration of the archives and memories of those involved at the time. While time blunts recall, for several resolutions a consistent picture emerges of drafts rotating between NGOs, WPS-friendly states, and UN gender bureaucracy, moving with some friction across a circuit that includes all three faces of the UN and draws in forces from beyond. At different times, there were seemingly entrenched divisions within as much as between each group. Civil society organizations were vehemently split over the desirability of a resolution on sexual violence specifically. Governments were divided between friendly, hostile, and incapable, with the same state sometimes occupying more than one position. As a whole, the network was intensely concentrated in Midtown Manhattan, but at tilting points would convene for intense deliberations elsewhere, forming a cosmopolitan archipelago of meeting houses and "seminars" from Windhoek to Wilton Park.

While we have suggested that the creation of 1325 was enabled by a particular coalition, there is no single origin point of WPS, nor is there a single consensus version of the arrayed resolutions twenty-three years later. The members of the Security Council as of October 2000 were not mere tribunes, but agencies of state reason, such as it was. Viewed in this light it becomes clearer that WPS was split from the start, and that it was even then heavy with possibility and unintended consequences. Discourses of duel and theater live on and are visible each year at the open debates that bear the title of the agenda (frequently encountered by scholars and practitioners alike as opportunities for geopolitics as normal in the guise of feminist peace).[129] We have also explored specific trigger points and phrases (like sexual and reproductive rights, or "SRHR"), the importance of changes of government and personnel, and the spurs to individual resolutions. At the heart of this lineage is the diplomatic WPS circuit, the network of actors moving in and out of offices and posts trailing gender expertise, connections, and commitment to pushing the agenda forward in all its many guises, whenever the opportunity is presented. Officials from government missions circulate early drafts, use civil society feedback to refine language, collaborate across space, draft text that they know other states will take credit for; for some resolutions, "it was a bit like having an entire orchestra of people contributing."[130] And we note also the roles of key individuals and the contingency of their appointments, interests, and performances, a cast increasingly recognized in the new histories of 1325's birth.[131]

The growth of WPS over the last two decades has produced a complex, interconnected system of policy and governance across and beyond the UN; in this regard, it can appear as if WPS is perpetually misdirected, pursuing feminist peace across the slippery circuits of the three UNs in a clumsy effort to keep up with the shell game of true security business. Fionnuala Ní Aoláin advances this argument, for example, in the context of the 2015 alignment of counterterrorism and countering violent extremism with WPS in resolution 2242.[132] Ní Aoláin cautions against a hasty celebration of "inclusion" because it also represents a danger that "is the greater precisely because the terms of inclusion have been set by male-dominated security institutions and states whose interest in a robust dialogue about the definition of terrorism, the causes conducive to the production of terrorism, and the relationship between terrorism and legitimate claims for self-determination by collective groups has been virtually nil."[133]

The impossibility of fixing the home of WPS at the UN in the council, the extent to which the agenda exceeds council business and spills out across the organization through its various entities and agencies and in policy and protocol, presents the appearance of a thriving, if heterogenous, agenda. But our investigations have also suggested that this energy is frequently met with equal and opposite resistance, blocked or sidestepped entirely. The vitality of WPS is often in search of the "right" committee, the seat of power, the ultimate locus of authority; in the early days of 1325, the grafting of feminist peace onto the agenda of the UN Security Council fostered hope for future blossoms even as the dangers of co-optation tempered those hopes. We have shown here how the agenda is being produced and reproduced through these relations at the council and across the UN system, mindful of the porosity of that institution's boundaries in world politics. In the chapters that follow, we explore other spaces and enactments of WPS that are also integral parts of the ecosystem, technologies of governance relationally constituted and with their own reproductive effects. To that end, we now turn to national expressions of WPS and efforts to "domesticate" the agenda.

5

DOMESTICATING
THE GENDER PERSPECTIVE

There is no document of civilization that is not at the same time a document of barbarism."[1] Writing from exile in Paris in 1940, as Europe's colonial and genocidal practices returned to devour it, Walter Benjamin distilled the critique of teleology, that reassuring justification of present arrangements, preferring instead the injunction to "brush history against the grain."[2] The conflagration of the Second World War yielded the United Nations Charter, which remains the indispensable reference point for multiple freedom horizons. Feminism has served as both a diagnosis of barbarism and a promise of civilization, increasingly present in the pages of national strategy, an interloper in the house of realpolitik. Today it is proposed that foreign policy itself might become feminist—as has been declared by at least ten governments, North and South—a designation cross-pollinated with the WPS agenda, which has been the primary means through which feminist arguments have entered ministries of defense and foreign affairs.[3]

At the time of writing, 183 National Action Plans guiding WPS engagement have been produced, 161 of which are included in our mapping (see chapter 3). Dozens of countries have issued multiple editions, and six boast four or more (Denmark, Italy, the Netherlands, Norway, Switzerland, and the United Kingdom). By the metric of the "norm cascade"—whereby adoption by a third of states triggers a tipping point, consolidating a new rule of international society—the articles of a feminist peace have become endemic.[4] The cascade entails a chronology and compass, ideals elaborated at a global level then gradually adopted and integrated by national governments, local authorities, social groups, and individuals. Of course, rules of conduct are first invented by individuals, oftentimes working within the apparatus of a state. For the WPS ecosystem, the global wellspring is more elusive still, with rival articulations of the agenda being the product of coalitions of diplomats, bureaucrats, experts, and transnational activist networks. Every NAP encodes vitality and failure, advocacy and resistance, a negotiated settlement typically forged by an uneasy and shifting social alliance, or alternatively is a product of the advocacy "boomerang," where national civil society groups partner with international organizations to pressure their own government.[5] Ours is a study of the generative, productive effects of NAPs as projections or mirrors of the sovereign self, sometimes implying but not reducible to the analysis of NAP implementation failures, the many urgent and necessary accounts of the WPS "paper tiger."[6]

Standard histories of the WPS agenda usually note the adoption of the NAP for the implementation of resolution 1325 by the Danish government in 2005. NAPs were first broached in the 2004 presidential statement on WPS as an indicator that UN member states were making efforts to implement the resolution in their national (domestic) contexts (S/PRST/2004/40, 3) and have since been widely interpreted as the preeminent signal by states of their investment in the WPS agenda, the level of action where the feminist peace ceases to be a list of pleas and urgings from the Security Council or other proxies of the "international community" and instead becomes *operational.*[7] The early generation of NAPs tended to be perfunctory and repetitive, but the genre has become increasingly elaborate, the release of new iterations carefully timed (e.g., to coincide with landmark anniversaries or International Women's Day, held every March 8), trailed and launched, shaped by stakeholders who are themselves increasingly sophisticated about the internal differentiation of the agenda and its links to other spheres of government.[8]

To "domesticate" has a double meaning, latterly connoting the importance of integrating the inner and outer aspects of the state, attending to participation and protection as much in ministries of home affairs and gender as in diplomacy and defense. On this front governments of the

Global North especially are failing, but when understood as recrafting the demands of the Security Council into the identity of a state, domesticated WPS is thriving. Such has been the success of moves to pursue the WPS agenda through the formation and adoption of NAPs that these have themselves become a synecdoche for implementation, the pulse of WPS measured by the rhythm of publication and ministerial announcement. To imprint a policy with the sovereign sign *is* to enact WPS. At the same time, NAPs can remake WPS, having "more creative licence than UNSC resolutions" because they are not products of international diplomatic consensus and thus present different opportunities for expansive interpretation of the agenda's concerns and remit.[9] NAPs may be a vehicle for implementation, of course, but we problematize the association of NAPs with implementation such that the two are presumed to stand in for each other, challenging not only the idea that NAPs are a form of implementation in and of themselves but also the premise that implementation best happens through NAPs. Even such strong signals as signatures to treaties are better thought of as *institutionalizing* policy, which need not lead to *implementation* in the sense of formal state mechanisms that ensure routine compliance.[10]

Action plans are today supplemented with other bespoke governance initiatives—the Women, Peace, and Security Caucus and Act in the United States Congress, Canada's feminist aid policy, the United Kingdom's Preventing Sexual Violence Initiative—which are to varying degrees caught by our ecosystem frame. Agents of WPS—especially from civil society—sometimes choose to engage with the agenda outside the NAP process, even where one exists.[11] More, states that do not produce NAPs are not necessarily "failing" to "do" WPS (or to do it correctly); the production of a NAP—indeed, repeated iterations, as is the case in many countries—is not necessarily evidence of vitality. In this chapter, we argue that the opposite can in fact be true: NAP production can be a way of stultifying feminist peace, or interpolating WPS into the machinery of the state. This is after all a key part of *governing*: delimiting, policing, calibrating, reconciling the interests of different interests and social forces. Likewise, the dynamics of NAP resistance, rather than being read as failure, should be examined on a contextual basis to investigate the quality of contention and its effect on the tensions and possibilities through which the agenda is structured.

Despite their apparently technical purpose—directing state spending, ranking priority areas, mandating quotas, establishing baselines and metrics of progress—national WPS policies are also beacons of national status, sites for the production and reproduction of foreign policy narratives. Gender equality is a standard of civilization, and NAPs promise to meet it. "Foreign policy" is the name given to the conscious strategy of states, fashioned in ministries, special interest groups, and thought collectives, articulated as a stable "national interest" or, alternatively, an admixture of "interests" and "values," material and ideational. It is practiced by a network of planners and emissaries, implementing instructions that may be secret or at least not openly debated. But foreign policy is at the same time, in public representations and justifications, a way of securing "the boundaries of the identity in whose name it operates."[12] Following the insights of relationalism, domestication is not only the transfer of fixed policy from the international or a partner national sphere, but an ongoing process of boundary making, a project in which practices and transactions are constantly being sorted into separate domains even as sovereignty is presented as an invariant fact.[13] NAPs, as policy documents, reproduce the inside/outside distinction on which "foreign" policy rests.[14] Unlike resolutions or statements of the Security Council, which must pay heed to convention and are engineered in a similar length and voice, national commitments are subject to no such regulation and are chaotic to encounter in their multiple forms, one sometimes bearing no resemblance to another, although there are echoes and traces of similarity across groups of NAPs within the set.

Our tour through national WPS thus foregrounds the interplay of technicality, statecraft, and performances of race/nation/state. That which is made central and that which is made surplus to WPS in national engagements are brought into focus as we explore the currents that reproduce WPS within and under the auspices of the state, reading NAPs against the grain. We proceed at three depths, and in three substantive sections: first, we comment on the most straightforward measure of national energy, the existence or nonexistence of a NAP; second, we elaborate on the evasion of the central object of WPS—war—in select NAPs and the counternarrative of WPS offered in others; and finally, we examine the boundary work of securing the national subject of foreign policy, with attention to the place of Indigeneity, race, and nation in the NAPs of primarily liberal democratic settler colonial states. Together, these NAP interrogations enable a thoroughgoing and novel critique of the domestication of WPS and provide further illustration of the contours of the WPS ecosystem.

NAPs AND THEIR DISCONTENTS

NAPs do not (only) describe the WPS agenda; they constitute it. Where NAPs begin to represent specific issues, or represent those issues either more or less consistently, those issues become part of what the WPS agenda *is*. For example, several national governments (Austria, the Netherlands, Côte d'Ivoire, and Uganda) joined regional organizations in referring to terrorism and extremism before the Security Council took up the issue substantively in resolution 2242, which in turn generated a spike in NAPs after 2015 (S/RES/2242, paras. 11–13). The articulation of an issue in one of the WPS resolutions need not generate dedicated uptake by member states: resolution 2242 also encouraged states to do more to recognize the insecurities and threats associated with climate degradation, but we observe no significant uptick in coverage on this front. Issues can also spread through national policy without an obvious UN parallel, as with internal displacement and forced migration, which remained a key topic despite the rise of terrorism and extremism.

As policy artifacts, NAPs might be expected to reflect and represent the interests and priorities of the state, however formulated, including whether the state in question has an interest in being part of the recognized community of WPS states. Figure 5.1 shows the concentration of NAPs in various regions; although there is some NAP activity in every region, the most policy energy is clearly to be observed in western Europe and North America (where there are the highest number of states shaded in darker grays, representing publication of more than one NAP). Eastern Europe, North Africa, Central America, and the Middle East have relatively low levels of NAP activity, although as we have noted, NAP activity should be presumed to stand in neither for implementation practices that transform peace and security "on the ground" nor for support and commitment to feminist principles. More, NAPs, despite their

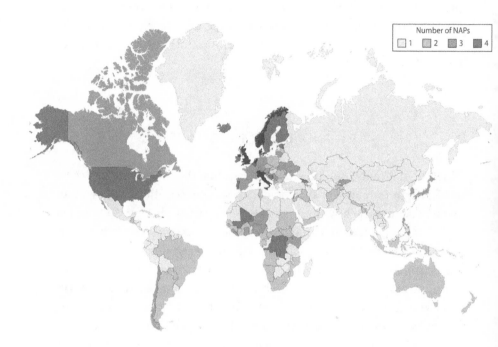

FIGURE 5.1 Concentration of NAP activity worldwide ($n = 161$).

Source: Map by the authors.

appearances, are not necessarily to be taken as discrete expressions of national WPS: at least some have been funded by other states, if through the mediating role of international agencies, expressions of the collaborative WPS circuit.[15]

There are some notable absences among the community of "NAP-having states," and some notable late adopters. South Africa, for example, only released its first NAP in 2020, which was, on the face of it, long overdue given the country's consistent expressions of support for the agenda at the Security Council. In 2008 South Africa cosponsored the adoption of resolution 1820, the second WPS resolution,[16] and oversaw the adoption of resolution 2493, the tenth resolution in the collection. Further, representatives from South Africa collectively have a remarkable record of contributions to the open debates on WPS (both those engaging the agenda in October and the debates on sexual violence in conflict that typically take place in April). Until 2020, in fact, South Africa was among the very few UN member states that had not (yet) developed a NAP but had nonetheless consistently attended the debates and made a statement, missing only two since 2002 (Lichtenstein is now the only state to hold a similar record).

Delays and disavowals of NAPs, despite evidence of a commitment to advancing the WPS agenda, should prompt a reconsideration of NAPs as the primary vehicle for implementation. It is also a useful reminder that within the WPS ecosystem important documents other than NAPs exist, many of which demonstrate ownership of and authority over the principles embedded in the WPS agenda. The African Union more broadly is not often centered in WPS analysis, despite being a locus of significant early activity in the development of the WPS agenda (see also chapter 3, pp. 67–69).[17] South Africa, even in the absence of a NAP, was considered "a frontrunner regarding levels of women in the military and on deployments . . . [,] rated as one of the top 20 troop-contributing countries to the UN."[18] During its term of office as an elected member of the Security Council (2019–2020), not only did South Africa shepherd through a resolution, it also engaged across the UN system. Even prior to its NAP adoption, therefore, South Africa was, in essence, "doing" WPS, along with many other African states, in ways that are not visible within the NAP population, thus encouraging a wider optic on WPS documents and protocols to understand the ways in which the agenda is being reproduced.

India is another state that has famously resisted the development of a NAP, while undertaking actions easily interpreted as in line with WPS provisions and principles. Like South Africa (though to a lesser extent), India has supported the WPS agenda at the UN Security Council through attendance and statements at WPS open debates, particularly in more recent years. More significantly, the Indian government pioneered the development of all-female formed police units (FFPU), which have been cited as a landmark in enhancing gender equality in peacekeeping;[19] Soumita Basu refers to the FFPU as a "concrete policy manifestation of the WPS agenda."[20] It is a manifestation that India should be credited for developing: "The first FFPU in UN peacekeeping emerged from an Indian context that has historically included, and continues to include, gendered approaches to policing. . . . Despite the global publicity around the FFPU, the Indian domestic factors that made it possible have not been well recognized abroad."[21] The FFPU and India's troop contributions are frequently cited by Indian representatives at the WPS open debates as evidence of the government's dedication to the agenda.[22]

The longstanding commitment to this element of the agenda sits at odds with the continued resistance to developing a NAP, a greater-than-normal degree of domestic policy contestation.[23] Moreover, the government refuses to permit the invocation of resolution 1325 or the principles of the WPS agenda as a normative framework through which to govern the ongoing conflicts in "disturbed areas" that are subject to (and whose designation as such is legitimized by) the Armed Forces Special Powers Act.[24] While the Indian government's concern may be related to sovereignty, as well as fears regarding interventionist actions from the international community, Indian WPS practices suggest that the government's denial or reluctance stems at least in part from the definition of conflict and the extent to which a NAP would sit uneasily in a context of ongoing violence or "disturbance."[25]

In fact, the relevance of WPS to the violence in particular in Nagaland, Manipur, and Jammu and Kashmir has been explicitly denied by the Indian government. At the WPS open debate in October 2019, the Pakistani representative made a strong statement about this issue, arguing that the WPS agenda

> applies to all women in conflict situations, especially in cases of foreign occupation, such as in occupied Jammu and Kashmir. For almost three months, the world has witnessed in horror as India's cruel clampdown on all civil liberties in occupied Kashmir and its illegal annexation of the disputed territory, in gross violation of international law and several Security Council resolutions, have exacerbated and compounded the suffering of people, especially women and girls.[26]

Subsequently, the Indian representative described his Pakistani counterpart as "regurgitating rhetoric" about the violations of women's rights and "*making baseless allegations without any relevance to the agenda under consideration.*"[27] WPS haunts the disputed territory, refused precisely because it would otherwise reveal something, would entail changes in international standing as much as new metrics of implementation, a political threat in policy garb.

The territorial sovereign authors WPS policy; but "national" WPS is also deployed as resistance, and in situations where the issuing entity does not enjoy the usual powers and recognition of a state. In the case of Palestine, the agenda has been adopted in large part to name an occupation (recall chapter 3, pp. 70). In 2005 an alteration to Israeli law and a Palestinian Presidential Decree on 1325—two NAP prototypes—indicated a potential dialogue. Yet the "harmony of interests" conception of women's role in peacemaking was to be confounded. The International Women's Commission lasted six years but disbanded over the possibility of collaborating in a context of occupation.[28] In the buildup to the issuing of the 2015 Palestinian National Strategic Framework, which we treat as equivalent to a first NAP despite the nomenclature, the overwhelming emphasis of civil society groups was on Palestinian women as "direct victims of occupation," stressing displacement, fragmentation of families, land confiscation, settlements, and arrests as key vectors, with a secondary emphasis on gender-based discrimination within a "conservative and traditional" Palestinian society.[29] Resolution 1325 was taken up as "a new tool for engaging against and exposing the policies of the aggressive occupying state that violates international resolutions and legitimacy."[30]

These emphases are strongly reflected in the most recent Palestinian NAPs, where strategic objectives relate overwhelmingly to gender-based discrimination linked to the occupation, such as imprisonment, house demolitions, and harassment at checkpoints; resilience against the occupation, through sponsorship of women's initiatives; and seeking to hold occupation forces accountable through legal redress, especially through UN and international bodies (Palestinian NAP I 2017, 12–43). The WPS ecosystem is situated in a larger infrastructure comprised of human rights treaties in a variant of the boomerang effect, with an occupied polity appealing to international frameworks against the intermediary occupying force (Palestine NAP II 2020, 29). Palestinian civil society groups continue to stress the relevance of 1325 to "a prolonged Israeli occupation system facilitated by militarism and violence."[31] In a more recent response to the WPS Global Study, the MIFTAH (the Palestinian Initiative for the Promotion of Global Dialogue and Democracy) group offered ten strategies for implementing 1325, nine of which relate to exposing, documenting, resisting, and lobbying international agencies on human rights violations related to the colonial occupation.[32] Palestinian feminists commenting on 1325 have likewise seen the barrier of patriarchal culture as secondary to, indeed exacerbated by, Israeli military authority: "The occupation reinforces the patriarchal structures of Palestinian society."[33] Direct appeals to the Security Council have been accomplished through the civil society medium, articulating WPS as requiring not just gender-responsive humanitarian relief or greater participation, but an end to occupation and settler expansion itself.

That the Palestinian Authority has developed three NAPs or equivalent instruments while the Israeli government has none may at the same time indicate that the uses of the agenda are not as straightforwardly hegemonic as some critics have suggested. As Sarai Aharoni has argued, WPS-related norms have been helpful in allowing activists to challenge domestic patriarchy within Israel, but their utility for peace building has been minimal.[34] A limited codification of WPS in Israeli national law regarding women's political participation may be read as an acknowledgment of feminist peace arguments at the same time that active opposition to Israeli occupation is articulated in the Palestinian NAP. Despite the prospect of a more constructive peace process founded on the meaningful participation of women on all sides, the agenda is instead fractured along the fault lines of the conflict. Though Israel still does not have a NAP of its own, despite civil society and international efforts over some years, Israeli legations at the United Nations regularly narrate the state as an advocate of WPS norms.[35] Diplomats have linked 1325 to the role of women in the Israel Defense Forces during debates on peacekeeping,[36] to women as agents of change against extremism,[37] and to the prophet Miriam in Jewish theology.[38] Military publicity celebrates the resonance with past feminist icons (see figure 5.2). The point is less to endorse or denounce these strategic framings than to note how they are disclosed when WPS is analyzed as a field of contention in which antagonistic parties may mobilize competing claims under a nominally common umbrella.

WRITING THE WPS STATE

Some governments resist the formalization of WPS in action plan form lest it trouble their counterinsurgency, pacification, or state-making programs; others proclaim their leadership while drawing on the agenda

FIGURE 5.2 "We Can Do It," released by the Israel Defense Forces on social media for International Women's Day 2015.

Source: Israel Defense Forces (@IDF), "#HappyWomensDay from the IDF! #MakeItHappen," Twitter, March 8, 2015, 12:37 p.m., https://twitter.com/IDF/status/574609954046345216.

selectively. In the literature that attends closely to national WPS policy, inconsistency is a recurrent mark of failure: insufficient political will or governance capacity frustrating the ambitions set out by the Security Council or social movements. Common remedies include monitoring against baseline indicators, consistent gender budgeting, and integration with national law and international treaty instruments. Optimists mark the progress that has been made, cynics the betrayal. The advent of WPS rankings encourages the sense of a contest: an ordinal hierarchy arraigning all governments from best to worst, most WPS to least. Assessment is doubtless necessary, selectivity tracked against some measure, though the practice can also obscure the constitutive plurality of WPS, the ways in which it is assembled anew.

The "production" of WPS in national discourse is a matter not just of laying claim to some trends in the field, some pillars or niches, but of reconceiving war and peace in a parochial frame. The failure that stalks the agenda includes the habits and decisions that prevent recognition, the omission of troubling facts and violent histories. Reading NAPs against the grain implies an *agnotology*, the study of patterned ignorance, or amnesia (as Paul Gilroy has called for, especially when it is colonialism that is being forgotten),[39] not least since the postcolonial is always post-conflict.[40] The specter of colonialism may seem wildly at odds with the proceduralism and egalitarianism of feminist advocacy, a grotesque and oversized horror. If there is an agreed complaint against WPS, it is that the project has been insufficiently implemented, not excessively enforced. Yet the temporal coincidence of the agenda with the "colonial present"[41] offers a natural experiment in foreign policy discourse, as may be illustrated by the place afforded to Iraq and Afghanistan in the plans of the United States and United Kingdom.

Both countries are recognized as WPS champions (the two penholders for canonical resolutions in the Security Council);[42] both have long been engaged with prominent gender issues through and beyond NAPs; and together, they were the leading partners in the two most significant wars of the early twenty-first century, in Afghanistan and Iraq beginning in 2001 and 2003, respectively. Between 276,000 and 308,000 deaths were directly caused by the Iraq War;[43] the United States alone expended $880 billion from 2003 to 2020 in theater.[44] In blood and sheer military labor "Iraq" was the defining geopolitical trauma of the 2000s, unfolding in

parallel with the nascent WPS agenda, with which it so obviously inter-
sected, touching every "pillar" and implicating swaths of the ecosystem.[45]
Even acknowledging that the machinery of state might be internally
divided in its attitude to recent wars, few sites could have mattered more
for American and British gender perspectives in the first two decades of
the WPS agenda. Feminist language figured in the arguments for both
wars, especially Afghanistan (as we explore in the next chapter), though
arguably more often against them.[46] "Gender" was everywhere in the conjoined wars: in political rhetoric; nationalist and sectarian sentiment;
combatant role and embodiment; the swell of protest and uprising; displacement and refuge; the toll and patterns of death and debility; the aesthetics of humanitarian appeals; in aid spending and blueprints for
peace; ethnic cleansing and genocide; the legacies of memory and haunt-
ing; and the figures of the terrorist and the veteran.

Certainly, Iraq appears in official national WPS. In the first U.S. plan,
it is a "country in transition," one of several where Washington "works
with the women of the region to ensure the successful transformation of
their countries into vital and vibrant democracies" (US NAP I 2011, 24).
The language of "partnership" remains in the next edition, with programs
for survivors of gender-based violence in Iraq alongside similar efforts in
Cameroon, Mali, and Ukraine (US NAP II 2016, 9; see figure 5.3). In UK
policy, Iraq is more present, twice named as a priority or focus country
(UK NAP II 2012 and IV 2018). Yet the conflagration is rendered in a
passive voice: "Iraq has suffered many years of conflict," "exacerbated and
prolonged" by unnamed external actors but at root sectarian (UK NAP
IV 2018, 21).[47] The particulars become more explicit the further any given
document is from the 2003 invasion, as Daesh/Islamic State becomes the
shared nemesis, the United Kingdom's plan announcing reconciliation
mechanisms for areas liberated from its control (UK NAP IV 2018, 18;
figure 5.4). For Afghanistan too, "emerging from more than 40 years of
conflict" (UK NAP IV 2018, 21), a long shadow obscures the identities of
the parties to the war. Britain's share of the state-building project may be
glimpsed, obliquely, in passages dedicated to professionalization of the
Afghan military (UK NAP IV 2018, 19) and in ministerial speeches that
celebrated the inclusion of female cadets in Afghan state forces.[48]

A naive reader could be forgiven for not realizing that the United Kingdom had been at war in Afghanistan or Iraq at all, still less that the

The United States is supporting partners in Iraq who are implementing programs that address the protection of vulnerable people, including women and children. Protection activities include the threat of unexploded ordnance, family separation, excessive security screenings and detention procedures, armed conflict, and sexual violence, which remain widespread throughout Iraq. *Photo credit: UN OCHA*

FIGURE 5.3   A partnership for gender protection in Iraq.

Source: Original caption, reprinted from U.S. NAP II, 28.

invasion of Iraq had so divided the same "international community" and Security Council otherwise seen as the wellspring of WPS; that legal consensus identified it as a war of aggression in violation of the UN Charter; or that "Operation Iraqi Freedom" had in turn spawned new geographies of insurgency and sectarianism. In launching NAPs, ministers were more likely to mention South Sudan, Somalia, or Burma than Iraq.[49] The example of Female Engagement Teams as a vector of women's participation and cultural sensitivity raised the relative profile of Afghanistan, though to the exclusion of any other aspect of gender.[50] For Iraqi feminists, WPS represents an irreducible tension: it is a source of energy

FIGURE 5.4 "Womenandchildren" taking refuge from Daesh in Iraq.

Source: Original caption, reprinted from UK NAP IV, 18.

and legitimacy indelibly linked to the invasion.[51] As Yasmin Chilmeran has shown, the NAP became a symbol of *Western feminist* desires, generating "anger on multiple levels, both in feelings of being robbed of ownership over the NAP, and at the implications for the perceived capacity of Iraqi actors themselves."[52] The WPS circuit, then, may mark the advent of a NAP as a sign of vitality—Iraq issued the Middle East's first—at the same time that the plan's nominal beneficiaries are ambivalent or bereft.

It was not preordained that the United Kingdom and the United States should demur from a fuller accounting. Foreign policy discourse might just as well celebrate Kurdish feminism in northern Iraq, take credit for the period of freedom from Taliban rule, or index military interventions as an extension of the suffragist peace. As many of its critics stress, the WPS policy field is not intrinsically antiwar, as is underscored by the place of gender balancing in the armed forces in these same plans. In a plural field, there is no contradiction in celebrating military feminism or postwar diversity initiatives as progress. Yet official U.S. and UK WPS documents have proved almost coy in detailing partners and beneficiaries, evidencing low-key support at odds with the undeniably transformative effects of war and its aftermaths in both countries. The silence works to disentangle the foreign policy of the United States and United Kingdom from the gendered coordinates of post-conflict Iraq and Afghanistan. In brevity and euphemism, NAPs separate histories of violence that are in truth conjoined. The NAP form is not just an anodyne schema; in its technical provisions and policy speak it hides relations and convergences, produces the image of the "friend of WPS" as outside and distant from the essence of conflict, always already resolving, assisting, protecting, evolving. Though strategic silence is a ubiquitous feature of national WPS, it is not a necessary effect of genre. Other NAPs do acknowledge the historical legacies of violence, whether in the aftermath of genocidal civil war (Guatemalan NAP, 15–17), the state's post-conflict record with international regimes (Libera NAP II, 6–11), or the ramifications of an independence struggle at fifty years remove (Bangladesh NAP, 2–5).

Critical accounts of the agenda have tended to focus on plans produced in the Global North for obvious reasons: capacity to deliver, proclamations of commitment, and the sheer volume of discourse about WPS emanating from institutions and movements located in the forty-two states that account for 55 percent of all plans.[53] Yet the Global South writes WPS too, in ways that indicate distinct visions of power and progress.[54] Brazil adopted its first NAP relatively late and in a moment of deep political turmoil. Developed under Dilma Rousseff, Brazil's first female president and a former revolutionary who had been tortured in the dictatorship years, it was officially issued by Michel Temer's caretaker administration following Rousseff's impeachment.[55] Symbolically released on International Women's Day 2017, the plan was initially limited to two years to reconcile the original vision with the deep skepticism of the military and to a lesser extent the Foreign Ministry.[56] Emphasizing women's participation in policing and combat, and excluding the references to internal conflict and human trafficking that had been briefly considered in early drafts, the plan celebrates the Brazilian way of peacekeeping, echoing a wider counter-discourse of Brazil's contribution to international order.[57]

Though its text is relatively conventional, the Brazilian NAP also includes an appendix of images, presenting a maternal lineage long predating 1325. Before the compulsory photos of smiling peacekeepers, a number of historical women are featured, beginning with Maria Quitéria de Jesus Medeiros, described in a caption as the first Brazilian woman to join the military (Brazil NAP I 2017, 73; see figure 5.5).[58] Quitéria had disguised herself as a man to join the then secessionist army of Dom Pedro against Portuguese rule in the 1820s. Born in Bahia, an area with a high Black and mulatto population, Quitéria was once described by an aristocratic British visitor in the following terms:

> Her dress is that of a soldier of one of the Emperor's battalions, with the addition of a tartan kilt, which she told me she had adopted from a picture representing a highlander, as the most feminine military dress. What would the Gordons and MacDonalds say to this? The "garb of old Gaul," chosen as a womanish attire!—Her father is a Portuguese. . . . Her mother was also a Portuguese; yet the young woman's features, especially her eyes and forehead, have the strongest characteristics of the Indians. . . . She is not particularly masculine in her appearance, and her manners are gentle and cheerful. She has not contracted any thing [sic] coarse or vulgar in her camp life, and I believe that no imputation has ever been substantiated against her modesty. One thing is certain, that her sex never was known until her father applied to her commanding officer to seek her.[59]

Her deception exposed, Quitéria continued to serve alongside male combatants, going on to lead an all-female force.[60] She is reported to have declared that she was fighting not only against rule from Lisbon but "for myself . . . to liberate Maria Quitéria de Jesus Medeiros from paternal tyranny, from the painful domestic chores, from an unsavoury life. Oh, I will fight with water over my breasts for the liberation of women, for the new woman that will emerge."[61] Quitériea has latterly been hailed as a "Brazilian version of Joan of Arc,"[62] a heroine of the "backlands,"[63] rebel, guerrilla, amazon—the Amazon River itself taking its name from the Indigenous women who attacked the first conquistadors traveling its waters.[64] When women were first allowed to enter the administrative branch of the army, the mixed cohort was named the "Maria Quitéria Group" (Brazil NAP, 11–13).

What does the inclusion of such a figure in a policy artifact signify? Initially released only in Portuguese, the Brazilian NAP arguably serviced a primarily domestic audience, though a deeply fractured one. Quitéria's androgyny, queer ethnicity, and martial prowess suggest an unconventional reading of the nation's founding, though she is at the same time well-known and celebrated in Brazilian military circles.[65] As the NAP

FIGURE 5.5 Maria Quitéria de Jesus Medeiros, foremother of Brazilian WPS.

Source: Reprinted from Brazil NAP official translation, 73.

process was initiated, a wider rediscovery of feminism was also under-way. Several academic professorships and inclusion initiatives, the NAP working group among them, took the name of Bertha Lutz, the Brazilian zoologist, feminist, and diplomat at the forefront of efforts to enshrine gender equality in the UN Charter.[66] Like Quitéria, Lutz was included in the NAP's gallery and referenced repeatedly by the Brazilian delega-tion at the Security Council in open debates on WPS and sexual violence in the years either side of the NAP's arrival, even being quoted in the chamber: "There will never be unbreakable peace in the world until women help to forge it."[67] Despite the last-minute narrowing of the NAP, and its subsequent fortunes under the Bolsonaro government, the fig-ures of Quitéria and Lutz remain, symbols of an alternate herstory around which the Brazilian military, Foreign Ministry, and civil society might find some common ground. As an intragovernmental tactic, recov-ering and elevating historical icons was one self-conscious way in which NAP drafters sought to reassure "the military and other actors that were resistant to the NAP that things wouldn't have to change."[68] The balance was precarious, requiring a tribute to foremothers that at the same time muted explicitly feminist symbols that would read as leftist in Brazilian political culture.[69]

As NAPs become longer and more sophisticated, national identity is increasingly signaled in visual terms.[70] In a quite different postcolonial context, the Polish plan offers a congruous prehistory. Like Brazil's issued relatively late, Poland's NAP was coordinated with its elected term on the UN Security Council (2018–2019) and drew on some years of preparatory diplomacy. As its permanent representative put the case during an ear-lier open debate,

In the past, Poland was a victim of many foreign aggressions and suf-fered the consequences of violent conflict. In that respect, I would like to highlight the role of the heroic women who led with vision, dedica-tion and courage, and stood up against aggression. One example of such a woman comes from the history of my own country, as well as that of a country rather far away from Poland—the island of Tonga. Queen Sālote of Tonga was the first foreign leader to officially oppose the German inva-sion of Poland on 1 September 1939. She and her action are a great exam-ple for us even now in the twenty-first century.[71]

Resistance to foreign colonial imposition orients Polish WPS, a participation agenda flowing from a variety of historical and contemporary
sources, ranging from the 1863 "January Uprising" against Russian suzer-
ainty and the Polish Legions of the First World War to women's involvement in border policing and the EU Frontex agency (Polish NAP, 16, 15; see
figures 5.6 and 5.7).[72] Against the focus of most NAPs on contemporary
conflict and assistance, the wellspring of Poland's engagement instead
becomes the legacy of women who resisted the Nazis and Soviets, an
inheritance continued in the institutional form in the countries membership in NATO, the European Union, and the Organization for Security
and Co-operation in Europe (Polish NAP, 6–8). The attempt to present a
specifically Polish prehistory to WPS coexists with complex regional
dynamics, from the rise of "anti-gender" movements, the Russian invasion of Ukraine (ongoing at the time of writing), and the wider politics of
a suspended colonial-postcolonial condition, neither Global North nor
Global South.[73]

FIGURE 5.6 Voluntary Legion of Women, Lviv, 1918.

Source: Reprinted from Polish NAP, 6.

FIGURE 5.7 Lieutenant Katarzyna Tomiak-Siemieniewicz, the first Polish woman to become a MiG-29 fighter pilot.

Source: Reprinted from Polish NAP, 9.

VICTIMS AND SOVEREIGNS

NAPs represent, and reproduce, the state's understanding of militarization and feminist peace, selectively engaging with dimensions of the agenda that align with the partial tellings of complex histories—and presents—that the state wishes to promote. The Brazilian and Polish NAPs are emblematic of feminism in the vernacular of women's combat and anticolonial resistance, which subverts a unidimensional appreciation of how feminist peace is disciplined through its incorporation into policy. Other policy artifacts broach and evade race and nation by other means. Indicting WPS as a manifestation of what she calls "securofeminism," Lila Abu-Lughod lays out the webs of connections between governance, security, and gender politics that weave together and hold much WPS vitality in the referential frame of Whiteness.[74] Chamindra Weer-awardhana explicitly links race and gender in her critique of WPS governance:

The problems inherent in the WPS agenda and gender mainstreaming primarily stem from the fact that the very authority that drafts these policy guidelines is also one that is largely spearheaded by influential states with power acquired through centuries of colonization, and by white settler-controlled authorities that are squarely responsible for the human, socioeconomic, cultural, and linguistic genocide of First Peoples, especially women and gender-plural peoples of Turtle Island and elsewhere.[75]

The operation of racialized power lies unexamined in most critiques of governance feminism, although this is not as true for critical WPS studies.[76] One largely unacknowledged failure of the WPS agenda is the apparent inability of liberal democratic governments in settler colonial states to grapple with the applicability of the agenda to the manifest insecurities that structures the lives of Indigenous people in majority-White societies.[77] Just as analyses and efforts to implement the WPS agenda have failed to satisfactorily engage racialized power, including its manifestation in imperial violence, the differential effects of peace and security governance on Indigenous communities are rarely discussed either in academic or policy spheres.[78] Moreover, despite apparent commitment in several settler colonial states to the inclusion of diverse groups of women in the formation of their NAPs, there is almost zero meaningful participation of Indigenous women in agenda-setting discussions and policy development consultation. Yet Indigenous peoples account for at least 12.3 million citizens in just five of the states with NAPs that we discuss in this chapter.[79] These exclusions exacerbate and entrench a profound tension in the WPS agenda, where liberal democratic settler colonial states project the imperative for the participation of diverse groups of women in peace and security processes outward through their foreign and security policies while simultaneously failing to enact similar measures for diversity and inclusion, still less decolonization, in their domestic governance.

When Indigenous women protested at the 2019 UN Climate Change Conference in Madrid—once outside the U.S. embassy highlighting the issue of missing and murdered Indigenous women, again within the main hall demanding a gender justice and rights dimension to the negotiations—they demonstrated the interplay of participation and protection across the nominally distinct policy domains of violence against women and girls, natural resources, and cultural recognition.[80] Coloniality and Indigeneity are intrinsic to considerations of gendered (in)security, if for no reason other than the fact that many contemporary conflicts are the outgrowth of historic or contemporary colonial violence. As Adrian Guelke notes, "deeply divided societies" very often rest on a "division of society into settlers and natives as a legacy of colonisation or conquest,"[81] and many continue to experience violent conflict. Others, however, do not, despite their unresolved colonial histories of genocide against Indigenous peoples, Australia and Canada being emblematic of these latter cases.[82] The "settler colonial" designation distinguishes settlement from other enactments of coloniality. While extractive colonialism seeks, for example, to plunder resources from a territory without necessarily residing permanently or even temporarily on that land, settler colonialism involves claiming sovereignty over the land—and its people. Crucially, "the colonizers come to stay—invasion is a structure not an event."[83]

The failure, or active refusal, to recognize the harms of colonization perpetrates a form of ongoing structural violence against Indigenous peoples, who in many contemporary liberal democracies are still experiencing a continuity of marginalization and oppression that dates from the original invasion of, and displacement from, their lands. Indigeneity relates specifically to place, and the connection of a people to territory, existing as a category of identity and a relation of power in connection to settler coloniality: it is the pronouncement and imposition of settlement, by settlers, that constitutes the binary of settler/native. But just as the dynamics of colonization and settlement were, and continue to be, different across the world,[84] the term "Indigenous describes what are in fact thousands of distinct societies with their own names, governments, territories, languages, worldviews, and political organisations."[85] The language for designating Indigeneity is in large part imposed from without, inscribed in legal regimes of the settler colonial state.[86] A mapping of Indigenous nations in Australia, for example, demonstrates the diversity of language groups. These groups have different customs, songlines, and lore as well as different language traditions; holding in mind this diversity is a guard against tokenistic inclusion of "*the* Indigenous perspective." It is almost four thousand kilometers from the stolen lands of the Eora nation on which the city of Sydney is built, on Australia's eastern coast, to Perth, which is located on the western coast in the country of the Whadjuk people; the United Kingdom sits a similar distance from Algeria, Azerbaijan, and Lebanon, and yet a single representative would not be expected to speak for all four of these places.

While Indigenous communities in Australia may share some commonalities, in terms of their cosmological relationship with nonhuman and more-than-human kin and their communitarian ontology,[87] and their survival in the face of genocidal violence perpetrated by settlers in many cases, their interests, priorities, and needs are not homogenous. Just as one woman cannot necessarily speak for all women, Indigenous people inhabit multiple intersecting identities that inform engagement with politics, including peace and security. Indigeneity is racialized, but it is not contained by analytical attention to race. While racial justice—much like gender justice—is frequently configured within the constraints of a liberal rights framework that envisions equality as the ultimate standard of justice, Indigenous justice implies a thoroughgoing reformulation of the framework and standards of justice itself. In short, "within the context of land and settler colonialism, the issues facing Indigenous women, as inseparable from the issues facing Indigenous peoples as a whole, are resolved via decolonization and sovereignty, not (just) parity."[88] Although social movements invested in gender and racial justice have sometimes leveraged the articulation of radical reform agendas, notably the call in 2020 by Black Lives Matter advocates to defund the police as a response to the carceral practices of the U.S. American state that disproportionately disadvantage Black people and people of color, Indigenous justice movements often start from the need for radical reconfiguration of the state and its apparatus.[89]

Though hardly mentioned since, Indigeneity *was* present at the birth of WPS. Resolution 1325 calls on actors involved in peace processes to adopt "measures that *support local women's peace initiatives and indigenous processes* for conflict resolution, and that involve women in all of the implementation mechanisms of the peace agreements" (S/RES/1325 2000, para. 8c; emphasis added). But that has been the extent of the Security Council's formal recognition of Indigenous knowledges and support of the inclusion of Indigenous women in peace and security governance (although the same language appears in the 2001 presidential statement; see S/PRST/2001/31, 1).[90] No subsequent resolutions affirm the importance of Indigenous representation and knowledge in the WPS agenda, nor does Indigeneity feature again in presidential statements of the Security Council (though it does appear whenever 1325 is appended to government or intergovernmental action plans).

The formal architecture of the agenda thus undoes an early moment of promise, a distinct if underplayed aspect of failure in the promise of the feminist peace. As is the case with various other issues for which there is limited support within the formal architecture of the agenda, however, some UN member states have identified the issue of Indigenous politics as (notionally) salient to peace and security governance in their national contexts, and have incorporated discussion of either the inclusion, and interests, of Indigenous women, or engagement with Indigenous knowledge, or both, in their NAPs.[91] In advocating for a Security Council seat in 2013, Australia had highlighted recognition and reconciliation with Indigenous peoples, though the topic was not raised again.[92] Figure 5.8 provides an overview of the relative weight given in NAPs to our interrelated term clusters for the words "colonialism," "Indigeneity," and "race," terms which we counted together for the purposes of our new issues survey in chapter 3. The level of formal curiosity about the workings of racism, settler occupation, apartheid, and imperialism is unsurprisingly low throughout, with spikes associated with deep interest from a handful of authorities more alive to historical legacies: Guatemala, Palestine, and Canada above all.[93]

The 2020–2024 Kenyan NAP is one example of a plan that emphasizes the incorporation of Indigenous knowledges in security planning and conflict prevention. Under the "prevention" pillar, it includes a commitment to "conduct research on the use of existing indigenous and traditional knowledge on women's roles in early warning and early response" (Kenyan NAP II 2020, 26). The implication is that proper engagement with "indigenous and traditional knowledge" in the sphere of conflict prevention will produce better outcomes—presumably (more) sustainable peace—than knowledge embedded in international community interventions. The idea of Indigenous peace knowledge has affinity with the valorization of Indigenous knowledges in development, the roots of which can be traced back to critical development scholarship and practice challenging the dominance of modernization theory.[94] Development has a particularly troubled and troubling relationship with

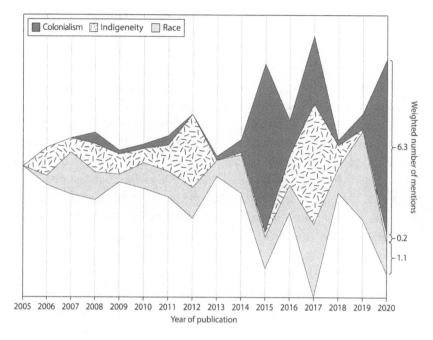

FIGURE 5.8 Mentions of colonialism, Indigeneity, and race in NAPs over time (2005–2020, *n* = 161, weighted by number of documents published each year).

Source: Graph by the authors.

Indigeneity (along with the discipline of anthropology, for obvious reasons); for many decades, development governance actors unquestioningly reproduced the dominance of Western knowledge systems, enacting a technocratic, top-down system of development that "dictated the marginalization and disqualification of non-Western knowledge systems," even though these latter might present effective "alternative rationalities to guide social action" and economic activity.[95]

The growth and empowerment of regulatory governance institutions, along with the assumption that development programs could be generated centrally and implemented through "structural adjustment" in contexts from Argentina to Zimbabwe without variation or much attention to the particularities of those contexts, is supported by the rejection of "non-Western knowledge systems"; such was the dominance of this ideological regime for many decades that it was not until late in the twentieth century that development actors began to take Indigenous knowledge seriously. In an eventual and somewhat unsurprising process of co-optation, contemporary development enterprise now includes the "deployment of indigenous knowledge as part of the armoury of some mainstream development agencies."[96] Although "Indigenous knowledge" is as varied as Indigenous communities themselves (and, further, should not be romanticized as somehow operating outside of existing structures of power),[97] its recognition—and therefore potential validation—in the context of WPS opens up the possibility of different ways of configuring peace and security, in line with what feminist scholars have suggested for twenty years is the impetus for the agenda: to realize a feminist vision of security and peace that is not reliant on the militarized, masculinized presumptions of conventional security institutions.

While the Kenyan NAP endorses the validation of Indigenous knowledges, the Canadian and Guatemalan plans, both launched in 2017, address Indigeneity through the specific representation of Indigenous women and discussion of their needs and interests. The Canadian NAP includes a commitment of "support to gender-responsive local and Indigenous processes for conflict resolution" (Canadian NAP II 2017, 8), which is similar to the emphasis in the Kenyan NAP, but it also presents a two-page discussion of the forms of violence and insecurity faced by Indigenous women and girls:

> Indigenous women and girls in particular face intersecting discrimination and violence based on gender, race, socioeconomic status and other identity factors, as well as underlying historic causes—in particular the legacy of colonialism and the devastation caused by the residential school system. While Indigenous women make up 4% of Canada's total number of women, 16% of all women murdered in Canada between 1980 and 2012 were Indigenous (Canadian NAP II 2017, 4–5).

The rates of violence against Indigenous women in Canada are indeed shocking, with the situation reported in the NAP described as a "crisis" of missing and murdered Indigenous women;[98] this crisis has been mobilized in support of social justice movements aimed at decolonial violence-prevention strategies that are attentive to intersecting axes of oppression. Indigenous women across the world are disproportionately affected by both violence and state responses to violence. In Australia, for example, one study revealed that in 2012 "Indigenous women comprised a staggering 34.2% of the female prisoner population . . . (compared with the equivalent Indigenous male proportion of 26.7%) while they represent[ed] only 2% of the female general population."[99] Many women's rights advocates in Australia link these forms of insecurity to the WPS agenda, which they see as essential to the use of the agenda in defense of rights for *all* women.

One possible interpretation of the representation of Indigenous women relates victimization to vulnerability. Just as the Canadian NAP highlights the specific violations endured by Indigenous women, the Guatemalan NAP emphasizes that "women have suffered" under patriarchy and explains that "indigenous women suffer from multiple and intertwined discrimination, which has meant for them experiencing violence in an extreme way" (Guatemalan NAP 2017, 16). The suffering of women, presumed to be a universal experience deriving from their sociopolitical positioning as a group, is represented as the foundation for political action under the auspices of WPS. This construction does not surface women's agency in peace and security governance. Further, there are echoes here of the only consistent way that Indigenous women are brought into discourse on WPS at the UN, which is as victims of violence in the annual reports by the secretary-general on sexual violence in conflict: in 2012, reporting on parties to conflict credibly suspected of committing sexual violence, the secretary-general noted that in Colombia "sexual violence disproportionately affects girls, displaced women and girls and Afro-Colombian and indigenous women and girls."[100] Similar constructions are presented in later reports, including the September/October reports on the WPS agenda. These representations are often but not exclusively related to the situation in Colombia.[101]

An alternative interpretation, however, makes visible the ways in which Indigenous women and community groups claim recognition of *both* the continued violence and insecurity that characterize life under colonisation *and* the agency and rights associated with a subject position that is not reducible to violence and victimization. There are many examples of Indigenous women working on conflict prevention and reconstruction. In Colombia, for example, "the National Association of Rural and Indigenous Women of Colombia . . ., a group of women rural leaders, has been working to identify damages Indigenous communities suffered during the conflict, and claim reparations benefits, including access to land."[102] Such community organizing takes seriously the ideas embedded in the concept of intersectionality, developed as a way to understand the complexities of oppression and antiviolence work not as additive but rather as intersecting, such that—per Kimberlé Crenshaw's original formulation[103]—a Black woman is never solely Black nor solely a woman, but is always embodied, encountered, as both Black *and* female. Moreover, these identity markers are inextricably intertwined, indivisible, although the political salience of each varies by context. At its most basic, attention to intersectionality involves recognizing that "women are not a homogenous group and face many and varied forms of discrimination including being a member of religious, cultural, ethnic, LGBTQI+ and migrant communities and as a result of experiencing a disability" (Irish NAP III 2019, 16). A more sophisticated approach extends this recognition by exploring how and in what ways forms of empowerment and agency, along with forces of oppression and discrimination, are structured and tempered by shifting identity formations, which "come into existence in and through contradictory and conflictual relations to each other."[104]

The partial inclusion of Indigeneity in the WPS field, deferred since that first fleeting acknowledgment in 1325, therefore takes a particular form, animated primarily by the figure of the Indigenous woman in NAPs, the most recognizable and assimilable object of protection. The addition at times represents a shift in the state's diagnosis of insecurity, an admission of colonial histories and an opening for a more introspective and comprehensive gender perspective. Yet Indigeneity remains demarcated even in these NAPs, displacing the challenge it poses to national identity, diplomacy, and memory. For one, the settler colonial state regulates authentic identity, and in profoundly gendered ways. Until 1985, Indigenous women in Canada lost their tribal status when marrying non-Indigenous men.[105] Until the late 1960s the residential school system—deployed with some variations in the United States, Canada, and Australia—disrupted kinship and tradition, exploited children's labor, and served as a site of nation building through coerced "integration."[106] Indigenous "status" itself—recognized through formal acts of state—produces forms of attachment and division by gender and race, in part sustaining patriarchal arrangements.[107]

Indigenous politics always already implied relations between nations. North America is the product of hundreds of conflicts between settlers and natives (and coalitions of the two) waged into the early twentieth century,[108] yielding a patchwork of conquest, treaty, reservation, and purchase that subtends contemporary Canada and the United States.[109] The post-conflict settlement lives on in government departments specializing in Indigenous affairs, regulating a "plurinational" sovereign order in which the sharp delineation of the foreign and domestic breaks down.[110] It is standard practice in Australia to acknowledge the Indigenous custodians of the country in any formal meeting or address, along with a recognition that sovereignty over that land and its people was never ceded; Aboriginal sovereignty is the foundation of rights-based claims to land and personhood.[111]

The Indigenous present—which Manuela Picq has characterized in terms of "vernacular sovereignties" that disrupt the putative Westphalian coincidence of territory and authority—undercuts the pretension of leading liberal democratic states that they exist beyond conflict.[112] To the extent that Indigenous people can be located elsewhere, drafted as a community to be consulted in peace talks, the orientation of a feminist *foreign* policy can be maintained. Where the settler colonial condition is admitted, other policy questions follow. The gulf can be seen in microcosm in Canadian WPS, where Indigenous women were first mentioned as subjects of "increased participation," exclusively in distant fragile states (Canada NAP I 2010, 3, 5, 8), but were later recognized as integral to Canada's own postcolonial history, from ongoing discrimination and violence to the residential school system and in as quintessential a post-conflict institution as the Truth and Reconciliation Commission (Canada NAP II 2017, 4–5). This second NAP coincided with the Trudeau government's National Inquiry Into Missing and Murdered Indigenous Women and Girls, which signaled the transition from a Conservative administration that had issued the first Canadian NAP while resisting calls for just such an inquiry.[113]

Notwithstanding Indigenous critiques of the liberal fix, and the question of how its promise has manifested in practice, admissions of the *intra*-national politics of Indigeneity are rare. Though on first glance a mirror of common WPS debates regarding victimhood and agency, the figure of the Indigenous women instead invites different possibilities for feminist policy. On the one hand, her explicit inclusion is itself a rebuke to civilizationist historiography, a kind of resistance given that settler colonial statecraft *requires* the disappearance of Indigenous women, whether in legal, reproductive, or physical terms.[114] In Guatemala, the recognition of state violence against Indigenous women acts as a channel for reparations measures and enables a variety of historical reckoning, as in the Sepur Zarco case, where Guatemalan military officers were convicted of crimes against humanity for a campaign of sexual violence and forced labor against Indigenous Maya Q'eqchi' women in the 1980s.[115] The discourse of the "disappeared" has been a major focus for several critical interventions on the gender of Indigeneity.[116] On the other hand, in WPS terms, Indigeneity has served primarily as a mark of individual vulnerability, a characteristic of women disproportionately at risk and therefore most in need of protection measures under the policy rubrics of sexual violence, trafficking, or occasionally at the nexus of domestic and collective violence. From these experiences, Indigenous women come to be valued for their standpoint, as people bearing "experiences of intersectional discrimination" and "unique perspectives on conflict," listed alongside other categories of women, but absent any acknowledgment of settler colonial dominion.[117]

Within the auspices of WPS, Indigeneity is frequently—not even consciously—excluded from consideration as not properly related to *international* peace and security at all, in line with the disciplinary histories of governance that obscure the colonial foundations of both international law and, later, IR. The settler colonial foundations of so many nation-states lie beyond the remit of "the Parliament of Man," in part diminished as too domestic a series of conflicts, and otherwise too significant a challenge to the sovereignty of the actor presumed to write WPS from a national perspective.[118] The "additive" model, including Indigenous women but not Indigenous polities, discounts the tension lines of resource and nation, militarism and extractivism, and memory and sovereignty that would situate settler colonial contexts as a post-conflict present.[119] The specific dynamics of *settler* colonialism qualify its enduring character as "an ongoing project that preserves intact its colonial, spatial and legal structures," which themselves have an obscure temporality, stretching back to the originary imperial architectures and forward to an assimilated future (or future of mutual acceptance), but obscuring the violences of everyday dispossession, accumulation, and extraction—of land and being.[120]

The matrix of vulnerability, double vulnerability, even triple vulnerability, explored in this section foregrounds the "event" of violence in ways that can displace the "structure" of settler colonialism.[121] But both event and structure can be rendered prominent in ways that nourish and reinforce WPS, which can be seen as the context and condition of its vitality and failure. The concept of sovereignty, as the foundational principle of international law, was enshrined in the lexicon of IR through the disavowal of Indigenous autonomy and the right to self-determination.[122] Moreover, the presumed domesticity of Indigenous rights and entitlements continues to erase the spatial and temporal ties to the project of contemporary international order—including international peace and security, with which WPS is centrally concerned. Historical and contemporary traces of coloniality—figured by Mazen Masri as the "colonial imprint"[123]—connect women to peace and peace to security in ways that complicate claims to *feminist* peace, as we have shown here, and, further, blur the boundaries between international and domestic spaces within which WPS can fail or flourish. WPS ineluctably bears this imprint in settler colonial contexts, but also arguably more broadly, as the system of international order on which the agenda relies for authority and authenticity is itself implicated in—indeed was produced by—coloniality.[124]

INSIDE/OUTSIDE WPS

Through the production of NAPs, through NAP avoidance, through the mobilization (and concomitant construction) of "feminist" imagery and iconography, and through its layering over existing conflicts about peace and security that bear the imprint of colonization, we have traversed the national estate of the ecosystem. The documents available for analysis, the NAPs on which we draw here, and which are widely held up as the preeminent performance of WPS commitments, are themselves nodes in different ecosystems of domestic politics and policy. The NAPs that are published are the remainder of extensive contestation, negotiation, and spoiling, frequently objects of great disappointment for advocates and others involved in national "consultations." Nevertheless, these plans circulate and resonate, acting as signals of *the* national position on, and engagement with, WPS. The contestation is hidden, the choices often improvised, but the text persists as an artifact and signal.

Focusing on the domestication of WPS in various registers demonstrates the presence, here as elsewhere, of contestation. We have traced what might be recognized as "femonationalism"—"the exploitation of feminist themes by nationalists and neoliberals"[125]—and shown how these practices enable prescriptive visions of WPS antithetical to feminist peace to thrive. Thrive they do, however, against the foil of, in tandem with, and parallel to those visions that might be more easily recognized as rooted in other feminist, anticolonial, and pacifist positions. The absence of a NAP should likewise be read not as failure but as a form of fractious vitality: a failure by some metrics and a form of active contestation by some others. It may be as an expression of agency against a monolithic or universalist agenda; the enactment of contestation regarding what the agenda is, where it applies, and who it governs, national and statist imaginaries reworked in the language of feminism. It is not just that it takes energy to instrumentalize or co-opt the feminist peace, but that the precondition of the exclusion is the articulation of WPS, its reproduction. Even the sense among advocates that NAPs have been undermined, or that national policy is unserious, points to the coexistence, rather than the antipathy, of vitality and failure. Domesticating WPS requires the energy of militaries and ministries that rearticulate WPS, factions that are eager for WPS even as their vision might differ starkly from that of feminist activists elsewhere. The work of agnotology is not only a complaint about delivery or demand for change but a clue about what sorts of feminist and quasi-feminist coalitions are possible.

In showing how elements of the agenda are rearticulated in the discourse of national history and identity, we reveal not only the plurality of the agenda in implementation, but its role in wider constitutions of self and other, the ways in which gender can both accentuate and obscure violent pasts. Questions of time, space, order, and justice enliven WPS at the national level more than anywhere, especially in settler colonial contexts where contestation over the when, and the what, of a "post-conflict environment" has a unique inflection. In her research on WPS in South Asia, Shweta Singh posits that Sri Lanka, along with other similarly militarized and insecure settings, "does not fit into the neat categories of conflict or post-conflict, but more aptly speaks to the category of post-war contexts."[126] We propose that many settler colonial states, and WPS "champions," may not easily qualify as "postwar," given their involvement in ongoing violence either internally or overseas. Though we have focused on Iraq and Afghanistan as wars coterminous with UK policy, we could have also included Northern Ireland, not formally recognized as "postconflict" or integral enough to feature in the first four strategies.[127] Elsewhere, WPS champions may too easily imagine themselves as good faith states, offering reconciliation and recognition but not reckoning with the present structure of dispossession or the multiplicity of inner sovereignties.[128]

These questions bring to the fore pressing considerations relating to claims of WPS "success," "championing," and "resistance." More specifically, our investigation draws attention to the need for careful interrogation of claims about race and coloniality in the WPS agenda and careful investigation of how racialized power operates within the ecosystem as a vector of both platitude and critique.[129] In the symbolism, instrumentalism, or negotiated minimalism of WPS, however, one can discern the coordinates for a reply to the Global North, the seeds of a counterhierarchy. In unsettling these accounts, we are better able to make out the relations between vitality and failure, and to map them onto broader dialogues about colonial legacies and North-South inequalities, tasks which are taken up again in chapter 6.

6

FRACTURES AND FRICTIONS OF A
POLICY ECOSYSTEM

I
n May 2012, the heads of the twenty-eight member states of the North
Atlantic Treaty Organization met in Chicago to deliberate on a range
of matters, including ballistic missile capability and the scheduled end
of combat operations in Afghanistan. Amnesty International—a founding member of the NGO Working Group on Women, Peace and Security
and a consistent advocate of gender justice—convened a shadow summit
in the same city, hosting Afghan feminists to warn against the effects of
a troop withdrawal. In an open letter to Presidents Barack Obama and
Hamid Karzai, signatories including Madeleine Albright, Gloria Steinem,
former U.S. ambassadors, defense secretaries, Supreme Court justices, and
several Nobel Peace Prize laureates cited Security Council resolution 1325
to demand such WPS fundamentals as women's participation in peace
talks, legal measures on violence against women and girls, funding for
independent civil society, and gender mainstreaming in the Afghan government.[1] In a coordinated public advocacy campaign, posters appeared
at Chicago bus stops demanding that NATO "Keep the Progress Going!,"
with that slogan set against an image of Afghan women in burqas (see
figure 6.1).[2] The campaign provoked a backlash, not least from antiwar
activists protesting NATO itself. Amnesty quickly issued a clarification:
"we're not calling for NATO to remain in the country."[3] Despite the denial,
the open letter had lauded the effects of military as much as development
spending, implying that women's meaningful participation was only possible under the protection afforded by U.S. and NATO troops.

FIGURE 6.1 Amnesty International, "Keep the Progress Going!" advocacy poster.

Source: Reproduced with permission from Amnesty International.

The linkages between women's rights and martial power—fraught and toxic, furiously disputed yet seldom deconstructed—would recur as farce and tragedy. Under the next administration, the U.S. national security adviser, General H. R. McMaster, persuaded President Donald Trump to expand U.S. forces in part by showing him a photo of women wearing miniskirts in the Kabul of the 1970s.[4] Over almost the same two-decade period we examine in this book the United States spent a minimum of, and likely much more than, \$787 million on programs for Afghan women and girls, with participation a major priority.[5] As we were completing our first draft of this manuscript, the last Western personnel and many desperate Afghans were fleeing the country in disarray as President Biden made good on Trump's compact with the Taliban. In the ensuing controversy over the timing and terms of U.S. withdrawal the status of women was again the focus of an intense quarrel, mobilized both by the activists long critical of the Western military presence and by those who proposed a limitless extension of it.[6] Afghan women—less singular in their experiences and opinions than the debate over Western strategy could allow—negotiated stark material realities they had little ability to shape at the same time that their rhetorical invocation signaled a renewed contest of feminisms and faux feminisms.

The Afghan scene is but the most vivid in a family of disputes—over militarism and resistance, coloniality and Whiteness, complicity and progress—that far exceeds the Women, Peace, and Security agenda but with which it has long been entangled. Though, as we have documented, WPS can claim sources in transnational feminist peace activism and postcolonial politics (see especially chapter 4), it has also been charged with entrenching the liberal innocence of the Global North, an ally of "White feminism" historically at ease with structural inequality and colonial domination.[7] In this chapter we address these disputes as they play out between civil society and security institutions, two species of the WPS ecosystem long in contention, returning recurrently to the intervention in Afghanistan as a salient case in point illustrating many of the dynamics we explore here.

We begin with the fracture between NATO and the Women's International League for Peace and Freedom (WILPF), a feminist and antimilitarist civil society group sometimes credited as the historical originator of the WPS agenda.[8] In liberal world order thinking, NATO is a guardian of democracy, human rights, and international law.[9] For skeptics and critics, it is something else: a relic of Cold War militarism and an ongoing threat to the peace. Military alliances and activist networks differ most obviously in their sources of power and authority, their founding purposes, and in the means available to them for advancing their agendas. At the same time, their estates overlap. NATO convenes an annual civil society advisory panel comprised of local women's groups (often from theaters where it operates) as well as household-name humanitarian agencies like Oxfam and CARE International and dedicated advocacy groups like Operation 1325. Activists simultaneously critique and construct policy, and some are subcontracted to teach gender to NATO.[10] Even the most skeptical activists today concede the need to "engage" other institutions of the WPS circuit, even those specializing in armed force.[11] Military gender advisers serve on the advisory boards of WPS Centres of Excellence while security professionals seek greater equality in their careers.[12] Both NATO and WILPF articulate a vision of WPS, each stressing the value of participation and the urgency of protection, viewing themselves as agents of conflict prevention and proffering models for post-conflict reconstruction on gender egalitarian terms. The fault line between them expresses in miniature fractures that lace the WPS field. We show in the sections that follow how both WILPF and NATO deploy the language of the agenda strategically in ways that defer fundamental tensions over the character and resolution of conflict.

The second half of the chapter explores race as a vector of power in WPS. We evaluate claims that the agenda has become (or has always been) colonial in its articulation and explore expressions of agency and resistance to hegemonic and homogenizing assertions of WPS. Examining these erased and unacknowledged historical inheritances and resonances, we show how the category of "civil society" includes degrees of accommodation with great powers and White feminism and that women's movements in the Global South engage with the agenda both strategically and in ways that generate friction and fractures. The structuring and performance of these acts of resistance is part of how the agenda—its ownership and constituency—is reproduced.

ALL THE ELEMENTS OF NATIONAL POWER

NATO's adoption of WPS is widely recognized as emblematic of the internal tensions of the field.[13] A significant site of policy production from relatively early in the WPS life story, the alliance also lays claim to a longer record of gender mainstreaming, dating to the Committee on Women in NATO Forces, founded in the mid-1970s, and its successor in the NATO Committee on Gender Perspectives (see table 6.1).[14] In ecosystem terms, the alliance has emphasized the most obviously "securitized" of issues: human trafficking, terrorism and extremism, and sexual violence. Sexual exploitation and abuse—a more inward-focused project of training and discipline—is also a major concern.[15] In an overlapping series of policies, plans, and directives it has produced more paperwork on the

TABLE 6.1 Time line of NATO WPS

1961	Female officers in NATO begin organizing ad hoc conferences, the first in Copenhagen
1973	Committee on Women in NATO Forces (CWINF) created at a Conference of Female Senior Officers
1976	NATO's Military Committee recognizes CWINF formally
1998	CWINF office established in NATO HQ
2003	Adoption of first NATO Equal Opportunities and Diversity Policy
2006	First NATO gender adviser role created
2007	First NATO Euro-Atlantic Partnership Council (EAPC) Policy on Implementing 1325
2008	NATO gender advisers first deployed with ISAF in Afghanistan
2009	Bi-strategic Command Directive 40-1 issued CWINF becomes NATO Committee on Gender Perspectives
2010	Lisbon Summit Declaration includes WPS reference First NATO/EAPC Action Plan First NATO field gender adviser position created for deployment in national militaries
2011	Second EAPC Policy
2012	Bi-strategic Command Directive updated. Previously ad hoc gender adviser positions in Allied Command Transformation (the learning and education part) becomes a permanent position Post of secretary-general's special representative for women, peace and security created, with Mari Skåre its first occupant Military Committee approves a strategy training plan on gender Nordic Centre for Gender in Military Operations is appointed as "gender department head," meaning it is responsible for delivery of all gender education and training SHAPE WoMen initiative to encourage understanding of gender among Supreme Allied HQ staff and their spouses inside or outside the military
2013	Both the North Atlantic Council and the defense ministers of the alliance approve the Bi-strategic Directive
2014	Third revised EAPC Policy Second NATO/EAPC Action Plan Marriët Schuurman becomes second special representative for WPS

2015	Military Guidelines on the Prevention of, and Response to, Conflict-Related Sexual and Gender-Based Violence released
2016	Third NATO/EAPC Action Plan Women's professional network established at Allied Command Transformation Civil Society Advisory Panel established
2017	Bi-strategic Command Directive updated again, among other things expanding SEA to include prostitution and forced labor
2018	Fourth NATO/EAPC Action Plan, issued jointly with policy Clare Hutchinson appointed third special representative for WPS
2020–2021	NATO 2030 Strategy launched, incorporated WPS as part of human security element
2021	Fourth NATO/EAPC Action Plan Policy on Preventing and Responding to Conflict-Related Sexual Violence issued Irene Fellin appointed as fourth special representative for WPS
2022	NATO Strategic Concept pledges to integrate WPS across all tasks

agenda than any other regional or security body, and has been taken as a "best practice" example to follow for its own member states and beyond.[16] NATO is itself a propagator of policy—the "teaching machine" in Cynthia Enloe's much-cited phrase[17]—with a staff of gender advisers, an informal "Friends of 1325" internal advocacy group,[18] a tranche of directives and manuals, and its own variant of military feminism. But the alliance is also a heterogenous creature, a shoal of thirty nation-states, most of which have NAPs or otherwise act in the agenda's name, as is the case with Poland (chapter 5, pp. 135–137).[19] As Enloe stressed, NATO is *not* a well-oiled, smoothly functioning inter-state machine"; learning was asymmetric and largely internal to the alliance as it navigated Cold War tensions, manpower shortages, and the rise of the women's movement.[20] The relationship between members and headquarters is not quite one of symbiosis: NATO doctrine feeds and is fed by national military culture, and the very introduction of the agenda has been attributed to the work of a wider security community, the first doctrine authorized by the Euro-Atlantic Partnership Council, encompassing partner nations as well as the then twenty-six NATO members, "the only document of its kind to have been endorsed" in this way.[21]

NATO's gender work began soon after the initial blooming of NAPs, the first nine of which were, not coincidentally, issued by member states of the alliance or—in the case of Austria, Sweden, and Switzerland—by partners. Several refinements of policy and doctrine have followed, accompanied by an increasing visibility of WPS in high-profile engagement from NATO's secretary-general and the growing importance of the special representative for WPS role.[22] Through the special representative, NATO has increasingly participated in, and contributed to, Security Council open debates on the state of the agenda and conflict-related sexual violence.[23] Over the same span, gender has become more embedded across its organizational tiers. By 2018, NATO member and partner states fielded at least 772 gender advisers (likely significantly more), up from 494 in 2014.[24] The tempo of adoption indicates enthusiasm for the gender perspective, yet another manifestation of the agenda's vitality, though uptake has been uneven: a review some years into NATO WPS practice found that "the overwhelming majority" of commanders were not aware of the relevant command directive.[25] The degree of transformation is measured by the implementation technologies of the scorecard and best practice, a pedagogy within the alliance.[26] Here, as elsewhere in the ecosystem, the agenda is suspended, forever making progress and endlessly in need of full and proper implementation.[27]

Despite its foundational purpose in securing western Europe from Soviet encroachment, no theater has been as generative for NATO's gender work as Afghanistan.[28] From the start, NATO's interest was operational, "to identify . . . how gender issues can be better taken into account to assist the efforts of the Provincial Reconstruction Teams in Afghanistan," as the secretary-general's cover note to the 2007 policy had it (NATO Policy I 2007, 1). In 2008, the very first NATO gender advisers were deployed to Afghanistan by Sweden and Norway, both major state proponents of WPS.[29] Sweden's experience with gender advisers and focal points especially served as an influential lesson for the alliance.[30] The gender perspective in this arena became inseparable from the rediscovery of counterinsurgency warfare by Western military intellectuals and an accompanying troop surge explicitly framed in protection-of-civilian terms. The new "war among the people" entailed a more concerted intelligence-gathering campaign, energized by military anthropology and the turn to culture of the U.S. Army's "Human Terrain" project operating also in Iraq.[31]

At the heart of NATO's integration and inclusivity program were Female Engagement Teams, or FETs, comprising small groups of female (and *only* female) U.S. Marines, later adopted in a British version.[32] Trained in combat but tasked primarily with influencing women to support ISAF (the UN-authorized International Stability and Assistance Force) and the Afghan government, FETs gathered intelligence on enemy activities but also provided medical, educational, and economic assistance. Inclusivity offered a solution to the faltering record of single-sex operations: "Our mostly all-male units were handicapped early on by their inability to interact with or serve half the Afghan population . . . [and] we lacked officers who could both serve in combat and interact with Afghan women."[33] At a point of military failure, WPS was an epiphany: "gender was key to understanding Afghanistan."[34]

In their ability to communicate with Afghan women, FETs were expected to intervene at the fundamental unit of society: "Win the women and you own the family," in the words of the preeminent counterinsurgency intellectual, David Kilcullen.[35] Oriented between violence and empathy, warrior masculinity and conservative femininity, FETs embodied a "third gender" who could traverse otherwise impassable social boundaries.[36] As has been extensively documented by Sippi Azarbaijani-Moghaddam, who served as an ISAF cultural adviser during this period, the FET program was liable to vastly inflate its successes and was congenitally naive in its appreciation of local gender politics.[37] The promise of "female engagement" was sustained by command enthusiasm: all combat teams were required to send "promising" women from their ranks for FET training in 2010.[38] The vitality generated contradictions: FETs were expected to gather intelligence for military use but also to win the trust of communities, and to tap into Afghan women's desire for freedom, but without being seen to "social engineer."[39]

In this manner, Afghan patriarchy became the cause for pursuing gender equality within Western liberal military institutions, an attribution of "backwardness" that sparked a progress otherwise lacking. Yet FETs were not originally a manifestation of WPS policy. As the facilitators of women's participation, gender advisers had in truth been marginal figures in ISAF.[40] Women's counterinsurgency work instead became more closely affiliated with "Women, Peace, and Security" over time, an affinity produced both by military practitioners in search of theory and by WPS advocates seeking common ground for policy influence. Early studies emphasized the intelligence and force-protection aspects, with provincial reconstruction expected "to help the Government of Afghanistan gain a monopoly over the legitimate use of force."[41] Robert Egnell, one of the most prominent military proponents of WPS, was drawn to the agenda having worked first on the history of irregular warfare, taking lessons from Britain's "rich history with counterinsurgency" in colonial Malaya and Northern Ireland.[42] Writing for the U.S. Army War College's in-house journal, Egnell reassured readers that the gender perspective would not alter combat culture.[43] Women's participation was no imposition from without, not an unwarranted extension of civilian control, but a functional imperative emerging from experiences in theater.[44] In responding to "tactical level challenges," female combatants and FETs had "served as force multipliers."[45] Their contribution to irregular war was, per Lawrence of Arabia, "far more intellectual than a bayonet charge."[46] Or, as the U.S. military's field manual famously had it, "counter-insurgency is the graduate level of war."[47]

The economy of force remains the most succinct argument for WPS within NATO, the tenet of "gender parity as an operational enhancer,"[48] inclusion "an operational necessity."[49] "Force multiplier" logic appears, too, in the WPS Directive covering all activity within alliance chains of command (NATO Directive I 2009, 1–2).[50] Every special representative has emphasized the unity of participation and protection (protection of the NATO force itself or of some population), orientated toward success in a concrete mission or mandate: "a planning machinery with gender baked into the practical tools that the military structure uses in daily life," in the words of the second NATO special representative for WPS, Marriët Schuurman.[51] In a more explicitly bellicose framing, women become a material resource: to exclude them is to enter battle without marshalling "all the elements of national power."[52] Whether the tactical benefit of women's inclusion can be so comprehensively proven is less important than the rhetorical purchase of linking "the right thing to do" with "the smart thing to do,"[53] to keep at bay any contradiction between inclusivity and efficiency.[54]

The presence of NATO/ISAF has been read as a precondition for progress on the basic structure of the agenda, through mechanisms such as the development of the Afghan NAP.[55] Where the mandate includes civilian protection, operational effectiveness may align with a feminist protection mandate, most obviously in relation to sexual violence.[56] Perhaps surprisingly, integration spurs an inner reckoning: some gender advisers have described their role as preventing violence that would otherwise have been perpetrated *by NATO forces*.[57] Still, preventing sexual violence by other armed groups is emphasized as "mission critical and essential to our operational effectiveness,"[58] and repeatedly invoked in policy and guidance (NATO Directive I 2009, 3–1; NATO Directive II 2012, 3, 7, 12, 13; NATO Policy III 2014, para. 19).[59] Tactics become politics: preventing sexual violence and gender equality are objectives fully compatible with, perhaps *the consequence of*, the use of force to establish order and triumph politically.[60] The grammar of policy establishes a coincidence between women's operational roles, including in deploying force, and the general improvement in women's lives globally. The linkage of "new" security dimensions to old is performative in the sense that NATO WPS champions do not just report a consensus but seek to create that reality with their words.

As its many critics have argued, NATO's turn to gender channels feminist arguments into heavily guarded streams. In one, a focus on the inner diversity work of leadership and inclusion;[61] in another, the deployment of femininity as tactical edge. Equal opportunity militarism meets armed social work.[62] These ends are not cynical: employees and deployees may believe strongly in women's right to participate in the alliance, and in their distinctive contributions on operations. The engagement can even be joyful, as in a mock interview with the foundational resolution published in *NATO Review*: "I meet the 19-year-old 1325 over coffee at NATO Headquarters in Brussels. She is touring Europe [and] asks me not to describe what she is wearing noting that 'male resolutions rarely have their appearance or age commented on.' "[63] In rare moments the desire for an egalitarian military bloc leads to points of connection with more radical ideas, like intersectionality, introduced for discussion in formal documents affiliated with the special representative.[64] These are signs of vitality, even as they serve a function in granting legitimacy.[65] In parceling the meaning of WPS in this way, the NATO articulation of WPS inevitably diverges from alternative conceptions of the feminist peace. Though more obviously compatible with civilizationist and elite feminisms, which retain the core institutions of the Western world order, the shift in institutional culture is nevertheless itself generative, more anxious in its founding that often appreciated and more unsettling of gender experience, at least for those within the alliance.

ABOLITION AND ACCOMMODATION

NATO special representatives have presented gender integration as the culmination of a process begun by the Women's International League for Peace and Freedom in 1915, making the alliance the latest participant in an "unstoppable revolution" of feminist activism.[66] In the choice between gender equality and more radical arguments, they have at times appeared to favor the latter, stating, for example, that "having women at the table is important, but it's only important if those women are feminist women."[67] Yet to credit a military alliance with revolutionary feminist progress is also to discredit antimilitarist feminisms, which appear in discussions of NATO's gender pedagogy as excessively "theoretical" or "purist,"[68] an "unchecked extreme position" mirroring traditional militarism,[69] and as lagging behind a "feminist scholarship [that] has grown and shed light on . . . the importance of engaging all actors."[70] The negativity of antimilitarism threatens failure, a risk to the agenda's implementation stemming from the "division that has emerged between WPS purists and *more progressive elements advocating a mandate that transcends the traditional.*"[71] In this way NATO is presented as an evolutionary vector of the ecosystem, its pragmatism pushing beyond tired dichotomies, less a narrow regional bloc than a tribune for the agenda's global ambitions, a feminist successor.[72]

Though not obvious from a survey of official WPS discourse, as a collective security organization NATO was in truth a major target of the feminist peace movement during and after the Cold War. That it could seem WILPF's inheritor is all the more instructive in tracing the fractures of the agenda, given WILPF's history of opposing NATO. Now established as perhaps *the* WPS civil society group, WILPF began in the bloody heat of the First World War, when over a thousand women peace activists gathered at The Hague in April 1915.[73] That first congress produced an International Women's Committee for Permanent Peace and a twenty-point resolution demanding, among other things, immediate peace negotiations, universal suffrage, democratic control of foreign policy, universal disarmament, the creation of a permanent international organization incorporating an international court of justice, and a democratic peace council (see also chapter 7, pp. 179–180 and 184–185).

What began as an alternative to the system of secret alliances that produced one world war continued into the post-1945 peace movement. The feminist case against NATO was put sharply and often by feminist activists, particularly Cynthia Cockburn, a prominent WILPF figure, member of the Women in Black activist network, and sociologist. According to this view, NATO's mainstreaming initiatives amounted to a veneer on the patriarchy of the nation-state, the trafficking and sex industry implications of foreign military bases, the diversion of public funds to military-industrial ends, and the perpetuation of war. Regarding the alliance's mission in Afghanistan, the configurations of women as passive victims of a brutal regime were extensively challenged at the time by feminists objecting to the diminution of Afghan women's agency and what was seen as a superficial commitment at best to the rights and interests of Afghan women,[74] their "liberation" described as no more than a "devious justification" for invasion.[75]

While supreme allied commanders were issuing the first NATO directive on gender perspectives, WILPF was actively participating in coalitions calling for the alliance to be dismantled, arguing that it was an obstacle to peace and an agent of expansionist militarism.[76] Opposing the notion that war could be reformed, prominent WILPF figures posed the challenge, on the sixtieth anniversary of the alliance's founding, of "whether NATO should exist at all."[77] It remains WILPF policy to "advocate against . . . military alliances such as NATO,"[78] and to outlaw the use of coercive force altogether,[79] by means of "stigmatis[ing] the very concept of 'military security.'"[80] The rejection has been put most strongly in resolutions of the triennial WILPF Congresses. Most recently these demanded the "closure and elimination" of all U.S. and NATO military bases; called on governments to end all arms transfers to conflict zones; and urged universal nuclear disarmament via the

Treaty on the Prohibition of Nuclear Weapons.[81] Opposed for fueling the arms race during the "Cold War," NATO has since been seen as a trigger for a new conflict, as in the judgment that Russia's annexation of Crimea and conflict with the Ukrainian government in the Donbas region of Ukraine had been "exacerbated and provoked by NATO military exercises and proposed expansion."[82] As the specter of war loomed, WILPF's secretary-general wrote to the Security Council, citing "the militarization and co-optation of the language of the Women, Peace and Security agenda by the UN, NATO and the Ukrainian authorities."[83] Once Russia invaded Ukraine in force in February 2022, WILPF branches argued against Swedish and Finish membership of NATO, placing them on one side of a deep fissure within feminists about the concrete politics of antimilitarism in the face of a war of aggression.[84]

A deep antipathy to NATO was the natural extension of a feminist analysis opposed to all military alliances and alert to the colonial infrastructure of "regional security." By the 1970s, WILPF convocations pointed to NATO bases in fascist Portugal's overseas empire to argue that military blocs undermined the United Nations and decolonization, and hence that citizens of NATO member states should agitate for the dissolution of the alliance as much as for the end of empire itself.[85] This logic implicated the economic system that NATO was in part tasked with defending, today figured as a capitalist, imperial, and racist, as well as patriarchal, international order.[86] The dispute is foundational. In NATO discourse as much as the common sense of much IR theory, military power is bound up with political order, such that "military strength and political solidarity" may together become the "basic ingredients" allowing for freedom and democracy.[87] Though WILPF came to recognize anticolonial violence as legitimate, its analysis owes most to a tradition of radical peace activism resisting not just war but the apparatus of martial values, weapons design, resource extraction and expenditure, defense preparedness, and geopolitical rivalry that is summed up under the term "militarism." The horizon is not inclusion but abolition.

Yet WILPF's rejection of the alliance system has also become less explicit in the last decade, over the same span as NATO's more active embrace of the WPS agenda. WILPF's appraisal of two decades of WPS offered only mild criticisms of military gender balancing as insufficiently holistic, demurring a call for disbandment.[88] In the form of the

PeaceWomen project, WILPF itemizes and tracks the behavior of NATO members and rival great powers, especially in the Security Council. Occupying the niche so characteristic of civil society groups on the WPS circuit, it provides granular scrutiny of the language of council resolutions and plans.[89] In this guise, WILPF offers encouragement and tutelage, at times even a brutally honest reckoning with promises made and betrayed, more than the radical alterity sketched in many earlier declarations. Ironically, implementation indexes like the "Security Council WPS Scorecard" may even have the effect of rehabilitating NATO's preeminent member, given that the United States tends to score significantly higher than Russia and China, which alternate in the role of the Western alliance's geopolitical nemesis (see figure 6.2).[90]

In this, WILPF's WPS work has diverged from its advocacy over nuclear weapons and the arms trade, which continues to name NATO as an opponent in respect of the nuclear weapons ban treaty.[91] WILPF's "Reaching Critical Will" project, inheritor of a century of agitation for total and universal disarmament,[92] and later allied with other activist groups in the International Campaign to Abolish Nuclear Weapons, had begun in 1999, just before the advocacy campaign that secured resolution 1325.[93] Drawing inspiration from women's historical contribution to the disarmament

	2010	2011	2012	2013	2014	2015	2016	2017	2018	2019
China	42.4 %	41.6 %	37.8 %	44.4 %	50.3 %	44.6 %	43.4 %	46.5 %	47.5 %	49.9 %
France	54.3 %	55.3 %	55.9 %	51.0 %	52.9 %	52.2 %	58.4 %	69.4 %	78.9 %	78.6 %
United Kingdom	55.0 %	60.4 %	60.5 %	54.8 %	62.4 %	64.8 %	57.1 %	70.1 %	74.3 %	78.6 %
Russia	38.9 %	30.1 %	36.7 %	34.4 %	33.2 %	34.9 %	35.5 %	40.8 %	43.1 %	41.7 %
United States of America	53.4 %	50.6 %	54.6 %	54.3 %	55.6 %	54.3 %	69.4 %	60.1 %	64.8 %	58.2 %

* In the graph above, the average performance of each country in all main categories for the period between 2010 and 2019 is reflected.

** In the graph above, the average performance of each country for the period between 2010 and 2019 is reflected.

FIGURE 6.2 Security Council WPS Scorecard, devised as part of WILPF's Women, Peace and Security program, also known as PeaceWomen.

Source: Reproduced with permission from PeaceWomen from "Security Council WPS Scorecard," Peace Women, accessed September 26, 2023, http://peacewomen.org/scorecards.

movement, the campaign secured references to the disproportionate impacts on women and girls in the treaty's preamble, where Indigenous peoples were also acknowledged.[94] WILPF arguments for a comprehensive ban on development, production, testing, hosting, and stockpiling had also worked to reverse conventional gender codes (according to which masculinity signifies rationality, and femininity emotionality) by insisting that nuclear weapons do not serve their official function, but are instead a prop to "possess and brandish" in support of dominion and status.[95]

In aspiring to a new norm of international society, the campaign was necessarily setting itself against NATO, whose cumulative nuclear arsenal was a major factor in WILPF's larger case against it.[96] Despite the end of the bipolar world for which nuclear parity was constructed, the nuclear weapon remains an undiminished deterrent and symbol. In NATO's 2030 initiative, which reported less than a month after resolution 1325's twentieth birthday, a gender-balanced group of experts recommended that NATO sustain its nuclear arsenal. The navigation was delicate: it was decided that the alliance should "reaffirm" nonproliferation commitments but without reducing its own capabilities, which would be renewed in response to violations by Russia, Iran, North Korea, and China, and moreover speak with a collective voice against the ban treaty, which "will never contribute to practical disarmament, nor will it affect international law."[97] WPS, by contrast, received lower billing in the call for a new "strategic concept," paired with human security and entailing the recognition of gender insofar as it contributed to "operations and counter terrorism activities" alongside "a diverse workforce."[98]

Despite the bold ambition of the nuclear weapons ban movement, WILPF's confrontation with NATO as such proceeded obliquely.[99] The point of tension became a weapon—albeit a weapon of megaton proportions and apocalyptic nightmares—that could in principle be decommissioned, rather than a military alliance that must be shuttered. The abolitionist vision, still vivid in the league's conference declarations, is muted in documents dedicated *to the agenda*. As both a fixture of the WPS policy landscape and a radical agitator for the feminist peace, WILPF has moved increasingly between engagement and rejection, code-switching by forum, negotiating an awkward partnership. The opportunity lies in the malleability of participation discourse, which for NATO can signify combat and leadership roles for women, as well as the subjects of the war-affected and information-yielding "human terrain," and for WILPF the grassroots potential of peacemaking and social transformation. The inclusive subject—the woman to be consulted, deployed, and empowered—offers a locus of compromise, if only for a time.

Arguments that NATO should not be treated as a "proper" WPS actor simply sidestep the analytical challenge posed by a variegated field and circuit. Nor can the tension between NATO and WILPF be read straightforwardly as a case of "norm decay" or as either party violating the fundamental norm.[100] Stéfanie von Hlatky has recently argued that "norm distortion" is at work to the extent that an "original meaning is transformed in the process of its implementation."[101] The term draws attention to the uneven resources of deployment, and the predominance of operational over equality concerns, though even here failure is a consequence of *insufficient* participation undercutting policy.[102] WPS is such a sprawling ecosystem, including such an array of artifacts and actors working in concert and opposition across political space, that a focus on norms alone, with its implication that all WPS agents seek the same change in values and rules, risks occluding profound differences by casting them as variations on a single theme. NATO is far from the only example. "WPS" has been produced by the Global North in forms compatible with militarism, racialized hierarchies, and the security state.[103] The security apparatus of the Global South—including such groups as the African Union—may likewise forge new accommodations between participation, pacification, and war. The degree of contestation and dynamism visible across so many different planes and axes suggests that fracture is a feature, not a bug, in the ecosystem.

PROVINCIALIZING WPS

Where militaries and militarism have always been fault lines of the WPS field, race was largely invisible in early analysis of resolution 1325, before "the WPS agenda" took shape as the object of analysis. Prominent and much-cited pieces on the significance of 1325 fail to mention race as a vector of power that structures the resolution and related implementation practices, even as they provide sharp insight into the process of the resolution's adoption.[104] Several of these analyses, which are among the small handful of early works on WPS that form the beginnings of the WPS episteme, elaborate quite extensively on the geographical situatedness and national identity of the women involved in advocacy for resolution 1325 in 1999 and 2000, but these considerations were only later extended in critique of the colonial dynamics of the encounters at the UN Security Council and beyond. Even the few studies that mention race do so seemingly in passing, and as a way of acknowledging "difference" within the category of "women," of whom the resolution purports to speak, rather than engaging in analysis of racialized power;[105] Dianne Otto perhaps comes closest to surfacing these racialized dynamics when she argues that "If women's participation is conditioned on repeating the gendered and raced stereotypes that underpin imperialism and militarism, it will be impossible for it to destabilise military ways of thinking."[106] Race thus emerges as a site of submerged fracture and friction.

In the last decade, there has emerged a literature that grapples with race and coloniality, drawing attention to the ways in which the agenda can be both complicit in the reproduction of forms of domination and progressive in its emphasis on inclusive and participatory peace and security governance and the need to ensure the protection of women's rights.[107] These critiques of coloniality directed at the WPS agenda should be situated in the broader context of critical feminist engagements with military and security interventions and the ways in which gender equality and women's rights were mobilized as justifications for imperial violence. There are two dimensions of these mobilizations of relevance to the discussion of race and coloniality in the WPS agenda to which we attend here: first, criticism of the strategic deployment of the rights of women as a justification for war fighting; and, second, alertness to the ways in which feminist advocates, academics, and activists have been complicit in such justifications, perpetuating divisions between communities of women and reproducing racialized subjectivities in line with colonial logics.

Feminist scholars of militarism and state security practices have focused attention on the "logic of masculinist protection" as a foundation of both statecraft and war fighting.[108] This concept builds on the feminist insight that war and statecraft are intrinsically gendered activities;

making states and prosecuting war—as separate but related activities—rely on, and reproduce, gendered norms and other structures of gendered power. At its most minimal, in war fighting, this involves a gendered distinction between combatant and civilian, which Jean Bethke Elshtain famously describes as the "Just Warrior" and the "Beautiful Soul."[109] Elshtain's early analysis of the construction of women in war, which also comments on the ways in which other war-involved subjectivities are gendered, depicts the legitimacy of war as being contingent on a series of binaries separating battleground from home front, combatant from civilian, warrior from innocent, protector from protected; these binaries map on to the presumed gender binary that similarly separates men/masculinity from women/femininity. Elshtain explains that the protection afforded to the "Beautiful Soul" by the "Just Warrior" is a crucial dimension of legitimacy in war, and feminist scholarship has built on these insights to develop an understanding of the gendered legitimacy of the state more broadly, extending the idea that protection is central to statecraft (including war fighting) and building on this idea to inform the theory of the state as a "protection racket." According to this view, "the protection racket is an underlying justification for states, governments, (even rebel groups), and their wars";[110] it is a "racket" because the myth of protection is not realized, as violence and insecurity continue to plague the lives of women and girls even as they submit to the requirements of protection by the patriarchal state. The "logic of masculinist protection" operates similarly: "the role of the masculine protector puts those protected, paradigmatically women and children, in a subordinate position of dependence and obedience."[111]

This theorization is where the relationship between WPS and the gendered logics of protection begins to emerge and take shape, as women's rights—and their protection—became common motifs in Western war rationales of the twenty-first century. But Black feminists, Indigenous feminists, and feminists of color have long analyzed the complicity of certain forms of feminism, and associated claims about the subjects who should be afforded protection, in the perpetration of violence against people of color. Chandra Mohanty, in this vein, offered a trenchant and compelling critique of the implication of Western feminist scholarship in the reproduction and perpetuation of structures of colonial power and dominance, arguing that "western feminist scholarship on the third world must be seen and examined precisely in terms of its inscription in these particular relations of power and struggle."[112] Western feminism was indicted by Mohanty and others[113] for failing to challenge—and in many cases actively supporting—the vilification of men of color and their configuration as "risky subjects" of security discourse, the agents of violence from whom "brown women" required protection (or "saving").[114] Similarly, in her analysis of the "war on terror" that began in 2001, Gargi Bhattacharyya situates the figure of the "dangerous brown man" in the center of her analytical frame, skillfully showing how logics of sexuality, gender, and race are central to the use of force in the guise of counterterrorism and how "imperial feminism" is implicated in this particular form of warcraft.[115] Critical engagement with discourse on "dangerous brown men," whether in relation to the "war on terror," or in relation to (efforts to counter) terrorism and violent extremism,[116] draws attention to the sexualized, gendered, and racialized logics of this discourse and "attempts to problematise the disparate levels and types of attention paid to similar violences globally, whereby violence against women in the developing world is seen as a security concern to the West, and yet violence against women in the West is minimised, ignored and/or individualised."[117]

This is the second dimension of critique related to the mobilization of women's rights as a justification for war: the protections afforded to women (and/or their rights) are applicable only to the (presumed passive) "victims of oppression" by (Western) agents of liberation, which both denies the various kinds of violence experienced by women in the West and further entrenches the domination of the West—including the positioning of women within the West as supraordinate to women elsewhere. Returning to the "logic of masculinist protection," Young argues that "feminists may identify with the stance of the masculine protector in relation to vulnerable and victimized women. The protector-protected relation is no more egalitarian, however, when between women than between men and women."[118] In the WPS agenda, the logic of *feminist* protection has given rise to what Vasuki Nesiah describes as "international conflict feminism,"[119] and which Negar Razavi terms "NatSec feminism";[120] we understand these as forms of governance feminism (discussed in chapter 1), and concur with Nesiah in identifying a particular brand of feminism as forging an "alliance with 'counter-terrorism' interventions as both rationale and remedy: i.e., on the one hand international conflict feminism provided a women's rights rationale for military intervention; on the other, it called for gender mainstreaming into post-conflict nation building initiatives as a necessary component of constructing liberal political society."[121]

Critiques of WPS coloniality direct attention to the violence done in the name of the agenda: the dangers of deploying women's rights in service of legitimizing intervention, keeping violent and militarized hierarchies intact but giving them "the legitimacy of gender inclusiveness and empowerment."[122] WPS emerges here as a stunted and deformed form of feminist peace, poisoned at root through association with the edifices of Western imperial power. Critics are entirely justified in targeting the WPS "champions" that simultaneously hold the pen in the Security Council on matters related to Women, Peace, and Security and maintain asylum and refugee policies that directly cause insecurity for thousands of women, or those that fail repeatedly to pursue justice for missing and murdered Indigenous women while they coordinate the informal "group of friends" of the WPS agenda. In a moral register, the variety of the ecosystem is not a license for hypocrisy. However, in line with the arguments we have presented throughout, where we diverge from this important critique is in the assumption that there is anything *inherent* in the WPS agenda, for good or ill. We seek to challenge not the essence of the agenda but its diverse practices—the idea that it *has* an essence at all. The friction between those aspects of the WPS enterprise that sustain and reproduce coloniality and those dimensions of WPS engagement that are actively antiracist, anticolonial, and motivated by a need to acknowledge the violence of imperialism and repair and recenter those written out of WPS's history and present is a feature of the agenda's chimerical form. Some parts of the WPS ecosystem, and the broader epistemic community that nourishes and is nourished by it, are animated by both the colonial shadow and the anticolonial form. The constitutive plurality of WPS denies us any appeal to singular readings of its failures, but we hold this alongside recognition of the deep fractures within the agenda concerning the implications of, and its imbrication with, colonial power.

RACE, AGENCY, GEOPOLITICS

The ways in which a veneer of inclusion and empowerment is mobilized within the WPS ecosystem, to legitimize both continuity and change over the agenda's lifetime, is also worthy of consideration. An additional important vector of critique relates to the erasure of the agency of southern states as actors in the histories and contemporaneous activities of the WPS agenda.[123] Swati Parashar refers to this erasure as a form of "epistemic violence."[124] Like Soumita Basu,[125] Parashar details the ways in which the implicit situatedness of the WPS agenda in the Global North denies the agency of actors in the Global South both to generate and build theory about the WPS agenda and to play an active role in its development and implementation. Instead, "for the WPS 'agenda' to acquire a discursive meaning and universal character, the Global South must perform the site of innumerable 'case studies' where people and societies are framed in a perpetual state of conflict and violence."[126] The subject position constructed for (all) southern states within WPS discourse, then, is a passive one: states and actors in and from the Global South are presumed to be recipients of WPS wisdom and freedoms rather than its producers; and scholarly theory is generated *about* rather than *in* southern states, such that locations in the Global South become visible only, as Parashar explains, as "case studies."[127]

Thus, expressions of agency are erased in scholarly stories of the history of WPS, and also in scholarly analysis of its contemporary enactment (see the discussion in chapter 4, pp. 93–96). The policy practices of WPS, moreover, frequently reproduce these same dynamics. "While individuals and organizations from the Global South are acknowledged and celebrated for their WPS work in local contexts, the authorship of the relevant reports and documents—at the global level—lies . . . with the relevant international body": the United Nations.[128] The conditions under which representatives of southern states become visible at the United Nations are limited, and their contribution constrained within narrow parameters of acceptable performance.[129] This disjuncture between North and South is well sedimented in the formations of the WPS agenda; it can be traced through the policy architecture of the WPS agenda as well as contemporary practices. But attending to the different ways in which southern states themselves articulate their engagement with WPS and agency in the development and implementation of the agenda can demonstrate the vitality of the agenda beyond, and in parallel to, those sites with which the agenda is conventionally associated. Assuming the dominance and centrality of subjects from the Global North as the primary populations of the WPS ecosystem reproduces the exclusionary and sometimes oppressive logics that permitted the racialized ignorance of the agenda and the pernicious marginalization of populations outside of the Global North.

Women in and from the Global South theorize and enact the WPS agenda in context-specific and transformative ways. Indeed, such women have always been among the populations of WPS actors. Again returning to the informative and important account of the development and adoption of resolution 1325 provided by Felicity Hill, Mikele Aboitiz, and Sara Poehlman-Doumbouya, it is clear that the civil society actors involved in those early discussions, in tandem with state representatives, wanted to create and hold space for women whose lives had been most affected by the issues on the agenda of the UN Security Council:

> The NGO Working Group invited women experts to bring their concerns and strategies to the open session. Inonge Mbikusita-Lewanika from the Organization of African Unity African Women's Committee on Peace and Democracy, Isha Dyfan from WILPF-Sierra Leone, Luz Mendez from the National Union of Guatemalan Women, and Somali delegate Faiza Jama Mohamed from the Africa Office of Equality Now in Kenya accepted the invitation and came to New York to address the Security Council in the Arria Formula and to observe the open session.[130]

The significance of the presence of these women at the inception of what became the WPS agenda does not simply reflect the narrow, liberal conceit that the participation in peace and security governance is important because women as fully human subjects have the same rights as others. Rather, or rather additionally, the presence of women and the experiences and insights they brought before the council were aimed at beginning to "develop an alternative, gendered view of society that will lead to the transformation at all levels of structures, practices and social relations, including gender relations," and these efforts demand attention still today.[131]

The agency of women from countries as diverse as Afghanistan, Georgia, and Sierra Leone is evident in the extent of their engagement with efforts to "localize" 1325 and bring WPS into their communities and societies in meaningful ways. The Localization Program implemented by the Global Network of Women Peacebuilders (GNWP) is consistently cited in the UN secretary-general's reports on WPS as a positive way to ensure that WPS actors at the subnational level lead the development of WPS initiatives and have the capacity to articulate a vision of WPS that resonates in their specific context. Since 2012, the GNWP has formalized this initiative, which began in Burundi and is now operational in twenty-seven countries across the world.[132] The local ownership of the guidelines enhances their efficacy as a 1325 implementation tool, but more importantly permits the expression of WPS in ways that work for the people whose lives are most directly affected by the agenda.

In Uganda, for example, localization action plans (LAPs) have been formulated in collaboration with, and include representation from, the Coalition for Action on Resolution 1325 (CoACT), an alliance of women's organizations working for full implementation of the agenda in the country. In Amuria District, Teso Women Peace Activists (TEWPA) are also collaborating partners; in fact, CoACT and TEWPA are credited by the local council chair with taking the initiative for developing the LAP, which—reflecting the priorities of these civil society organizations— includes objectives related to intra-district, community-level conflict resolution and ensuring the availability of education for women and girls. These objectives, with accompanying actions, strategies, and indicators, are well justified in the LAPs on the basis of existing strengths and opportunities presented by working with CoACT and TEWPA. There are links being drawn between, for example, TEWPA's peace and human rights clubs in local schools (which are under the supervision of teachers trained by TEWPA in being vigilant for signs of gender-based violence), advocating for the rights of children, encouraging children to stay in school, and finding ways for school dropouts to return safely and complete their education. TEWPA's WPS work includes these efforts toward broader human rights attainment and personal safety; a focus on issuing WPS from the Global North, or more specifically from the Security Council, with its prior assumptions about what matters in pursuit of security and whose security matters, overlooks these subnational visions and articulations of the agenda. Another example of the plurality of WPS from the study of LAPs comes from Maryland County in Liberia, where the two issues identified for urgent action under the protection pillar are the effect of sea erosion, given that Maryland County is a coastal region, and the abuse of drugs in the community. A further objective relates to securing rights to land and cattle ownership for women. These objectives were set through community consultation and represent a kind of "vernacular" WPS that diverges sharply from the vision of WPS animating, for example, the NATO policies discussed above.

The example of LAPs helps us sketch a counter-dynamic in which the local is generative, the council or ministry above it merely a locale. The local may also serve as a site of critique, not just of top-down efforts but of the hasty shorthand of "Global North" and "Global South" itself, with its exclusion of imperial and patriarchal histories in the forgotten "Second World."[133] Localization is an under-studied and underappreciated vector of the agenda, and at the same time a term deserving of contention. As chapter 2 argued, in the explanatory vocabulary of norms, the local is too easily assigned a derivate position, downstream or subsequent to the properly deliberative space of the "global," laundering as universal what is always already the product of the West.[134] Where agency features, it is as the pragmatic adjustments needed to make an idea work in foreign lands or unideal times. Implementation discourse is most often just this: a chronicle of the failure of the local to follow the script provided. The hierarchy is a product of the canonization of the agenda at the council and in government policy. But for many an early advocate, 1325 was in itself the basis for peacemaking, to be distributed and translated into conflict zones. This more horizontal vision—in which WPS was forged by a transnational women's movement, and then put to use in its service—was displaced by vitalities of state and organizational practice.

In the reproduction of the WPS agenda over time the space available to women from conflict-affected settings to participate in peace and security governance has shrunk, even as the WPS enterprise has grown; this is a form of failure intrinsically related to the racialized power structures that affix authority in the WPS agenda to the institutions and entities of the Global North. Again erasing the foundational contribution of women in and from the Global South in creating the conditions for the emergence of the WPS agenda, expressions of agency in practice are heavily disciplined in line with the vision of the WPS agenda that sees these women as victims for the agenda to save rather than its architects. The recognition of women as fully human and agential subjects with space to be angry, disappointed, active in their own lives creates a different perspective on women in and from the Global South as a population within the WPS ecosystem. Moreover, this fullness must include space for women to reshape, reform, criticize, and reject the WPS agenda entirely—and for this to be cast as both vitality and failure. Against the national-domestic frame of WPS, differences between constituencies of women—urban and rural, secular and religious, liberal and otherwise—affect uptake of the agenda. This population within the WPS ecosystem—peace activists who are suspicious of, disinclined to engage with, or not invested in the WPS agenda, as well as women in and from the Global South whose participation is conditional on their limited, passive, polite form of engagement—is a field of potential vitality. Their agency as agenda setters and architects of the agenda could usefully be centered in analysis as a means of undoing the overpowering Whiteness of the agenda's scholarly representation and the coloniality of its architectures of knowledge.

PLURALITY AND FRACTURE

In chapter 4, we proposed that the adoption of WPS resolutions at the Security Council can be read as an inexorable series of attempts to clarify the agenda; an antagonistic duel between competing visions of its truth; and various acts of geopolitical theater, involving different players by turns, spotlighting different areas and issues. All these interpretations are defensible and, in much the same way, the contestation we have mapped out here between NATO and WILPF imaginings of WPS articulated over time bear the same hallmarks. In embracing the agenda, NATO officials have worked to position the organization as a leader in some aspects of WPS (namely, protection from sexual violence and gender balancing of armed forces) while occluding others (antimilitarism and conflict prevention). Where NATO is seen as progressing the gender perspective at the same time that it sustains hegemonic military masculinity, it cannot but be "underpinned by contradictions."[135] Yet the contradictions are managed, *governed*, recrafted as a distinct version of WPS commitment, and so may operate as much within the WPS field as within the institution itself.

These practices, even as they represent "NATO WPS," *reproduce* WPS within the broader ecosystem. Even though an institutionalized NATO commitment to gender equality may seem minimal from some angles, far down the hierarchy of concerns that preoccupy its members and leadership, the significance of the organization and the energy it expends in propagating WPS is much more central. The differences in WPS practice and belief—both actual and assumed—between NATO and WILPF demonstrate both plurality and fracture under the common umbrella of WPS, and hence lend weight to our proposition that we must give up on the illusion of the agenda's singularity. The primary arena of contestation relates to the securitization or militarization of the agenda, with NATO's endorsement of the agenda seen by some inside and beyond WILPF as emblematic of this process and, further, evaluating this development as a failure of the agenda to realize the promise of (a "true," pacifist and antimilitarist, possibly antiestablishment) *feminist* peace. The narrowing of the debate between NATO and WILPF such that it now primarily revolves around militarism, and specifically nuclear weapons technology, is indicative of accommodations, the ebb and flow of political emphasis, and the internal tensions that structure and form organizations, as much as they enliven encounters between them.

These pluralities and fractures are neither resolvable by establishing the "right" WPS to endorse, nor reducible to political commitment—manifestations of competing feminisms, for example. Arguably, both NATO and WILPF articulations of WPS contain elements of standpoint feminism, visible in the idea that experience determines epistemology, and liberal feminism, visible in the frequent emphasis on balancing and equality of opportunity for women in national military machineries and other institutions of war's governance. There are even surprising offshoots in each: moments of a more deconstructive gender analysis in NATO against the radical feminism of WILPF (even its diverse national chapters). But neither offers "pure" WPS, and such a thing is beyond reach: WILPF can lay claim to a history of feminist organizing, and these activities might be foundational to the agenda, but the organization has also been criticized for a Eurocentric/White feminist inheritance; NATO, as well as being a significant actor acknowledged by many others in the ecosystem, making progress on some indicators beyond that observed in, for example, UN peacekeeping missions, also perhaps articulates the version of WPS closest to what the Security Council thought it was signing up to in 2000. We hold space in our analysis for both reproductions of WPS, both domains within the ecosystem that we take as our analytical target in this book.

The contestation over the militarization of the agenda spills over into other spheres of WPS, with the structuring dynamics of race, gender, and geopolitics linking the struggle between NATO and WILPF over competing visions of WPS to the broader institutionalization of WPS in the guise of international conflict feminism and the erasure of other kinds of (differently racialized) feminisms beyond the imaginaries of national security. In the final sections of the chapter, we picked up on the theme of coloniality introduced in chapter 5, and examined the willful forgetting of racialized geo-positioning in accounts of the agenda's formation. Examining these often unacknowledged historical inheritances and resonances, we showed how the agenda includes degrees of accommodation with great powers and White feminism, and how women's movements in the Global South engage with the agenda both strategically and in ways that generate friction and fractures. Recovering decentered, displaced, and erased wellsprings of WPS activity—and investigating those places where WPS is worked in parallel to other complementary visions of feminist peace—not only mitigates against any easy association of WPS with Whiteness and the institutions of the Global North, but also demonstrates its plurality and fractures. The field is unfolding and dynamic, with space for emphasis and energy growing and shrinking—we see WPS simultaneously dying back, fossilizing, and being nurtured into new life, in new forms. In the final substantive chapter, to which we now turn, we explore some of these new frontiers of WPS, examining the borderlands where long-standing feminist concerns are being regrafted onto the agenda, which we continue to use as vehicles for the discussion of the vitality of the agenda and the proclamations of its failures.

7

BORDERLANDS OF THE FEMINIST PEACE

As established in preceding chapters, there are areas within the WPS ecosystem that enjoy a far greater vitality than other areas: populations recognized as legitimate WPS actors while others fail to achieve such recognition; practices that are seen to "naturally" fall under the auspices of WPS while contestation continues over the validity of labeling others as such; and even extensions of WPS work that are accepted as seamless with the original architecture of the agenda (however estimated). In this chapter, our interest is in areas where long-standing feminist concerns are being regrafted to the agenda, border zones that we use as sites for the discussion of the vitality of the agenda—its claimed "successes," presumed "natural" affinities, and prospective evolution. At the edges of the ecosystem, performative identity blurs; we observe a permeable boundary with other fields and circuits, some of which promise new alliances, even the subordination of one policy domain within another.

The first case we explore is the increasing reference to different dimensions of (women's, human) rights in the WPS ecosystem, including sexual and reproductive health rights (SRHR), the rights of lesbian, gay, bisexual, trans, queer, intersex, and asexual people and others of minoritized genders and sexualities (LGBTQIA+) in conflict and conflict-affected settings, and the subject of "women human rights defenders" (WHRD) in the WPS ecosystem. These all represent points of some contestation, with different populations of WPS actors invested in very different ways in discourses of rights, but there is visible energy in them today. We navigate the borderland between the WPS ecosystem and the women's rights ecosystem that takes the Convention on the Elimination of all forms of Discrimination Against Women as its linchpin, to provide the foundation of our analysis of the space, and points of contact, between CEDAW and WPS. In part this returns us to the resolution texts of chapter 4, which acquire a different valence when viewed as the membrane between governance domains. We then chart the articulation of these various rights discourses into WPS, exploring first the efforts by some WPS actors to diminish provisions related to SRHR in the agenda, then the limited engagement with LGBTQIA+ rights, and finally the agenda's reification of "women's civil society organizations" as a subject to confer legitimacy and authority on WHRD as WPS actors.

Our second ecological effort is at the interface of WPS and contemporary arms control campaigns. For historically minded activists, gender equality and disarmament have always been conjoined. The WPS agenda is in some respects responsible for divorcing them, the politics of the Security Council being inadequate to a proper deconstruction of the arms economy. The point is often made that the duel between protection from sexual violence on the one hand and an expansive project of demilitarization and freedom on the other has been settled in favor of the former. Nevertheless, WPS has been brought into the orbit of attempts to gender arms control, with a common coalition shaping both the agenda and the Arms Trade Treaty. In exploring this affinity, we are able to show how feminist peace concerns have been energized outside of (or overlapping) the WPS circuit, and in turn been limited by a regime permissive of significant arms transfers, so long as they do not result in the most physically proximate atrocities. The ongoing war in Yemen demonstrates the work of closure in the arms control ecosystem that distinguishes between harmful effects, constraining the basis on which gender is permitted to count.

HUMAN RIGHTS, WOMEN'S RIGHTS

Although there have been limited human rights principles embedded in treaties and conventions throughout history, at least since the formation of the "modern state system,"[1] the establishment of a universal human rights regime gained impetus at the Hague Peace Conference of 1889.[2] The development of what has become known as international humanitarian law, as well as the more obviously relevant international human rights law, co-occurred with the solidification of the broader framework of international law that requires as its subject the sovereign state. The rights of states within the international system are thereby intertwined with the rights of the human subject within the state's territorial boundaries. It was not until the 1940s, however, that momentum developed for the articulation of a universal human rights regime. Although there were local rights discourses that afforded specific protections to populations and individuals within states, and notwithstanding the Eurocentricity of both the international legal system and the predication of universal human rights on opposition to the Holocaust,[3] it was the adoption of the Universal Declaration of Human Rights in 1948 that created a cohesive governance system in the sphere of human rights. The legal and policy framework supporting human rights protection is far more variegated and complex in many ways than the WPS ecosystem; it is tricky analytically to work with human rights as a single frame given its plurality and magnitude, so here we focus tightly on women's rights and associated laws and policies.

Against the backdrop of the human rights governance systems that began to proliferate in the second half of the twentieth century, there emerged networks of actors, practices, and texts concerned with women's human rights in particular. CEDAW was adopted in 1979 as a wide-ranging statement concerning the equal rights of women and men; the preamble to the convention explains that

> discrimination against women violates the principles of equality of rights and respect for human dignity, is an obstacle to the participation of women, on equal terms with men, in the political, social, economic and cultural life of their countries, hampers the growth of the prosperity of society and the family and makes more difficult the full development of the potentialities of women in the service of their countries and of humanity.[4]

CEDAW is widely held to be a historic moment in women's rights protections, developing out of the UN designation of 1975 as the "International

Women's Year," in which the first World Conference on Women was held in Mexico City in 1975, and which culminated in the United Nations Decade for Women (1976–1985). Moreover, CEDAW is increasingly interlinked with WPS in contemporary articulations.[5] As one interviewee mused, "I created a matrix to link it [WPS] to CEDAW. . . . For me, the CEDAW has to relate. . . . You don't have gender equality separate."[6]

Activism and advocacy related to the recognition of women's rights as human rights throughout the 1980s mobilized the power of the (by then consolidated) human rights governance framework and sought to challenge "biased interpretations of supposedly universal norms (human rights, equality, rule of law, etc.) and their role in perpetuating practices that systematically disadvantage women and marginalized groups in society."[7] These efforts created the conditions for "extraordinary success" at the 1993 World Conference on Human Rights in Vienna,[8] with the adopted Vienna Declaration and Programme of Action, which affirms, among other provisions relating to women's rights, that "The human rights of women should form an integral part of the United Nations human rights activities, including the promotion of all human rights instruments relating to women."[9]

The Vienna Declaration was supported later in 1993 by the Declaration on the Elimination of Violence Against Women and these tracks of advocacy and activism continued to carry momentum through to the Fourth World Conference on Women in Beijing in 1995, a powerful organizing event, both in the sense of the energies that were harnessed there and the subsequent place of the "Beijing juncture" in feminist discourse (but see chapter 4, pp. 93–97, on unacknowledged precursors).[10] Proximity to the WPS ecosystem of the human rights ecosystem is thus visible where the human rights universe features actors, activities, and policy and legislative architecture related to women's human rights, as the Beijing Declaration and Platform for Action—the outcome document of the Beijing conference—is cited in the preamble of resolution 1325. As Sanam Naraghi Anderlini and Judy El-Bushra argue,

> The BPFA [Beijing Platform for Action] is not only comprehensive but has also set clear benchmarks and a vision for improving women's lives. With 188 states as signatories, it is an influential international document on women's rights. At Beijing, the impact of armed conflict on women was noted as a specific emerging issue requiring attention. Its inclusion

in the Platform for Action spurred the growth of a global women's peace movement.[11]

Eight of the ten WPS resolutions reference the Beijing Declaration and Platform for Action in the preambular material (Security Council resolutions 1960 and 2106 do not include reference to the Beijing conference or documents, perhaps because these are narrower "sexual violence" resolutions). The same eight WPS resolutions also reference CEDAW, although citation of the convention moves from the operative body text in resolution 1325 (para. 9) to the preamble in resolutions 1820, 1888, 1889, 2122, 2242, and 2493, with reference again to the convention in an operative paragraph in resolution 2467. It is intriguing, given that the text was so contested (as we discuss in chapter 4), that resolution 2467 includes a reminder to states of "their obligations under the Convention on the Elimination of All Forms of Discrimination Against Women and the Convention on the Rights of the Child" in a paragraph concerning the reproductive health needs of women and girls who become pregnant as a result of sexual violence in conflict.

CEDAW contains important provisions on sexual and reproductive health, and women's rights groups within various national contexts have been very effective at leveraging the power of CEDAW to motivate policy change in the sphere of women's sexual and reproductive health.[12] A significant point of contestation in the drafting of resolution 2467 related to SRHR, which have not been foregrounded effectively in the WPS agenda thus far,[13] although resolution 1889 includes explicit reference to the need for states to ensure "access to basic services, in particular health services, including sexual and reproductive health and reproductive rights" (S/RES/1889 2009, para. 10; this language was reaffirmed in the preambular material of resolutions 2106 and 2122). Beyond a straightforward—and somewhat obligatory—recitation of a reaffirmation of the provisions of the existing WPS resolutions in the preamble to resolution 2467, the inclusion of reference to CEDAW and states' obligations under the convention is a way of including rights provisions related to sexual and reproductive health without using that explicit language.

There is if anything a greater power in invoking the agenda's roots at "Beijing," though the conditions were crucially different. There were fierce disagreements among delegations at the Beijing conference regarding language and representation, particularly related to the distinction between 'sex" and "gender" and regarding the recognition of women's bodily autonomy: in coalition with other religious organizations and conservative Catholic state representatives, "the Vatican sought to undo and roll back the achievements women had made in Cairo" at the International Conference on Population and Development, which took place in 1994,[14] using what became known as the "holy brackets."[15] The practice of bracketing contested text, signaling the need for further negotiation, was used extensively in the preparation for and throughout the Beijing conference itself. At one stage almost 40 percent of the preparatory text was in brackets, with the most profound tension emerging over the concept of gender.[16] As Doris Buss explains, "gender" was threatening to the conservative coalition because it is inimical to the view of "essentially complementary" binary sex categories and it opens up the possibility of "different and fluid sexuality identities which are not constrained by biological identification."[17] While concerted advocacy, lobbying, and clever negotiating tactics prevented most of the significant rollback of language, the citation of Beijing not only brings with it the traces of successful women's rights advocacy, but also the contestation.[18] In one genealogy, the WPS agenda is thus constituted always already in relation to women's human rights claims.

Another element of proximity and interconnection between the women's human rights ecosystem and the WPS ecosystem relates to justice mechanisms. Particularly in the sphere of sexual violence prevention, and accountability for sexual violence crimes, there is synergy between the two governance systems. Resolution 1325 includes an operative paragraph on the significance of the Rome Statute as an artifact of international law, in the same paragraph that invokes CEDAW calling "upon all parties to armed conflict to respect fully international law applicable to the rights and protection of women and girls, especially as civilians, . . . and to bear in mind the relevant provisions of the Rome Statute of the International Criminal Court" (S/RES/1325 2000, para. 9). All subsequent sexual violence resolutions mention the Rome Statute and its significance to the governance of sexual violence crimes.

Other areas of the WPS ecosystem also connect with this area of the women's human rights ecosystem. In a statement to the 2016 open debate in June, for example, human rights advocacy director for MADRE and

NGO Working Group member Lisa Davis linked the practices of the International Criminal Court to the WPS agenda:

> The recent landmark conviction of former Chadian President Hissène Habré is a reminder that while the wheels of justice turn slowly, they do turn, and it is possible to achieve accountability for crimes that include rape and sexual slavery. The Security Council and other Member States should expand political and financial support to accountability efforts, including through referrals to the International Criminal Court and ensuring that those with arrest warrants against them face trial in The Hague.[19]

Similarly, the secretary-general's reports make numerous references over time to the international legal frameworks addressing conflict-related sexual violence, even prior to the adoption of resolution 1820 and the subsequent bifurcation of reporting (after the adoption of resolution 1820, the secretary-general was required to report to the council on sexual violence in conflict, according to the mandate of resolution 1820, separately to his report on the implementation of resolution 1325).

The establishment of the ICC and the ratification of the Rome Statute, which includes "Rape, sexual slavery, enforced prostitution, forced pregnancy, enforced sterilization, or any other form of sexual violence of comparable gravity" as crimes against humanity,[20] provides a context within which sexual violence in conflict—as a violation of women's human rights—can be prosecuted. The prosecution of such acts, both at the ICC and in conflict-affected countries, is frequently listed in the secretary-general's reports on WPS and sexual violence in conflict.[21] These prosecutions are reported as successes related to the WPS agenda,[22] despite the fact that in the case of Jean-Pierre Bemba, the verdict was eventually overturned.[23] This association of WPS with advances in jurisprudence and an implied commitment to the rule of law produces a connection with human rights governance, as well as security, contributing to the sense of an emerging regime (chapter 4, pp. 109–111). Though we touch fleetingly on the border work here, the intermingling with international criminal tribunals is fractious: just as sexual violence has been treated as one side in a duel with participation and rights, so, too, have prosecutions at the ICC and elsewhere been challenged not just by their own failings but in comparison to alternative modalities of justice and preferences to devote resources to reparations.[24] The entanglement here is not only with a proximate ecosystem of universal rights, but with deep contentions over what is increasingly called "carceral feminism."

There is much more cross-pollination between the women's human rights and WPS ecosystems. We have not touched, for example, on the right to political participation, and other civil and political rights, which are enshrined in the International Covenant on Civil and Political Rights,[25] or women's rights in political settlement and conflict transition;[26] there are many other connections, both tenuous and strong. The WPS ecosystem is nourished by its connections with these human rights systems and structured at least in part through the documentary architecture it shares with the human rights governance frameworks. Here we have elaborated the shared root systems to shed light on the dynamics of the WPS agenda at its borderlands. These dynamics, drawing on the women's human rights ecosystem, produce and reproduce the WPS agenda in particular ways, with specific political effects. They must therefore become visible in analysis as proximate to, and potentially a merging part of, the WPS ecosystem if we wish to understand its establishment and governance.

SEX AND SEXUALITY IN WPS

In 2009, the Security Council adopted resolution 1889, which

> Encourages Member States in post-conflict situations, in consultation with civil society, including women's organizations, to specify in detail women and girls' needs and priorities and design concrete strategies, in accordance with their legal systems, to address those needs and priorities, which cover inter alia support for greater physical security and better socio-economic conditions, through education, income generating activities, access to basic services, in particular health services, *including sexual and reproductive health and reproductive rights* and mental health, gender-responsive law enforcement and access to justice. (S/RES/1889 2009, para. 10; emphasis added)

Thus, the formal architecture of the WPS agenda clearly, if briefly, articulated a normative position on the provision of SRHR for women in postconflict situations. This position was reinforced in both resolutions adopted in 2013. Resolution 2106 encouraged "United Nations entities and donors to provide non-discriminatory and comprehensive health services, including sexual and reproductive health, psychosocial, legal, and livelihood support and other multi-sectoral services for survivors of sexual violence" (S/RES/2106 2013, para. 19), while the preamble to resolution 2122 notes "the need for access to the full range of sexual and reproductive health services, including regarding pregnancies resulting from rape, without discrimination" in conflict and post-conflict situations (S/RES/2122 2013, preamble). Thus, even though SRHR are not mentioned again in the text of WPS resolutions, there is a compelling case to be made that existing resolutions commit the council to upholding these rights in conflict and conflict-affected settings. In other words, SRHR represents a successful splicing of women's rights governance with the WPS agenda.

This area of WPS practice budded in the middle years of WPS development (with resolutions adopted in 2009 and 2013) but has not since thrived. To the contrary, there have been determined efforts to pick off this area of potential growth by undermining the existing commitments to SRHR documented in the resolutions cited above. The negotiation of resolution 2467, for example, was highly charged; there was intense scrutiny of the process and an unprecedented level of media attention paid to council activity in the period before the resolution was adopted in April 2019. Information was leaked in the days before the resolution was due to be tabled at the annual Security Council open debate on sexual violence in conflict and discussions on social media and among other populations of WPS advocates and practitioners; these disclosures and related discourse focused on whether the language in the draft resolution about sexual and reproductive health care for survivors of wartime sexual violence could be protected, while attempting to strengthen accountability for sexual violence in conflict, in the face of serious opposition, primarily from representatives of the Trump administration.[27] As it turned out, it could not.

The zero draft of resolution 2467 refers to "comprehensive sexual and reproductive health care such as access to emergency contraception, safe termination of pregnancy and HIV prevention and treatment." By the time the text of the resolution was put "in blue" (that is, by the time a draft was ready for negotiation), this language had been removed. Further changes to the negotiation draft were demanded by U.S. government representatives, so that phrases that drew attention to "lack of availability of services for survivors" and the need for all women and girls to have "access to education, livelihoods, employment, land, and health services," as well as direct reference to "sexual and reproductive health, psychosocial, legal, and livelihood support," were excised. In a last-minute change to the previously agreed text, even the replacement language was deleted: in place of direct mention of SRHR, the resolution urged member states to provide services "in line with Resolution 2106." The entire clause was gone from the adopted resolution, at the behest of the U.S. government, which otherwise threatened to veto. Within the formal architecture of the WPS agenda as it currently stands, efforts to foster growth in the area of SRHR by expanding these provisions in the agenda's resolutions are being met with significant resistance.

LGBTQIA+ rights have had a different trajectory than that of sexual and reproductive health rights in the WPS ecosystem; these specific rights have not been articulated in the formal UN architecture of the agenda at any point (see chapter 3, pp. 80–81). What recognition exists has come via momentary flashes and subterranean passages. For one, mention of LGBTQIA+ rights in the 2019 secretary-general's report on WPS is grafted on to a discussion of men and boys:

> Violations against men were reported in Burundi, the Central African Republic, the Democratic Republic of the Congo, South Sudan, Sri Lanka and the Syrian Arab Republic, occurring primarily in villages and detention facilities. Men and boys also face reporting barriers owing to the stigma relating to perceived emasculation, as well as particular physical and psychological consequences. There are often no legal provisions regarding the rape of men. Instead, the criminalization of adult consensual same-sex conduct may impede reporting for fear of prosecution, despite being a victim. Lesbian, gay, bisexual, transgender and intersex (LGBTI) individuals who are survivors of conflict-related sexual violence are negatively affected by such laws and risk penalties when reporting their experiences.[28]

Previous efforts to rethink the subjects of WPS discourse and practice thus offers opportunity for further hybridizing moves. Mixing in LGBTQIA+ rights claims with other forms of rights discussion has the potential to create more inclusive WPS practice and also to fundamentally reshape some of the cis- and heteronormative logics of the agenda.[29] At another level of contestation linking WPS to contemporary feminist and feminist-adjacent disputes, the politics of recognition and inclusion are confronted with the deconstructive energies of queer theory, which can just as often critique rights discourse, against the bestowing of "an adjectival gloss on a stable noun, like capitalism with its human face."[30]

Expansive moves have thus been successful in some governance niches and encountered aggressive countermeasures in other, as shown through the consideration of different kinds of rights and different rights-bearing subjects. Another example relates to the concept and representation of women human rights defenders, or WHRD. These are a specific population of WPS actors frequently though not exclusively identified as a sub-population of women's civil society organizations. These same organizations have consistently been represented in the WPS ecosystem as an influential, and therefore significant, population. From the adoption of the foundational resolution, the role of women's civil society organizations has been consistently and repeatedly emphasized as part of resolution 1325's unique character: "It may well be the only Security Council resolution for which the groundwork, the diplomacy and lobbying, the drafting and redrafting, was almost entirely the work of civil society, of non-governmental organisations."[31]

While most Security Council resolutions, presidential statements, and reports of the secretary-general mention civil society (though notably resolution 1325 does not), there has been increasing energy around WHRDs in the last decade, as a discrete population distinct from other civil society or political actors. To the best of our knowledge, the precise phrase "women human rights defenders" was first used in the context of WPS by Jadranka Kosor, Croatia's vice prime minister and minister of the family, veterans affairs, and intergenerational solidarity, at the June 2008 open debate.[32] Kosor noted in her statement that "without ensuring women's physical safety and economic security through social norms, efforts to engage them in decision-making processes will not succeed. Due to a lack of such norms, we have witnessed the assassination of many women human rights defenders worldwide."[33]

In the following year, the executive director of the UN Development Fund for Women (UNIFEM, now UN Women) also spoke out in support of "women defenders of human rights,"[34] and her words were quoted by the representative from the United Kingdom in his statement to the April open debate in 2010.[35]

From 2011, WHRDs are routinely mentioned in reports of the secretary-general, as both subjects in need of protection (vulnerable to violence intended to silence or derail them) and as agents of change within society, champions of equality, and—obviously—defenders of women's human rights. The formulation of "women human rights defenders" is itself as curious as it is grammatically muddled. It is not clear from that wording whether the human rights defenders themselves are female, or whether they are multi-gendered defenders of women's human rights. There is sufficient ambivalence in the way that the phrase is used and repeated to suggest that either interpretation is plausible, and even that those using the phrase mean to invoke *female* defenders of women's human rights. All of these uses are present in the reports and statements from member states; in 2011, for example, the secretary-general's report mentions three cases of "human rights violations against women promoting women's rights."[36] What is clearer is the emergence of the figure of the "WHRD" as a subject of WPS re-grounding the *women* of "Women, Peace, and Security" in peace building and resistance. As our story of vitality and failure has indicated, the growth of activity on the WPS circuit has been twinned with a sense that the WPS field is being denuded. The agency of the defender becomes in response a leading example of how participation may be transformative and "full and meaningful" (the adjective added to canonical WPS from 2013 onward), rather than shallow or tokenistic.

The WPS ecosystem supports the pluralization of WPS actors, hybridizing civil society organizations with human rights actors to produce two distinct and separate subjects with legitimacy and authority within the sphere of WPS practice: "Civil society organizations and women human rights defenders are key actors for implementation, often being the only ones delivering services and sustaining dialogue in conflict-affected communities."[37] The discourse around WHRD has shifted from where it was five or ten years earlier. More frequently mentioned by those working on and around WPS in New York, WHRD are also more frequently mentioned across the ecosystem, as shown in figure 7.1.

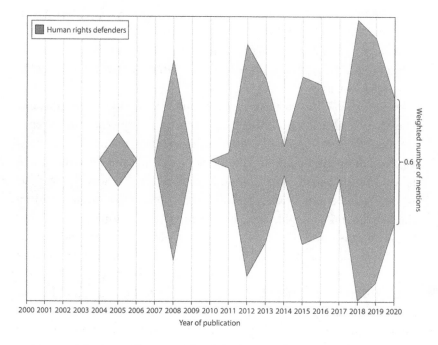

FIGURE 7.1 Mentions of human rights defenders in all ecosystem documents over time (2005–2020, $n = 237$, weighted by number of documents produced each year).

Source: Graph by the authors.

From interviews we have undertaken and conversations we have had with WPS practitioners, there is, however, a perception that WHRD are not universally accepted as legitimate and authoritative WPS actors by virtue of their evolution through human rights governance. That is, although there are increasing numbers of references to WHRD in reports of the secretary-general, and even in statements by some UN member states to the annual open debates, the Security Council (specifically some of the five permanent members) remain deeply resistant to this language.

In one conversation in 2014, with reference to the negotiation of resolution 2122, our interlocutor noted, "there's five paras that mention civil society but there's nothing on women's human rights defenders or human rights defenders, and in earlier drafts there were. That's a real shame because the G8 declaration [on sexual violence in conflict] actually does have [language on] women human rights defenders. And the P5 are all members of the G8."[38] Several years later, discussing the negotiation of resolution 2467 with a different person, we were advised that although the initial text of the resolution "was quote unquote, 'ambitious,' meaning they did put in a lot of issues that we had asked for, they put in language on women human rights defenders, they put in language on LGBTQI+. They put in language on SRHR, and all this stuff. When you looked at the zero draft of the text, to me it was clear as day that all this was language that they had very little intention of throwing their political capital behind."[39]

What we identify here, then, is another example of contentious diversity within the ecosystem: there is widespread use of the concept of WHRD by some UN member states, in NAPs and statements to the open debates each year; and yet there is profound resistance to the inclusion of WHRDs in the text of Security Council resolutions and presidential statements, to the extent that language on WHRD is included in negotiation drafts as a concessionary point. Such is the shifting circuit that WHRD both are and are not key actors within the field of WPS practice, subjects of WPS discourse, and primary drivers of change under the auspices of the WPS agenda.

The generative connections with the human rights ecosystem, shown here to be in close proximity to the WPS ecosystem that is our focus, are thus a source of nourishment for the agenda. There are multiple points of contact between the two ecosystems, and through our analysis of CEDAW, LGBTQIA+ rights claims, and the increasing emphasis on the role—and precarity—of WHRDs, particularly in conflict-affected settings, we have shown that these borderlands infuse the agenda with a rights focus that is a powerful illustration of the paucity of a security approach. Though the Security Council may be the institutional home of WPS, for many of the civil society actors involved in its genesis, it was envisioned as a rights agenda, and this founding vision has not thrived over the last two decades. Indeed, the council has frequently worked against the realization of WPS as a matter of women's rights, instead securitizing responses to issues such as gender-based violence and trafficking in persons.[40] It is thus politically important to note both the energy of exchange between these proximate ecosystems, and the simultaneous failure to grow the rights dimensions of the agenda in ways that are transformative and that do not reproduce security's stranglehold on WPS possibilities.

MAKING WAR SAFE FOR WOMEN

When the first International Congress of Women met at The Hague in 1915, it declared itself for universal disarmament, to be achieved at first by an international alliance empowered to "take over the manufacture of arms and munitions of war and . . . control all international traffic in the same,"[41] and later by the general shedding of stockpiles. This early call for abolition was intended as a foundation of the international feminist order to come, what Jane Addams at the time called "the subordination of an isolated nationalism to general international interests. It is hoped this new approach . . . will be vital enough to assert itself at the end of this war as over against the militaristic and 'armed peace' relationship."[42] A successor regime to the armed peace did not materialize, neither after that war nor after those that followed, but the regulatory imperative has since been reprised by critics of the Security Council,[43] and more rarely in the pragmatics of security sector reform.[44] Though feminist, antimilitarist arms control proposals have been largely excluded from WPS, which has tended in many of its manifestations to emphasize "making war safe for women" over defunding war as such,[45] the same impetus has bubbled up in parallel policy fields. As we documented in the last chapter, arguments over the proper scope and form of participation in military-security institutions and conflict resolution have displaced the antimilitarist case against the global arms economy. But where the contention between NATO and WILPF indicated a fracture within the WPS ecosystem, we now foreground how activists and some states have built an imperfect bridge between the gender perspective and the arms control regime, navigating this borderland to pursue the feminist peace in non-WPS space.

The Arms Trade Treaty (ATT)—negotiated in the early 2010s and entering into force just before the fifteenth anniversary of 1325—is the most significant global instrument limiting a heterogenous set of weapons and military technologies.[46] Under its article 7(4) exporting states must assess the risks of arms "being used to commit or facilitate serious acts of gender-based violence or serious acts of violence against women and children." The provision applies to the "the broadest range of conventional arms,"[47] and includes eight named categories: tanks; combat vehicles; artillery; combat aircraft; attack helicopters; warships; missiles and their launchers; and small arms and light weapons.[48] Facilitation has been understood to mean a significant contribution to violence, even at "one or more steps remove."[49] The tethering of an export to a violent event may involve several links: for instance, an original state recipient passing weapons to private actors who guard detention facilities where sexual violence is used to torture prisoners, or who make use of an armored vehicle to transport them to such a site.[50] An assessment might include such factors as a government's willingness or ability to punish gender-based violence, the listing of armed groups with the special representative of the secretary-general on sexual violence in conflict, and the prevalence of threats to female activists.[51] States are expected to collate data on end users, their human rights and gender equality records, in authorizing or mitigating sales.[52]

The explicit reference to "gender-based violence" has been celebrated as a first in the history of treaty making, won by pressure from a hundred countries at the tail end of negotiations.[53] Though the treaty does not itemize differences or intersections between "GBV" and "violence against women and children"—the two terms it uses—the recognition of men and boys has been understood as an implied innovation, opening up the "broader spectrum of harm,"[54] a movement in rhyme with the contemporaneous WPS resolutions that sought the same. And the regulatory web thickens: gender was the focus for the Fifth Conference of Parties of the ATT.[55] Such vitality has been elaborated in guides to best practice, indicators, and refined legal definitions,[56] where the density of gender governance reaches as far into weapons system chains as the ammunition life cycle.[57]

Where WPS horizons have been limited by the domestic-international frontier, export assessments in the ATT in theory require states to consider *innenpolitik* as much as realpolitik: the degree of trust in authorities, the treatment of Indigenous peoples, and the state of domestic discrimination law in an arms-importing partner.[58] And yet five years in, there was no indication that gender-based violence had ever been the explicit reason for denying an export license (though it may have featured implicitly in general human rights assessments).[59] In the absence of a true global regime, states are self-regulating, and the diplomatic compromise on a threshold of undefined "overriding risk" in the final treaty replaced both the "substantial" danger of earlier drafts and the original activist criterion that it be "reasonably foreseen that . . . users are likely to use the arms to perpetuate patterns of abuse."[60]

The affinity between WPS and arms control may be discerned in the history of activism and resonances between state practice across the ecosystems. Both the transnational advocacy network behind 1325 and that which agitated for the ATT share common members: Amnesty International, WILPF (in the form of the Reaching Critical Will project), GAPS UK (Gender Action for Peace and Security), the Centre for Women's Global Leadership, and Oxfam.[61] Others—like the Women's Network of International Action on Small Arms—contribute to an overlapping coalition even as they focused exclusively on one policy domain. The Control Arms campaign began in 2003, soon after the "watershed" of 1325, and shared some of the same state allies: Finland, Iceland, Kenya, and Norway—all of which have a NAP—have been credited as the strongest supporters of a gender provision.[62] As with the prehistory of 1325, governments of the Global South played a leading role that was overshadowed in subsequent narratives; for the arms transfer regime Costa Rica, for WPS Namibia and Bangladesh.[63]

The two agendas were also anticipated by the same summits and taken up in the same councils. At the Beijing World Conference on Women, states also endorsing a call to "reduce excessive military expenditures and control the availability of armaments."[64] In 2013, the Commission on the Status of Women would agree a more limited charge, that *illicit* arms "aggravated" violence against women and girls.[65] Five General Assembly resolutions on gender and arms control, adopted in the years either side of the ATT entering into force, implicitly and then explicitly found common cause with WPS resolutions emanating from the Security Council.[66] There, resolutions 2106, 2122, and 2467 all "noted" or "acknowledged" the ATT's article 7(4) in their preambles. After an effort to include explicit reference to women's participation in the treaty failed,[67] resolution 2122 included an operative paragraph on women's participation in "efforts to combat and eradicate the illicit transfer and misuse of small arms and light weapons" (S/RES/2122 2013, o.p. 14). Resolution 2242 was stronger, advocating a more fulsome role for women and diagnosing the "destabilizing accumulation" of arms and the wide-ranging impact on mobility, education, and economic opportunity as well as physical safety (S/RES/2242 2015, o.p. 15). The WPS supplement to arms control negotiations was reciprocated by references to WPS in Security Council resolutions 2117 and 2220 on small arms.[68]

As the ATT was taking form, the CEDAW committee formally declared in favor of a gender provision, citing the "proliferation and illicit trade of arms and ammunition" in harming women and children.[69] A year later its General Recommendation 30 advocated measures to "address the gendered impact of international transfers of arms" through the ATT (CEDAW/C/GC/30 2013, 9), while General Recommendation 35 identified "the accessibility and availability of arms" as increasing vulnerability to gender-based violence.[70] In at least three periodic reviews the committee has regarded progress on arms exports as an imperative for states otherwise seen as champions of WPS.[71] These assessments were arguably a dilution of the 1979 convention, which had identified "general and complete disarmament"—and not just an end to "illicit" weapons—as a tributary of gender equality.[72] Still, the prominence of CEDAW indicates the cross-fertilization of domains, a merging of human rights, arms control, and WPS ecosystems around a long-muted demand of the feminist peace.

Like the ream of WPS resolutions, the ATT has been welcomed as "a new global norm,"[73] evidence of a horizon of women's participation in arms control negotiations and disarmament programs,[74] and as one feature of an "emerging arms control regime."[75] The map of state parties to the ATT—and thereby bound to its specific gender-based violence provision—might indeed be mistaken for one of WPS adoption.[76] Ratification and implementation are clustered in Europe and West Africa, Latin America and Australasia; of the ninety-four states with NAPs on WPS, 72 percent are also parties to the ATT, outnumbering both WPS-implementing states that are not parties and state parties lacking a WPS plan.[77] There are, however, some striking exceptions and caveats. The United States is not a signatory, the only one of the seventeen states that have issued three or more NAPs not to be. Canada only acceded to the treaty in 2019. In several conflict-affected states—the Democratic Republic of the Congo, Iraq, Sudan, South Sudan, Ukraine—there are currently no arms control measures to match WPS commitments. A more significant undercutting of the treaty's feminist peace credentials is the vagueness of key terms, and the reliance on states to create their own method of self-regulation.[78]

The junction of WPS and arms control is unstable. Though expressing a convergence of the gender perspective, the ATT itself does not mention 1325 or its successor resolutions.[79] Arms control activists have
invoked WPS surprisingly rarely, and at minimal length, even where gender was their focus.[80] To be sure, WPS resolutions were seen as relevant
in the case for rights and participation.[81] At other times, gender work in
the ATT process has been said to "echo" WPS motives and networks,[82] a
movement in parallel, availing "synergies" of mutual implementation.[83]
In the vitality story of the ATT, the prior success of campaigns on land
mines and cluster munitions in the late 1990s is often to the fore;[84] elsewhere gender is seen as a bridge to human rights law or CEDAW.[85] State
parties to the ATT are lagging in developing measures of gendered security for export decisions,[86] precisely the variety of intelligence that WPS
research and monitoring could provide, for example through NAP and
UN mechanisms.[87] But twenty years in, arms control and WPS remain
ecosystems in need of symbiotic nurture.[88]

The neglect is all the more surprising given the accolades offered to the
agenda as a blueprint for changing state practice.[89] Though resolution 1325
urged conflict *prevention*, recalled the Beijing Declaration—which had
come out in favor of "general and complete disarmament under strict and
effective international control"[90]—and invoked the UN Charter, with its
call for "the regulation of armaments, and possible disarmament,"[91] by its
second decade WPS was not strongly associated with the regulation of
weapons flows. In part this reflected the duel between participation and
protection, and the sense that WPS now stood for action (including armed
actions) against sexual violence by rebel groups and others outside of the
putatively liberal world order. But even before the ecosystem had developed its various niches, the governing logic of the Security Council had
imposed limits on grafting and dynamism, as explored above in relation
to the proximate human rights ecosystem. The "international peace and
security" domain allowed for the rearticulation of violence against women
and girls *as* a security problem, but not at the expense of established
parameters of military expenditure and reasons of state.

Despite prominent declarations of a feminist foreign policy, evidence
to date does not suggest a meaningful shift in arms export patterns.[92]
More, as figure 7.2 indicates, the arms trade is a major fracture line
within the intergovernmental coalition, with fifteen of the top twenty

arms-exporting states during the first two decades of the agenda also being declared WPS champions. They are also the largest funders of the agenda.[93] Some friends of WPS are prime beneficiaries of the arms trade in revenue terms; others are significant advocates for its regulation and even closure. As well as Iceland's sponsorship of the gender provision, Ireland and Switzerland in their most recent NAPs both stress the link between women's participation and the nonproliferation regime (Ireland NAP III 2019, 17, 29; Swiss NAP IV 2018, 22). Fourteen NAPs within our time frame mention the ATT; of these, seven may be read as adopting a more comprehensive approach to arms control, while four focus exclusively on small arms.[94] Recent EU-level commitments have gestured to the wider horizon of disarmament and arms control (EU Policy IV 2018, 26),

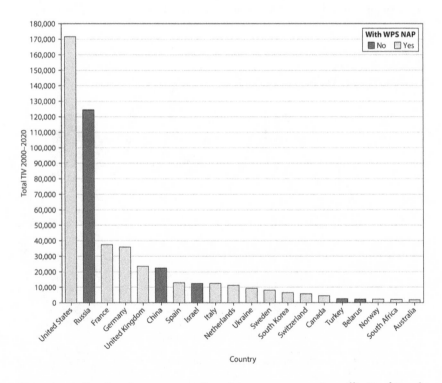

FIGURE 7.2 Top twenty arms-exporting states, 2000–2020, in millions of trend-indicator value (TVI) units. Those with a National Action Plan on Women, Peace, and Security are marked in light gray.[95]

Source: Graph by the authors.

yet the general object of policy remains the AK-47 assault rifle more than the drone or the nuke, tools of diffuse and idiosyncratic violence more than industrial warfare.

The asymmetry is evident in our ecosystem analysis, where references to "small" arms consistently outstrip mentions of heavy weapons and weapons of mass destruction, despite the broad categories used to capture the latter (see figure 7.3). In the first twenty years of the agenda, policy documents were over five times more likely to mention "small arms," "light weapons," "guns" or "disarmament, demobilization, and reintegration" than the "arms trade," "arms transfer," "arms control," "nonproliferation," or "nuclear."[96] Other research confirms that references to weapons in WPS policy are overwhelmingly about small arms and light weapons, with occasional references to land mines and cluster munitions along-side recognition of the ATT.[97] Though it may be read as most convenient

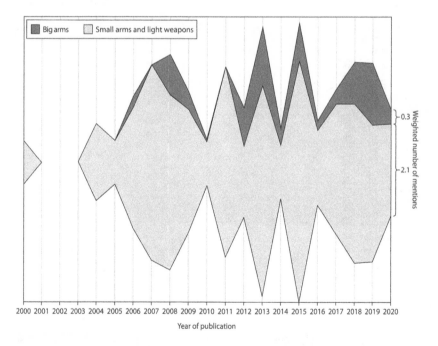

FIGURE 7.3 Big and small arms in all ecosystem documents over time (2000–2020, $n = 237$, weighted by number of documents published each year).

Source: Graph by the authors.

for the major powers, the consensus around small arms also follows from feminist advocacy. For the ATT especially, the role of small arms in increasing the prevalence and gravity of domestic and family violence was a fundamental concern.[98] The linkage contained a radical analysis, breaking the conceptual boundary between security proper and the domestic sphere, and drawing the "intimate" into war and peace accounting. Yet it has also constrained the more ambitious strains of the WPS agenda that would undo the systemic coincidence of states, militarism, and the arms industry. In this way policy announcements targeting arms can reinforce existing geopolitical circuits, as when Germany opted not to export small weapons beyond its NATO and EU partners,[99] consolidating a Global North bloc rather than reducing the circulation of weapons as such.[100]

GENDERING AIR WAR

The general intersection of arms control and the feminist peace is, then, fraught. Perhaps the most catastrophic contemporary fissure is in Yemen, where prevention discourse and the provisions of the ATT collide with high geopolitics. Following an uprising in 2011 and the failure of national reconciliation initiatives, internationalized civil war has raged since March 2015, pitting the insurgent Houthi (or Ansarallah) movement against the recognized government and a coalition led by Saudi Arabia and materially supported by its allies, including the United States and the United Kingdom.[101] Despite widespread abuses by the Houthis against Yemeni civilians and their targeting of some Saudi infrastructure,[102] the worst suffering flows from the coalition's bombing campaign, which has become the primary culprit for a transnational advocacy coalition seeking an end to the war.[103] UN sources estimate that 233,000 deaths were caused by the war in its first six years, 131,000 of those indirectly through starvation and the destruction of critical infrastructure.[104] Four million people have been forcibly displaced to date,[105] the vast majority of them women and their children. As the calamity deepened in 2018, UN offices began to repeatedly refer to Yemen as "the world's worst humanitarian crisis." In parallel, Yemenis was assessed as facing the most patriarchal of crises on measures of inclusion, justice, and security for women, above only Syria and Afghanistan, and lowest ranked in the 2019 WPS Index.[106]

Supply lines for weaponry facilitate gender-based violence in the sense anticipated by the ATT. Multiple studies attest to the increase in armed group sexual violence and the waning of what protections had existed.[107] Security Belt Forces backed by the United Arab Emirates have been judged responsible for "widespread cases of rape and other forms of sexual violence" against migrants and for abuses against gender-nonconforming persons in South Yemen.[108] In less organized form, the ready availability of small arms enabled exploitation and abuse in domestic and communal spaces, including sexual slavery and extortion targeting young boys.[109] The experience of other conflicts is strongly suggestive of a rise in domestic violence.[110]

In its updates on Yemen, the Informal Experts Group on WPS has consistently cited the spread in sexual and gender-based violence, and traced the brutal variety of conflict-linked rape, torture, trafficking, forced marriage, and "honor killing," committed with impunity by all parties against political activists, migrants, detainees, girls and boys, women and men, and persons of diverse gender identity.[111] The distinct UN Group of Eminent Experts on Yemen concluded before its mandate was terminated that members of the coalition had committed rape and sexual violence, among numerous other war crimes.[112] Again, though Houthi forces have committed similar violations, the coalition strategy is directly and indirectly implicated in gender violence at scale, with clear causal links to the effects of weaponry deployed, and transferred to it by other states, including numerous WPS champions.[113]

In short, the very nexus of arms and gender violence envisioned by arms control advocates, and animating one fundamental antecedent of WPS, is at work in Yemen. Yet, despite the coalition's intervention benefiting from the license of the Security Council, in a resolution adopted in the same anniversary year of the agenda that also saw the "mainstreaming" of gender across all council business, WPS remains strangely absent from the scene, operational only in the latest stages and in hamstrung form.[114] Yemen's National Action Plan on WPS, issued at the close of the agenda's second decade and five years into the conflict by the country's embattled government, covers the standard four pillars of participation, protection, prevention, and post-conflict relief and recovery, but does not explicitly mention arms transfers, the coalition bombing campaign, or the identity of protagonists beyond the Houthi insurgents.[115] Saudi Arabia has no NAP or equivalent commitments. Other governments have championed the participation of Yemeni women in politics, but eschew any comment on the fundamental drivers of gendered harm (e.g., Germany NAP II 2017, 7; Switzerland NAP IV 2018, 23; UK NAP IV 2018, 23). Before the coalition intervention, when the end of Ali Abdullah Saleh's rule was still classifiable as a revolution-cum–civil war, the Security Council *had* recalled the WPS series in preamble as it created a sanctions committee;[116] in 2021 it designated one individual—a Houthi police chief—for command responsibility and direct infliction of sexual torture and intimidation.[117] The experts on conflict-related sexual violence identified by the special representative of the secretary-general address their demands to "all parties" and note the contribution of the conflict at large to an increase in prevalence,[118] yet measures have been taken late in the day against some protagonists only, and within the remit so associated with one side in the "duel" over the scope of WPS.

The war in and on Yemen poses such a test for the gendering of arms control precisely because the harms far outstrip the conventional attention to sexual violence. With nearly 24,000 air strikes in under seven years, the conditions of everyday survival themselves have become a target.[119] The effect of bombardment at this scale is the collapse of sanitary and energy infrastructure, in turn stoking infant mortality, acute malnutrition, and generalized debility. On one measure, in the first three and a half years of the war, 85,000 children died prematurely from malnutrition exacerbated by the war.[120] Communications submitted to the ICC prosecutor allege the joint responsibility of licensing authorities and weapons company executives in disregarding prevention measures, gender being an implicit aspect of war crimes and international humanitarian law violations in Yemen.[121] More, the coalition has plausibly been pursuing a starvation strategy, targeting agriculture and blockading ports.[122]

Advocacy briefs have attributed these unarguable gender *effects* (disproportionate as they are in shrinking the life spans and lifeworlds of Yemeni women and girls) to failures in implementing the risk-assessment strictures of the ATT.[123] Since explosive weaponry, deployed indiscriminately by the coalition, wrecks infrastructure and lives, transfers should evidently cease.[124] The charge of indiscrimination at the population level entails a creative slippage: where treaty texts forbid violence that has a gendered "basis," they are less explicit on gender-unequal death and debility, even where this is inseparable from the deployment of weapons systems or the military strategy of arms importers. Though war crimes and crimes against humanity may turn on a lack of discrimination, and may draw attention to gendered wreckage to prove it, "gender" itself—as a distinct treaty article and category—is instead still articulated as a motive or a vector of "the sexual" inextricably linked to the bodily site of an attack.

The movement of gender in ATT advocacy mimics that of WPS at large, where tightly negotiated diplomatic text that would not exist without the efforts of feminist social movements is after the fact leveraged by the same movements for more ambitious and systemic ends, deepening the resonances and prospective operational forms in the policy field. In the swirl of activism mobilizing the ATT, we make out the long-standing contestation of the feminist peace at two levels: in the first a radical antimilitarist impulse confronts the bleeding edge of business as usual; in a second, sexual and gender-based violence receives some recognition when understood as a weapon of war, but does not alter the course of state behavior when the nexus with weaponry is more structural, when the regular running of the international order depends on flow and exchange. Yet the ongoing conflict in Yemen demonstrates not just the calculated neglect of some WPS norms by some WPS champions, but also the ongoing labor of grafting, as provisions are interpreted and extended, paired with the tools available in WPS space, in claim making before national and international courts and in the appeals of advocacy. Gender is made legible in these sites, even as the meaning of the text is blurred in arguing over "gender-based" harms and what it means to facilitate them. Though there is no reason to suppose that arms control and WPS will coevolve, the inclusion of gender in the ATT suggests a connective tissue, a potential often latent but sometimes semi-active, the outline of something adequate to the *systemic* coincidence of weaponry and patriarchy.

PROXIMITY AND DISTANCE

The vital plurality we have traced within WPS is evident also in its borderlands, as are a new set of tensions. Though the policy domains we have explored in this chapter—the human rights system, the attempt to integrate sexual and reproductive health and rights, recognition of human rights defenders and those living in ways that complicate and challenge binary gender norms, the arms control regime—all have their own significant complexity and life outside of WPS, they nevertheless cross-pollinate, producing new wellsprings as well as dead ends. The process is often one of self-conscious grafting, as when practitioners inscribe references to other legally authoritative texts—such as the Convention on the Elimination of All Forms of Discrimination Against Women—in WPS text. Elsewhere an elective affinity, rather than a foundational grounding, is at work. Arms control predates the agenda and need not appeal to it for legitimacy. Still, to be alive to the gender coordinates of violence in the twenty-first century is necessarily to consider the affordances of the agenda, as coalition network, alternative forum, or enforcement mechanism.

Rights-based encounters with, and challenges to, the WPS agenda are multiplying. As outlined above, sexual and reproductive health rights in conflict-affected and post-conflict settings are a site of significant contestation as well as a motivator for new and different forms of WPS engagement. Queer rights similarly mobilize communities of action that overlap with and challenge WPS in profound ways. Although we have not had space to attend to it here, human rights approaches to WPS are also tilting the ecosystem away from security in the governance of terrorism and violent extremism: the 2021 report of the special rapporteur on the promotion and protection of human rights and fundamental freedoms while countering terrorism directly expresses concern "about the extension of militarized and carceral counter-terrorism approaches into areas such as domestic violence regulation."[125] The same report notes that "Regrettably, some women claim to function as feminist voices within those security frameworks instrumentalizing and appropriating a securitized version of the women and peace and security agenda to advance the narrow aims of countering terrorism or securitized countering violent extremism."[126]

The borderland between WPS and human rights ecosystems are thus being both marked and actively contested as the agenda continues its sprawling development. Within the WPS field, translation has been shaped by the imperatives and limits of security work. Small arms may be encompassed with little difficulty, coding for action against rebels and insurgents rather than renewed effort at arms reduction and nonproliferation of weapons of mass destruction. But this form of "making war safe for women"—prioritizing action on sexual violence above all other insights of the gender perspective—does not imply simple failure. Here we have made out a creative impetus to produce new regulatory forms, vitality marked by the spread of an idea through the policy field, generative even within its clear limits. Where activists are able to mount campaigns against such catastrophes as the war in Yemen these may be effectively sealed off from WPS commitments by the political character of the Security Council and the threat that the feminist peace might at last impinge on fundamentals of world order. For Yemen, the wider contradictions allow for some energies to be directed against abuses, while obscuring structural links between a bombing campaign and gender-unequal death and debility.

Nevertheless, WPS aims—or the ambition of one fundamental animating spirit of the agenda, traceable to 1915 at least—are pursued in non-WPS space. The ATT has offered one opportunity for a common coalition to forge new horizons beyond the Security Council and national plans. In some senses they have succeeded, laying the groundwork for WPS metrics to serve gender-sensitive arms control. Current WPS is neither a veneer on geopolitical business as usual nor a radical assault on the military-industrial complex. There remain many consequential ambivalences in the language of "misuse" and the "illicit," underscoring the critical complaint that the mention of weapons too often acts to shore up business as usual, the "liberal" guarantee of continuing circulation.[127] Moreover, attitudes to weapons cross and fracture the coalition, expose contradictions for great powers, but also serve as common grounds for a grouping of states that have worked against the arms trade in the name of gender. These points of equivocation are, as we have argued throughout, a feature and not a bug of the WPS agenda. Duel and duality constitute the agenda: the ecosystem is characterized by tensions, fractures, and outright opposition. In our final chapter, we therefore argue that feminist peace might be contingent on forgetting WPS.

8

FORGET WPS

I n the opening years of its third decade, the Women, Peace, and Security agenda is again in bloom—though perhaps not in the United Nations Security Council, still incapacitated by the Russian delegation's October 2020 draft resolution, received by the WPS community as an act of birthday sabotage, a pretend engagement designed to fail (see chapter 4, pp. 108). Rumors of a new resolution—perhaps a consolidation of the sexual violence regime—have not yet borne fruit. But elsewhere, the ecosystem continues to expand its borders, sinking new roots. At the strata of policy and institutional commitment, text continues to proliferate. Seventeen new NAPs were issued after the 2020 cutoff of our ecosystem dataset, the majority in countries without a prior policy or protocol (Bulgaria, Chad, Egypt, Ethiopia, Kazakhstan, Malawi, Mexico, Morocco, Peru, Slovakia, Somalia, Sri Lanka, the United Arab Emirates, and Uruguay). The long-anticipated Israeli NAP is scheduled; NATO released a new action plan; climate change is increasingly identified as a critical nexus of gendered peace and security.[1] Advocates continue to refine new applications of participation and protection: for cybersecurity, reproductive health, and private military corporations, among others.[2] The end of the Trump presidency reanimated hegemonic investments in WPS, raising the profile of groups like Women of Color Advancing Peace, Security, and Conflict Transformation, whose founder became U.S. undersecretary for arms control and international security in the Biden administration (thus also renewing debates about the politics of representation). The final exit of Western forces from Afghanistan seemed to signal the abandonment of a promise indelibly marked as "WPS." Only a few months later the Russian invasion of all Ukraine drew worldwide attention to wartime sexual violence, female combat, the politics of machismo, and the lurking danger of nuclear war, even as existing WPS policy proved inadequate to the catastrophe.[3] In the preeminent threat paradigms of global health security and climate change, a gender perspective was often lacking, inviting new campaigns for learning and synthesis. The WPS governance project turns in a greater orbit than ever before, the ceaseless return of vitality and failure.

This book was born of confusion, frustration, and stubbornness. As aspiring political ecologists, we have been persistently confused by the mercurial "WPS" in scholarly and practitioner discourse, frustrated not only by the absence of clarity about what WPS *is* but also the general lack of interest in the multiplicity of WPS and its implications. We have stubbornly resisted the pressure to bring to bear an illusory coherence on the agenda, instead committing to sitting with its "beautiful chaos."[4] In short, the plurality of WPS is constitutive. Confusion, frustration, and stubbornness have also at times characterized the process of researching and writing this book. The agenda—unsurprisingly—refused to fit comfortably within the neat chapters we had planned to compose; desirable snippets of data eluded us (mostly in the form of WPS memorabilia and similar artifacts); interviewing across time zones was at times logistically challenging and always accompanied by an acute awareness of what might have been lost as a result of remote connection. And then there was collaborating from opposite sides of the world during a devastating global pandemic.

In the wake of all this, the conclusion we offer is in some ways a simple one: forget WPS.

Readers may be forgiven for thinking that the pressure has gotten to us. To clarify: We are not proposing that supporters, advocates, and practitioners should abandon their posts; to the contrary, there is a pressing need for feminist arguments, perhaps now more than ever in the face of state and popular support for the erosion of women's rights and the continued exclusion and marginalization of women from formal and informal institutions. Rather, we seek to give up on the concept of "the WPS agenda" as a singular political project or vision and instead apprehend and engage with the agenda always as a plural object of knowledge and practice. The polycentric, polyvalent, polysemic qualities of the policy ecosystem that we have contoured and explored here confound neat prescriptions. They confound even attempts to monitor and evaluate success or failure, leaving conventional tools of policy studies and the study of regulation and governance insufficient to the task. The instability is even more profound when moving past the flat surface of political discourse to which we have largely confined ourselves.

To forget the image of WPS as a capacious and settled norm is to revive feminist curiosity: What does the agenda do with—and to—gender otherwise? The lapse enables a new suppleness, working along lines of fracture and difference rather than emphasizing the unity of either a hegemonic project or a feminist revolution deferred. It is to expect metastasis and seismic break. Though we share with many others a commitment to feminist ends, we have come to doubt the effort to lend WPS coherence through engaged scholarship. Studies of the implementation gap and normative architecture have often emphasized what the agenda was *supposed* to be, its motive and promise, and so kept the faith in the pages of academic journals and on the expert circuit. That the agenda has never managed to be what it was supposed to be should give us pause. In his article "Is Good Policy Unimplementable?," anthropologist David Mosse proposes that policy frameworks exist to mobilize political support, to secure relationships between organizations, and to maintain themselves in representational as much as operational terms.[5] They so often "fail" in implementation precisely because vague and even contradictory elements nevertheless allow different protagonists pursuing differing ends to collaborate under the same umbrella. This is not to say that a script is set in advance, but rather that the idea of a common enterprise covers for the fact that there is no script. By this metric, WPS is exceptional policy. In the same spirit as Mosse, we seek not to debunk WPS but to account for the constant labor of making it signify, of composing it despite its heterogeneity. The manifestations we have traced in the course of this book are not just deviations and imperfect efforts, but in each niche a form of feminist governance at work. That this variety includes equal opportunity militarism and climate justice efforts, gender essentialism and antiessentialism, transnational radicalism and statist chauvinism, indicates only that feminism has never existed without adjectives. Abandoning what we are supposed to know about, say, the authority of the Security Council, enriches not just the study of WPS as an academic subfield but the contemporary diagnostics of gender at large.[6]

Forgetting is also a form of fidelity. WPS has become a canon and a paradigm. Yet, for its earliest champions, resolution 1325 was merely one more means to facilitate a revolution from below. Feminists intended less to justify and buttress a new international regime than to provide a wedge against the patriarchal bargain that shut women out at every level. This was classic boomerang politics: activists would appeal to a declaration of the Security Council to force open doors to local or national government blocked by belligerents and diplomats. The gambit had its contradictions, most obviously that of accepting the Security Council's self-image as supreme arbiter of peace and ultimate source of power. Feminist analysis at the same time located real power elsewhere, in the everyday webs of gender politics, and the organizational energies of women. Still, the early efforts to translate and disseminate 1325 spoke to a belief in the abilities of grassroots peace builders that is less and less evident in the professionalized circuit of the agenda today. What if the policy formalism of WPS is as much a sign of petrification as maturity? What if forgetting is a way to keep the possibilities of WPS alive? As Judith Jack Halberstam comments, "from the perspective of feminism, failure has often been a better bet than success."[7] This book's wager is that we may learn, and even thrive, in a landscape of inadequacies.

In this concluding chapter, we reflect on the vitality, vibrancy, and plurality that we have elaborated on throughout the book. By returning to vitality and failure—by applying ourselves to understanding how both are enacted and instantiated in and through the WPS ecosystem and with what effects—we can show not only how "the WPS agenda" breaks the bounds of the present governance architecture, but also that it is no static monolith to feminist activism, and that by forgetting "the WPS agenda" we might remember and renew different futures of feminist peace. We first revisit scholarship on the governance of peace and security, drawing in particular on feminist legal research and feminist interrogations of international organizations to foreground the tensions, discontinuities, and ruptures that characterize the agenda and associated modes of governmentality. We go on to elaborate the themes of vitality and failure that we have threaded through our analysis, weaving with these threads an account of the agenda that in many ways defies the kind of summary that would conventionally be found in a conclusion. We also revisit our guiding theoretical proposition in this section, restating the contribution to scholarship on governance that we offer, which is a way of making sense of complexity by focusing on its relational and reproductive effects and constitution. In the final section, we speculate on the possibilities of feminist peace that might be engendered by giving up on "the WPS agenda" and explore what kinds of worlds could be conjured in place of a presumption of coherence, an illusion of regulatory efficacy, and a fiction of failure—or success.

FEMINIST FRUSTRATIONS, FEMINIST RESISTANCE

Part of our motivation for undertaking the investigations on which we report here was to reconnect WPS work with feminist scholarship on security and human rights. As we have commented elsewhere, writing with Soumita Basu, an extensive field of feminist research and engagement supported and nourished the incipient WPS agenda, but these connections have not always and wholly been uncomplicated.[8] The feminist frustrations reside primarily in the tension between those engagements that seek to rehabilitate the institutions of governance that regulate and order peace and security and those that are avowedly skeptical, even critical, of the possibility that these institutions can be transformed.[9] These frustrations are not new, and have haunted the WPS agenda since its inception, as we outlined in chapter 1. The ambivalence felt by many feminist activists and scholars regarding whether and how to intervene in machineries and mechanisms of governance in pursuit of feminist peace is a consistent through line traceable back to the preliminary consideration of articulating rights concerns in the language of security. Natalie Hudson neatly summarized the dilemma when she noted that "employing the security language may be advantageous in the short term, but it also situates many actors in the WPS network in positions where more fundamental critiques challenging the traditional security paradigm become impossible and even unthinkable."[10] The productive effects of this tension are therefore not only visible in the long-running debates about what the WPS agenda *is* (a rights/security agenda, with the slash doing a lot of intellectual work), but also in how critiques can be articulated. This book has been an attempt not to resolve this tension but rather to sit with it, to work at it, to elaborate both the multiplicity of the agenda and the multiplicity of critique.

Feminist practitioners were always acutely aware of the simplifications of the agenda.[11] Again, Dianne Otto summarized the stakes for many when she described the "power and danger" of the encounter between women's rights and the Security Council as the hegemonic institution of security governance.[12] The power lay in recognizing the council as a reservoir of legitimacy: its symbolic power is after all also what states desire, cognizant as they are that social capital thus acquired increases their status, and the likelihood of their perspective gaining support.[13] The regular attention of the Security Council, even where perfunctory, generates a signal that reverberates throughout global politics. The long-term presence of an issue on the council's docket creates a common, consensual knowledge, and facilitates the emergence of a caste of credentialed experts who interpret, implement, and modify the techniques of feminist governance. The "danger," on the other hand, lay in the prospect that the Security Council would extract legitimacy from feminist associations without altering the patriarchal foundations of world order.[14] More sharply, WPS advocates have been accused of participating in the "securitization" of sexual violence, helping produce the weapon talk that figures women as abject victims and military or police forces as rescuers.[15] The increasingly statist inflection of the agenda, while arguably an internalization of WPS arguments into foreign policy practice,[16] also indicates that activists may have misjudged the nature of power in the council.[17] The caution that Otto identifies has continued to animate, motivate, and sometimes restrain feminist engagements with WPS, and has been both cause and condition of some of the dynamics of vitality and failure that we have traced.

These tensions regarding entry, co-optation, investment, and critique persist. We have not sought to take a position on whether engaging with governance institutions is generically the "right" thing to do for feminist peace activists and advocates, nor whether feminist encounters with governance inevitably nourish the kinds of (faux) feminism that "have used a focus on harm to women—particularly sexual harm—to aid in the legitimization and extension of coercive state power, often against marginalized individuals and communities, and less powerful states."[18]

Feminist resistance, disinvestment, and conscientious objection is both visible and understandable in light of these important realizations. But the plurality of the ecosystem—no less than the paradoxical mosaic of feminism itself[19]—allows for no solution to these tensions, no general truth of WPS to be realized. Governance institutions are themselves plural, acting as often in discord as in unison, and less static bodies than clearing houses for other social bargains and conflicts. The point may be taken as a plea for objective consideration of the history of advocacy and policy in its rich variety, posed against narrow politicizations of one or other lineage. But it is also a conscious refusal of the seductive logics of claims about tendencies to order.

We encounter a cacophony of WPS across the ecosystem, a hectic and frequently discordant soundscape that reveals the extent to which WPS is sung in different voices. Our ambition is not to bring these into tune, but to listen attentively to the various calls that marshal WPS activity. In this, we travel alongside Gina Heathcote, who argues persuasively for acknowledgment of "the value of existing gender justice projects within institutions while raising additional dialogues with respect to the fundamental nature of the organisations themselves via an array of feminist accounts of power, of gender, and of privileged knowledge within feminist approaches, as well as within global governance."[20] Hearing, seeing, doing WPS (and undoing WPS, as our deconstructive effort reveals): these are reproductive technologies that renew the ecosystem in whole and in part in each time. Given our central focus on the agenda's constitutive plurality, we cannot appeal to an originary truth of WPS to deliver feminist peace. There is no singular, righteous WPS to guide feminist peace work, but nor is there support for total abdication of all political commitment to the same. And so we hold on to feminist frustrations and feminist resistance.

TRACING VITALITY AND FAILURE

Let us briefly recap our argument. Our epistemological proposition was quite straightforward. As we argued in chapter 1, practically every sympathetic scholarly account of the agenda to date presumes a coherent WPS of lively possibility. Yet the agenda is deeply marked by failures both historic and anticipated. This observation encouraged us to look otherwise at unrealized success, and we adopted the twin motifs of vitality and failure. Following the lines of this epistemological prompt, we hypothesized that as the agenda has developed—grown in scope and depth and energy—it has also de-cohered into the dappled microhabitats and niches of the ecosystem. Such an array of practices, documents, positions statements, and enactments requires similarly varied methods of data collection and analysis, which we described as a *bricolage*: the construction of an artifact (this book, and the formations of knowledge we present) through the assembly or arrangement of already existing and new descriptions, insights, and practices.

Chapter 2 continued the development of our conceptual framework. Given the prevalence of scholarship on WPS as a norm, or normative framework, we first mapped out our encounter with this body of work. Although we acknowledge the utility—and, indeed, the appeal—of anchoring engagement with the WPS agenda in the theoretical architecture developed around the political life of norms, we highlighted the limits of norms as a framework for understanding the multiple practices of WPS. While an expansive concept of normative framework might fit the WPS agenda, WPS norms have not cohered in the way they are expected to, and currently do not weigh heavily on state behavior. Almost since its formal inception, with the adoption of resolution 1325 in 2000, critics and supporters alike have bemoaned the chronic gap in implementation of the agenda. Such failings are articulated overwhelmingly in terms of lack of resources and political will, but the slippage between failing the agenda and upholding its constitutive norms is rarely observed. Merely acknowledging this slippage is not sufficient. We therefore elaborated the model of the policy ecosystem, which we offer as an alternative to the concept of normative or legal framework. Ours is not a simple acknowledgement that there is a lot of WPS activity going on. Rather, ecology is a way of apprehending the whole and its parts and its constitutive plurality, wagering that through such examination the WPS agenda can be better apprehended.

The conceptual work presented in chapter 2 was brought to bear on the empirical manifestations of the WPS agenda in chapter 3, as we both introduced the dataset we have curated to represent two decades of WPS policy and presented a surface-level analysis of the ecosystem as a whole. In approaching WPS as an ecosystem, we wanted to draw attention to a universe of practice and relational connections behind and beyond the textual surface of official operative paragraphs and national strategies, or what we have called the canopy. In chapter 3, however, we laid out our map, the coordinates for the shape of the agenda as expressed in the documents that provide visions and mandates for what WPS is and how it should be done. We then extended the ecosystem concept to accommodate the idea of proximate ecosystems, illustrating the relationship of the WPS ecosystem to adjacent others. Each of these proximate ecosystems has its own discursive formations, its own embedded strata of principles and priorities, its own archaeologies of practice and intellectual ancestry.

From this generative foundation, we proceeded to open up the first of our detailed interrogations of various aspects of the agenda, commencing in chapter 4 with a historiography of the ten WPS resolutions and WPS at the UN Security Council more broadly. Foregrounding the role of contingency, of move and countermove, we explored the iterative process of agents mutually shaping the field of production and reproduction and traced out the ebb and flow of WPS priorities over time. We drew on interviews with policymakers and practitioners and analysis of how resolutions changed across drafts to excavate the political meaning of the resolutions at the time, and how they are now remembered in the WPS sequence. We also investigated WPS resolutions that were drafted but never passed in showing how the core of the agenda has been produced. Expressed by participants as variations on series, duel, and theater, the instantiation of the WPS agenda at the council was never a foregone conclusion, yet neither is the realization of each new resolution merely a technical or bureaucratic process. Our analysis illuminates the complexity of the agenda's formal policy architecture and the relational connections through which it is reproduced.

In this same chapter, we also examined the emergence of parallel and overlapping policy work within the UN system, such as in the splitting off of peacekeeper "sexual exploitation and abuse" into a human resources issue, to show how apparently central WPS themes travel under different governance rubrics. The development of an anti–sexual violence regime based in the UN system is the aspect of the WPS agenda that has most closely followed standard models of global governance, with the creation of dedicated offices, a consolidating mechanism for sanctioning perpetrators, and a collaborative exercise across UN entities and member states in developing standards and conducting investigations. Against views of the UN as the owner of the agenda, or accounts of the primacy of the Security Council, we showed how the agenda manifests differently across the layers of international institutions. Through our *bricolage* of institutional practice, texts, and observations, we opened the production of resolutions beyond the council to critical scrutiny, and explained the both products and production of the WPS resolutions, including those that never were.

Chapter 5 turned to national practices and productions of WPS, including both performances that document WPS principles in policy and those that uphold such principles without formal articulation. One of the key themes that animated our discussion in this chapter is that of the interplay of race and nation, the multiple and sometimes conflicting ways in which violences of racism—including racialized exclusions—and coloniality are erased or ignored in WPS practice. The tour through national WPS thus foregrounded the interplay of technicality, statecraft, and performances of race/nation/state. That which is made central and that which is made surplus to WPS in national engagements were brought into focus as we explored the currents of vitality and failure that locate and reproduce WPS within and under the auspices of the state, reading National Action Plans for the implementation of the agenda against the grain. We proceeded at three depths, and in three substantive sections: first, we commented on the most straightforward measure of national energy, the existence or nonexistence of a NAP; second, we elaborated on the evasion of the central object of WPS—war—in select NAPs and counternarratives of WPS offered in others; and finally, we examined the boundary work of securing the national subject of foreign policy, with attention to the place of Indigeneity in the NAPs of primarily liberal democratic settler colonial states. Together, these NAP interrogations enabled a novel critique of the domestication of WPS and provided further illustration of the contours of the WPS ecosystem that is our object of study.

Turning from national articulations of WPS, in chapter 6 we refocused on WPS actors beyond the state, transnational and international. We sat with the friction between WILPF and NATO, arguing that the fault line between them expresses in miniature fractures across the WPS field. Both WILPF and NATO deploy the language of the agenda strategically in ways that defer fundamental tensions over the purpose of WPS itself. We went on to evaluate claims that the agenda has become (or has always been) colonial in its articulation. Examining these erased and unacknowledged historical inheritances and resonances, we showed how "civil society" operates by degrees of accommodation with great powers and White feminism, while also showing that women's movements in the Global South engage with the agenda both strategically and in ways that generate friction and fractures. The structuring and expression of these acts of resistance is part of how the agenda—its ownership and constituency—is reproduced.

In the final substantive chapter, our interest is in the borderlands of the agenda, its horizons and the extent of future possibilities. We identified two areas where long-standing feminist concerns are being regrafted to the agenda, which we used as vehicles for the discussion of continuing vitality and failure. The first case we explored was the increasing reference to different dimensions of (women's/ human) rights in the WPS ecosystem, including sexual and reproductive health rights, the rights of LGBTQIA+ people in conflict and conflict-affected settings, and the subject of "women human rights defenders" in the WPS ecosystem. These all represent points of some contestation, with different populations of WPS actors very differently invested in discourses of rights, but there is visible energy in these fields of activity at the present moment in WPS development. Our second case at the borderlands of WPS was the governance of the global arms trade. Radical versions of WPS have long stressed the necessity of disarmament; contemporary security articulations have tended to displace arms control. In this liminal space, a common coalition shapes both the agenda and the Arms Trade Treaty. In exploring this affinity, we showed how feminist peace concerns have been energized outside of (or overlapping with) the WPS circuit, and in turn have been limited by a regime permissive of significant arms transfers, so long as they do not result in the most physically proximate atrocities. The ongoing war in Yemen demonstrates the work of closure in the arms control ecosystem that distinguishes between the means of wartime harm, constraining the basis on which gender is permitted to count.

AFTER WPS

And so we end almost where we began: unable to provide a satisfactory, or satisfactorily unified, account of our object of study. Even as we write, WPS is shifting. UN member states are articulating different visions of WPS, as we saw in October 2021 when the representative from Saint Vincent and the Grenadines commented during the annual open debate on "the need to apply anti-colonial-intersectional gender analysis as the standard in every aspect of the work of the Security Council" as a foundation or cornerstone of WPS work.[21] As we have shown in our discussion, particularly in chapters 5 and 6, such a call is likely to be both enthusiastically welcomed and to cause deep, if unacknowledged, consternation among WPS advocates and practitioners. As we have also shown, this is a feature, and not a bug, of the WPS agenda.

From our vantage point on the other side of our ecosystem map, WPS continues to be structured by at least six fundamental tensions.

The first is over what *gender* even entails. It is a critical commonplace that the WPS circuit indulges the gender binary, with its clean and indelible opposition of the masculine and feminine in male and female bodies, respectively. Though latterly of importance for queer and trans scholarship and activism on WPS, the complaint is a long-standing one, attentive to how often feminist discourse evokes a monolithic figure of the "woman" against an undifferentiated violent and domineering masculinity. Inevitably, theory is implicitly at stake in the sometimes starkly different ideas of "the work that gender does," to take up Marysia Zalewski's prompt.[22] The friction is not, or not *only*, that of academic feminism against feminist advocacy, but plays out in everyday conceptualization. WPS relies on the adoption of "the gender perspective," a kind of consensus shorthand that says little about what gender explains, what the insights of the perspective might be, or what standing its findings should be given in the eventual calculus of decision making. It does not specify the proper treatment of masculinity, nor acknowledge the challenge of intersectionality. Where the unifying force of "women" as a collective subject of peace is frayed—say, by reference to differences of privilege, power, and place—the agenda becomes necessarily multiple.

Second, there is the seeming clash of *vulnerability* and *agency*. This— much more than the interplay of vitality and failure—has been the explicit defining theme of decades of WPS scholarship. Participants in the WPS circuit have emphasized the horizon of rights, knowledge, and leadership that positions women as the impetus for peace and the engine of change, but have also relied on women's marginality, violation, and hurt to make the case for the agenda. Consider the WPS theater of the "woman in conflict"—the exact woman and the exact conflict vary—who appears before the Security Council, performing her suffering or suppressing her anger in an appeal for assistance.[23] The tension is at the heart of the duel narrative in which "protection" measures emerge in ways that displace and even suppress the grander potentialities of "participation." Building in part from differing accounts of gender, observers have seen in the agenda the tell-tale signs of the patriarchal protection racket, reinforcing rather than alleviating gender hierarchies. Though vulnerability need not be simply opposed in a zero-sum choice, the recurrence of the dueling narrative indicates a stubborn political division.

Third, the feminist peace project is caught between *hegemony* and *multiplicity*. When viewed as a Western feminist endeavor, whether in terms of its origin or evolution, the WPS field is rendered partial and parochial. Though proclaiming itself a transformative project for all peoples, led by local women peacemakers, it may be better understood as an elite foreign policy disposition forged in the United States and Europe in the lapse between great power conflict. To the extent that WPS has served as cover for Western military actions in Afghanistan, Iraq, or Libya, it leaks legitimacy. Though we have questioned monocausal and monovocal histories of the agenda, there is no doubting the hierarchies of expert and beneficiary, donor and recipient, savior and damned, that shape it. An alternative agenda begins from below—as many advocates for 1325 intended—with reigning powers acting in response as needed, through close consultation or on the terms outlined by a transnational WPS activist network: a romanticism of the grassroots against an idealism of benevolent power. Yet multiplicity comes not exclusively from below; it also captures the emergence of distinct regional approaches, a multipolar order in which we might think of WPS with Latin American characteristics as much as Scandinavian ones.

Fourth, there is the contest between an ethos of *inclusion* and one of *abolition*. Most evident in the case of military institutions and blocs like NATO, the feminist demand might be understood as one of equal opportunity or radical critique. The opposition is not as simple as that between continuity and change, as for advocates of inclusion an increase in the quantity of women creates a change in the quality of an institution. Nevertheless, where some seek the end of patriarchy through techniques of balancing, mainstreaming, quotas, and regulations, others identify a structural linkage in which patriarchy persists even once it is no longer populated exclusively by men. In a different register, this is the question of whether WPS is for or against the state, with its established basis in ministries of defense and gender, its place in the global circulation of arms, its near monopoly on the legitimate use of force, and its location at the apex of political organization.

Fifth, there are clashing *issue hierarchies*. In most sketches of the agenda, this is a question of the interrelationship of the four "pillars" (participation, protection, prevention, and post-conflict relief and recovery). The duel becomes a multi-protagonist standoff, as resource and attention economies imply chronic competition. Though conceptually unsatisfying given the many complementarities, the clash reminds outsiders that governance is also about concrete choices, inviting a study of pragmatism and least worst outcomes. As the agenda has diversified, issue hierarchies have also been about the sheer range of possible connections between the agenda and its relatives, whether in terms of governance or themes. WPS becomes associated with policy domains conceivable as natural allies or strange bedfellows: migration, terrorism, climate change, transitional justice, organized crime, arms control, labor rights, cybersecurity, international criminal law, global health. Growth need not imply success or purity: countering violent extremism doesn't "belong" to the original conception, but then neither do reproductive rights.

Finally, there is a foundational and perpetual tension over *peace* and *security* that has both spatial and temporal dimensions. Like gender, peace and security is oddly un-, or at least under-, specified in WPS, a fault line running through the agenda dividing those who see its form and function as a means to make war safe(r), to enable the mitigation of harm and limitation of violence, and those who (still) espouse a vision of a world without war, offering a thoroughgoing antimilitarist critique. Meanwhile, within-world delineations of spaces of peace and security from spaces of peacelessness and insecurity are both critiqued and reinforced in WPS practices. Moreover, the agenda assumes a peace/conflict dichotomy, enshrining a linear temporality of conflict in the repeated articulations of "during" and "after" conflict. (Perhaps as a result of its institutional home in the Security Council, there is little mention in the WPS resolutions of *before* as a meaningful temporal zone.) Some WPS resolutions offer glimpses of resistance to the stubborn linearity of the presumed progression from conflict to that which comes "after,"[24] but otherwise, it is assumed by the architecture and many proponents of the agenda alike that time can be divided neatly and ascribed the status of "conflict" or "peace," even if there is no agreement on what "peace" looks like.

We have suggested that these oppositions are not mere differences of perspective, but constitutive paradoxes, resulting from the agenda's logic of governance and the potential of its ambition. Rhetorical strategies indicate political stakes: the antagonistic temporalities of, on the one hand, a WPS that was originally vibrant but has been perverted, and at the other extreme, a feminism that has long been tainted by colonial baggage, essentialism, and liberal pieties and is only now becoming properly radical and intersectional. WPS must be at once essentialist and antiessentialist, irreverent and paternalistic, hegemonic and diverse, inclusive and abolitionist, narrow and plural, armed and pacificist. An alternative response is to see the WPS frame as a convenient fiction, where the positions that draw so much criticism from activists and scholars are merely the palatable surface for a more dynamic and radical program. Gayatri Spivak is often cited for her use of "strategic essentialism," the tactic of adopting a stereotype or mimicking a crass figuration even while knowing that it is false, that the ambitions of WPS far exceed the protection of vulnerable women or inclusion in the offices of state. As we have in part documented, the WPS field is marked by the trail of this subversive vitality. But less noted is Spivak's subsequent regret that "my notion just simply became the union ticket for essentialism. As to what is meant by strategy, no one wondered about that."[25]

Our insight that the agenda is plural and complex is not novel per se: earlier research that analyzed WPS work at United Nations Headquarters as a series of narratives governed by undecidable logics concluded that "recognizing the undecidability of these logics not only reaffirms their plurality but also acknowledges the ambiguity of the agenda: its regressive as well as its transformative possibilities, the moments of its silence as well as its potential as a platform for amplifying the voices of those marginalized or dispossessed by security practices that too often ignore insecurity, and its violences as well as its solutions for peace."[26] This ambiguity characterizes the agenda at the UN, but our contribution is not simply to show that such ambiguity goes beyond the United Nations: rather, we foreground constitutive plurality. This is to argue both for the utility of the ecosystem as a model in the study of governance and for the consideration of different questions about the effects of relational governance. Through our investigation, we have encountered significant political questions about what and how we measure, and how we conceive of existence and effect, against which evaluations of "success" and "failure" seem meager or mean (and certainly partial). We have reevaluated what can be known and how we can know it, driven by an underlying acceptance of the unknowability of the social world in its entirety.

Moreover, we wish to redeem complexity from those who describe it as "a superficially appealing but theoretically vacuous metaphor."[27] Nor is our commitment to policy ecology a generically post-structural view of irreducible discourses. Scholars of international organizations, global governance, and regimes have examined different forms of complex governance systems to understand what insights can be gleaned from centering and working with complexity.[28] Complexity in governance has been taken as an object of study in its own right, not to develop explanatory theory but to provide a context or framework for theorizing the interplay of specific contexts, mechanisms, and practices.[29] A key insight from this literature is that "complex systems are not merely adaptive but co-adaptive. This means that actors are not only shaped by the system but can also shape the system itself."[30] The WPS ecosystem is enacted in and by every text authored or statement delivered in its name, as well as by our scholarly interference; WPS documents, actors, institutions, and analysts take on meaning in ever-shifting constellations of relational connections. These conditions may have partial equivalents in other governance spheres, but on our account are specific to the history and development of WPS. The ecosystem, for all its confounding plurality, is a web of substance.

For scholars of governance, the fractured "case" of WPS sits uneasily in reigning models. Neither a robust new norm nor an old practice, the agenda lies somewhere between the first breakthrough of a transnational advocacy network and the end point of a robust regime. Though it is in many ways less technical and embedded than other governance projects it is also more sprawling, appearing explicitly and implicitly across the terrain of security, development, and human rights. This form deserves

attention from outside the field of feminists drawn to the agenda's promise, not least because the agenda shows no signs of dissipating. For students of feminism, WPS has too often appeared as a technocratic apparatus from above, co-opted or instrumentalized, disengaged from struggles
over identity and justice. Our history instead situates it as always entangled in a web of feminist contentions over everything from sexuality to
carcerality. This is the practical face of relationality, a continual attention
to transactions and coalitions of governors. The analytical move is paradoxical, since it is precisely by forgetting a pristine WPS that the myriad
connections to contemporary feminist movements become visible again.
For the future practice of war and peace, we anticipate an expanding fracture. Failures of implementation are not always errors: where they privilege some dimensions of the agenda over others they may be better understood as confounding examples of vitality, rearticulations of the agenda
in increasingly rivalrous form. The identification of foreign policy with
feminism—of which the National Action Plan is one methodologically
convenient symptom—allows for a new variety. The demand that states
adopt the agenda invites accommodations, whether as "femonationalism,"
"national security feminism," or "securitization." The greater the demand,
the more energy is available for particularity. The concomitant intensifi-
cation of feminist investments in abolitionism, intersectionality, and freedom will produce new contradictions and alliances.

We opened this book with the impossibility of WPS. We have written
many thousands of words about something that we have argued doesn't
really exist, at least in the commonly presumed form. We are now, having
dwelled on plurality and fracture, exhorting you to forget WPS. Forget
the idea that those three neat letters can contain the multitude of feminist
peace. Give up on—or, following Janet Halley,[31] just take a break from—
the will to know WPS. Forcing the coherence of the agenda is itself a form
of violence, an erasure or dismissal of those not counted by that which is
captured in any partial vision or presumed faithful representation of the
agenda. Every entity, connection, surface, and contribution within the
ecosystem is a fragment of peace potential because the adaptation of the
system to the part (and vice versa) is inevitably nonlinear, unpredictable,
and replete with possibility. We have, we hope, broken "the WPS agenda,"
displaying now its shards, which can be recomposed but not recovered,
shifting kaleidoscopically, dizzyingly, to illuminate feminist peace.

APPENDIX 1

ECOSYSTEM POLICY DOCUMENTS

O ur policy ecosystem map is based on a collection of 237 policy documents issued between October 31, 2000, and December 31, 2020 (see chapter 3). To distinguish these documents, we adopt abbreviations for in-text citations, as listed below for each of our three document sets (the UN system, National Action Plans, and regional/other WPS). Documents are dated by their year of release, even if this precedes the beginning of the period covered by the plan (e.g., Philippines 2009 sets policy for 2010–2016).

Our selection criteria are outlined in appendix 2. In applying them we have produced a set that differs somewhat from our prior effort.[1]

Several NAPs were translated into English as part of a research project investigating the formation and implementation of the WPS agenda. These are not official translations. For more information about this project, please see the project's website, Women, Peace and Security: Rethinking Policy, Advocacy and Implementation, at https://www.lse.ac.uk/women-peace-security/research/Rethinking-Policy-Advocacy-Implementation.

TABLE A.1 The United Nations

Ecosystem abbreviation	Official title
S/RES/1325	United Nations Security Council, Resolution 1325, S/RES/1325, October 31, 2000.
S/PRST/2001/31	United Nations Security Council, "Statement by the President of the Council," S/PRST/2001/31, October 31, 2001.
S/PRST/2002/32	United Nations Security Council, "Statement by the President of the Council," S/PRST/2002/32, October 31, 2002.
S/PRST/2004/40	United Nations Security Council, "Statement by the President of the Council," S/PRST/2004/40, October 28, 2004.
S/PRST/2005/52	United Nations Security Council, "Statement by the President of the Council," S/PRST/2005/52, October 27, 2005.
S/PRST/2006/42	United Nations Security Council, "Statement by the President of the Council," S/PRST/2006/42, October 26, 2006.
A/RES/61/143	United Nations General Assembly, Resolution 61/143, A/RES/61/143, January 30, 2007.
S/PRST/2007/5	United Nations Security Council, "Statement by the President of the Council," S/PRST/2007/5, March 7, 2007.
S/PRST/2007/40	United Nations Security Council, "Statement by the President of the Council," S/PRST/2007/40, October 24, 2007.
A/RES/62/134	United Nations General Assembly, Resolution 62/134, A/RES/62/134, February 7, 2008.
A/HRC/RES/7/24	United Nations Human Rights Council, Resolution 7/24, A/HRC/RES/7/24, March 28, 2008.
S/RES/1820	United Nations Security Council, Resolution 1820, S/RES/1820, June 19, 2008.
S/PRST/2008/39	United Nations Security Council, "Statement by the President of the Council," S/PRST/2008/39, October 29, 2008.
A/HRC/RES/11/2	United Nations Human Rights Council, Resolution 11/2, A/HRC/RES/11/2, June 17, 2009.
S/RES/1888	United Nations Security Council, Resolution 1888, S/RES/1888, September 30, 2009.

Ecosystem abbreviation	Official title
S/RES/1889	United Nations Security Council, Resolution 1889, S/RES/1889, October 5, 2009.
S/PRST/2010/8	United Nations Security Council, "Statement by the President of the Council," S/PRST/2010/8, April 27, 2010.
A/HRC/RES/14/12	United Nations Human Rights Council, Resolution 14/12, A/HRC/RES/14/12, June 30, 2010.
S/PRST/2010/22	United Nations Security Council, "Statement by the President of the Council," S/PRST/2010/22, October 26, 2010.
S/RES/1960	United Nations Security Council, Resolution 1960, S/RES/1960, December 16, 2010.
S/PRST/2011/20	United Nations Security Council, "Statement by the President of the Council," S/PRST/2011/20, October 28, 2011.
S/PRST/2012/3	United Nations Security Council, "Statement by the President of the Council," S/PRST/2012/3, February 23, 2012.
S/PRST/2012/23	United Nations Security Council, "Statement by the President of the Council," S/PRST/2012/23, October 31, 2012.
S/RES/2106	United Nations Security Council, Resolution 2106, S/RES/2106, June 24, 2013.
S/RES/2122	United Nations Security Council, Resolution 2122, S/RES/2122, October 18, 2013.
CEDAW/C/GC/30	United Nations Convention on the Elimination of All Forms of Discrimination against Women, General Recommendation No. 30 on Women in Conflict Prevention, Conflict and Post-Conflict Situations, CEDAW/C/GC/30, November 1, 2013.
S/PRST/2014/21	United Nations Security Council, "Statement by the President of the Council," S/PRST/2014/21, October 28, 2014.
S/RES/2242	United Nations Security Council, Resolution 2242, S/RES/2242, October 13, 2015.
S/PRST/2016/9	United Nations Security Council, "Statement by the President of the Council," S/PRST/2016/9, June 15, 2016.

(continued)

TABLE A.1 The United Nations (*continued*)

Ecosystem abbreviation	Official title
UN PBC 2016	United Nations Peacebuilding Commission, Peacebuilding Commission's Gender Strategy, September 2016.
S/RES/2467	United Nations Security Council, Resolution 2467, S/RES/2467, April 23, 2019.
S/RES/2493	United Nations Security Council, Resolution 2493, S/RES/2493, October 29, 2019.
A/HRC/45/L.24	United Nations Human Rights Council, Agenda 45/L.24, A/HRC/45/L.24, September 30, 2020.

TABLE A.2 National Action Plans

Ecosystem abbreviation	Official title
Denmark NAP I 2005	Ministry of Foreign Affairs of Denmark and the Ministry of Defence, *Denmark's Action Plan on Implementation of Security Council Resolution 1325 on Women and Peace and Security.* English summary. September 2005.
Norway NAP I 2006	Norwegian Ministry of Foreign Affairs, *The Norwegian Government's Action Plan for the Implementation of UN Security Council Resolution 1325 (2000) on Women, Peace and Security.* March 2006.
Sweden NAP I 2006	Swedish Ministry of Foreign Affairs, *The Swedish Government's Action Plan to Implement Security Council Resolution 1325 (2000) on Women, Peace and Security.* English summary. 2006.
United Kingdom NAP I 2006	Government of the United Kingdom, *UNSCR1325—United Kingdom High Level National Action Plan.* 2006.
Austria NAP I 2007	Austrian Federal Ministry for European and International Affairs, *Austrian Action Plan on Implementing UN Security Resolution 1325 (2000).* August 2007.
Netherlands NAP I 2007	Ministry of Foreign Affairs of the Netherlands, *Dutch National Action Plan on Resolution 1325: Taking a Stand for Women, Peace and Security.* December 2007.
Spain NAP I 2007	Spanish Ministry of Foreign Affairs, *Action Plan of the Government of Spain for the Implementation of Resolution 1325 of the Security Council of the United Nations (2000), on Women, Peace and Security.* 2007.
Switzerland NAP I 2007	Swiss Federal Department of Foreign Affairs, *National Action Plan for the Implementation of UN Security Council Resolution 1325 (2000) on Women, Peace and Security.* February 2007.
Côte d'Ivoire NAP 2008	Ivorian Ministry of the Family, Women and Social Affairs and Gender Equality and Promotion Directorate, *National Action Plan for the Implementation of Resolution 1325 of the Security Council (2008–2012) Background Document.* 2008.

(continued)

TABLE A.2 National Action Plans (*continued*)

Ecosystem abbreviation	Official title
Denmark NAP II 2008	Ministry of Foreign Affairs of Denmark, Ministry of Defence, and Danish National Police, *Denmark's National Action Plan for Implementation of UN Security Council Resolution 1325 on Women, Peace and Security 2008–2013*. 2008.
Finland NAP I 2008	Ministry for Foreign Affairs of Finland, *UN Security Council Resolution 1325 (2000) "Women, Peace and Security" Finland's National Action Plan 2008–2011*. September 2008.
Iceland NAP I 2008	Icelandic Ministry for Foreign Affairs, *Women, Peace and Security: Iceland's Plan of Action for the Implementation of United Nations Security Council Resolution 1325 (2000)*. March 2008.
Uganda NAP I 2008	Ugandan Ministry of Gender, Labour and Social Development, *The Uganda Action Plan on UN Security Council Resolutions 1325 & 1820 and the Goma Declaration*. December 2008.
Belgium NAP I 2009	Belgian Federal Public Service (FPS) for Foreign Affairs, Foreign Trade and Development Cooperation, Ministry of Defence, FPS Justice, and the Institute for the Equality of Men and Women, for the Minister of Equal Opportunities Commission Women and Development, *Women, Peace and Security: Belgian National Action Plan on the Implementation of UN Security Council Resolution 1325*. 2009.
Chile NAP I 2009	Chilean Ministry of Foreign Affairs, Ministry of National Defense, and Women's National Service, *National Plan of Action for Implementation of the UN Security Council Resolution 1325/2000 "Women, Security and Peace."* English translation. August 2009.
Guinea NAP 2009	Guinean Ministry of Social Affairs, of Women and Childhood Promotion, *National Plan of Strategic Actions for the Implementation of the 1325 and 1820 Resolutions of the United Nation Security Council—2009–2013*. English translation. November 2012.
Liberia NAP I 2009	Liberian Ministry of Gender and Development, *The Liberian National Action Plan for the Implementation of United Nations Resolution 1325*. 2009.

Ecosystem abbreviation	Official title
Philippines NAP I 2009	Government of the Philippines, *The Philippine National Action Plan on UNSCRS 1325 & 1820: 2010–2016*. 2009.
Philippines NAP II 2017	Office of the Presidential Adviser on the Peace Process, *National Action Plan on Women, Peace and Security 2017–2022*. 2017.
Portugal NAP I 2009	Portuguese Ministry of Foreign Affairs, *National Action Plan for Implementation of the UNSC Resolution 1325 (2000) on Women, Peace and Security (2009–2013)*. 2009.
Sweden NAP II 2009	Swedish Ministry of Foreign Affairs, *The Swedish Government's Action Plan for 2009–2012 to Implement Security Council Resolution 1325 (2000) on Women, Peace and Security*. February 2009.
Bosnia and Herzegovina NAP I 2010	Gender Equality Agency of Bosnia and Herzegovina and Ministry of Human Rights and Refugees of BiH, *Action Plan for the Implementation of UNSCR 1325 in Bosnia and Herzegovina 2010–2013*. January 2010.
Canada NAP I 2010	Government of Canada, *Building Peace and Security for All: Canada's Action Plan for the Implementation of United Nations Security Council Resolutions on Women, Peace and Security*. 2010.
DRC NAP I 2010	DRC Ministry of Gender, Family and Children, *The Government's Action Plan of the Democratic Republic of the Congo for the Purposes of Resolution 1325 of the United Nations Security Council*. January 2010.
Estonia NAP I 2010	Estonian Ministry of Foreign Affairs, *Estonia's Action Plan for the Implementation of UN Security Council Resolution 1325 "Women, Peace and Security" in Estonia 2010–2014*. 2010.
France NAP I 2010	French Ministry for Europe and Foreign Affairs, *National Action Plan for France: Implementation of the "Women, Peace and Security" Resolutions of the United Nations Security Council*. 2010.
Guinea-Bissau NAP 2010	Guinea-Bissau Institute for Women and Children, *National Action Plan for the Implementation of Resolution 1325 (2000)*. 2010.

(continued)

TABLE A.2 National Action Plans (*continued*)

Ecosystem abbreviation	Official title
Italy NAP I 2010	Italian Ministry of Foreign Affairs, *National Action Plan of Italy on "Women, Peace and Security" 2010–2013*. December 2010.
Rwanda NAP I 2010	Rwandan Ministry of Gender and Family Promotion, *Republic of Rwanda National Action Plan 2009–2012: The United Nations Security Council Resolution 1325/2000 on Women, Peace and Security*. English translation. May 2010.
Serbia NAP I 2010	Organization for Security and Co-operation in Europe Mission to Serbia, *National Action Plan to Implement United Nations Security Council Resolution 1325—Women, Peace and Security in the Republic of Serbia (2010–2015)*. 2010.
Sierra Leone NAP 2010	Sierra Leonian Ministry of Social Welfare, Gender and Children's Affairs, *The Sierra Leone National Action Plan for the Full Implementation of United Nations Security Council Resolutions 1325 (2000) & 1820 (2008)*. 2010.
Slovenia NAP I 2010	Slovenian Ministry of Foreign Affairs, *Action Plan of the Republic of Slovenia for the Implementation of UN Security Council Resolutions No. 1325 and 1820 on Women, Peace and Security for the Period 2010–2015*. 2010.
Switzerland NAP II 2010	Swiss Federal Department of Foreign Affairs, *Women, Peace and Security National Action Plan to Implement UN Security Council Resolution 1325 (2000)*. 2010.
Burundi NAP I 2011	Burundian Ministry of National Solidarity, Human Rights and Gender, *National Action Plan 2012–2016: Action Plan for the Implementation of Resolution 1325 (2000) of the Security Council of the United Nations*. Unofficial translation. December 2011.
Croatia NAP I 2011	Government of the Republic of Croatia, *National Action Plan for the Implementation of UN Security Council Resolution 1325 (2000) on Women, Peace and Security, and Related Resolutions (for the Period from 2011 to 2014)*. Draft. 2011.
Georgia NAP I 2011	Parliament of Georgia, *Resolution of the Georgian Parliament on Approval of 2012–2015 National Action Plan for Implementation of the UN Security Council Resolutions ## 1325, 1820, 1888, 1889 and 1960 on "Women, Peace and Security."* Unofficial translation. December 2011.

Ecosystem abbreviation	Official title
Ireland NAP I 2011	Irish Department of Foreign Affairs and Trade, *Ireland's National Action Plan for Implementation of UNSCR 1325, 2011–2014.* 2011.
Lithuania NAP 2011	Ministry of Foreign Affairs of the Republic of Lithuania, *Lithuania's Action Plan for the Implementation of UN Security Council Resolution 1325 on Women, Peace and Security.* December 2011.
Nepal NAP 2011	Nepalese Ministry of Peace and Reconstruction, *National Action Plan on Implementation of the United Nations Security Council Resolutions 1325 & 1820 (2011/12–2015/16).* February 2011.
Netherlands NAP II 2011	Ministry of Foreign Affairs of the Netherlands, *Women: Powerful Agents for Peace and Security—Dutch National Action Plan (2012–2015) for the Implementation of UN Security Council Resolution 1325 on Women, Peace & Security.* 2011.
Norway NAP II 2011	Norwegian Ministry of Foreign Affairs, *Women, Peace and Security: Norway's Strategic Plan 2011–13.* 2011.
Senegal NAP 2011	Senegalese Ministry of Gender and Relations with African and Foreign Women's Associations, *National Action Plan Implementation of Resolution 1325 (2000) of the Security Council of the United Nations.* Unofficial translation. May 2011.
Togo NAP 2011	Government of the Togolese Republic, *National Action Plan for the Involvement of Togolese Women in Conflict Resolution and Peacebuilding: Implementation Strategies for Resolutions 1325 and 1820 of the Security Council of the United Nations.* Unofficial translation. 2011.
Uganda NAP II 2011	Ugandan Ministry of Gender, Labour and Social Development, *The Ugandan Action Plan on UN Security Council Resolutions 1325 & 1820 and the Goma Declaration (Revised Version).* September 2011.
U.S. NAP I 2011	The White House, *United States National Action Plan on Women, Peace, and Security.* December 2011.
Australia NAP I 2012	Australian Department of Families, Housing, Community Services and Indigenous Affairs, *Australian National Action Plan on Women, Peace and Security 2012–2018.* 2012.

(*continued*)

TABLE A.2 National Action Plans (*continued*)

Ecosystem abbreviation	Official title
Austria NAP II 2012	Austrian Federal Ministry for European and International Affairs, *Revised National Action Plan on Implementing UN Security Council Resolution 1325 (2000)*. January 2012.
Burkina Faso NAP 2012	Burkina Faso Ministry for the Promotion of Women and Ministry of Human Rights and Civic Promotion, *National Action Plan of Burkina Faso for the Implementation of Resolutions 1325 and 1820 of the Security Council of the United Nations*. Unofficial translation. December 2012.
Finland NAP II 2012	Ministry for Foreign Affairs of Finland, *UN Security Council Resolution 1325 (2000) "Women, Peace and Security": Finland's National Action Plan 2012–2016*. 2012.
Gambia NAP 2012	Government of the Republic of the Gambia, *The Gambia National Action Plan on United Nations Security Council Resolution 1325*. 2012.
Germany NAP I 2012	Federal Government of Germany, *Action Plan of the Government of the Federal Republic of Germany on the Implementation of United Nations Security Council Resolution 1325 for the Period 2013–2016*. Translation. December 2012.
Ghana NAP I 2012	Ghanaian Ministry for Women and Children's Affairs, Ministry for Defence, Ministry of Interior, and Ministry of Foreign Affairs and Regional Integration, *Ghana National Action Plan for the Implementation of the United Nations Security Council Resolution 1325 on Women Peace and Security (GHANAP 1325)*. October 2010.
Mali NAP I 2012	Malian Ministry for the Promotion of Women, Children and Families, *National Action Plan for the Implementation of Resolution 1325 of the Security Council of the United Nations on Women, Peace and Security 2012–2014*. Unofficial translation. March 2012.
North Macedonia NAP 2012	Macedonian Ministry of Labour and Social Policy, Ministry of Foreign Affairs, Ministry of the Interior, Ministry of Defense, and Center for Crisis Management, *Women, Peace and Security National Action Plan of the Republic of Macedonia for Implementation of the UN Resolution 1325*. December 2012.

Ecosystem abbreviation	Official title
UK NAP II 2012	United Kingdom Foreign and Commonwealth Office and Department for International Development, *UK Government National Action Plan on UNSCR 1325 Women, Peace & Security—November 2010 to November 2013.* February 2012.
Belgium NAP II 2013	Belgian Government, *Second National Action Plan "Women, Peace, Security" (2013–2016), Implementing UN Security Council Resolution 1325.* Unofficial translation. 2013.
Bosnia and Herzegovina NAP II 2013	BiH Ministry for Human Rights and Refugees and Gender Equality Agency of Bosnia and Herzegovina, *Action Plan for Implementation of UNSCR 1325 in Bosnia and Herzegovina for the Period 2014–2017.* December 2013.
DRC NAP II 2013	DRC Ministry of Gender, Family and Children, *Action Plan of the Government of the Democratic Republic of the Congo for the Implementation of United Nations Security Council Resolution 1325.* Unofficial translation. March 2013.
Iceland NAP II 2013	Icelandic Ministry for Foreign Affairs, *Iceland's National Action Plan for the Implementation of UN Security Council Resolution 1325 on Women, Peace and Security 2013–2016.* 2013.
Kyrgyzstan NAP I 2013	Government of the Kyrgyz Republic, *National Action Plan on the Implementation of the UN Security Council Resolution 1325 on Women and Peace and Security.* Unofficial translation. 2013.
Nigeria NAP I 2013	Nigerian Ministry of Women Affairs and Social Development, *National Action Plan for the Implementation of UNSCR 1325 and Related Resolutions in Nigeria.* 2013.
Switzerland NAP III 2013	Swiss Federal Department of Foreign Affairs, *Women, Peace and Security National Action Plan to Implement UN Security Council Resolution 1325 (2000).* 2013.
CAR NAP 2014	Central African Republic Ministry of Social Affairs, National Solidarity and Gender Promotion, *National Action Plan for the Implementation of Resolution 1325 of the Security Council of the United Nations on Women, Peace and Security 2014–2016.* Unofficial translation. 2014.

(continued)

TABLE A.2 National Action Plans (*continued*)

Ecosystem abbreviation	Official title
Denmark NAP III 2014	Ministry of Foreign Affairs of Denmark, Danish Ministry of Defence, and Justice Ministry, *Denmark's National Action Plan for Implementation of UN Security Council Resolution 1325 on Women, Peace and Security 2014–2019*. 2014.
Indonesia NAP 2014	Coordinating minister of people's welfare of the Republic of Indonesia, *The National Action Plans for the Protection and Empowerment of Women and Children During Social Conflicts of 2014–2019*. June 2014.
Iraq NAP I 2014	Ministry of Women's Affairs, Ministry of Interior, and Ministry of Defense in Baghdad, Ministry of Interior and Women's High Council in Kurdistan, and Iraqi NAP1325 Initiative, *National Action plan for Implementation of the United Nation Security Council Resolution 1325 Women, Peace and Security 2014–2018*. English translation. 2014.
Italy NAP II 2014	Italian Ministry of Foreign Affairs, *National Action Plan of Italy "Women, Peace and Security—WPS" 2014–2016*. February 2014.
Kosovo NAP 2014	Kosovo Agency of Gender Equality and Office of the Prime Minister, *Working Plan to Implement Resolution 1325, "Women, Peace and Security" 2013–2015*. English translation. March 2014.
Portugal NAP II 2014	Portuguese Commission for Citizenship and Gender Equality, *II National Action Plan for the Implementation of the United Nations Security Council Resolution 1325 (2000) on Women, Peace and Security*. December 2014.
Republic of Korea NAP I 2014	Korean Ministry of Foreign Affairs, *The National Action Plan of the Republic of Korea for the Implementation of United Nations Security Council Resolution 1325 on Women, Peace and Security*. 2014.
Romania NAP 2014	Romanian Ministry of National Defense, *Ministry of National Defense Plan for the Implementation of the "Women, Peace and Security" UN Security Council Resolution 1325 (UNSCR 1325) and of the Related Resolutions as well as of the Complementary Documents Approved by Various International Organizations of Which Romania Is a Member—2014–2024*. Unofficial translation. 2014.

Ecosystem abbreviation	Official title
Tajikistan NAP 2014	Government of the Republic of Tajikistan, *A National Review of the Republic of Tajikistan and the Implementation of the Beijing Declaration and the Platform for Action (1995) and the Final Documents of the Twenty-Third Special Session of the General Assembly (2000) in the Context of the Twentieth Anniversary of the Fourth World Conference on Women and the Adoption of the Beijing Declaration and Platform Action in 2015*. 2014.
UK NAP III 2014	United Kingdom Foreign and Commonwealth Office, *United Kingdom National Action Plan on Women, Peace & Security 2014–2017*. 2014.
Afghanistan NAP 2015	Afghan Ministry of Foreign Affairs, Directorate of Human Rights, and Women's International Affairs, *Afghanistan's National Action Plan on UNSCR 1325—Women, Peace, and Security 2015–2022*. June 2015.
Argentina NAP 2015	Argentinian Government, *National Action Plan of the Argentine Republic for the Implementation of Resolution No. 1325 (2000) of the United Nations Security Council et Seq.* Unofficial translation. 2015.
Chile NAP II 2015	Chilean Ministry of Foreign Affairs, Ministry of National Defence, and Ministry of Women's Affairs and Gender Equality, *"Women, Security and Peace": Second National Action Plan for the Implementation of Resolution 1325/2000 of the Security Council of the United Nations*. Unofficial translation. 2015.
Estonia NAP II 2015	Estonian Ministry of Foreign Affairs, *Estonia's Action Plan for the Implementation of the United Nations Security Council Resolution 1325 on Women, Peace and Security in Estonia 2015–2019*. 2015.
France NAP II 2015	French Ministry for Europe and Foreign Affairs, *France's Second National Action Plan: Implementation of United Nations Security Council "Women, Peace and Security" Resolutions 2015–2018*. 2015.
Ireland NAP II 2015	Government of Ireland, *Ireland's Second National Action Plan on Women, Peace and Security 2015–2018*. 2015.

(continued)

TABLE A.2 National Action Plans (*continued*)

Ecosystem abbreviation	Official title
Japan NAP I 2015	Japanese Government, *National Action Plan on Women, Peace and Security*. Provisional translation. September 2015.
Mali NAP II 2015	Malian Ministry for the Advancement of Women, Children, and the Family, *Mali National Action Plan for the Implementation of UN Security Council Resolution 1325 (2000) and Related Issues on Women, Peace, and Security 2015–2017*. Unofficial translation. June 2015.
New Zealand NAP 2015	New Zealand Ministry of Foreign Affairs and Trade, New Zealand Police, and the New Zealand Defence Force, *New Zealand National Action Plan for the Implementation of United Nations Security Council Resolutions, Including 1325, on Women, Peace & Security 2015–2019*. 2015.
Norway NAP III 2015	Norwegian Ministries, *National Action Plan: Women, Peace and Security 2015–18*. 2015.
Palestine Strategic Framework 2015	Palestinian Ministry of Women's Affairs, *National Strategic Framework for the Implementation of UNSCR 1325*. Unofficial translation. April 2015.
Paraguay NAP 2015	Paraguayan Ministry of Foreign Affairs, *National Action Plan Implementation of Resolution 1325 of the United Nations Security Council in the Republic of Paraguay*. Unofficial translation. December 2015.
South Sudan NAP 2015	South Sudanese Ministry of Gender, Child, Social Welfare, Humanitarian Affairs and Disaster Management, *South Sudan National Action Plan 2015–2020 on UNSCR 1325 on Women, Peace and Security and Related Resolutions*. 2015.
Bougainville NAP 2016	Bougainvillean Ministry for Community Development, *The Autonomous Region of Bougainville Policy for Women's Empowerment, Gender Equality, Peace and Security*. August 2016.
Georgia NAP II 2016	Government of Georgia, *2016–2017 National Action Plan of Georgia for Implementation of the UN Security Council Resolutions on Women, Peace and Security*. Official translation. July 2016.

Ecosystem abbreviation	Official title
Italy NAP III 2016	Italian Ministry of Foreign Affairs and Inter-ministerial Committee for Human Rights, *Italy's Third National Action Plan, in Accordance with UN Security Council Resolution 1325 (2000), 2016–2019*. December 2016.
Kenya NAP I 2016	Kenyan Ministry of Public Service, Youth, and Gender Affairs and Ministry of Interior and Coordination of National Government, *National Action Plan for the Implementation of United Nations Security Council Resolution 1325 and Related Resolutions*. 2016.
Netherlands NAP III 2016	1325 Dutch NAP Partnership, *The Netherlands National Action Plan on Women, Peace and Security 2016–2019*. 2016.
Niger NAP 2016	Nigerien Ministry for Population, Women Promotion and Child Protection and General Directorate for Women and Gender Promotion, *National Action Plan of the Niger for Implementation of the Resolution 1325 of the United Nations Security Council in the Ecowas Area 2016–2018*. Unofficial translation. December 2015.
Sweden NAP III 2016	Government of Sweden, *Women, Peace & Security: Sweden's National Action Plan for the Implementation of the UN Security Council Resolutions on Women, Peace and Security 2016–2020*. 2016.
Timor-Leste NAP 2016	Ministry of Interior Democratic Republic of Timor-Leste, *National Action Plan on United Nations Security Council Resolution 1325 (2000) on Women, Peace and Security (2016–2020)*. October 2016.
Ukraine NAP 2016	Cabinet of Ministries of Ukraine, *National Action Plan on Implementation of UN Security Council Resolution #1325 "Women, Peace, Security" till 2020*. February 2016.
U.S. NAP II 2016	The White House, *The United States National Action Plan on Women, Peace, and Security*. June 2016.
Angola NAP 2017	Angolan Ministry for Family and Promotion of Women and the Ministry of National Defense and Interior, *National Plan of Action for the Implementing of Resolution Number 1325/2000, of the 31st of October, of the Security Council of the United Nations Pertaining to Women, Peace, and Safety*. Unofficial translation. June 2017.

(*continued*)

TABLE A.2 National Action Plans (*continued*)

Ecosystem abbreviation	Official title
Belgium NAP III 2017	Belgian Government, *Third National Action Plan: "Women, Peace, Security" (2017–2021)*. Unofficial translation. 2017.
Bosnia and Herzegovina NAP III 2017	BiH Ministry of Human Rights and Refugees and Gender Equality Agency of Bosnia and Herzegovina, *Action Plan for the Implementation of UNSCR 1325 "Women, Peace and Security" in Bosnia and Herzegovina for the Period 2018–2022*. Unofficial translation. October 2017.
Brazil NAP 2017	Brazilian Ministry of Foreign Affairs, *National Action Plan on Women, Peace and Security*. 2017.
Burundi NAP II 2017	Republic of Burundi Ministry of Human Rights, Social Affairs and Gender, *2017–2021 National Action Plan for the Implementation of United Nations Security Council Resolution 1325 on Women, Peace and Security*. July 2017.
Cameroon NAP 2017	Cameroonian Ministry of Women's Empowerment and the Family, *Republic of Cameroon: National Action Plan for the 1325 Resolution and Companion Resolutions of the United Nations Security Council on Women, Peace and Security (2018–2020)*. August 2017.
Canada NAP II 2017	Government of Canada, *Gender Equality: A Foundation for Peace—Canada's National Action Plan 2017–2022 for the Implementation of the UN Security Council Resolutions on Women, Peace and Security*. 2017.
Czech Republic NAP 2017	Czech Government, *The Action Plan of the Czech Republic to Implement Security Council Resolution UN Security Council no. 1325 (2000) on Women, Peace and Security and Related Resolutions for the Years 2017–2020*. 2017.
Djibouti NAP 2017	Republic of Djibouti Ministry of Women and the Family, *National Action Plan for the Implementation of Security Council Resolution 1325 (2000) and Related Resolutions of the United Nations on Women, Peace, and Security*. November 2017.
El Salvador NAP 2017	Ministry of Foreign Affairs of El Salvador, *National Action Plan for Resolution 1325 "Women, Peace and Security" 2017–2022*. Unofficial translation. 2017.

Ecosystem abbreviation	Official title
Germany NAP II 2017	Federal Government of Germany, *Action Plan of the Government of the Federal Republic of Germany on the Implementation of United Nations Security Council Resolution 1325 on Women, Peace and Security for the Period 2017–2020.* 2017.
Guatemala NAP 2017	Inter-Agency Roundtable on Women, *National Action Plan for the Implementation of Resolution 1325 of the United Nations Security Council and Related Resolutions on Women, Peace and Security.* Unofficial translation. 2017.
Jordan NAP 2017	Jordanian National Commission for Women, *Jordanian National Action plan (JONAP) for the Implementation of UN Security Council Resolution 1325 on Women, Peace and Security 2018–2021.* December 2017.
Montenegro NAP 2017	Montenegrin Ministry of Defence, *Action Plan for Implementation of United Nations Security Council Resolution 1325 Women, Peace and Security in Montenegro (2017–2018).* February 2017.
Nigeria NAP II 2017	Nigerian Federal Ministry of Women Affairs and Social Development, *National Action plan for the Implementation of UNSCR 1325 and Related Resolutions on Women, Peace and Security in Nigeria 2017–2020.* 2017.
Palestine NAP I 2017	Palestinian Ministry of Women's Affairs, *The National Action Plan for the Implementation of UNSCR 1325 Women, Peace and Security—Palestine 2017–2019.* 2017.
Philippines NAP II 2017	Philippine Office of the Presidential Adviser on the Peace Process, *National Action Plan on Women, Peace and Security 2017–2022.* 2017.
Serbia NAP II 2017	Organization for Security and Co-operation in Europe Mission to Serbia and Ministry of Defence of the Republic of Serbia, *National Action Plan for the Implementation of UN Security Council Resolution 1325—Women, Peace and Security in the Republic of Serbia (2017–2020).* 2017.
Solomon Islands NAP 2017	Solomon Islands Ministry of Women, Youth, Children and Family Affairs, *Solomon Islands Women, Peace and Security National Action Plan 2017–2021.* 2017.

(continued)

TABLE A.2 National Action Plans (*continued*)

Ecosystem abbreviation	Official title
Spain NAP II 2017	Spanish Government, *2017–2023 Second National Action Plan on Women, Peace and Security*. 2017.
Albania NAP 2018	Albanian Government, *Inter-institutional Action Plan on the Implementation of the United Nations Security Council Resolution 1325, on Women, Peace and Security 2018–2020, in the Republic of Albania*. August 2018.
DRC NAP III 2018	DRC Ministry of Gender, Family and Children, *National Action Plan for Implementing United Nations Security Council Resolution 1325 on Women, Peace, and Security, 2nd Generation 2019–2022*. Unofficial translation. September 2018.
Finland NAP III 2018	Ministry for Foreign Affairs of Finland, *Women, Peace and Security: Finland's National Action Plan 2018–2021*. March 2018.
Georgia NAP III 2018	Government of Georgia, *2018–2020 National Action Plan of Georgia for Implementation of the UN Security Council Resolutions on Women, Peace and Security*. 2018.
Iceland NAP III 2018	Icelandic Ministry for Foreign Affairs, *Iceland's National Action Plan on Women, Peace and Security 2018–2022*. November 2018.
Kyrgyzstan NAP II 2018	Government of the Kyrgyz Republic, *Action Plan for the Implementation of Resolution 1325 of the United Nations Security Council on the Role of Women in Ensuring Peace and Security*. September 2018.
Luxembourg NAP 2018	Luxembourg Ministry of Foreign and European Affairs, *National Action Plan "Women and Peace and Security" 2018–2023 for the Implementation of United Nations Security Council Resolution 1325 (2000)*. Unofficial translation. 2018.
Moldova NAP 2018	Moldovan Government, *National Implementation Program of the United Nations Security Council Resolution 1325 on Women, Peace and Security for 2018–2021*. March 2018.
Mozambique NAP 2018	Mozambican Ministry of Gender, Child and Social Action, *National Action Plan on Women, Peace and Security (2018–2022)*. May 2018.

Ecosystem abbreviation	Official title
Poland NAP 2018	Polish Ministry of Foreign Affairs, *Polish National Action Plan on Women, Peace and Security 2018–2021*. October 2018.
Republic of Korea NAP II 2018	Korean Government, *The Second National Action Plan of the Republic of Korea for the Implementation of United Nations Security Council Resolution 1325 on Women, Peace and Security*. 2018.
Rwanda NAP II 2018	Rwandan Ministry of Gender and Family Promotion, *Rwanda National Action Plan (2018–2022) for the Implementation of the United Nations Security Council Resolutions 1325 (2000) and Subsequent Resolutions*. 2018.
Slovenia NAP II 2018	Slovenian Ministry of Foreign Affairs, *Action Plan of the Republic of Slovenia for the Implementation of the UN Security Council Resolutions on Women, Peace and Security for the 2018–2020*. Unofficial translation. October 2018.
Switzerland NAP IV 2018	Swiss Federal Department of Foreign Affairs, *Women, Peace and Security: Switzerland's Fourth National Action Plan to Implement UN Security Council Resolution 1325 (2018–2022)*. 2018.
Tunisia NAP 2018	Tunisian Ministry of Women, Family, Children and Seniors, *National Action Plan 2018–2022 to Implement the UNSC's Resolution No. 1325 on "Women and Peace and Security" and Its Complementary Resolutions*. Unofficial translation. 2018.
UK NAP IV 2018	Government of the United Kingdom, *UK National Action Plan on Women, Peace & Security 2018–2022*. January 2018.
Armenia NAP 2019	Armenian Government, *2019–2021 National Action plan of the Republic of Armenia on the United Nations Security Council Resolution 1325 on Women, Peace and Security and Timetable for its Implementation*. Unofficial translation. 2019.
Bangladesh NAP 2019	Bangladeshi Ministry of Foreign Affairs, *National Action Plan on Women, Peace and Security 2019–2022*. 2019.
Croatia NAP II 2019	Croatian Ministry of Foreign and European Affairs, *National Action Plan for the Implementation of United Nations Security Council Resolution 1325 (2000) on Women, Peace and Security and Related Resolutions for the Period 2019–2023*. Unofficial translation. August 2019.

(continued)

TABLE A.2 National Action Plans (*continued*)

Ecosystem abbreviation	Official title
Ireland NAP III 2019	Irish Ministry for Foreign Affairs and Trade, *Women, Peace and Security: Ireland's Third National Action Plan for the Implementation of UNSCR 1325 and Related Resolutions 2019–2024*. 2019.
Japan NAP II 2019	Japanese Government, *National Action Plan on Women, Peace and Security Second Edition (2019–2022). Provisional translation*. March 2019.
Lebanon NAP 2019	National Commission for Lebanese Women, *Lebanon National Action Plan on United Nations Security Council Resolution 1325: The Path to a Fair and Inclusive Society Through the Women, Peace and Security Agenda 2019–2022*. 2019.
Liberia NAP II 2019	Liberian Ministry of Gender, Children and Social Protection, *Liberia's Second Phase National Action Plan on Women, Peace and Security 2019–2023*. 2019.
Mali NAP III 2019	Malian Ministry for the Advancement of Women, Children and Families, *National Action Plan for the Implementation of Resolution 1325 and Related Resolutions of the United Nations Security Council on the Agenda for Women, Peace and Security in Mali (2019–2023). Unofficial translation*. 2019.
Namibia NAP 2019	Namibian Government, *Namibia National Action Plan on Women Peace and Security: Moving United Nations Security Council Resolution 1325 Forward 2019–2024*. March 2019.
Norway NAP IV 2019	Norwegian Ministries, *The Norwegian Government's Action Plan: Women, Peace and Security (2019–2022)*. 2019.
Portugal NAP III 2019	Portuguese Government, *III National Action Plan for the Implementation of United Nations Security Council Resolution Number 1325 (2000) Concerning Women, Peace and Security 2019–2022. Unofficial translation*. February 2019.
Sierra Leone NAP II 2019	Sierra Leone Ministry of Social Welfare, Gender and Children's Affairs, *The Sierra Leone National Action Plan (SiLNAP) II for the Full Implementation of United Nations Security Council Resolutions 1325 (2000) and 1820 (2008) (2019–2023)*. 2019.

Ecosystem abbreviation	Official title
U.S. NAP III 2019	President of the United States, *United States Strategy on Women, Peace, and Security.* June 2019.
Bulgaria NAP 2020	Ministry of Foreign Affairs of the Republic of Bulgaria, *Women, Peace and Security National Action Plan 2020–2025.* March 2020.
Cyprus NAP 2020	Office of the Commissioner for Gender Equality and Ministry of Foreign Affairs of the Republic of Cyprus, *Women, Peace and Security National Action Plan 2020–2024 of the Republic of Cyprus Implementing the United Nations Resolution 1325.* December 2020.
Denmark NAP IV 2020	Ministry of Foreign Affairs of Denmark, Danish Ministry of Defence and Justice Ministry, *Denmark's National Action Plan on Women, Peace and Security 2020–2024.* 2020.
Estonia NAP III 2020	Ministry of Foreign Affairs of the Republic of Estonia, *Estonia's Action Plan for the Implementation of UN Security Council Resolution 1325 on Women, Peace and Security, 2020–2025.* May 2020.
Gabon NAP 2020	Gabon Ministry of Social Affairs and Women's Rights, *Gabon National Action Plan for the Implementation of Resolution 1325 and Related United Nations Security Council Resolutions on Women, Peace and Security (2020–2023).* March 2020
Ghana NAP II 2020	Ghanaian Ministry of Gender, Children and Social Protection, *Ghana National Action Plan for the Implementation of UN Security Council Resolution 1325 (2000) on Women, Peace & Security (2020–2025).* 2020.
Italy NAP IV 2020	Italian Inter-ministerial Committee for Human Rights, *Italy's IV Plan of Action on Women, Peace and Security (2020–2024), in Accordance with UN Security Council Resolution 1325 (2000).* December 2020.
Kenya NAP II 2020	Kenyan Ministry of Public Service, Youth, and Gender Affairs and Ministry of Interior and Coordination of National Government, *Kenya National Action Plan for the Advancement of United Nations Security Council Resolution 1325 on Women, Peace and Security 2020–2024.* 2020.

(*continued*)

TABLE A.2 National Action Plans (*continued*)

Ecosystem abbreviation	Official title
Latvia NAP 2020	Latvian Ministry of Foreign Affairs, *National Action Plan on the Implementation of the UN Security Council Resolution 1325 on Women, Peace and Security in Latvia for the Period of 2020–2025*. 2020.
Lithuania NAP II 2020	Minister of Foreign Affairs of the Republic of Lithuania, *Action Plan for the Implementation of the Women, Peace and Security Agenda for 2020–2024*. June 2020.
Malta NAP 2020	Malta Ministry for Foreign and European Affairs, *Women, Peace & Security: Malta's National Action Plan for the Implementation of United Nations Security Council Resolution 2020–2024*. 2020.
Niger NAP II 2020	Republic of Niger Ministry for the Promotion of Women and Child Protection, *National Action Plan on Women, Peace and Security, Second Generation, 2020–2024*. September 2020.
Palestine NAP II 2020	State of Palestine Ministry of Women's Affairs, *The Second National Action Plan on Women, Peace and Security for the Implementation of United Nations Security Council Resolution 1325 and Subsequent Resolutions 2020–2024*. October 2020.
South Africa NAP 2020	Republic of South Africa Department of International Relations and Cooperation, *National Action Plan on Women, Peace and Security—2020 to 2025*. 2020.
Sudan NAP 2020	Republic of the Sudan Ministry of Labour and Social Development, *National Action Plan for the Implementation of UN Security Council Resolution 1325 on Women, Peace and Security 2020–2022*. March 2020.
Ukraine NAP II 2020	Cabinet of Ministers of Ukraine, *National Action Plan for the Implementation of UN Security Council Resolution 1325 on Women, Peace, Security until 2025*. October 2020.
Yemen NAP 2020	Yemen Ministry of Social Affairs and Labor, *National Plan to Implement Security Council Resolution 1325 Women, Security and Peace 2020–2022*. Informal translation (Peace Track Initiative). 2020.

TABLE A.3 Regional and Other WPS

Ecosystem abbreviation	Official title
OAU Plan 2003	Organisation of African Unity, *Maputo Protocol to the African Charter on Human and People's Rights on the Rights of Women in Africa*. Assembly of the Union, July 11, 2003.
AU Declaration 2004	African Union, *Solemn Declaration on Gender Equality in Africa*, July 6–8, 2004.
ICPSDD Plan 2004	International Conference for Peace, Security, Democracy and Development in the Great Lakes Region, *Dar Es-Salaam Declaration on Peace, Security, Democracy and Development in the Great Lakes Region*, November 20, 2004.
OSCE Plan 2004	Organization for Security and Co-operation in Europe, *Decision No. 14/04 2004 OSCE Action Plan for the Promotion of Gender Equality*. MC.DEC/14/04. Ministerial Council, December 7, 2004.
EU Policy I 2005	Council of the European Union, *Implementation of UNSCR 1325 in the Context of ESDP*. 11932/2/05 REV 2, September 29, 2005.
PNA Declaration 2005	Palestinian National Authority, *Presidential Decree # () for the Year 2005*. Chairman of the PLO Executive Committee, president of the Palestinian National Authority, September 26, 2005.
NATO Policy I 2007	North Atlantic Treaty Organization, *Implementing UNSCR 1325 on Women, Peace and Security*. EAPC(C)D(2007)0022, December 10, 2007.
SADC Plan 2007	Southern African Development Community, *SADC Gender Policy (English)*, 2007.
EU Policy IIa 2008	Council of the European Union, *Comprehensive Approach to the EU Implementation of the United Nations Security Council Resolutions 1325 and 1820 on Women, Peace and Security*. 15671/1/08 REV 1, December 1, 2008.
EU Policy IIb 2008	Council of the European Union, *Implementation of UNSCR 1325 as Reinforced by UNSCR 1820 in the Context of ESDP*. 15782/3/08 REV 3, 3 December 2008.
SADC Plan 2008	Southern African Development Community, *SADC Protocol on Gender and Development*, 2008.

(*continued*)

TABLE A.3 Regional and Other WPS (*continued*)

Ecosystem abbreviation	Official title
NATO Directive I 2009	North Atlantic Treaty Organization, *Bi-strategic Command Directive 40-1 (Public Version): Integrating UNSCR 1325 and Gender Perspectives in the NATO Command Structure Including Measures for Protection During Armed Conflict.* September 2, 2009.
AU Plan 2009	African Union, *African Union Gender Policy,* 2009.
ECOWAS Plan 2010	Economic Community of West African States, *The Dakar Declaration & ECOWAS Plan of Action for the Implementation of United Nations Security Council Resolutions 1325 and 1820 in West Africa,* September 2010.
EU Plan I 2010	European Commission, *EU Plan of Action on Gender Equality and Women's Empowerment in Development 2010–2015.* SEC(2010) 265. Commission Staff Working Document, March 8, 2010.
NATO Policy II 2011	North Atlantic Treaty Organization, *NATO/EAPC Policy for Implementing UNSCR 1325 on Women, Peace and Security, and Related Resolutions,* July 13, 2011.
EU Policy III 2012	Council of the European Union, *Implementation of UNSCRs on Women, Peace and Security in the Context of CSDP Missions and Operations.* 7109/12, March 6, 2012.
NATO Directive II 2012	North Atlantic Treaty Organization, *Bi-strategic Command Directive 40-1 (Public Version): Integrating UNSCR 1325 and Gender Perspective Into the NATO Command Structure,* August 8, 2012.
Pacific Islands Plan 2012	Pacific Islands Forum, *Pacific Regional Action Plan: Women, Peace and Security 2012–2015,* 2012.
League of Arab States Plan I 2012	League of Arab States, Arab Women Organization, and UN Women, *Regional Strategy: Protection of Arab Women: Peace and Security,* 2012.
G8 Declaration 2013	United Kingdom Foreign and Commonwealth Office, Group of Eight Industrialized Nations, *Declaration on Preventing Sexual Violence in Conflict,* April 11, 2013.
IGAD Plan 2013	Intergovernmental Authority on Development, *Running with the Baton! Regional Action Plan for Implementation of United Nations Security Council Resolutions 1325 (2000) an 1820 (2008),* 2013.

Ecosystem abbreviation	Official title
ACHPR/Res.283	African Commission on Human and Peoples' Rights, *283 Resolution on the Situation of Women and Children in Armed Conflict*. ACHPR/Res.283, May 12, 2014.
NATO Policy III 2014	North Atlantic Treaty Organization, *NATO/EAPC Policy for the Implementation of UNSCR 1325 on Women, Peace and Security and Related Resolutions*, April 1, 2014.
NATO Plan I 2014	North Atlantic Treaty Organization, *NATO/EAPC Action Plan for the Implementation of the NATO/EAPC Policy on Women, Peace and Security*, 2014.
EU Plan II 2015	Council of the European Union, *Gender Action Plan 2016–2020: Council Conclusions*. 13201/15, October 26, 2015.
EU Commission Framework 2015	European Commission and High Representative of the Union for Foreign Affairs and Security Policy, *Gender Equality and Women's Empowerment: Transforming the Lives of Girls and Women through EU External Relations 2016–2020*. Joint Staff Working Document SWD(2015) 182, September 21, 2015.
League of Arab States Plan II 2015	League of Arab States, Arab Women Organization, and UN Women, *Strategic Framework for the Executive Action Plan "Protection of Arab Women: Peace and Security" 2015–2030*, September 13, 2015.
NATO Plan II 2016	North Atlantic Treaty Organization, *NATO/EAPC Action Plan for the Implementation of the NATO/EAPC Policy on Women Peace and Security*, 2016.
ASEAN Declaration I 2017	Association of Southeast Asian Nations, *Joint Statement on Promoting Women, Peace and Security in ASEAN*, November 13, 2017.
Global Affairs Canada Policy 2017	Global Affairs Canada, *Canada's Feminist International Assistance Policy*, 2017.
NATO Directive III 2017	North Atlantic Treaty Organization, *Bi-strategic Command Directive 040-001 (Public Version): Integrating UNSCR 1325 and Gender Perspective into the NATO Command Structure*. SH/SAG/GEN/JC/17-317874/1, October 17, 2017.

(continued)

TABLE A.3 Regional and Other WPS *(continued)*

Ecosystem abbreviation	Official title
United States Act 2017	United States Congress, *Women, Peace, and Security Act of 2017.* Public Law 115-68, October 6, 2017.
ECCAS Plan 2018	Economic Community of Central African States, *ECCAS Regional Action Plan for the Implementation of Resolution 1325 of the Security Council and Resolutions Related to Women, Peace and Security,* June 2018.
EU Policy IV 2018	Council of the European Union, *Women, Peace and Security— Council Conclusions (10 December 2018).* Outcome of Proceedings, 15086/18, December 10, 2018.
ICGLR Plan 2018	International Conference of the Great Lakes Region, *Great Lakes Region of Africa Regional Action Plan for the Implementation of United Nations Resolution 1325 (2000), 2018–2023,* 2018.
NATO Plan III 2018	North Atlantic Treaty Organization, *NATO/EAPC Women, Peace and Security Policy and Action Plan,* 2018.
SADC Plan II 2018	South African Development Community, *Regional Strategy on Women, Peace and Security 2018–2022,* July 2018.
ASEAN Declaration II 2019	Association of Southeast Asian Nations, *Joint Statement on Promoting Women, Peace and Security Agenda at the ASEAN Regional Forum,* August 2, 2019.
EU Policy IVb 2019	Council of the European Union, *EU Action Plan on Women, Peace and Security (WPS) 2019–2024.* 11031/19, July 5, 2019.
ACHPR/Res.467 2020	African Commission on Human and Peoples' Rights, *467 Resolution on the Need for Silencing the Guns in Africa Based on Human and Peoples' Rights.* ACHPR/Res.467, December 3, 2020.
ASEAN Declaration III 2020	Association of Southeast Asian Nations, *East Asia Summit Leaders' Statement on Women, Peace and Security,* November 14, 2020.
EU Plan III 2020	European Commission, *EU Gender Action Plan III: An Ambitious Agenda for Gender Equality and Women's Empowerment in EU External Action.* High representative of the union for foreign affairs and security policy, 25 November 2020.

APPENDIX 2

POLICY ECOSYSTEM SELECTION CRITERIA

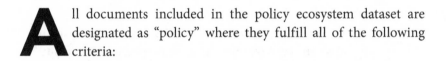 ll documents included in the policy ecosystem dataset are designated as "policy" where they fulfill all of the following criteria:

1. Explicit reference to the WPS agenda in the form of:
   a. Inclusion of the phrase "Women, Peace, and Security," the initialism "WPS," or any of the core ten resolutions[1] as a rationale for the policy in the framing or preambular sections of the document; or
   b. Inclusion of the phrase "Women, Peace, and Security," the initialism "WPS," or any of the core ten resolutions in the document title (e.g., "National Action Plan on 1325"); or
   c. Inclusion of the phrase "Women, Peace, and Security," the initialism "WPS," or any of the core ten resolutions in a section of the document setting out the mandate for the policy outlined in the document (i.e., where a document does not commence with this framing).
2. Policy language, comprising the following:
   a. Explicit commitment to implementation of the WPS agenda in whole or part, commonly signaled by prominent use of terms such as "agreeing," "declaring," "urging," "calling on," "encouraging," "affirming," "deciding," "mandating," "enforcing," "implementing," or "requesting"; and

    b. Some operational element setting out what the promise of implementation consists of, such as new resources or initiatives, a focus on a particular theme or pillar of the agenda, targets to be achieved, benchmarks, or other indicators of progress. Plans may involve direction to other government entities to implement elements of the policy or otherwise share responsibility for successful implementations.

3. Issued by a national or international government entity of the following types:

    a. A national government;

    b. The leader or official representative of a national government, acting in an official capacity;

    c. A government department or ministry (or several departments or ministries acting together);

    d. The legislative branch of a polity, mandating action by a national government;

    e. A national authority apart from a national government that is widely recognized as representative of a people, nation, or polity;

    f. The decision-making body of an intergovernmental organization with some authority over the actions of the organization or the organization's member states;

    g. A specialized office or agency of an intergovernmental organization, where this has the authority to instruct or advise member states on matters within the office or agency's remit;

    h. A treaty body with a formal role in instructing or advising state parties on matters within the treaty's remit;

    i. An intergovernmental network or forum, where states reach official agreements at summits or equivalent gatherings.

4. Issued or published between October 31, 2000, and December 31, 2020, regardless of whether the policy covered a period exceeding that date range.

APPENDIX 3

CODEBOOK FOR POLICY ECOSYSTEM ANALYSIS

	Concept	Actual search term
Pillar issues	participation	participat*
	prevention	prevent*
	protection	protect*
	relief & recovery	relief and recovery *or* humanitarian *minus all instances of* humanitarian law
Non-pillar new issues	refugee/IDP	asylum *or* refugee *or* displaced
	disasters	disasters
	LGBTQIA+	LGB* *or* gay *or* lesbian *or* queer *or* homosexual* *or* transgender *or* sexuality
	sexual and reproductive health	reproductive *or* family planning *or* contraception *or* abortion *or* sexual health

(continued)

TABLE A.4 *(continued)*

Concept	Actual search term
human trafficking	traffick* *or* slave*
climate change	climate
transitional justice mechanisms	transitional justice *or* reconciliation *or* reparation
men and boys	men and boys *or* masculin*
human rights defenders	human rights defenders
small arms and light weapons	small arms *or* guns *or* disarmament, demobilisation and reintegration *or* disarmament, demobilization and reintegration *or* DDR *or* SALW
terrorism/extremism	terror* *or* extremi* *or* radicali*
disability	disability *or* disabled
cyber	cyber*
age	elderly
sexual violence	sexual violence *or* rape *or* sexual and other violence *or* gender-based violence *or* gender-based persecution *or* violence against women *or* SGBV *or* GBV *or* VAW *or* VAWG
sexual exploitation and abuse	sexual exploitation *or* sexual abuse *or* SEA
big arms	nuclear *or* arms trade *or* arms transfer *or* arms control *or* non-proliferation
colonialism	coloni* *or* imperial* *or* occupation *or* settler *or* apartheid
Indigeneity	Indigenous *or* Indigeneity *or* First Nation *or* Aboriginal *or* Native
race	race *or* racism *or* ethnic* *or* intersectional*

APPENDIX 4

UNITED NATIONS TREATIES, CONVENTIONS, AND RESOLUTIONS

Beijing Declaration and Platform for Action. Adopted at the Sixteenth Plenary Meeting of the Fourth World Conference on Women (September 15, 1995). https://www.un.org/womenwatch/daw/beijing/pdf/BDPfA%20E.pdf.

Commission on the Status of Women. Results of the fifty-first, fifty-second, and fifty-third sessions of the Committee on the Elimination of Discrimination Against Women. E.CN.6.2013.CRP.1 (December 3, 2012). https://www2.ohchr.org/english/bodies/cedaw/docs/E.CN.6.2013.CRP.1_en.pdf.

Commission on the Status of Women. Zero Draft: Achieving Gender Equality and the Empowerment of All Women and Girls in the Context of Climate Change, Environmental and Disaster Risk Reduction Policies and Programmes. Draft Agreed Conclusions. Sixty-sixth session (March 14–25, 2022).

Committee on the Elimination of Discrimination Against Women. Concluding Observations on the Combined Seventh and Eighth Periodic Reports of Germany. CEDAW/C/DEU/CO/7-8 (March 9, 2016). https://undocs.org/en/CEDAW/C/DEU/CO/7-8.

Committee on the Elimination of Discrimination Against Women. Concluding Observations on the Combined Seventh and Eighth Periodic Reports of France. CEDAW/C/FRA/CO/7-8 (July 25, 2016). https://undocs.org/en/CEDAW/C/FRA/CO/7-8.

Committee on the Elimination of Discrimination Against Women. Concluding Observations on the Combined Eighth and Ninth Periodic Reports of Sweden. CEDAW/C/SWE/CO/8-9 (March 10, 2016). https://undocs.org/en/CEDAW/C/SWE/CO/8-9.

Committee on the Elimination of Discrimination Against Women. General Recommendation No. 35 on Gender-Based Violence Against Women. Updating General Recommendation No. 19. CEDAW/C/GC/35 (July 14, 2017). https://digitallibrary.un.org/record/1305057?ln=en.

Convention on the Elimination of all forms of Discrimination Against Women (CEDAW) (1979). Adopted and opened for signature, ratification, and accession by General

Assembly resolution 34/180 (December 18, 1979). https://www.ohchr.org/Documents
/ProfessionalInterest/cedaw.pdf.

Economic and Social Council. Commission on the Status of Women Report on the Fifty-
Seventh Session. E/2013/27 (March 4–15, 2013). https://undocs.org/E/2013/27.

Treaty on the Prohibition of Nuclear Weapons. CN.476.2017.TREATIES-XXVI-9 (2017). [Cer-
tified True Copy]. https://treaties.un.org/doc/Treaties/2017/07/20170707%2003-42%20 p.m./
Ch_XXVI_9.pdf.

UN Development Program. Human Development Report, 1994 (1994). https://hdr.undp.org
/system/files/documents/hdr1994encompletenostatspdf.pdf.

United Nations Economic and Social Council. Kampala Action Plan on Women and Peace:
Adopted by the Regional Conference on Women, Peace and Development, E/ECA/ATRCW/
ARCC.XV/94/7 (April 1994).

UN General Assembly. Human Rights Impact of Counter-Terrorism and Countering (Vio-
lent) Extremism Policies and Practices on the Rights of Women, Girls and the Family:
Report of the Special Rapporteur on the Promotion and Protection of Human Rights and
Fundamental Freedoms While Countering Terrorism, Fionnuala Ní Aoláin. A/HRC/46/36
(January 22, 2021). https://www.ohchr.org/en/documents/thematic-reports/ahrc4636
-human-rights-impact-counter-terrorism-and-countering-violent.

UN General Assembly. Human Rights Council Report of the Independent Investigative Mechanism for Myanmar. A/HRC/42/66 (August 7, 2019). https://undocs.org/en/A/HRC/42/66.

UN General Assembly. Resolution Adopted by the General Assembly on 16 September 2005.
60/1. 2005 World Summit Outcome. A/RES/60/1 (September 16, 2005). https://undocs.org
/A/RES/60/1.

UN General Assembly. Resolution Adopted by the General Assembly on 6 December 2006.
A/RES/61/89 (December 18, 2006). https://undocs.org/A/RES/61/89.

UN General Assembly. Resolution Adopted by the General Assembly on 2 July 2010. A/
RES/64/289 (July 21, 2010). https://undocs.org/en/A/RES/64/289.

UN General Assembly. Resolution Adopted by the General Assembly on 8 December 2010. A/
RES/65/69 (January 13, 2011). https://undocs.org/A/RES/65/69.

UN General Assembly. Resolution Adopted by the General Assembly on 24 December 2012.
A/RES/67/234 (January 4, 2013). https://undocs.org/A/RES/67/234.

UN General Assembly. Resolution Adopted by the General Assembly on 3 December 2012. A/
RES/67/48 (January 4, 2013). https://undocs.org/A/RES/67/48.

UN General Assembly. Resolution Adopted by the General Assembly on 5 December 2013. A/
RES/68/33 (December 9, 2013). https://undocs.org/A/RES/68/33.

UN General Assembly. Resolution Adopted by the General Assembly on 2 December 2014. A/
RES/69/61 (December 11, 2014). https://undocs.org/A/RES/69/61.

UN General Assembly. Resolution Adopted by the General Assembly on 5 December 2016. A/
RES/71/56 (December 13, 2016). https://undocs.org/A/RES/71/56.

UN General Assembly. Resolution Adopted by the Human Rights Council 14/12. A/HRC/
RES/14/12 (June 30, 2010). https://undocs.org/A/HRC/RES/14/12.

UN General Assembly. Resolution Adopted by the Human Rights Council on 22 June 2020.
A/HRC/RES/43/39 (July 6, 2020). https://undocs.org/A/HRC/RES/43/39.

UN General Assembly/UN Security Council. Letter Dated 12 July 2000 from the Permanent Representative of Namibia to the United Nations Addressed to the Secretary-General; Annex 1: Windhoek Declaration on the Tenth Anniversary of the United Nations Transition Assistance Group; Annex 2; Namibia Plan of Action on Mainstreaming a Gender Perspective in Multidimensional Peace Support Operations. A/55/138-S/2000/693 (July 14, 2000). https://undocs.org/en/A/55/138.

UN General Assembly/UN Security Council. Sexual Violence in Conflict: Report of the Secretary-General. A/67/792–S/2013/149 (March 14, 2013). https://undocs.org/A/67/792.

UN General Assembly/UN Security Council. Women's Participation in Peacebuilding: Report of the Secretary-General. A/65/354–S/2010/466 (September 7, 2010). https://undocs.org/A/65/354.

UN Human Rights Council. Situation of Human Rights in Yemen, Including Violations and Abuses Since September 2014: Report of the Group of Eminent International and Regional Experts on Yemen. A/HRC/48/20 (September 13, 2021). https://undocs.org/A/HRC/48/20.

UN Security Council. Conflict-Related Sexual Violence: Report of the Secretary-General. S/2019/280 (March 29, 2019). https://undocs.org/S/2019/280.

UN Security Council. Conflict-Related Sexual Violence: Report of the Secretary-General. S/2020/487 (June 3, 2020). https://undocs.org/S/2020/487.

UN Security Council. S/PV.4852 (October 29, 2003). https://undocs.org/en/S/PV.4852.

UN Security Council. S/PV.5066 (October 28, 2004). https://undocs.org/en/S/PV.5066.

UN Security Council. S/PV.4589 (July 25, 2002). https://undocs.org/en/S/PV.4589.

UN Security Council. S/PV.4635 (October 28, 2002). https://undocs.org/en/S/PV.4635.

UN Security Council. S/PV.4402 (October 31, 2001). https://undocs.org/en/S/PV.4402.

UN Security Council. Letter Dated 16 April 2021 from the President of the Security Council Addressed to the Secretary-General and the Permanent Representatives of the Members of the Security Council. S/2021/375 (April 16, 2021). https://undocs.org/en/S/2021/375.

UN Security Council. Letter Dated 17 March 2021 from the Permanent Representatives of Ireland, Mexico and the United Kingdom of Great Britain and Northern Ireland to the United Nations Addressed to the Secretary-General. S/2021/264 (March 17, 2021). https://undocs.org/S/2021/264.

UN Security Council. Letter Dated 18 July 2017 from the Permanent Representatives of Sweden, the United Kingdom of Great Britain and Northern Ireland and Uruguay to the United Nations Addressed to the Secretary-General. S/2017/627 (July 21, 2017). https://undocs.org/S/2017/627.

UN Security Council. Letter Dated 21 July 2020 from the President of the Security Council Addressed to the Secretary-General and the Permanent Representatives of the Members of the Security Council. S/2020/727 (July 21, 2020). https://undocs.org/S/2020/727.

UN Security Council. Report of the Secretary-General on Conflict-Related Sexual Violence. S/2018/250 (March 23, 2018). https://undocs.org/S/2018/250.

UN Security Council. Report of the Secretary-General on Women, Peace and Security. S/2007/567 (December 12, 2007). https://undocs.org/S/2007/567.

UN Security Council. Report of the Secretary-General on Women, Peace and Security. S/2011/598 (September 29, 2011). https://undocs.org/S/2011/598.

UN Security Council. Report of the Secretary-General on Women, Peace and Security. S/2015/716 (September 16, 2015). https://undocs.org/S/2015/716.

UN Security Council. Resolution 1612 (2005). S/RES/1612 (July 26, 2005). https://undocs.org/S/RES/1612(2005).

UN Security Council. Resolution 1645 (2005). S/RES/1645 (December 20, 2005). https://undocs.org/S/RES/1645(2005).

UN Security Council. Resolution 2140 (2014). S/RES/2140 (February 26, 2014). https://www.undocs.org/S/RES/2140%20(2014).

UN Security Council. Resolution 2564 (2021). S/RES/2564 (February 25, 2021). https://undocs.org/S/RES/2564(2021).

UN Security Council. Russian Federation: Draft Resolution. S/2020/1054 (October 30, 2020). https://undocs.org/en/S/2020/1054.

UN Security Council. Security Council Unanimously Adopts Resolution 2242 (2015) to Improve Implementation of Landmark Text on Women, Peace and Security Agenda. SC/12076 (October 13, 2015). https://www.un.org/press/en/2015/sc12076.doc.htm

UN Security Council. S/PV.7428 (April 15, 2015). https://undocs.org/en/S/PV.7428.

UN Security Council. S/PV.7533 (October 13, 2015). https://undocs.org/en/S/PV.7533.

UN Security Council. S/PV.7704 (June 2, 2016). https://undocs.org/en/S/PV.7704.

UN Security Council. S/PV.7793 (October 25, 2016). https://undocs.org/en/S/PV.7793.

UN Security Council. S/PV.8514 (April 23, 2019). https://undocs.org/en/S/PV.8514.

UN Security Council. S/PV.8649 (Resumption 1) (October 29, 2019). https://undocs.org/S/PV.8649%20(Resumption%201).

UN Security Council. S/PV.8649 (Resumption 2) (October 29, 2019). https://undocs.org/S/PV.8649%20(Resumption%202).

UN Security Council. S/PV.8079 (October 27, 2017). https://undocs.org/en/S/PV.8079.

UN Security Council. S/PV.8886 (October 21, 2021). https://undocs.org/en/S/PV.8886.

UN Security Council. S/PV.8234 (April 16, 2018). https://undocs.org/en/S/PV.8234.

UN Security Council. S/PV.8382 (October 25, 2018). https://undocs.org/en/S/PV.8382.

UN Security Council. S/PV.5294 (October 27, 2005). https://undocs.org/en/S/PV.5294.

UN Security Council. S/PV.7044 (October 18, 2013). https://undocs.org/en/S/PV.7044.

UN Security Council. S/PV.6302 (April 27, 2010). https://undocs.org/en/S/PV.6302.

UN Security Council. S/PV.5556 (October 26, 2006). https://undocs.org/en/S/PV.5556.

UN Security Council. S/PV.6196 (October 5, 2009). https://undocs.org/en/S/PV.6196.

UN Security Council. S/PV.6877 (November 30, 2012). https://undocs.org/en/S/PV.6877.

UN Security Council. S/PV.5916 (June 19, 2008). https://undocs.org/en/S/PV.5916.

UN Security Council. Women and Peace and Security: Report of the Secretary-General. S/2020/946 (September 25, 2020). https://undocs.org/en/S/2020/946.

UN Security Council. Women, Peace and Security: Report of the Secretary-General. S/2004/814 (October 13, 2004). https://undocs.org/S/2004/814.

United Nations. Rome Statute of the International Criminal Court, Volume 2187, 1–38544 (1998). https://treaties.un.org/doc/Treaties/1998/07/19980717%2006-33%20 p.m./volume-2187-I-38544-English.pdf.

United Nations. Secretary-General's Statement to the Open Debate of the Security Council on Security Council Resolution 1325 (October 5, 2009). https://www.un.org/sg/en/content /sg/statement/2009-10-05/secretary-generals-statement-open-debate-security-council -security.

United Nations. The Arms Trade Treaty (2014). https://unoda-web.s3-accelerate.amazonaws .com/wp-content/uploads/2013/06/English7.pdf.

United Nations. United Nations Charter (1945). https://www.un.org/en/about-us/un-charter /full-text.

Vienna Declaration and Programme of Action, adopted by the World Conference on Human Rights in Vienna on June 25 (1993). https://www.ohchr.org/sites/default/files/vienna.pdf.

NOTES

1. THE IMPOSSIBILITY OF WOMEN, PEACE, AND SECURITY

1. Carol Cohn, Helen Kinsella, and Sheri Gibbings, "Women, Peace and Security: Resolution 1325," *International Feminist Journal of Politics* 6, no. 1 (2004): 130. Emphasis in original.
2. Karen Barnes and 'Funmi Olonisakin, "Introduction," in *Women, Peace and Security: Translating Policy Into Practice*, ed. 'Funmi Olonisakin, Karen Barnes, and Eka Ikpe (London: Routledge, 2011), 3.
3. Radhika Coomaraswamy et al. *Preventing Conflict, Transforming Justice, Securing the Peace: A Global Study on the Implementation of United Nations Security Council Resolution 1325* (New York: UN Women, 2015), 28.
4. Sara E. Davies and Jacqui True, "WPS: A Transformative Agenda?," in *The Oxford Handbook of Women, Peace and Security*, ed. Sara E. Davies and Jacqui True (Oxford: Oxford University Press, 2019), 4.
5. Noha Shawki, "Implementing the Women, Peace and Security Agenda," *Global Affairs* 3, nos. 4–5 (2017): 455–467; Jacqui True and Antje Wiener, "Everyone Wants (a) Peace: The Dynamics of Rhetoric and Practice on 'Women, Peace and Security,'" *International Affairs* 95, no. 3 (2019): 553–574; Soumita Basu, Paul Kirby, and Laura J. Shepherd, eds., *New Directions in Women, Peace and Security* (Bristol, UK: Bristol University Press, 2020); Rita Manchanda, "Introduction," in *Women and Politics of Peace: South Asia Narratives on Militarization, Power, and Justice*, ed. Rita Manchanda (New Delhi: SAGE, 2017), xv–xl; Rita Manchanda, "Difficult Encounters with the WPS Agenda in South Asia: Re-scripting Globalized Norms and Policy Frameworks for a Feminist Peace," in Basu, Kirby, and Shepherd, *New Directions in Women, Peace and Security*, 61–82.
6. The title of this chapter refers to a parallel argument about the tensions in cohering a field of knowledge and instruction under the auspices of "women's studies": "Why,

when we looked closely at this project for which we had fought so hard and that was now academically institutionalized, could we find no *there* there?" See Wendy Brown, "The Impossibility of Women's Studies," *differences: A Journal of Feminist Cultural Studies* 9, no. 3 (1997): 82.

7. Though there is a clear resonance in the emphasis on relations, this is not the technical meaning of "field" found in the work of Pierre Bourdieu. See David McCourt, "Practice Theory and Relationalism as the New Constructivism," *International Studies Quarterly* 60, no. 3 (2016): 479.

8. Michael Barnett and Raymond Duvall, "Power in Global Governance," in *Power in Global Governance*, ed. Michael Barnett and Raymond Duvall (Cambridge: Cambridge University Press, 2005), 2.

9. Coomaraswamy et al., *Preventing Conflict*, 28.

10. Against the caricature of academic detachment, WPS scholars are frequent collaborators with civil society, international organizations, and governments, and so coproduce their object of study in a direct sense.

11. Dianne Otto, "Power and Danger: Feminist Engagement with International Law Through the UN Security Council," *Australian Feminist Law Journal* 32, no. 1 (2010): 97–121.

12. See Columba Achilleos-Sarll, "Women, Peace and Security Advocacy in the UK: Resisting and (Re)producing Hierarchies of Gender, Race and Coloniality" (PhD diss., University of Warwick, 2020).

13. Stephanie A. Shields, *Speaking from the Heart: Gender and the Social Meaning of Emotion* (Cambridge: Cambridge University Press, 2002); Sara Ahmed, *The Cultural Politics of Emotion* (Edinburgh: Edinburgh University Press, 2004); Linda Åhäll, "Affect as Methodology: Feminism and the Politics of Emotion," *International Political Sociology* 12, no. 1 (2018): 36–52; Sarah Amsler and Sara C. Motta, "The Marketised University and the Politics of Motherhood," *Gender and Education* 31, no. 1 (2019): 82–99.

14. Åhäll, "Affect as Methodology," 39; Emma Hutchison and Roland Bleiker, "Theorizing Emotions in World Politics," *International Theory* 6, no. 3 (2014): 502. We do not here seek to resolve the ongoing debate about how best to theorize the location and causal influence of affect, or to settle the boundaries between affect and emotion, but see Hutchison and Bleiker, "Theorizing Emotions"; Rose McDermott, "The Body Doesn't Lie: A Somatic Approach to the Study of Emotions in World Politics," *International Theory* 6, no. 3 (2014): 557–562; Åhäll, "Affect as Methodology."

15. Anna Elomäki et al., "Affective Virtuosity: Challenges for Governance Feminism in the Context of the Economic Crisis," *Gender, Work and Organisation* 26, no. 6 (2019): 827.

16. Clare Hemmings, "Affective Solidarity: Feminist Reflexivity and Political Transformation," *Feminist Theory* 13, no. 2 (2012): 147–161. But see Shirin Saeidi and Heather M. Turcotte, "Politicizing Emotions: Historicizing Affective Exchange and Feminist Gatherings," *International Studies Review* 13, no. 4 (2011): 693–695.

17. Hemmings, "Affective Solidarity," 150. Emphasis added.

18. Nina J. Lahoud, "What Fueled the Far-Reaching Impact of the Windhoek Declaration and Namibia Plan of Action as Milestone for Gender Mainstreaming in UN Peace

Support Operations and Where Is Implementation 20 Years Later?," *Journal of International Peacekeeping* 24, nos. 1–2 (2020): 44. The reference is to the chain of events linking the Windhoek Seminar on gender mainstreaming in May 2000 to the passage of resolution 1325, on which more detail is available in chapter 4.

19.   Coomaraswamy et al., *Preventing Conflict*, 14.

20.   Felicity Ruby, "Security Council Resolution 1325: A Tool for Conflict Prevention?," in *Rethinking Peacekeeping, Gender Equality and Collective Security*, ed. Gina Heathcote and Dianne Otto (Basingstoke, UK: Palgrave Macmillan, 2014), 173–184; Laura J. Shepherd, "Making War Safe for Women? National Action Plans and the Militarisation of the Women, Peace and Security Agenda," *International Political Science Review* 37, no. 3 (2016): 324–335; Soumita Basu and Catia C. Confortini, "Weakest 'P' in the 1325 Pod? Realizing Conflict Prevention through Security Council Resolution 1325," *International Studies Perspectives* 18, no. 1 (2017): 43–63.

21.   Cohn, Kinsella, and Gibbings, "Women, Peace and Security"; Laura J. Shepherd, *Gender, Violence and Security: Discourse as Practice* (London: Zed Books, 2008); Laura J. Shepherd, "Sex, Security and Superhero(in)es: From 1325 to 1820 and Beyond," *International Feminist Journal of Politics* 13, no. 4 (2011): 504–521; Chamindra Weerawardhana, "Profoundly Decolonizing? Reflections on a Transfeminist Perspective of International Relations," *Meridians: Feminism, Race, Transnationalism* 16, no. 1 (2018): 184–213.

22.   In this sweeping summary, we do not disentangle the differing positions from which a feminist critique of WPS is made; these concerns are taken up at points throughout the rest of the book.

23.   Sheri Lynn Gibbings, "No Angry Women at the United Nations: Political Dreams and the Cultural Politics of United Nations Security Council Resolution 1325," *International Feminist Journal of Politics* 13, no. 4 (2011): 522–538; Sam Cook, "The 'Woman-in-Conflict' at the UN Security Council: A Subject of Practice," *International Affairs* 92, no. 2 (2016): 353–372.

24.   The discomfort with "WPS" may be seen in microcosm in the naming of research institutions as centers of "gender, peace, and security" even as they work predominantly on the agenda, a signal to keep essentialist associations at bay.

25.   Paul Kirby and Laura J. Shepherd, "The Futures Past of the Women, Peace and Security Agenda," *International Affairs* 92, no. 2 (2016): 373–392; Shepherd, *Gender, Violence and Security*; Shepherd, "Sex, Security and Superhero(in)es"; Shepherd, "Making War Safe for Women?"; Laura J. Shepherd, *Narrating the Women, Peace and Security Agenda: Logics of Global Governance* (New York: Oxford University Press, 2021); Paul Kirby, "Sexual Violence in the Border Zone: The EU, the Women, Peace and Security agenda and Carceral Humanitarianism in Libya," *International Affairs* 96, no. 5 (2020): 1209–1226.

26.   Judith Halberstam, *The Queer Art of Failure* (Durham, NC: Duke University Press, 2011), 3. Where low theory encourages frivolity and irrelevance—precisely as routes to new ways of understanding and being—we recognize the ongoing tension between thinking within and outside of hegemonic categories. Halberstam's examples of failure

are also invariably revelatory and productive by an alternative standard, becoming case studies in art *about* or *expressive of* failure rather than that which fails to connect with an audience or convey its intended meaning. Failure is no simple remedy.

27.   Halberstam's art is quietly circumscribed: "*Under certain circumstances* failing, losing, forgetting, unmaking, undoing, unbecoming, not knowing may in fact offer more creative, more cooperative, more surprising ways of being in the world." Halberstam, *The Queer Art of Failure*, 2–3. Emphasis added.

28.   In a different context, failure has been identified as a major source of policy change. See Susan Park and Antje Vetterlein, "Owning Development: Creating Policy Norms in the IMF and the World Bank," in *Owning Development: Creating Policy Norms in the IMF and the World Bank*, ed. Susan Park and Antje Vetterlein (Cambridge: Cambridge University Press, 2010), 18.

29.   "By exploring and mapping, I also mean detouring and getting lost." Halberstam, *The Queer Art of Failure*, 24.

30.   Halberstam, *The Queer Art of Failure*, 2.

31.   Sanam Naraghi Anderlini, *Women Building Peace: What They Do, Why It Matters* (Boulder, CO: Lynne Rienner, 2007); Shepherd, *Gender, Violence and Security*; Natalie Florea Hudson, *Gender, Human Security and the United Nations: Security Language as a Political Framework for Women* (London: Routledge, 2010).

32.   See Jane Addams, Emily G. Balch, and Alice Hamilton, eds., *Women at The Hague: The International Congress of Women and Its Results* (Urbana: University of Illinois Press, 2003); J. Ann Tickner and Jacqui True, "A Century of International Relations Feminism: From World War I Women's Peace Pragmatism to the Women, Peace and Security Agenda," *International Studies Quarterly* 62, no. 2 (2018): 221–233; see also chapters 6 and 7 in this book. On IR's origin stories, see Benjamin de Carvalho, Halvard Leira, and John M. Hobson, "The Big Bangs of IR: The Myths that Your Teachers Still Tell You About 1648 and 1919," *Millennium: Journal of International Studies* 39, no. 3 (2011): 735–758; Peter Wilson, "The Myth of the 'First Great Debate,'" *Review of International Studies* 24 (1998): 1–15.

33.   Helena Swanwick, *Women and War* (London: Union of Democratic Control, 1915), 3–4. See also Lucian Ashworth, "Feminism, War and the Prospects for Peace: Helena Swanwick (1864–1939) and the Lost Feminists of Inter-War International Relations," *International Feminist Journal of Politics* 13, no. 1 (2011): 25–43. In Swanwick may be found not only a critical engagement with world order proposals, but succinct expressions of what would later become the "participation" pillar of WPS: "Women will then be more effective peace-makers. . . . No one can doubt that they have been more opposed to war than men, because they have nothing to gain and all to lose in war. But they have been subjected, ignorant, inarticulate, disorganised. Those who have kept them so should be the last to blame them." Swanwick, *Women and War*, 6.

34.   Claudia Jones, *Women in the Struggle for Peace and Security* (New York: National Women's Commission of the Communist Party, 1950).

35.   Elisabeth Armstrong, "Before Bandung: The Anti-imperialist Women's Movement in Asia and the Women's International Democratic Federation," *Signs: Journal of Women in Culture and Society* 41, no. 2 (2016): 305–331.

36. Francisca de Haan, "Continuing Cold War Paradigms in Western Historiography of Transnational Women's Organisations: The Case of the Women's International Democratic Federation (WIDF)," *Women's History Review* 19, no. 4 (2010), 566nn8–9.

37. Valerie Hudson and Patricia Leidl, *The Hillary Doctrine: Sex and American Foreign Policy* (New York: Columbia University Press, 2015), 336.

38. Sara R. Farris, *In the Name of Women's Rights: The Rise of Femonationalism* (Durham, NC: Duke University Press, 2017). See also chapter 5.

39. See, for example, Soumita Basu, "The Global South Writes 1325 (Too)," *International Political Science Review* 37, no. 3 (2016): 362–374. See also chapters 5 and 6.

40. On gender in militaries, see Laleh Khalili, "Gendered Practices of Counterinsurgency," *Review of international Studies* 37, no. 4 (2011): 1471–1491, and Synne L. Dyvik, "Women as 'Practitioners' and 'Targets': Gender and Counterinsurgency in Afghanistan," *International Feminist Journal of Politics* 16, no. 3 (2014): 410–429. See also chapter 6.

41. The Wonder Woman campaign was pulled after protests at the use of a fictional comic book heroine. In a sign of the contradictions of public advocacy, we were denied permission by DC Comics to reproduce the image in this book. Girl Security works to achieve systematic change through the significant representation of women and gender minorities to shift discriminatory norms within national security institutions. Their work is based on the reformative social movement approach (email correspondence between Paul Kirby and Lauren Buitta, October 18, 2022).

42. Otto, "Power and Danger," 97; Carol Cohn, "Mainstreaming Gender in UN Security Policy: A Path to Political Transformation?," in *Global Governance: Feminist Perspectives*, ed. Shirin M. Rai and Georgina Waylen (Basingstoke, UK: Palgrave Macmillan, 2008), 202.

43. Ruby, "Security Council Resolution 1325," 181.

44. Cohn, "Mainstreaming Gender," 201. On governance feminism, see Janet Halley, *Split Decisions: How and Why to Take a Break from Feminism* (Princeton, NJ: Princeton University Press, 2006). See also Janet Halley et al., "From the International to the Local in Feminist Legal Responses to Rape, Prostitution/Sex Work, and Sex Trafficking: Four Studies in Contemporary Governance Feminism," *Harvard Journal of Law & Gender* 29 (2006): 335–423; Otto, "Power and Danger"; Elisabeth Prügl, "Diversity Management and Gender Mainstreaming as Technologies of Government," *Politics & Gender* 7, no. 1 (2011): 71–89; Janet Halley et al., *Governance Feminism: An Introduction* (Minneapolis: University of Minnesota Press, 2018); Janet Halley et al., eds., *Governance Feminism: Notes from the Field* (Minneapolis: University of Minnesota Press, 2019); Negar Razavi, "NatSec Feminism: Women Security Experts and the US Counterterror State," *Signs: Journal of Women in Culture and Society* 46, no. 2 (2021): 361–386.

45. Karen Engle, Vasuki Nesiah, and Dianne Otto, "Feminist Approaches to International Law," in *International Legal Theory: Foundations and Frontiers*, ed. Jeffrey Dunoff and Mark Pollack (Cambridge: Cambridge University Press, 2022), 174–196, x.

46. Aiko Holvikivi, "Gender Experts and Critical Friends: Research in Relations of Proximity," *European Journal of Politics and Gender* 2, no. 1 (2019): 136.

47. Dianne Otto, "Beyond Stories of Victory and Danger: Resisting Feminism's Amenability to Serving Security Council Politics," in Heathcote and Otto, *Rethinking Peacekeeping*, 166–167.

48. Halley, *Split Decisions*, 21, 33.

49. Sarah Smith and Elena B. Stavrevska, "A Different Women, Peace and Security Is Possible? Intersectionality in Women, Peace and Security Resolutions and National Action Plans," *European Journal of Politics and Gender* 5, no. 1 (2022): 63–82.

50. Sam Cook, "Encountering Metis in the Security Council," *Women, Peace and Security Working Paper Series*, no. 15 (Centre for Women Peace and Security, London School of Economics and Political Science, 2018), http://www.lse.ac.uk/women-peace-security /assets/documents/2018/wps15Cook.pdf; Aiko Holvikivi, "Gender Experts and Critical Friends: Research in Relations of Proximity," *European Journal of Politics and Gender* 2, no. 1 (2019): 131–147; Minna Lyytikäinen and Marjaana Jauhola, "Best Practice Diplomacy and Feminist Killjoys in the Strategic State: Exploring the Affective Politics of Women, Peace and Security," in Basu, Kirby, and Shepherd, *New Directions in Women, Peace and Security*, 83–90.

51. See, for example, Sahla Aroussi, *Rethinking National Action Plans on Women, Peace and Security* (Amsterdam: IOS Press, 2017); Hudson, *Gender, Human Security and the UN*; 'Funmi Olonisakin and Awino Okech, eds., *Women and Security Governance in Africa* (Cape Town: Pambazuka Press, 2011); Louise Olsson and Theodora-Ismene Gizelis, eds., *Gender, Peace and Security: Implementing UN Security Council Resolution 1325* (London: Routledge, 2015).

52. For a partial exception looking to institutional coalitions in policymaking, see Roberta Guerrina and Katharine A. M. Wright, "Gendering Normative Power Europe: Lessons of the Women, Peace and Security Agenda," *International Affairs* 92, no. 2 (2016): 293–312. Of course, there are studies of the WPS implementation of policy in differing domains, but none reflect on the broader character of policy transfer. See Maria-Adriana Deiana and Kenneth McDonagh, " 'It Is Important, but . . .': Translating the Women, Peace and Security (WPS) Agenda Into the Planning of EU Peacekeeping Missions," *Peacebuilding* 6, no. 1 (2018): 34–48.

53. On conceptual ambiguity, see Robbie Waters Robichau, "The Mosaic of Governance: Creating a Picture with Definitions, Theories, and Debates," *Policy Studies Journal* 39, no. 1 (2011): 113–131. On governance in IR theory, see John Gerard Ruggie, "On the Problem of 'the Global Problematique': What Roles for International Organizations?," *Alternatives* 5, no. 4 (1980): 517–550; Saul Mendlovitz, "On the Creation of a Just World Order: An Agenda for a Program of Inquiry and Praxis," *Alternatives* 7, no. 3 (1981): 355–373; Friedrich Kratochwil and John Gerard Ruggie, "International Organization: A State of the Art on an Art of the State," *International Organization* 40, no. 4 (1984): 753–775.

54. Kratochwil and Ruggie, "International Organization," 760.

55. Barnett and Duvall, "Power in Global Governance," 1. See also Rorden Wilkinson, "Global Governance: A Preliminary Interrogation," in *Global Governance: Critical Perspectives*, ed. Rorden Wilkinson and Steve Hughes (Routledge: London, 2002), 1–4; Shirin Rai and Georgina Waylen, eds., *Global Governance: Feminist Perspectives* (Basingstoke, UK: Palgrave Macmillan, 2008), 1–2; Thomas G. Weiss and Rorden Wilkinson, "Rethinking Global Governance? Complexity, Authority, Power, Change,"

International Studies Quarterly 58, no. 1 (2014): 207–215; Thomas G. Weiss and Rorden Wilkinson, *Rethinking Global Governance* (Cambridge: Polity, 2019).

56. Iver B. Neumann and Ole Jacob Sending, *Governing the Global Polity: Practice, Mentality, Rationality* (Ann Arbor: University of Michigan Press, 2010), 4.

57. Deborah D. Avant, Martha Finnemore, and Susan K. Sell, eds., *Who Governs the Globe?* (Cambridge: Cambridge University Press, 2010).

58. John Gerard Ruggie, "Reconstituting the Global Public Domain—Issues, Actors, and Practices," *European Journal of International Relations* 10, no. 4 (2004): 519.

59. Neumann and Sending, *Governing the Global Polity.* The rapid proliferation of literature on governmentality is one indication of the analytical purchase of this approach. See Mitchell Dean, *Governmentality: Power and Rule in Modern Society* (London: SAGE, 1999); Wendy Larner and William Walters, eds., *Global Governmentality: Governing International Spaces* (London: Routledge, 2004); Ronnie Lipschutz, "Global Civil Society and Global Governmentality: Or, the Search for Politics and the State Amidst the Capillaries of Social Power," in *Power in Global Governance,* ed. Michael Barnett and Raymond Duvall (Cambridge: Cambridge University Press, 2005), 229–248; Cerasela Voiculescu, *European Social Integration and the Roma: Questioning Neoliberal Governmentality* (London: Routledge, 2017); Jan Busse, *Deconstructing the Dynamics of World-Societal Order: The Power of Governmentality in Palestine* (London: Routledge, 2018).

60. On regimes, see Kratochwil and Ruggie, "International Organization."

61. James Rosenau, "Governance, Order and Change in World Politics," in *Governance Without Government: Order and Change in World Politics,* ed. James Rosenau and Ernst Czempiel (Cambridge: Cambridge University Press, 1992), 4.

62. David McCourt, "Practice Theory and Relationalism as the New Constructivism," *International Studies Quarterly* 60, no. 3 (2016): 475–485; Chih-Yu Shih, "Affirmative Balance of the Singapore-Taiwan Relationship: A Bilateral Perspective on the Relational Turn in International Relations," *International Studies Review* 18, no. 4 (2016): 681–701; Yaqing Qin, "A Relational Theory of World Politics," *International Studies Review* 18, no. 1 (2016): 33–47; Marysia Zalewski, "Forget(ting) Feminism? Investigating Relationality in International Relations," *Cambridge Review of International Affairs* 32, no. 5 (2019): 615–635.

63. Zalewski, "Forget(ting) Feminism?," 626.

64. Ananya Sharma, "Decolonizing International Relations: Confronting Erasures Through Indigenous Knowledge Systems," *International Studies,* 58, no. 1 (2021): 25–40; Tamara A. Trownsell et al., "Differing About Difference: Relational IR from Around the World," *International Studies Perspectives,* 22, no. 1 (2021): 25–64; Morgan Brigg, Mary Graham, and Martin Weber, "Relational Indigenous Systems: Aboriginal Australian Political Ordering and Reconfiguring IR," *Review of International Studies* 48, no. 5 (2022): 891–909.

65. Qin, "A Relational Theory of World Politics," 36.

66. Matthias Hofferberth, "Get Your Act(ors) Together! Theorizing Agency in Global Governance," *International Studies Review* 21, no 1 (2018): 127–145.

67. These examples are drawn from Avant, Finnemore, and Sell, *Who Governs the Globe?*
68. Mustafa Emirbayer, "Manifesto for a Relational Sociology," *American Journal of Sociology* 103, no. 2 (1997): 287.
69. Emirbayer, 294–297.
70. Paraphrasing Somers and Gibson in Emirbayer, 288. Importantly, the alternative of so-called substantialist theorizing *does* recognize the importance of relations, but only as they unfold among entities that are prior and ontologically fixed. See Patrick T. Jackson and Daniel H. Nexon, "Relations Before States: Substance, Process and the Study of World Politics," *European Journal of International Relations* 5, no. 3 (1999): 291–332.
71. It follows that readers need not adopt a processual relational account of, say, the state in order to follow our argument. The deep processes that generate what otherwise appear to be fixed entities may make little concrete difference in explaining how an individual National Action Plan came to be written.
72. Martin Weber, "The Normative Grammar of Relational Analysis: Recognition Theory's Contribution to Understanding Short-Comings in IR's Relational Turn," *International Studies Quarterly* 64, no. 3 (2020): 644.
73. Emery Roe, *Narrative Policy Analysis: Theory and Practice* (Durham, NC: Duke University Press, 1994), 3. See also Dvora Yanow, *How Does a Policy Mean? Interpreting Policy and Organizational Actions* (Washington, DC: Georgetown University Press, 1996), 8–9; Carol Bacchi, *Analysing Policy* (French's Forest, NSW: Pearson Australia, 2009).
74. Colin J. Bennett and Michael Howlett, "The Lessons of Learning: Reconciling Theories of Policy Learning and Policy Change," *Policy Sciences* 25, no. 2 (1992): 275–294; David P. Dolowitz and David Marsh, "Who Learns What from Whom: Review of the Policy Transfer Literature," *Political Studies* 44, no. 2 (1996): 343–357; David P. Dolowitz and David Marsh, "Learning from Abroad: The Role of Policy Transfer in Contemporary Policy-Making," *Governance* 13, no. 1 (2000): 5–24; Keith Dowding, "Model or Metaphor? A Critical Review of the Policy Network Approach," *Political Studies* 43, no. 1 (1995): 136–158; Mark Evans, "Policy Transfer in Critical Perspective," *Policy Studies* 30, no. 3 (2009): 243–268.
75. David Marsh and Jason C. Sharman, "Policy Diffusion and Policy Transfer," *Political Studies* 30 no. 3 (2009): 269–288.
76. The mechanics of the council, with its five veto-wielding permanent members (the so-called P5), obviously militates against democracy, as does the identity of the P5 and the cloistering of diplomacy from public opinion. More, the decisions of the council have an unparalleled reach, making them the most impactful undemocratic decisions around.
77. Cook, "Encountering Metis in the Security Council," 3.
78. John Law, *After Method: Mess in Social Science Research* (London: Routledge, 2004), 145.
79. Marcus B. Weaver-Hightower, "An Ecology Metaphor for Educational Policy Analysis: A Call to Complexity," *Educational Researcher* 37, no. 3 (2008): 155.
80. Cf. Richard K. Ashley, "The Poverty of Neorealism," *International Organization* 38, no. 2 (1986): 225–286; Steve Smith, "The Discipline of International Relations: Still an

American Social Science?," *British Journal of Politics and International Relations* 2, no. 3 (2000): 374–402; Steve Smith, "Singing Our World Into Existence: International Relations Theory and September 11," *International Studies Quarterly* 48, no. 3 (2004): 499–515; Patrick T. Jackson, *The Conduct of Inquiry in International Relations: Philosophy of Science and Its Implications for the Study of World Politics* (London: Routledge, 2010).

81. Claudia Aradau and Jef Huysmans, "Critical Methods in International Relations: The Politics of Techniques, Devices and Acts," *European Journal of International Relations* 20, no. 3 (2014): 598.

82. Donna J. Haraway, "Situated Knowledges: The Science Question in Feminism and the Privilege of Partial Perspective," *Feminist Studies* 14, no. 3 (1988): 589.

83. On the political affordances of collaboration, see Xavier Guillaume, "Collaboration," in *Critical Security Methods: New Frameworks for Analysis*, ed. Claudia Aradau et al. (London: Routledge, 2014), 189–207.

84. Ken Gale and Jonathan Wyatt, *Between the Two: A Nomadic Inquiry Into Collaborative Writing and Subjectivity* (Newcastle, UK: Cambridge Scholars Press, 2019), 5.

85. Law, *After Method*, 143. Emphasis added.

86. Aradau and Huysmans, "Critical Methods in International Relations," 598.

87. Halberstam, *The Queer Art of Failure*, 15. Emphasis added.

88. Law, *After Method*, 6. Emphasis in original.

89. Law, 2.

90. Michael J. Shapiro, *Studies in Trans-disciplinary Method: After the Aesthetic Turn* (London: Routledge, 2012). See also, among others, Roland Bleiker, *Aesthetics and World Politics* (Basingstoke, UK: Palgrave Macmillan, 2009); Marysia Zalewski, *Feminist International Relations: Exquisite Corpse* (London: Routledge, 2013); William A. Callahan, *Sensible Politics: Visualizing International Relations* (New York: Oxford University Press, 2020).

91. Saara Särmä, "Collage: An Art-Inspired Methodology for Studying Laughter in World Politics," in *Popular Culture and World Politics: Theories, Methods, Pedagogies*, ed. Federica Caso and Caitlin Hamilton (Bristol, UK: E-International Relations Publishing, 2015), 110–119.

92. Joe L. Kincheloe, "Describing the Bricolage: Conceptualizing a New Rigor in Qualitative Research," *Qualitative Inquiry* 7, no. 6 (2001): 679–692. On renewed interpretations of Lévi-Strauss, see Francis Gooding, "Wolf, Turtle, Bear," *London Review of Books* 44, no. 10 (2022), https://www.lrb.co.uk/the-paper/v44/n10/francis-gooding/wolf-turtle-bear. On collage as a "cut-and-paste" genre juxtaposing high and low theory, see Halberstam, *The Queer Art of Failure*, 136.

93. Kincheloe, "Describing the Bricolage," 681.

94. Särmä, "Collage," 112.

95. Christian Bueger and Manuel Mireanu, "Proximity," in Aradau et al., *Critical Security Methods*, 120.

96. Fritjof Capra cited in Antoine Bousquet and Simon Curtis, "Beyond Models and Metaphors: Complexity Theory, Systems Thinking and International Relations," *Cambridge Review of International Affairs* 24, no. 1 (2011): 45.

2. BECOMING POLICY ECOLOGISTS

1. UN Security Council, S/PV.8514 (April 23, 2019), https://undocs.org/en/S/PV.8514. Open debates differ from other meetings of the Security Council in that representatives of states that do not currently hold a council seat are invited to attend, though they do not gain voting rights. At the April 2019 debate, sixty-four state representatives attended with the fifteen members of the council and the Vatican (the latter enjoying permanent observer status).

2. UN Security Council, S/PV.8514.

3. We have both been associated with the center, Paul as staff and Laura as a visiting fellow and long-term affiliate.

4. The others are the Georgetown Institute for Women, Peace and Security in the United States (founded in 2011), the WPS Institute at the Kofi Annan Peacekeeper Training Centre, Accra, Ghana (also from 2011), the Centre on Gender, Peace and Security program of the Peace Research Institute Oslo, Norway, and the Monash Gender, Peace and Security Centre, Australia (both since 2015).

5. See variously Peter M. Haas, "Introduction: Epistemic Communities and International Policy Coordination," *International Organization* 46, no. 1 (1992): 1–35; Margaret E. Keck and Kathryn Sikkink, *Activists Beyond Borders: Advocacy Networks in International Politics* (Ithaca, NY: Cornell University Press, 1998); Rebecca Sanders, "Norm Spoiling: Undermining the International Women's Rights Agenda," *International Affairs* 94, no. 2 (2018): 271–291; Graham T. Allison, "Conceptual Models and the Cuban Missile Crisis," *American Political Science Review* 63, no. 3 (1969): 689–718; Sara E. Davies and Jacqui True, "Norm Entrepreneurship in Foreign Policy: William Hague and the Prevention of Sexual Violence in Conflict," *Foreign Policy Analysis* 13, no. 3 (2017): 701–721; and Jeremy Youde, "The Role of Philanthropy in International Relations," *Review of International Studies* 45, no. 1 (2019): 39–56.

6. Deborah D. Avant, Martha Finnemore, and Susan K. Sell, "Who Governs the Globe?," in *Who Governs the Globe?*, ed. Deborah D. Avant, Martha Finnemore, and Susan K. Sell (Cambridge: Cambridge University Press, 2010), 11–14.

7. Dianne Otto, "The Security Council's Alliance of Gender Legitimacy: The Symbolic Capital of Resolution 1325," in *Fault Lines of International Legitimacy*, ed. Hilary Charlesworth and Jean-Marc Coicaud (Cambridge: Cambridge University Press, 2010), 240.

8. Martha Finnemore and Kathryn Sikkink, "International Norm Dynamics and Political Change," *International Organization* 52, no. 4 (1998): 891.

9. Simon Frankell Pratt, "From Norms to Normative Configurations: A Pragmatist and Relational Approach to Theorizing Normativity in IR," *International Theory* 12, no. 1 (2020): 61; Martin Weber, "The Normative Grammar of Relational Analysis: Recognition Theory's Contribution to Understanding Short-Comings in IR's Relational Turn," *International Studies Quarterly* 64, no. 3 (2020): 643.

10. See Torunn Tryggestad, "Trick or Treat? The UN and Implementation of Security Council Resolution 1325 on Women, Peace, and Security," *Global Governance* 15, no. 4

(2009): 539–557; Susan Willett, "Introduction: Security Council Resolution 1325: Assessing the Impact on Women, Peace and Security," *International Peacekeeping* 17, no. 2 (2010): 142–158; Sarai B. Aharoni, "Internal Variation in Norm Localization: Implementing Security Council Resolution 1325 in Israel," *Social Politics: International Studies in Gender, State & Society* 21, no. 1 (2014): 1–25; Jacqui True, "Explaining the Global Diffusion of the Women, Peace and Security Agenda," *International Political Science Review* 37, no. 3 (2016): 307–323; Annika Björkdahl and Johanna Mannergren Selimovic, "WPS and Civil Society," in *The Oxford Handbook of Women, Peace and Security*, ed. Sara E. Davies and Jacqui True (Oxford: Oxford University Press, 2019), 428–438; and Paul Kirby and Laura J. Shepherd, "Women, Peace and Security: Mapping the (Re)Production of a Policy Ecosystem," *Journal of Global Security Studies* 6, no. 3 (2021): ogaa45.

11. Cf. Phumzile Mlambo-Ngcuka, "Foreword," in *Preventing Conflict, Transforming Justice, Securing the Peace: A Global Study on the Implementation of United Nations Security Council Resolution 1325*, ed. Radhika Coomaraswamy et al. (New York: UN Women, 2015); Roberta Guerrina and Katharine A. M. Wright, "Gendering Normative Power Europe: Lessons of the Women, Peace and Security Agenda," *International Affairs* 92, no. 2 (2016): 294; Maria Martín De Almagro, "Lost Boomerangs, the Rebound Effect and Transnational Advocacy Networks: A Discursive Approach to Norm Diffusion," *Review of International Studies* 44, no. 4 (2018): 673; Mathew Hurley, "Watermelons and Weddings: Making Women, Peace and Security 'Relevant' at NATO Through (Re)Telling Stories of Success," *Global Society* 32, no. 4 (2018): 443; Jutta Joachim and Andrea Schneiker, "Changing Discourses, Changing Practices? Gender Mainstreaming and Security," *Comparative European Politics* 10, no. 5 (2012): 528–563; and Willett, "Security Council Resolution 1325," 149.

12. Cf. Torunn Tryggestad, "The UN Peacebuilding Commission and Gender: A Case of Norm Reinforcement," *International Peacekeeping* 17, no. 2 (2010): 159–171; Coomaraswamy et al., *Preventing Conflict*, 27–35; Amy Barrow, "Operationalizing Security Council Resolution 1325: The Role of National Action Plans," *Journal of Conflict and Security Law* 21, no. 2 (2016): 247–275; True, "Explaining the Global Diffusion"; Jacqui True and Antje Wiener, "Everyone Wants (a) Peace: The Dynamics of Rhetoric and Practice on 'Women, Peace and Security,'" *International Affairs* 95, no. 3 (2019): 553–574.

13. Per Sara E. Davies and Jacqui True, "WPS: A Transformative Agenda?" in *The Oxford Handbook of Women, Peace and Security*, ed. Sara E. Davies and Jacqui True (Oxford: Oxford University Press, 2019).

14. Elisabeth Rehn and Ellen Johnson Sirleaf, *Women, War, Peace: The Independent Experts' Assessment of the Impact of Armed Conflict on Women and Women's Role in Peace Building* (New York: UN Women, 2002), 3; Nina J. Lahoud, "What Fueled the Far-Reaching Impact of the Windhoek Declaration and Namibia Plan of Action as Milestone for Gender Mainstreaming in UN Peace Support Operations and Where Is Implementation 20 Years Later?," *Journal of International Peacekeeping* 24 (2020): 3.

15. Keck and Sikkink, *Activists Beyond Borders*. See also chapter 3, pp. 66–67, and chapter 5, pp. 117–121.

16. Of the 107, only 103 had issued documents available in the public domain by the end of 2022. For more information about the NAPs and their contents, see "WPS National Action Plans," LSE Centre for Women, Peace and Security and University of Sydney, accessed August 25, 2023, https://www.wpsnaps.org.

17. The vitality of WPS is also marked by its movement through the international system, as norms are said to "travel." See Susanne Zwingel, "How Do Norms Travel? Theorizing International Women's Rights in Transnational Perspective," *International Studies Quarterly* 56, no. 1 (2012): 115–129.

18. Quoted in Ian Somerville and Sahla Aroussi, "Campaigning For 'Women, Peace and Security': Transnational Advocacy Networks at the United Nations Security Council," in *Gender and Public Relations: Critical Perspectives on Voice, Image and Identity*, ed. Christine Daymon and Kristin Demetrious (Abingdon, UK: Routledge, 2013), 160.

19. Sanam Naraghi Anderlini, *The A-B-C to UN Security Council Resolution 1325 on Women, Peace and Security* (London: International Alert, 2000), 1. But see also Christy Fujio, "From Soft to Hard Law: Moving Resolution 1325 on Women, Peace and Security Across the Spectrum," *Georgetown Journal of Gender and Law* 9, no. 1 (2008): 215–236, and Christine Chinkin and Madeleine Rees, *Commentary on Security Council Resolution 2467: Continued State Obligation and Civil Society Action on Sexual Violence in Conflict* (London: LSE Centre for Women, Peace and Security, 2019).

20. Sarah Kenny Werner and Elena B. Stavrevska, *Where Are the Words? The Disappearance of the Women, Peace and Security Agenda in the Language of Country-Specific UN Security Council Resolutions* (London: Women's International League for Peace and Freedom/LSE Centre for Women, Peace and Security, 2020), 3.

21. See, for example, Marriët Schuurman, "NATO and the Women, Peace and Security Agenda: Time to Bring It Home," *Connections* 14, no. 3 (2015), 1. See also chapter 6.

22. "Global Norms and Standards: Peace and Security," UN Women, accessed August 25, 2023, https://www.unwomen.org/en/what-we-do/peace-and-security/global-norms-and-standards.

23. Felicity Hill, Mikele Aboitiz, and Sara Poehlman-Doumbouya, "Nongovernmental Organizations' Role in the Build-Up and Implementation of Security Council Resolution 1325," *Signs: Journal of Women in Culture and Society* 28, no. 4 (2003): 1256.

24. Coomaraswamy et al., *Preventing Conflict*, 28.

25. "Statement of Shared Commitments," Permanent Mission of Norway to the United Nations, April 4, 2022, https://www.norway.no/contentassets/1b036f2777f74bd3b8ff47 3555c63a98/statement-of-shared-commitments-2022.pdf.

26. True and Wiener, "Everyone Wants (a) Peace."

27. Sakiko Fukuda-Parr and David Hulme, "International Norm Dynamics and the 'End of Poverty': Understanding the Millennium Development Goals," *Global Governance* 17, no. 1 (2011): 18. A different understanding of "clustering"—where distinct norms become associated with each other—has recently been proposed, but it operates at a higher level of abstraction than we are concerned with here. See Eglantine Staunton and Jason Ralph, "The Responsibility to Protect Norm Cluster and the Challenge of Atrocity Prevention: An Analysis of the European Union's Strategy in Myanmar," *European Journal of International Relations* 26, no. 3 (2020): 660–686.

28. Audie Klotz, *Norms in International Relations: The Struggle Against Apartheid* (Ithaca, NY: Cornell University Press, 1995), 26–27.

29. Nina Tannenwald, "The Nuclear Taboo: The United States and the Normative Basis of Nuclear Non-Use," *International Organization* 53, no. 3 (1999): 433–468.

30. See, for example, Dominik Zaum, *The Sovereignty Paradox: The Norms and Politics of International Statebuilding* (Oxford: Oxford University Press, 2007), 7–8. See also J. Samuel Barkin and Bruce Cronin, "The State and the Nation: Changing Norms and the Rules of Sovereignty in International Relations," *International Organization* 48, no. 1 (1994): 107–130, and Gregory A. Raymond "Problems and Prospects in the Study of International Norms," *Mershon International Studies Review* 41, no. 2 (1997): 205–245.

31. Tannenwald, "The Nuclear Taboo."

32. Aharoni, "Internal Variation in Norm Localization," 2–3.

33. Mona Lena Krook and Jacqui True, "Rethinking the Life Cycles of International Norms: The United Nations and the Global Promotion of Gender Equality," *European Journal of International Relations* 18, no. 1 (2012): 123. Again, the aspiration to such a norm does not mean that legitimacy is dependent on it in practice, a part of the chronic confusion between ethical argument and behavioral regularity that we turn to below.

34. See Laura Pantzerhielm, Anna Holzscheiter, and Thurid Bahr, "Power in Relations of International Organisations: The Productive Effects of 'Good' Governance Norms in Global Health," *Review of International Studie* 46, no. 3 (2020): 395–414. This points to another distinction, between norms that are substantive and those that are procedural. See Anette Stimmer and Lea Wisken, "The Dynamics of Dissent: When Actions Are Louder than Words," *International Affairs* 95, no. 3 (2019): 518.

35. In discussing the antipoverty supernorm, Fukuda-Parr and Hulme note that the strength in unifying more discrete policies under an abstract general aim can also prove a weakness, as major political disagreements go unresolved. Fukuda-Parr and Hulme, "International Norm Dynamics," 29. This characteristic of supernorms is also evident in the case of WPS.

36. Antje Wiener, *Contestation and Constitution of Norms in Global International Relations* (Cambridge: Cambridge University Press, 2018), 190–204.

37. On customary law, see Chinkin and Rees, *Commentary.*

38. Carol Cohn, "Mainstreaming Gender in UN Security Policy: A Path to Political Transformation?," in *Global Governance: Feminist Perspectives*, ed. Shirin M. Rai and Georgina Waylen, 185–206 (Basingstoke, UK: Palgrave Macmillan, 2008); Sam Cook, "Security Council Resolution 1820: On Militarism, Flashlights, Raincoats, and Rooms with Doors—a Political Perspective on Where It Came from and What It Adds," *Emory International Law Review* 23, no. 1 (2009): 125–140; Otto, "The Security Council's Alliance of Gender Legitimacy."

39. See, for example, Nicole George and Laura J. Shepherd, "Women, Peace and Security: Exploring the Implementation and Integration of UNSCR 1325," *International Political Science Review* 37, no. 3 (2016): 297–306; Sara E. Davies and Jacqui True, eds., *The Oxford Handbook of Women, Peace and Security* (Oxford: Oxford University Press, 2019), pt. 2; "What Is UNSCR 1325? An Explanation of the Landmark Resolution on Women, Peace and Security," United States Institute of Peace, accessed August 25, 2023,

https://www.usip.org/gender_peacebuilding/about_UNSCR_1325; Henri Myrttinen, Laura J. Shepherd, and Hannah Wright, *Implementing the Women, Peace and Security Agenda in the OSCE Region* (Vienna: Organization for Security and Co-operation in Europe and LSE Centre for Women, Peace and Security, 2020).

40. Soumita Basu and Catia C. Confortini, "Weakest 'P' in the 1325 Pod? Realizing Conflict Prevention Through Security Council Resolution 1325," *International Studies Perspectives* 18, no. 1 (2017): 55; Felicity Ruby, "Security Council Resolution 1325: A Tool for Conflict Prevention?," in *Rethinking Peacekeeping, Gender Equality and Collective Security*, ed. Gina Heathcote and Dianne Otto (Basingstoke, UK: Palgrave Macmillan, 2014), 173–184.

41. See also Marie O'Reilly, "Where the WPS Pillars Intersect," in Davies and True, *Oxford Handbook of Women, Peace and Security*. Also see chapters 6 and 7 of this book.

42. The percentage of women in parliaments is however one aspect of "inclusion" measured in the WPS Index produced by the Georgetown Institute for Women, Peace and Security. See, for example, Georgetown Institute for Women, Peace and Security and Peace Research Institute Oslo, *Women, Peace and Security Index 2019/20* (Washington, DC: GIWPS and PRIO, 2020).

43. Norms are widely seen as limits on actions that would otherwise be possible, and for many thus offer alternative explanations than may be derived from purely "rationalist" or "materialist" premises. A selection of pieces that shaped discussion of norms in IR include Martha Finnemore, "International Organizations as Teachers of Norms: The United Nations Educational, Scientific, and Cultural Organization and Science Policy," *International Organization* 47, no. 4 (1993): 565–597; Finnemore and Sikkink, "International Norm Dynamics"; Peter J. Katzenstein, ed., *The Culture of National Security: Norms and Identity in World Politics* (New York: Columbia University Press, 1996); Jeffrey W. Legro, "Which Norms Matter? Revisiting the 'Failure' of Internationalism," *International Organization* 51, no. 1 (1997): 31–63; Keck and Sikkink, *Activists Beyond Borders*; Neta C. Crawford, *Argument and Change in World Politics: Ethics, Decolonization, and Humanitarian Intervention* (Cambridge: Cambridge University Press, 2002); and Ann Towns, *Women and States: Norms and Hierarchies in International Society* (Cambridge: Cambridge University Press, 2010).

44. See Towns, *Women and States*.

45. Jana Krause, Werner Krause, and Piia Bränfors, "Women's Participation in Peace Negotiations and the Durability of Peace," *International Interactions* 44, no. 6 (2018): 994, 1006.

46. "Women's Participation in Peace Processes," Council on Foreign Relations, accessed August 25, 2023, https://www.cfr.org/womens-participation-in-peace-processes/.

47. UN Security Council, *Report of the Secretary-General on Women, Peace and Security*, S/2020/946 (September 25, 2020), https://undocs.org/S/2020/946, para. 8.

48. Data compiled from using published gender statistics at "Gender," United Nations Peacekeeping, accessed August 25, 2023, https://peacekeeping.un.org/en/gender, with annual comparisons from latest reporting month (November 2021).

49. Sabrina Karim and Kyle Beardsley, "Female Peacekeepers and Gender Balancing: Token Gestures or Informed Policymaking?," *International Interactions* 39 (2013): 461–488; Marsha Henry, "Peacexploitation? Interrogating Labor Hierarchies and Global

Sisterhood Among Indian and Uruguayan Peacekeepers," *Globalizations* 9, no. 1 (2012): 15–33; Nina Wilén, "Female Peacekeepers' Added Burden," *International Affairs* 96, no. 6 (2020): 1585–1602.

50. See Coomaraswamy et al., *Preventing Conflict*, 47–48. Assessments of the agenda often take the level of women's participation in peace processes and mediation as a key metric of progress, though there are of course many other sites of decision making as set out by resolution 1325.

51. See Sophie Huvé, *The Use of UN Sanctions to Address Conflict-Related Sexual Violence* (Washington, DC: Georgetown Institute for Women, Peace and Security, 2018); Chinkin and Rees, *Commentary*, 7; Wiener, *Contestation and Constitution*. See also Sahla Aroussi, "'Women, Peace and Security': Addressing Accountability for Wartime Sexual Violence," *International Feminist Journal of Politics* 13, no. 4 (2011): 576–593, and the discussion in chapter 4.

52. Nicole Deitelhoff and Lisbeth Zimmermann, "Norms Under Challenge: Unpacking the Dynamics of Norm Robustness," *Journal of Global Security Studies* 4, no. 1 (2019): 3.

53. See the discussion in Alexander Betts and Phil Orchard, "Introduction: The Normative Institutionalization-Implementation Gap," in *Implementation and World Politics: How International Norms Change Practice*, ed. Alexander Betts and Phil Orchard (Oxford: Oxford University Press, 2014), 1–26.

54. Wiener, *Contestation and Constitution*, 7.

55. The two norms are not exactly opposites, as gender integration need not mean a prescription that women *should* engage in combat. Nevertheless, the two norms are clearly in tension, as the exclusion of women from militaries is more pronounced the closer the role is to combat.

56. Sarah Percy, "What Makes a Norm Robust: The Norm Against Female Combat," *Journal of Global Security Studies* 4, no. 1 (2019): 124.

57. André Broome, "Stabilizing Global Monetary Norms: The IMF and Current Account Convertibility," in *Owning Development: Creating Policy Norms in the IMF and the World Bank*, ed. Susan Park and Antje Vetterlein (Cambridge: Cambridge University Press, 2010), 114–117.

58. Broome, 115–118.

59. Broome. For the parallel capital account story see Ralf J. Leiteritz and Manuela Moschella, "The IMF and Capital Account Liberalization: A Case of Failed Norm Institutionalization," in Park and Vetterlein, *Owning Development*, 153–180.

60. Jeffrey M. Chwieroth, "Normative Change from Within: The International Monetary Fund's Approach to Capital Account Liberalization," *International Studies Quarterly* 52, no. 1 (2008): 129–158; Leiteritz and Moschella, "The IMF and Capital Account Liberalization."

61. Chwieroth, "Normative Change from Within," 148–150.

62. See, for example, Vivienne Jabri, "Disarming Norms: Postcolonial Agency and the Constitution of the International," *International Theory* 6, no. 2 (2014): 372–390.

63. Finnemore and Sikkink, "International Norm Dynamics," 895; Ayşe Zarakol, "What Made the Modern World Hang Together: Socialisation or Stigmatisation?," *International Theory* 6, no. 2 (2014): 328. See also Charlotte Esptein, "Stop Telling Us How to

Behave: Socialization or Infantilization?," in *Against International Relations Norms: Postcolonial Perspectives*, ed. Charlotte Epstein (Abingdon, UK: Routledge, 2017), 74–86, and Megan H. MacKenzie and Mohamed Sesay, "No Amnesty from/for the International: The Production and Promotion of TRCs as an International Norm in Sierra Leone," *International Studies Perspectives* 13, no. 2 (2012): 146–163.

64. See, for example, True, "Explaining the Global Diffusion"; Barrow, "Operationalizing Security Council Resolution 1325"; Björkdahl and Selimovic, "WPS and Civil Society."

65. See the discussion in Zarakol, "What Made the Modern World Hang Together"; on the application to WPS, see Martín De Almagro, "Lost Boomerangs." It is not always appreciated that Finnemore and Sikkink borrowed the cascade notion from its uses in legal scholarship to refer to a process *within* states, though in both arenas the movement implies hierarchy. See Finnemore and Sikkink, "International Norm Dynamics," 895–896.

66. See, for example, Amitav Acharya, "How Ideas Spread: Whose Norms Matter? Norm Localization and Institutional Change in Asian Regionalism," *International Organization* 58, no. 2 (2004): 239–275. For critiques, see Charmaine Chua, "Against Localization: Rethinking Compliance and Antagonism in Norm Dynamics," in Epstein, *Against International Relations Norms*, 87–105, and Arjun Chowdhury, "International Norms in Postcolonial Time," in Epstein, *Against International Relations Norms*, 106–122.

67. Leiteritz and Moschella, "The IMF and Capital Account Liberalization."

68. Keck and Sikkink, *Activists Beyond Borders*, 168. We broach white feminism in more detail in chapters 5 and 6.

69. Chua, "Against Localization"; MacKenzie and Sesay, "No Amnesty."

70. Chowdhury, "International Norms in Postcolonial Time." For a related argument at the level of states and stressing the history of stigmatization in explaining apparent refusals of "international" norms, see Zarakol, "What Made the Modern World Hang Together."

71. We discuss this further in chapter 5. See also Toni Haastrup and Jamie J. Hagen, "Global Racial Hierarchies and the Limits of Localization Via National Action Plans," in *New Directions in Women, Peace and Security*, ed. Soumita Basu, Paul Kirby, and Laura J. Shepherd (Bristol, UK: Bristol University Press, 2020), 133–151.

72. On transitional justice, see MacKenzie and Sesay, "No Amnesty."

73. Epstein, "Stop Telling Us How to Behave"; Robbie Shilliam, "'Open the Gates Mek We Repatriate': Caribbean Slavery, Constructivism, and Hermeneutic Tensions," *International Theory* 6, no. 2 (2014): 349–372.

74. Towns, *Women and States*.

75. Crawford, *Argument and Change*, 291–342.

76. Martín De Almagro, "Lost Boomerangs"; Rita Manchanda, "Difficult Encounters with the WPS Agenda in South Asia: Re-scripting Globalized Norms and Policy Frameworks for a Feminist Peace," in Basu, Kirby, and Shepherd, *New Directions in Women, Peace and Security*, 61–82.

77. Nicola Pratt, "Reconceptualizing Gender, Reinscribing Racial—Sexual Boundaries in International Security: The Case of UN Security Council Resolution 1325 on 'Women, Peace and Security,'" *International Studies Quarterly* 57, no. 4 (2013): 772–783.

78. See, among many others, Chandra Talpade Mohanty, "Under Western Eyes: Feminist Scholarship and Colonial Discourses," *Feminist Review* 30, no. 1 (1988): 61–88; Chandra Talpade Mohanty, " 'Under Western Eyes' Revisited: Feminist Solidarity Through Anticapitalist Struggles," *Signs: Journal of Women in Culture and Society* 28, no. 2 (2003): 499–535; Antony Anghie, *Imperialism, Sovereignty and the Making of International Law* (Cambridge: Cambridge University Press, 2004); Robbie Shilliam, ed., *International Relations and Non-Western Thought: Imperialism, Colonialism, and Investigations of Global Modernity* (London: Routledge, 2011); Sara de Jong, *Complicit Sisters: Gender and Women's Issues Across North-South Divides* (Oxford: Oxford University Press, 2017); Oumar Ba, *States of Justice: The Politics of the International Criminal Court* (Cambridge: Cambridge University Press, 2020).

79. Epstein, "Stop Telling Us How to Behave," 80.

80. See the discussion in Crawford, *Argument and Change*, 40–43.

81. Nicholas Onuf, "The New Culture of Security Studies," *Mershon International Studies Review* 42, no. 1 (1998): 134.

82. See, for example, Beth A. Simmons and Hyeran Yo, "Measuring Norms and Normative Contestation: The Case of International Criminal Law," *Journal of Global Studies* 4, no. 1 (2019): 29–31; Stimmer and Wisken, "The Dynamics of Dissent."

83. See, for example, Wiener, *Contestation and Constitution*, 13, 191.

84. Wiener, 42–45.

85. Wiener, 8, 50.

86. Park and Vetterlien hint at the contrast with the better-known norm *cycle*, which generally sidelines decay and contestation.

87. Susan Park and Antje Vetterlein, "Owning Development: Creating Policy Norms in the IMF and the World Bank," in Park and Vetterlein, *Owning Development*, 18.

88. Chweiroth, "Normative Change from Within," 131–132; Jeffrey T. Checkel, "International Institutions and Socialization in Europe: Introduction and Framework," *International Organization* 59, no. 4 (2005): 801–826.

89. At the time of writing, this is the situation only for the United States, though a draft WPS act is being considered by the British Parliament.

90. Though references to an "ecosystem" or "ecology" are not uncommon when describing complex interactions, we know of no attempt to explore this concept in relation to WPS. A recent paper by Aiko Holvikivi and Audrey Reeves describes WPS as "a dynamic, fast growing, and globalising ecosystem of national and international legislation, policies, and advocacy efforts," and the support system for survivors in the Democratic Republic of Congo was described as an "ecosystem" by Julienne Lusenge at an open debate on WPS in 2015, but neither engaged with the concept in the terms presented here. See Aiko Holvikivi and Audrey Reeves, "Women, Peace and Security After Europe's 'Refugee Crisis,' " *European Journal of International Security* 5, no. 2 (2020): 136, and Julienne Lusenge, "Statement at the UN Security Council Open Debate on Women, Peace and Security," NGO Working Group on Women, Peace and Security, October 13, 2015. https://www.womenpeacesecurity.org/files/NGOWG_UNSC_OpenDebate_Statement_Lusenge_10-2017.pdf.

91.   This formulation clearly owes an intellectual debt to Austinian speech act theory and
      its reworking by Judith Butler. For a discussion of uses of performativity in manage-
      ment and organizational studies, see Jean-Pascal Gond et al., "What Do We Mean by
      Performativity in Organizational and Management Theory? The Uses and Abuses of
      Performativity," *International Journal of Management Reviews* 18, no. 4 (2016): 440–
      463. Our sense integrates the original Austinian interest in "doing things with words"
      with the more post-structural approach to "constituting the self."

92.   Patrick T. Jackson, *The Conduct of Inquiry in International Relations: Philosophy of Sci-
      ence and Its Implications for the Study of World Politics* (London: Routledge, 2010),
      28–29.

93.   We draw on Weaver-Hightower's conceptualization of *policy ecology* as a perspective
      on education policy (a similarly variegated field of practice), which he puts forward as
      part of "a call to complexity for policy research, an appeal to researchers to theorize
      and account for the many interconnections that create, sustain, hold off, or destroy pol-
      icy formation and implementation." Marcus B. Weaver-Hightower, "An Ecology Met-
      aphor for Educational Policy Analysis: A Call to Complexity," *Educational Researcher*
      37, no. 3 (2008): 152.

94.   This distinguishes our approach to ecology from others who have recently invoked the
      term. One such effort integrates insights from the sociology of organizations to explore
      "aggregate changes in the types and numbers of organizations," where ecology is the
      study of interactions among a population of entities in a given environment and the
      relevant entities are organizations. See Kenneth W. Abbott, Jessica F. Green, and Rob-
      ert O. Keohane, "Organizational Ecology and Institutional Change in Global Gover-
      nance," *International Organization* 70, no. 2 (2016): 249. Our approach differs in that
      we are interested in the full range of actors and entities in the WPS field, understand
      interactions to include practices, habits, speech acts, and activities beyond the entry
      and growth conditions for organizations, and ask constitutive questions about how
      WPS actors are themselves produced, rather than treating organizations as sharply dis-
      tinct actors.

95.   Weaver-Hightower, "An Ecology Metaphor," 155.

96.   On some broader attempts to grapple with "complexity" in governance relations, see
      Thomas G. Weiss and Rorden Wilkinson, "Rethinking Global Governance? Complex-
      ity, Authority, Power, Change," *International Studies Quarterly* 58, no. 1 (2014):
      207–215.

97.   Klaus Dingworth and Philipp Pattberg, "World Politics and Organizational Fields: The
      Case of Transnational Sustainability Governance," *European Journal of International
      Relations* 15, no. 4 (2009): 707–743; Pantzerhielm, Holzscheiter, and Bahr, "Power in
      Relations."

98.   See International Commission on Intervention and State Sovereignty, *The Responsi-
      bility to Protect: Report of the International Commission on Intervention and State Sov-
      ereignty* (Ottawa, ON: International Development Research Centre, 2001), vii;
      Thomas G. Weiss, *Humanitarian Intervention* (Cambridge: Polity Press, 2007), 88.

99.   See Alex J. Bellamy, "The Responsibility to Protect and the Problem of Military Inter-
      vention," *International Affairs* 84, no. 5 (2008): 615–639; Alex J. Bellamy, *Responsibility
      to Protect: The Global Effort to End Mass Atrocities* (Cambridge: Polity Press, 2009);
      Mónica Sarrano, "The Responsibility to Protect and Its Critics: Explaining the Con-
      sensus," *Global Responsibility to Protect* 3, no. 4 (2011): 425–437.
100. See, for example, Cristina G. Badescu and Thomas G. Weiss, "Misrepresenting R2P and
      Advancing Norms: An Alternative Spiral?," *International Studies Perspectives* 11, no. 4
      (2010): 354–374; Amitav Acharya, "The R2P and Norm Diffusion: Towards A Frame-
      work of Norm Circulation," *Global Responsibility to Protect* 5, no. 4 (2013): 466–479;
      Jason G. Ralph and James Souter, "Is R2P a Fully-Fledged International Norm?," *Poli-
      tics and Governance* 3, no. 4 (2015): 68–71; and Luke Glanville, "Does R2P Matter? Inter-
      preting the Impact of a Norm," *Cooperation and Conflict* 51, no. 2 (2016): 184–199.
101. See, for example, Kjell Engelbrekt, "Responsibility Shirking at the United Nations Secu-
      rity Council Constraints, Frustrations, Remedies," *Global Policy* 6, no. 4 (2015): 369–
      378; Alex J. Bellamy, "UN Security Council," in *The Oxford Handbook of the Responsi-
      bility to Protect*, ed. Alex J. Bellamy and Tim Dunne (Oxford: Oxford University Press,
      2016), 249–268; Tor Dahl-Eriksen, "R2P and the UN Security Council: An 'Unreliable
      Alliance,'" *International Journal on World Peace* 36, no. 1 (2019): 33–59.
102. See Mojtaba Mahdavi, "A Postcolonial Critique of Responsibility to Protect in the Mid-
      dle East," *Perceptions: Journal of International Affairs* 20, no. 1 (2015): 7–36; Faith
      Mabera and Yolanda Spies, "How Well Does R2P Travel Beyond the West?," in Bellamy
      and Dunne, *The Oxford Handbook of the Responsibility to Protect*, 208–226; Noele
      Crossley, "Is R2P Still Controversial? Continuity and Change in the Debate on 'Human-
      itarian Intervention,'" *Cambridge Review of International Affairs* 31, no. 5 (2018): 415–
      436; Coralie Pison Hindawi, "Decolonizing the Responsibility to Protect: On Perva-
      sive Eurocentrism, Southern Agency and Struggles Over Universals," *Security Dialogue*
      53, no. 1 (2022): 38–56.
103. On the complexity of R2P, see Lloyd Axworthy and Allan Rock, "R2P: A New and
      Unfinished Agenda," *Global Responsibility to Protect* 1, no. 1 (2009): 54–69.
104. Indeed, Weaver-Hightower warns against "extrapolating from an ecological view that
      policy is somehow 'natural' or that it should be seen as an organic, inevitable outgrowth
      of human needs for regulation." Weaver-Hightower, "An Ecology Metaphor," 157.

3. MAP, TERRITORY, TEXT

1.   Matthias Hofferberth, "Get Your Act(ors) Together! Theorizing Agency in Global Gov-
     ernance," *International Studies Review* 21, no. 1 (2018): 139. See the discussion in chap-
     ter 1, pp. 18–24.
2.   For close examinations of the multi-scalar political geography of WPS, see Yasmin
     Chilmeran, "Women, Peace and Security Across Scales: Exclusions and Opportunities
     in Iraq's WPS Engagements," *International Affairs* 98, no. 2 (2022): 747–765; Stéphanie

Martel, Jennifer Mustapha, and Sarah E. Sharma, "Women, Peace and Security Governance in the Asia Pacific: A Multi-scalar Field of Discourse and Practice," *International Affairs* 98, no. 2 (2022): 727–746.

3. Deborah D. Avant, Martha Finnemore, and Susan K. Sell, "Who Governs the Globe?," in *Who Governs the Globe?*, ed. Deborah D. Avant, Martha Finnemore, and Susan K. Sell (Cambridge: Cambridge University Press, 2010), 2.

4. See especially Michael Barnett and Raymond Duvall, "Power in Global Governance," in *Power in Global Governance*, ed. Michael Barnett and Raymond Duvall (Cambridge: Cambridge University Press, 2005), 1–32. Productive power (diffuse, constitutive) is distinguished from more compulsory power (direct, interactive), structural power (direct, constitutional), and institutional power (diffuse, interactive).

5. We have conducted this kind of analysis before, though with some different choices. See Paul Kirby and Laura J. Shepherd, "Women, Peace and Security: Mapping the (Re) Production of a Policy Ecosystem," *Journal of Global Security Studies* 6, no. 3 (2021): apps. 2 and 3.

6. On this last, see Catherine O'Rourke and Aisling Swaine, "CEDAW and the Security Council: Enhancing Women's Rights in Conflict," *International and Comparative Law Quarterly* 67, no. 1 (2018): 167–199. We count thirty-three WPS policy documents generated by the UN system. We do not include reports of the secretary-general, high-level reviews (e.g., Radhika Coomaraswamy et al., *Preventing Conflict, Transforming Justice, Securing the Peace: A Global Study on the Implementation of United Nations Security Council Resolution 1325* [New York: UN Women, 2015]), or downstream implementation guidelines. Though in later chapters we note the cross-pollination of governance domains, for the purposes of this subset we include only the recognized ten "thematic" WPS resolutions, and not the other resolutions of the council that refer to WPS but fall within other technical categories, such as peacekeeping or country situations. See chapter 4, pp. 93–144.

7. The first NAP was released in 2005, pursuant to the 2004 recommendation of the UN secretary-general and endorsed by the Security Council. Ninety-four states produced at least one iteration of a NAP in our research period (including Bougainville and Tajikistan; these autonomous regions or states are often counted in assessments of extant NAP states as they have produced NAP-like documents). Forty-three of those formulated multiple iterations, producing a dataset of 161 individual government-issued documents produced over the period 2000–2020. There are in addition some domestic approaches to WPS that do not rise to the level of policy, and which we are therefore not able to include, as in the case of India. See Soumita Basu, "Civil Society Actors and the Implementation of Resolution 1325 in India," in *Openings for Peace: UNSCR 1325, Women and Security in India*, ed. Asha Hans and Swarna Rajagopalan (New Delhi: SAGE, 2016), 33–50.

8. We have chosen to include these national documents in this third category rather than along with the NAPs in order to preserve comparability between NAPs, which are to some extent written in a common policy "style," a point we expand on below. The 2019 United States Strategy on Women, Peace and Security, however, is included in the NAP

count, because it was intended, and styled, as a replacement for the 2016 NAP, despite the change in nomenclature.

9.   Documents that cover a range of years—true for almost all NAPs—are dated by the first year of coverage, which sometimes varies from the year of issue (e.g., Niger I 2016 was released in December 2015).

10.   On norm cascades and tipping points, see Martha Finnemore and Kathryn Sikkink, "International Norm Dynamics and Political Change," *International Organization* 52, no. 4 (1998): 901–902. This is also discussed in chapter 5.

11.   See also Jacqui True, "Explaining the Global Diffusion of the Women, Peace and Security Agenda," *International Political Science Review* 37, no. 3 (2016): 307–323.

12.   Of course, scholars of WPS are keenly aware of the existence of NAPs, and numerous studies take NAPs as their central focus. See, for example, Aisling Swaine, "Assessing the Potential of National Action Plans to Advance Implementation of United Nations Security Council Resolution 1325," *Yearbook of International Humanitarian Law* 12 (2009): 403–433; Katrina Lee-Koo, "Implementing Australia's National Action Plan on United Nations Security Council Resolution 1325," *Australian Journal of International Affairs* 68, no. 3 (2014): 300–313; Zeynep Kaya, *Women, Peace and Security in Iraq: Iraq's National Action Plan to Implement Resolution 1325* (London: LSE Middle East Centre, 2016); Toni Haastrup and Jamie J. Hagen, "Global Racial Hierarchies and the Limits of Localization Via National Action Plans," in *New Directions in Women, Peace and Security*, ed. Soumita Basu, Paul Kirby, and Laura J. Shepherd (Bristol, UK: Bristol University Press, 2020), 133–151. However, it is still remarkably common to see the agenda analyzed as occurring within the UN Security Council alone. For a related use of the term "domestication," see Josephine Beoku-Betts, "Holding African States to Task on Gender and Violence: Domesticating UNSCR 1325 in the Sierra Leone National Action Plan," *Current Sociology* 64, no. 4 (2016): 654–670. As we note in chapter 5, this sense of "domestication" should not be confused with the campaign to encourage states of the Global North to apply WPS principles internally on issues from refugee and asylum policy to the arms trade.

13.   See Tim Dunne, "Good Citizen Europe," *International Affairs* 84, no. 1 (2008): 13–28; Torunn L. Tryggestad, "International Norms and Political Change: 'Women, Peace and Security' and the UN Security Agenda" (PhD diss., University of Oslo, 2014); Minna Lyytikäinen and Marjaana Jauhola, "Best Practice Diplomacy and Feminist Killjoys in the Strategic State: Exploring the Affective Politics of Women, Peace and Security," in Basu, Kirby, and Shepherd, 83–90.

14.   The set of "regional organization" documents for this period includes the first NATO directive on 1325. Note that in figure 3.2, NATO is listed as a separate class from other regional organizations to more clearly indicate its outsized influence.

15.   See, for example, Soumita Basu, "The Global South Writes 1325 (Too)," *International Political Science Review* 37, no. 3 (2016): 362–374.

16.   Before even holding their first official assembly, a MARWOPNET (Mano River Women's Peace Network) delegation had attended the Beijing+5 meeting at the United Nations. The timeline bears stressing alongside the energies flowing from the

Windhoek Seminar in Namibia the month before (see chapter 4, pp. 93 and 95). See also Jennifer F. Klot, "The United Nations Security Council Agenda on 'Women, Peace and Security': Bureaucratic Pathologies and Unrealised Potential" (PhD diss., London School of Economics and Politics Science, 2015), 150–154; Filomina Chioma Steady, *Women and Leadership in West Africa: Mothering the Nation and Humanizing the State* (New York: Palgrave Macmillan, 2011), 41–42.

17. See Ecoma Alaga, *"Pray the Devil Back to Hell": Women's Ingenuity in the Peace Process in Liberia*, background brief (Ottawa, ON: Peacebuild, 2011); Inclusive Peace and Transition Initiative, *Case Study: Women in Peace and Transition Processes: Liberia (2003–2011)* (Geneva: Graduate Institute of International and Development Studies, 2018).

18. Elisabeth Rehn and Ellen Johnson Sirleaf, *Women, War, Peace: The Independent Experts' Assessment of the Impact of Armed Conflict on Women and Women's Role in Peace Building* (New York: UN Women, 2002), 77–78.

19. In addition to several mentions by UN officials, we count at least fifteen references to the Mano River Women Peace Network from state representatives in the first five years following the passage of 1325, weighted toward national representatives from Africa and the Global South (Guinea, Mauritius, Nigeria, Indonesia, Algeria, South Africa, Denmark, Ireland, France, and the United States). See UN Security Council, S/PV.4402 (October 31, 2001), https://undocs.org/en/S/PV.4402; UN Security Council, S/PV.4589 (July 25, 2002), https://undocs.org/en/S/PV.4589; UN Security Council, S/PV.4635 (October 28, 2002), https://undocs.org/en/S/PV.4635; UN Security Council, S/PV.4852 (October 29, 2003), https://undocs.org/en/S/PV.4852; UN Security Council, S/PV.5294 (October 27, 2005), https://undocs.org/en/S/PV.5294; UN Security Council, S/PV.5066 (October 28, 2004), https://undocs.org/en/S/PV.5066; UN Security Council, S/PV.5556 (October 26, 2006), https://undocs.org/en/S/PV.5556.

20. See especially Steady, *Women and Leadership in West Africa*, 39–52.

21. Côte d'Ivoire in 2008; Guinea and Liberia in 2009; Sierra Leone in 2010, when three other African states also published plans.

22. Though its conflict and post-conflict sites are central to many studies of WPS implementation, the African *sources* of WPS—from Windhoek to the Mano River to the African Union—remain unforgivably under-studied, though see 'Funmi Olonisakin and Awino Okech, eds., *Women and Security Governance in Africa* (Cape Town: Pambazuka Press, 2011); 'Funmi Olonisakin, Karen Barnes, and Eka Ikpe, eds., *Women, Peace and Security: Translating Policy Into Practice* (London: Routledge, 2011); Cheryl Hendricks, "Women, Peace and Security in Africa," *African Security Review* 24, no. 4 (2015): 364–375; Heidi Hudson, "The Power of Mixed Messages: Women, Peace, and Security Language in National Action Plans from Africa," *Africa Spectrum* 52, no. 3 (2017): 3–29; Toni Haastrup, "WPS and the African Union," in *The Oxford Handbook of Women, Peace, and Security*, ed. Sara E. Davies and Jacqui True (Oxford: Oxford University Press, 2019), 375–387.

23. The 2015 Palestinian document is included in our set but was technically a "strategic framework," with the first NAP branded as such in 2017.

24. Rehn and Sirleaf, *Women, War, Peace*, 58.

25. The commission itself illustrates the difficulty of separating out the influence of nominally distinct WPS actors: its 2010 meeting was funded by Spain and cosponsored by UNIFEM, at the same time that Spain held the presidency of the EU, and was attended by international WPS champions like Ellen Johnson Sirleaf, then president of Liberia and onetime chair of the Mano River Union, Jody Williams (the Nobel laureate best known for her work on the land-mine ban), and the celebrity feminist Gloria Steinem. See International Women's Commission for a Just and Sustainable Palestinian-Israeli Peace, *Advancing Women's Leadership for Sustainable Peace in the Palestinian-Israeli Conflict and Worldwide*, United Nations Development Fund for Women and International Women's Commission, Madrid, June 1–2, 2010), https://www.nwci.ie/download /pdf/isreali_conflict.pdf; International Women's Commission for a Just and Sustainable Palestinian-Israeli Peace, *Charter of Principles*, International Women's Commission, Istanbul, July 27, 2005, https://www.un.org/unispal/document/auto-insert-200863 /; International Women's Commission for a Just and Sustainable Palestinian-Israeli Peace, *Political Vision—Paper of Understanding*, International Women's Commission, August 30, 2008, https://www.un.org/unispal/document/auto-insert-197024/; Vanessa Farr, "UNSCR 1325 and Women's Peace Activism in the Occupied Palestinian Territory," *International Feminist Journal of Politics* 13, no. 4 (2011): 546–547; Sarai B. Aharoni, "Internal Variation in Norm Localization: Implementing Security Council Resolution 1325 in Israel," *Social Politics: International Studies in Gender, State & Society* 21, no. 1 (2014): 14.

26. These pillars are generally deemed to derive from resolution 1325, but they were first laid out in the September 2007 *Report of the Secretary-General on Women and Peace and Security*. Originally a fifth "normative" thematic area was listed, but after 2010 this became incorporated throughout as a "cross-cutting" element, and it has largely fallen away in subsequent policy practice.

27. Our full dataset also includes counts for other terms—"disasters," "human trafficking," "disability," "cyber," and "age"—that we do not include in graphics here because of the low count or because they are less relevant to our analysis.

28. As a simple measure of textual growth, in the first two years of our NAP set, plans averaged 10 pages in length. By 2010, it was 37 pages, by 2015, 39, dipping to 26 pages by 2020.

29. Each expressed the same point in different language—for the United Kingdom by encouraging identification of "suitably qualified female candidates," and the Guinean in references to women's "involvement" and "integration."

30. See Anna Holzscheiter, "Between Communicative Interaction and Structures of Signification: Discourse Theory and Analysis in International Relations," *International Studies Perspectives* 15, no. 2 (2014): 142–162.

31. In this and subsequent figures we indicate the weighted mentions for search terms in the final year of analysis to give an impression of frequency in each document category. In this figure we have provided values for each of the four pillar search terms. In the remaining figures we indicate the highest- and lowest-value search terms for 2020

and also include a third value for a search term in the middle range for that document category. Full details on the breakdown of mentions per document and the exact values for each year of analysis are available in the accompanying dataset, available from the authors on request.

32. See, for example, Soumita Basu and Laura J. Shepherd, "Prevention in Pieces: Representing Conflict in the Women, Peace and Security Agenda," *Global Affairs* 3, nos. 4–5 (2017): 441–453.

33. See Nadine Puechguirbal, "Women and Children: Deconstructing a Paradigm," *Seton Hall Journal of Diplomacy and International Relations* 5, no. 1 (2004): 5–16; Dianne Otto, "The Security Council's Alliance of Gender Legitimacy: The Symbolic Capital of Resolution 1325," in *Fault Lines of International Legitimacy*, ed. Hilary Charlesworth and Jean-Marc Coicaud (Cambridge: Cambridge University Press, 2010), 239–275; Sahla Aroussi, "'Women, Peace and Security': Addressing Accountability for Wartime Sexual Violence," *International Feminist Journal of Politics* 13, no. 4 (2011): 576–593; Jamie J. Hagen, "Queering Women, Peace and Security," *International Affairs* 92, no. 2 (2016): 313–332; Fionnuala Ní Aoláin, "The 'War on Terror' and Extremism: Assessing the Relevance of the Women, Peace and Security Agenda," *International Affairs* 92, no. 2 (2016): 275–291; Soumita Basu and Catia C. Confortini, "Weakest 'P' in the 1325 Pod? Realizing Conflict Prevention through Security Council Resolution 1325," *International Studies Perspectives* 18, no. 1 (2017): 43–63.

34. Aroussi, "Women, Peace and Security"; Laura J. Shepherd, "Sex, Security and Superhero(in)es: From 1325 to 1820 and Beyond," *International Feminist Journal of Politics* 13, no. 4 (2011): 504–521.

35. In descending order of mentions of our sexual violence term set, the ten are Uganda NAP I 2008; South Sudan NAP 2015; CAR NAP 2014; Sierra Leone NAP II 2019; Uganda NAP II 2011; Liberia NAP II 2019; Burkina Faso NAP 2012; Rwanda NAP II 2018; Ukraine NAP II 2020; and UK NAP III 2014.

36. See also Hagen, "Queering Women, Peace and Security."

37. The attention was predominantly on sexual violence (UK NAP III 2014, 6, 12, 16, 21), but men are also included as allies (UK NAP III 2014, 2, 11, 29). The focus faded somewhat, and by the time of its fourth plan the United Kingdom included fewer mentions than contemporaneous efforts from Ireland and the EU (Ireland NAP III 2019; EU Policy IV 2018). Resolution 2106 was the first to *explicitly* list men and boys as prospective victims (see chapter 4, pp. 105–106). See Paul Kirby, "Ending Sexual Violence in Conflict: The Preventing Sexual Violence Initiative and Its Critics," *International Affairs* 91, no. 3 (2015): 457–472.

38. For further context, see Henri Myrttinen, "Locating Masculinities in WPS," in Davies and True, *The Oxford Handbook of Women, Peace and Security*, 88–97; Hannah Wright, "'Masculinities Perspectives': Advancing a Radical Women, Peace and Security Agenda?," *International Feminist Journal of Politics* 22, no. 5 (2020): 652–674; David Duriesmith, "Engaging Men and Boys in the Women, Peace and Security Agenda: Beyond the 'Good Men' Industry," *Women Peace and Security Working Paper Series*, no. 11 (Centre for Women Peace and Security, London School of Economics and

Political Science, 2017), https://www.lse.ac.uk/women-peace-security/assets/documents
/2017/wps11Duriesmith.pdf; Philipp Schulz and Heleen Touquet, "Queering Explanatory Frameworks for Wartime Sexual Violence Against Men," *International Affairs*
96, no. 5 (2020): 1169–1187.

39.   See Ní Aoláin, "The 'War on Terror' and Extremism."

40.   The periodization excludes the first ever NAP, Denmark's, as it is the only one in the
2000–2005 window, but this short document (seven pages of large typescript with several images) touches on only some terms that later became common currency.

41.   See also Paul Kirby, "Sexual Violence in the Border Zone: The EU, the Women, Peace
and Security Agenda and Carceral Humanitarianism in Libya," *International Affairs*
96, no. 5 (2020): 1209–1226.

42.   There are also references in SADC documents in the same period, but here "sexuality"
is in a definition, and not self-evidently meant to encompass LGBTQIA+ persons. See
SADC Plan 2007, 36; SADC Plan 2008, 9.

43.   The multiple iterations of WPS policy by the U.S. government make for an instructive
case study in the contestation of the agenda's content. While there were several references to LGBTQIA+ issues in the 2011 and 2016 U.S. NAPs, there were none in the most
recent U.S. Strategy on Women, Peace and Security, issued by the Trump administration in 2019. See also chapters 4 and 5.

44.   Jamie Hagen and Catherine F. O'Rourke, "Forum-Shifting and Human Rights: Prospects for Queering the Women, Peace and Security Agenda," *Human Rights Quarterly*
45, no. 3 (2023): 406–430.

45.   See United Nations Development Programme, *Human Development Report 1994* (New
York: UNDP, 1994).

46.   Johan Galtung, *Essays in Peace Research*, vol. 1 (Copenhagen: Eljers, 1975), 2.

47.   D. Conor Seyle, "Operationalizing Positive Peace: Canadian Approaches to International Security Policy and Practice," in *The Palgrave Handbook of Global Approaches
to Peace*, ed. Aigul Kulnazarova and Vesselin Popovski (Cham, CH: Palgrave Macmillan, 2019), 193–213.

48.   United Nations General Assembly and United Nations Security Council, *Women's Participation in Peacebuilding: Report of the Secretary General*, A/65/354–S/2010/466 (September 7, 2010), https://undocs.org/S/2010/466.

49.   United Nations General Assembly and United Nations Security Council, *Women's Participation in Peacebuilding*, o.p. 53.

4. PRODUCING AN AGENDA AT THE UNITED NATIONS

1.   For references to the "inauguration" of WPS, see Nicole George, Katrina Lee Koo, and
Laura J. Shepherd, "Gender and the UN's Women, Peace and Security Agenda," in *Rout-
ledge Handbook of Gender and Security*, ed. Caron E. Gentry, Laura J. Shepherd, and
Laura Sjoberg (London: Routledge, 2019), 311–322; Paul Kirby and Laura J. Shepherd,
"The Futures Past of the Women, Peace and Security Agenda," *International Affairs*

92, no. 2 (2016): 376; Catherine O'Rourke, "'Walk[ing] the Halls of Power?' Understanding Women's Participation in International Peace and Security," *Melbourne Journal of International Law* 15, no. 1 (2014): 128; Lourdes Peroni, "Women's Human Rights in Conflict: The WPS Agenda Twenty Years On," *Questions of International Law*, October 31, 2020, http://www.qil-qdi.org/womens-human-rights-in-the-wps-agenda-twenty -years-on/; Dipti Tamang, "Rethinking 'Participation' in Women, Peace and Security Discourses: Engaging with 'Non-participant' Women's Movements in the Eastern Borderlands of India," *International Feminist Journal of Politics* 22, no. 4 (2020): 485.

2.   PeaceWomen, for example, has reports and analysis going back as far as 2002, while the NGO Working Group on Women, Peace and Security continues to monitor the cycle of council decision making for WPS integration. See also Sarah Kenny Werner and Elena B. Stavrevska, *Where Are the Words? The Disappearance of the Women, Peace and Security Agenda in the Language of Country-Specific UN Security Council Resolutions* (London: Women's International League for Peace and Freedom/LSE Centre for Women, Peace and Security, 2020).

3.   See, for example, Louise Allen, "The WPS Agenda Is Almost 20, But It's Not Time to Celebrate Yet," in *Women, Peace and Security: Defending Progress and Responding to Emerging Challenges*, ed. Lisa Sharland and Genevieve Feely (Canberra: Australian Strategic Policy Institute, 2019), 12–13; Soumita Basu, "The United Nations' Women, Peace and Security Agenda," in *Handbook on Gender and War*, ed. Simona Sharoni et al. (Cheltenham, UK: Edward Elgar, 2016), 572–590; Elin Martine Doeland and Inger Skjelsbæk, "Narratives of Support and Resistance: A Political Psychological Analysis of the Implementation of UNSCR 1325 in Bosnia and Herzegovina," *Political Psychology* 39, no. 5 (2017): 995–1011; Claire Duncanson, "Beyond Liberal vs Liberating: Women's Economic Empowerment in the United Nations' Women, Peace and Security Agenda," *International Feminist Journal of Politics* 21, no. 1 (2019): 111–130; George, Lee-Koo, and Shepherd, "Gender and the UN's Women, Peace and Security Agenda"; Toni Haastrup, "Creating Cinderella? The Unintended Consequences of the Women, Peace and Security Agenda for EU's Mediation Architecture," *International Negotiation* 23, no. 2 (2018): 218–237; Katrina Lee-Koo and Barbara K. Trojanowska, "Does the United Nations' Women, Peace and Security Agenda Speak With, For, or To Women in the Asia Pacific? The Development of National Action Plans in the Asia Pacific," *Critical Studies on Security* 5, no. 3 (2017): 287–301; Elizabeth Seymore Smith, "Climate Change in Women, Peace and Security National Action Plans," *SIPRI Insights on Peace and Security*, no. 2020/7 (June 2020): 2; Albert Trithart, "The Women, Peace and Security Agenda Is Not Just for Straight Cisgender Women," *IPI Global Observatory*, October 13, 2020, https://theglobalobservatory.org/2020/10/the-women-peace-and-security-agenda -is-not-just-for-straight-cisgender-women/; Jacqui True, "A Tale of Two Feminisms in International Relations: Feminist Political Economy and the Women, Peace and Security Agenda," *Politics and Gender* 11, no. 2 (2015): 421–423.

4.   Duncanson, "Beyond Liberal vs Liberating," 112.

5.   Ian Hurd, *After Anarchy: Legitimacy and Power in the United Nations Security Council* (Princeton, NJ: Princeton University Press, 2007), 5.

6. Thomas G. Weiss, Tatiana Carayannis, and Richard Jolly, "The 'Third' United Nations," *Global Governance* 15, no. 1 (2009): 123–142.

7. On these dynamics and their link to imperial power, see especially Mark Mazower, *No Enchanted Palace: The End of Empire and the Ideological Origins of the United Nations* (Princeton, NJ: Princeton University Press, 2009).

8. Inis L. Claude, "Collective Legitimization as a Political Function of the United Nations," *International Organization* 20, no. 3 (1966): 372.

9. With respect to norms and law, the council has been described as a four-tier delibera- tive setting, with the P5 as the top level, nested in the full council with its ten elected members with their two-year terms, and influenced by the full state membership that can on occasion enter or otherwise lobby the council; and ending with a circle of NGO advocates and international public opinion. Ian Johnstone, *The Power of Deliberation: International Law, Politics and Organizations* (Oxford: Oxford University Press, 2011), 60–61. In this chapter, and indeed throughout this book, we endeavor to trace WPS growth and stultification across all four of these tiers.

10. Hurd, *After Anarchy*, 3.

11. See, for example, Johnstone, *The Power of Deliberation*. On ethical argument, see Neta C. Crawford, *Argument and Change in World Politics: Ethics, Decolonization, and Humanitarian Intervention* (Cambridge: Cambridge University Press, 2002).

12. Carol Cohn, Helen Kinsella, and Sheri Gibbings, "Women, Peace and Security: Reso- lution 1325," *International Feminist Journal of Politics* 6, no. 1 (2004): 138.

13. On the "utopian vision" of WPS, see Sheri Lynn Gibbings, "No Angry Women at the United Nations: Political Dreams and the Cultural Politics of United Nations Security Council Resolution 1325," *International Feminist Journal of Politics* 13, no. 4 (2011): 522–538.

14. Felicity Hill, "*How* and *When* Has Security Council Resolution 1325 (2000) on Women, Peace and Security Impacted Negotiations Outside the Security Council?" (master's the- sis, Uppsala University, 2005), 32–33. On file with authors.

15. Victoria Brittain, "The Impact of War on Women," *Race & Class* 44, no. 4 (2003): 41.

16. On relationality and the microscopic, see chapter 1, p. 20.

17. As befits our bricolage approach, we draw on interviews conducted for several over- lapping projects over many years, as well as new interview data coproduced for this project. The recent interviews focused primarily on the drafting conditions for each resolution, where we spoke to direct participants in the negotiating and drafting pro- cess from the worlds of diplomacy, civil society, and the UN system. These have been anonymized, with all interview material cited by a single alphabetical identifier and the date of the interview. Where relevant, we have included mention of interviewees' roles in parentheses; in some cases, this information has been withheld in order to bet- ter preserve the subject's anonymity.

18. On determining the character of obligations, see Gregory H. Fox, Kristen E. Boon, and Isaac Jenkins, "The Contributions of United Nations Security Council Resolutions to the Law of Non-international Armed Conflict: New Evidence of Customary Interna- tional Law," *American University Law Review* 67, no. 3 (2018): 658–663.

19. Interviewee C (civil society project leader), 2020; interviewee F (civil society actor), 2020. See also Ian Somerville and Sahla Aroussi, "Campaigning For 'Women, Peace and Security': Transnational Advocacy Networks at the United Nations Security Council," in *Gender and Public Relations: Critical Perspectives on Voice, Image and Identity*, ed. Christine Daymon and Kristin Demetrious (London: Routledge, 2013), 171; Gina Heathcote, "Security Council Resolution 2242 on Women, Peace and Security: Progressive Gains or Dangerous Development?," *Global Society* 32, no. 4 (2018): 382.

20. This compounds a problem of norm language. Whether states frequently appeal to or argue for a principle of law is one way of establishing whether a legal norm exists, but this is *the norm of citing a norm*, which differs from both a norm as a shared rule and a norm as a pattern of behavior beyond the iteration of the rule itself.

21. Fox, Boon, and Jenkins, "The Contributions of United Nations Security Council Resolutions," 665, 692–713.

22. Laura J. Shepherd, *Narrating the Women, Peace and Security Agenda: Logics of Global Governance* (New York: Oxford University Press, 2021), 119–122.

23. Interviewee F (civil society actor), 2013.

24. Interviewee C (civil society project leader), 2020.

25. Interviewee G, 2020.

26. Edward Luck, *UN Security Council: Practice and Promise* (London: Routledge, 2006), 4.

27. Morocco, for example, was relatively disengaged from WPS performance at the council until serving as an elected member in 2012, presenting only four statements in nine years (2002–2011). Representatives from Morocco made statements to the WPS and sexual violence debates during both years of their E10 tenure (the E10 being the elected members of the council, sitting for two years at a time), but, more significantly, continued to make statements to both debates every year thereafter. Azerbaijan's participation was similarly sporadic also until 2012, with only two statements in the period 2002–2011. Azerbaijan was also an elected member during the 2012–2013 term and made statements to both debates in both years, and this engagement carried over to subsequent years, although with less consistency than Morocco—from 2014 onward, Azerbaijan presented statements at least once a year. Ethiopia is another interesting case, with no participation in the debates until 2013, a gap from 2013 until 2016, and then statements in every debate thereafter; we observe a similar pattern from Iran. Uruguay deserves particular mention because several of the countries mentioned here seemed to have consistent engagement triggered by serving as an elected member for a two-year period, and that does not seem to be the case for Uruguay. The country's first statement was on the ten-year anniversary of the adoption of resolution 1325, followed by a gap until 2013, but thereafter representatives made statements every year, preceding the Uruguayan E10 tenure (2016–2017), after which point they continued to present statements to every debate.

28. A different sense of prevention that obtains for avoiding war as such or anticipating terrorism. See Soumita Basu and Catia C. Confortini, "Weakest 'P' in the 1325 Pod?

Realizing Conflict Prevention Through Security Council Resolution 1325," *International Studies Perspectives* 18, no. 1 (2017): 43–63.

29. Interviewee G, 2020.

30. Interviewee F (civil society actor), 2020.

31. See, for example, interviewee D, 2020; and see Shepherd, *Narrating the Women, Peace and Security Agenda*, 119–122.

32. Interviewee A, 2020.

33. Sanam Naraghi Anderlini, *Women Building Peace: What They Do, Why It Matters* (Boulder, CO: Lynne Rienner, 2007), 5; Carol Cohn, "Mainstreaming Gender in UN Security Policy: A Path to Political Transformation?," in *Global Governance: Feminist Perspectives*, ed. Shirin M. Rai and Georgina Waylen (Basingstoke, UK: Palgrave Macmillan, 2008), 187; Laura J. Shepherd, *Gender, Violence and Security: Discourse as Practice* (London: Zed Books, 2008), 110; Natalie Florea Hudson, *Gender, Human Security and the United Nations: Security Language as a Political Framework for Women* (London: Routledge, 2010), 8; Karen Barnes, "The Evolution and Implementation of UNSCR 1325: An Overview," in *Women, Peace and Security: Translating Policy into Practice*, eds, 'Funmi Olonisakin, Karen Barnes, and Eka Ikpe (London: Routledge, 2011), 16–17.

34. Nandi-Ndaitwah went on to serve as Namibia's foreign minister and, at the time of writing, is its deputy prime minister and minister of international relations and cooperation (the renamed foreign minister post), from which position she continues to champion the agenda. It is all the more striking—and revealing of the limits of policy text analysis—that Namibia did not adopt its first NAP until 2019.

35. UN General Assembly and UN Security Council, "Letter Dated 12 July 2000 from the Permanent Representative of Namibia to the United Nations Addressed to the Secretary-General," annex 1: "Windhoek Declaration on the Tenth Anniversary of the United Nations Transition Assistance Group," and annex 2: "Namibia Plan of Action on Mainstreaming a Gender Perspective in Multidimensional Peace Support Operations," A/55/138-S/2000/693 (July 14, 2000), https://undocs.org/en/A/55/138. Attendees were drawn from the wider set: government diplomats, civil society representatives, and academics, as well as UN officials, gathered under the aegis of the UN DPKO Lessons Learned Unit.

36. Nina J. Lahoud, "What Fueled the Far-Reaching Impact of the Windhoek Declaration and Namibia Plan of Action as Milestone for Gender Mainstreaming in UN Peace Support Operations and Where Is Implementation 20 Years Later?," *Journal of International Peacekeeping* 24, nos. 1–2 (2020): 7.

37. Lahoud, 6.

38. Cornelia Weiss, "Creating UNSCR 1325: Women Who Served as Initiators, Drafters, and Strategists," in *Women and the UN: A New History of Women's International Human Rights*, ed. Rebecca Adami and Dan Plesch (London: Routledge, 2022), 143.

39. Lahoud, "What Fueled the Far-Reaching Impact," 46.

40. Weiss, "Creating UNSCR 1325," 139–140. At the fifteenth-anniversary open debate, Nandi-Ndaitwah drew attention to the formative commonality between "armed

liberation struggle," peacekeeping, "silencing the gun" by ending the arms industry, and ending "male dominated culture" through women's participation. UN Security Council, S/PV.7533 (October 13, 2015), https://undocs.org/en/S/PV.7533.

41. Felicity Hill, Mikele Aboitiz, and Sara Poehlman-Doumbouya, "Nongovernmental Organizations' Role in the Build-Up and Implementation of Security Council Resolution 1325," Signs: Journal of Women in Culture and Society 28, no. 4 (2003): 1265.

42. Karen Maters, "The Nairobi World Conference," supplement no. 24 to Women of Europe (Brussels: Commission of the European Communities, 1986), 40–41.

43. United Nations Economic and Social Council, Kampala Action Plan on Women and Peace, E/ECA/ATRCW/ARCC.XV/94/7 (April 1994), 2, https://repository.uneca.org/ds2 /stream/?#/documents/e6c4cc69-6dd2-5a72-9d70-5edd7bea44a1/page/1.

44. United Nations Economic and Social Council, 7.

45. Hill, Aboitiz, and Poehlman-Doumbouya, "Nongovernmental Organizations' Role"; Jutta Joachim, "Framing Issues and Seizing Opportunities: The UN, NGOs, and Women's Rights," International Studies Quarterly 47, no. 2 (2003): 247–274; Somerville and Aroussi, "Campaigning For 'Women, Peace and Security' "; Lahoud, "What Fueled the Far-Reaching Impact."

46. At the time of writing, the NGO Working Group has expanded to eighteen members, including some of the world's largest development, humanitarian, and rights organizations—such as Oxfam, Care International, and Human Rights Watch— alongside more radical and grassroots women's groups like MADRE and the Global Network of Women Peacebuilders. Apart from the defunct Hague Appeal, the original members continue. We explore the politics of civil society advocacy in more detail in chapters 6 and 7.

47. The Ford Foundation, Annual Report 2000: October 1, 1999, to September 30, 2000 (New York: Ford Foundation, 2000), 113; Sanam Naraghi Anderlini, "Civil Society's Leadership in Adopting 1325 Resolution," in The Oxford Handbook of Women, Peace and Security, ed. Sara E. Davies and Jacqui True (Oxford: Oxford University Press, 2019), 43: Weiss, "Creating UNSCR 1325," 144.

48. Somerville and Aroussi, "Campaigning For 'Women, Peace and Security,' " 165.

49. Cohn, Kinsella, and Gibbings, "Women, Peace and Security," 135. Emphasis added.

50. Hill, Aboitiz, and Poehlman-Doumbouya, "Nongovernmental Organizations' Role," 1258–1259; Somerville and Aroussi, "Campaigning For 'Women, Peace and Security,' " 170–172; Weiss, "Creating UNSCR 1325," 145. See also International Alert, "The Role of Women in Achieving Peace and Maintaining International Security—NGO Statement Read Out at the Arria Formula Meeting of the UNSC," International Alert, October 23, 2000, https://reliefweb.int/report/afghanistan/role-women-achieving-peace-and -maintaining-international-security.

51. Weiss, "Creating UNSCR 1325," 145; Anderlini, "Civil Society's Leadership," 45.

52. The NGO groups were WILPF Sierra Leone, the NGO Coalition, the Africa office of Equality Now, and the National Union of Guatemalan Women. Weiss, "Creating UNSCR 1325," 146; Hill, Aboitiz, and Poehlman-Doumbouya, "Nongovernmental Organizations' Role," 1259.

53. Hill, Aboitiz, and Poehlman-Doumbouya, "Nongovernmental Organizations' Role," 1256; Maha Muna cited in Somerville and Aroussi, "Campaigning For 'Women, Peace and Security,' " 169.

54. Noleen Heyzer quoted in Weiss, "Creating UNSCR 1325," 144.

55. Elisabeth Rehn and Ellen Johnson Sirleaf, *Women, War, Peace: The Independent Experts' Assessment of the Impact of Armed Conflict on Women and Women's Role in Peace Building* (New York: UN Women, 2002), 3.

56. Hill, "*How* and *When*," 1. Emphasis added.

57. Antje Wiener, *Contestation and Constitution of Norms in Global International Relations* (Cambridge: Cambridge University Press, 2018), 185–186.

58. Nekwaya Iileka and Julia Imene-Chanduru, "How Namibia Helped Birth UN Resolution 1325 on Women, Peace and Security," *Africa Renewal*, October 27, 2020, https://www.un.org/africarenewal/magazine/october-2020/how-namibia-helped-birth-un-resolution-1325-women-peace-and-security.

59. The feminist coordinates of WPS have overtaken this rather obvious question of state interest and motive, as if it was the duty of Security Council members to support the draft.

60. Field note of a comment made by a prominent WPS advocate, closed seminar, May 20, 2020.

61. Interviewee D, 2020.

62. Michael C. Wood, "Security Council Working Methods and Procedure: Recent Developments," *International and Comparative Law Quarterly* 45, no. 1 (1996): 154.

63. Operative paragraphs 1 and 2 of January 18, 2006, draft, on file with authors.

64. Sam Cook, "Security Council Resolution 1820: On Militarism, Flashlights, Raincoats, and Rooms with Doors—A Political Perspective on Where It Came from and What It Adds," *Emory International Law Review* 23, no. 1 (2009): 127 and 127n13. Emphasis added.

65. Interviewee C (civil society project leader), 2020. The explanation is supported by our review of correspondence between NGOs, November–December 2005.

66. In contrast to the 2006 draft, resolution 1820 did not use the phrase "gender-based violence" at all.

67. Interviewee D, 2020.

68. Interviewee D, 2020; interviewee C (civil society project leader), 2020. The Astoria summits were cited by several respondents as key to mobilizations in 2007–2008, along with the screenings of films like *The Greatest Silence* organized alongside (interviewee E, 2021). These events underscore the importance of unofficial gatherings to the early WPS circuit, which generated its own frictions, a sense of UN professionals called to account for themselves by the wife of a powerful male diplomat from the United States. Though we do not pursue the point further here, the apparent role of a group of "ambassador's wives" (interviewee C, 2020) and their social milieu itself provokes intriguing questions about the role of gender across amateur/professional and advocacy/bureaucracy boundaries.

69. Interviewee D, 2020.

70. Interviewee D, 2020; interviewee B, 2021; interviewee C (civil society project leader), 2020.

71. Interviewee D, 2020.

72. Interviewee D, 2020.

73. Following the first major WPS report within the UN system—which had highlighted the impact of UN personnel on conflict zone sexual economies, including through acts of trafficking, abuse, and violence—the sensitivity of "peacekeeper conduct" was such that it threatened to torpedo progress altogether in at least one informed view (interviewee D, 2020). See also Rehn and Sirleaf, *Women, War, Peace.*

74. Interviewee E, 2021.

75. Interviewee F (civil society actor), 2020. See also Kerry Crawford, *Wartime Sexual Violence: From Silence to Condemnation of a Weapon of War* (Washington, DC: Georgetown University Press, 2017).

76. Interviewee C (civil society project leader), 2019.

77. The role is designated as "under-secretary-general" level, sitting alongside emissaries on other global themes (such as climate change, disarmament, or children in armed conflict), heads of UN entities (like UNFPA and UNICEF), and special crisis envoys.

78. Interviewee F (civil society actor), 2020.

79. See Hillary Clinton, "Remarks on the Adoption of a United Nations Security Council Resolution to Combat Sexual Violence in Armed Conflict," U.S. Department of State Archive, September 30, 2009, https://2009-2017.state.gov/secretary/20092013clinton/rm/2009a/09/130041.htm.

80. Interviewee E, 2021.

81. Interviewee E, 2021; interviewee F (civil society actor), 2020.

82. Interviewee D, 2020; interviewee F (civil society actor), 2020.

83. Interviewee F (civil society actor), 2020.

84. This growth in "state WPS" may also be tracked via the domestication of NAPs, which we discuss in chapters 3 and 5. For a contemporary discussion of how states are claiming WPS positions, see Jacqui True and Antje Wiener, "Everyone Wants (a) Peace: The Dynamics of Rhetoric and Practice on 'Women, Peace and Security,'" *International Affairs* 95, no. 3 (2019): 553–574.

85. Interviewee J, 2019.

86. Several of our interviewees made comments of this sort, varying in the level of malevolence attributed depending on whether it was Vietnam, South Africa, or Russia under discussion.

87. Interviewee C (civil society project leader), 2019.

88. Interviewee D, 2020; interviewee F (civil society actor), 2020.

89. Interviewee E, 2021; interviewee B, 2021.

90. Interviewee F (civil society actor), 2020.

91. Sarah Taylor, "Women, Peace, and Politics at the UN Security Council," *IPI Global Observatory,* July 17, 2013, https://theglobalobservatory.org/2013/07/women-peace-and-politics-at-the-un-security-council/.

92. Though resolution 2106 noted that sexual violence "also affect[ed] men and boys," previous resolutions had condemned "all sexual and other forms of violence committed against civilians in armed conflict, in particular women and children" (in the words of resolution 1820), recognizing adult men implicitly. Only 1325 had taken a strictly monolithic view, expressing concern for all "civilians" as affected by armed conflict, but seeking "special measures to protect women and girls from gender-based violence" only.

93. Interviewee B, 2021; interviewee F (civil society actor), 2020. See also Paul Kirby, "Acting Time; or, the Abolitionist and the Feminist," *International Feminist Journal of Politics* 17, no. 3 (2015): 508–513.

94. Interviewee B, 2021.

95. Interviewee K, 2014.

96. "Sexual violence" here encompasses our grouping of terms to include abbreviations and synonyms. See the discussion in chapter 3 and appendix 3.

97. Interviewee F (civil society actor), 2020.

98. Interviewee B, 2021.

99. Interviewee A, 2020.

100. Interviewee A, 2020.

101. Interviewee D, 2020. The reputational value of WPS had by this stage grown to such proportion that the Spanish government produced a glossy booklet announcing the agenda as its top priority for 2015–2016. See Government of Spain, Ministry of Foreign Affairs, *Spain in the United Nations Security Council: A Comprehensive Review, 2015–2016* (Madrid: Government of Spain, 2017), https://www.exteriores.gob.es/es /ServiciosAlCiudadano/PublicacionesOficiales/2017_BALANCE%20CSNNUU%20 ENG.pdf.

102. Interviewee A, 2020. See also UN Security Council, S/PV.7533 (October 13, 2015), https:// undocs.org/en/S/PV.7533, 22.

103. Interviewee D, 2020.

104. Heiko Maas, "Speech by Federal Minister for Foreign Affairs Heiko Maas at the United Nations Security Council—'Pledge of Commitment on Women, Peace and Security,'" Federal Foreign Office of Germany, April 23, 2019, https://www.auswaertiges-amt.de /en/newsroom/news/maas-speech-security-council-pledge-of-commitment-on -women-peace-and-security/2212520.

105. Interviewee A, 2020.

106. Interviewee A, 2020.

107. Interviewee F (civil society actor), 2020; interviewee G, 2020. The very language of "mechanism" was taken to be "toxic" at least as far back as 2005 (interviewee F [civil society actor], 2020), immediately eliciting comparisons to the Children and Armed Conflict Working Group and the sanctions process, and underscoring the extreme care taken with language in council deliberations.

108. Fionnuala Ní Aoláin, "Gutting the Substance of a Security Council Resolution on Sexual Violence," *Just Security*, April 24, 2019, https://www.justsecurity.org/63750/gutting-the -substance-of-a-security-council-resolution-on-sexual-violence/; Susan Hutchinson,

"US Undermines UN Security Council Resolution Against Wartime Rape," *The Interpreter*, April 24, 2019, https://www.lowyinstitute.org/the-interpreter/us-undermines-un-resolution-against-wartime-rape.

109. Interviewee G, 2020.

110. Interviewee A, 2020.

111. Interviewee B, 2021; interviewee G, 2020.

112. Interviewee G, 2020. There is a countervailing view—namely, that Russia and China have worked constructively with the IEG at least (interviewee B 2021), and that the plurality of WPS politics may legitimately allow for a partisan stress on some linkages (say, with livelihoods or development) over others. We take up the question of national WPS in the next chapter.

113. UN Security Council, *Report of the Secretary-General on Women, Peace and Security*, S/2007/567 (December 12, 2007), https://undocs.org/S/2007/567, para. 42a.

114. Interviewee L, 2016.

115. See Sophie Huvé, *The Use of UN Sanctions to Address Conflict-Related Sexual Violence* (Washington, DC: Georgetown Institute for Women, Peace and Security, 2018).

116. Interviewee M (civil society actor), 2014.

117. Karen Engle, "Judging Sex in War," *Michigan Law Review* 106, no. 6 (2008): 942; Doris E. Buss, "The Curious Visibility of Wartime Rape: Gender and Ethnicity in International Criminal Law," *Windsor Yearbook of Access to Justice* 25, no. 1 (2007): 3–22.

118. "Peace operations" are conventionally understood as peacemaking, peacekeeping, and peace building, though these phases are neither linear nor universal. See, for example, Kate Grady, "Sexual Exploitation and Abuse by UN Peacekeepers: A Threat to Impartiality," *International Peacekeeping* 17, no. 2 (2010): 216–219; Ragnhild Nordås and Siri C. A. Rustad, "Sexual Exploitation and Abuse by Peacekeepers: Understanding Variation," *International Interactions* 39, no. 4 (2013): 512–514; Sabrina Karim and Kyle Beardsley, "Explaining Sexual Exploitation and Abuse in Peacekeeping Missions: The Role of Female Peacekeepers and Gender Equality in Contributing Countries," *Journal of Peace Research* 53, no. 1 (2016): 101–102; Jasmine-Kim Westendorf, "WPS and SEA in Peacekeeping Operations," in Davies and True, *The Oxford Handbook of Women, Peace and Security*, 222–236.

119. Jasmine-Kim Westendorf, *Violating Peace: Sex, Aid, and Peacekeeping* (Ithaca, NY: Cornell University Press, 2020), 24.

120. Although underreporting remains a persistent and widespread problem. See Grady, "Sexual Exploitation and Abuse," 218.

121. Jasmine-Kim Westendorf and Louise Searle, "Sexual Exploitation and Abuse in Peace Operations: Trends, Policy Responses and Future Directions," *International Affairs* 93, no. 2 (2017): 367.

122. Westendorf and Searle, "Sexual Exploitation and Abuse," 368.

123. Quoted in Westendorf, "WPS and SEA," 226.

124. Sarah Smith, "Accountability and Sexual Exploitation and Abuse in Peace Operations," *Australian Journal of International Affairs* 71, no. 4 (2017): 409.

125. UN Security Council, Resolution 2272 (2016), On Sexual Exploitation and Abuse by United Nations Peacekeepers, S/RES/2272 (March 11, 2016), https://undocs.org/S/RES /2272(2016), o.p. 13.

126. Westendorf and Searle, "Sexual Exploitation and Abuse"; Westendorf, "WPS and SEA"; Westendorf, *Violating Peace.*

127. Westendorf, "WPS and SEA," 232.

128. Dianne Otto, "Power and Danger: Feminist Engagement with International Law Through the UN Security Council," *Australian Feminist Law Journal* 32, no. 1 (2010): 97–121.

129. See Soumita Basu, "Gender as National Interest at the UN Security Council," *International Affairs* 92, no. 2 (2016): 255–273; Caitlin Hamilton, Rhaíssa Pagot, and Laura J. Shepherd, "BRICS Countries and the Construction of Conflict in the Women, Peace and Security Open Debates," *International Affairs* 97, no. 3 (2021): 739–757; Shepherd, *Narrating the Women, Peace and Security Agenda*, 71–72 and 173n1.

130. Interviewee E, 2021.

131. Lahoud, "What Fueled the Far-Reaching Impact"; Weiss, "Creating UNSCR 1325,"

132. Fionnuala Ní Aoláin, "The 'War on Terror' and Extremism: Assessing the Relevance of the Women, Peace and Security Agenda," *International Affairs* 92, no. 2 (2016): 275–291.

133. Ní Aoláin, 276.

5. DOMESTICATING THE GENDER PERSPECTIVE

1. Walter Benjamin, *Illuminations: Essays and Reflections*, trans. Harry Zohn (1955; repr., New York: Schocken Books, 2007), 256.

2. Benjamin, *Illuminations*, 257.

3. Those are Sweden (since renounced), Canada, Luxembourg, France, Mexico, Spain, Libya, Germany, Chile, and the Netherlands. See Columba Achilleos-Sarll, Jennifer Thomson, Toni Haastrup, Karoline Färber, Carol Cohn, and Paul Kirby, "The Past, Present and Future(s) of Feminist Foreign Policy," *International Studies Review* 25, no. 1 (2023): viaco68, https://doi.org/10.1093/isr/viaco68.

4. Martha Finnemore and Kathryn Sikkink, "International Norm Dynamics and Political Change," *International Organization* 52, no. 4 (1998): 901–902. As mentioned in chapter 3, WPS crossed this point in October 2016, when Timor-Leste released its first NAP.

5. Margaret E. Keck and Kathryn Sikkink, *Activists Beyond Borders: Advocacy Networks in International Politics* (Ithaca, NY: Cornell University Press, 1998), 13.

6. Míla O'Sullivan and Katerina Krulišová, "Women, Peace and Security in Central Europe: In Between the Western Agenda and Russian Imperialism," *International Affairs* 99, no. 2 (2023): 638.

7. Amy Barrow, "Operationalizing Security Council Resolution 1325: The Role of National Action Plans," *Journal of Conflict and Security Law* 21, no. 2 (2016): 247–275.

8. Many scholarly interventions have explored the dynamics of NAP production and implementation, both in general terms and in specific national contexts. Generally, see, among many others, Aisling Swaine, "Assessing the Potential of National Action Plans to Advance Implementation of United Nations Security Council Resolution 1325," *Yearbook of International Humanitarian Law* 12 (2009): 403–433; Jan Marie Fritz, Sharon Doering, and F. Belgin Gumru, "Women, Peace, Security and the National Action Plans," *Journal of Applied Social Science* 5, no. 1 (2011): 1–23; Barbara Miller, Milad Pournik, and Aisling Swaine, "Women in Peace and Security Through United Nations Security Resolution 1325: Literature Review, Content Analysis of National Action Plans, and Implementation" (Working Paper no. 13, Institute for Global and International Studies, George Washington University, Washington, DC, 2014), https://giwps .georgetown.edu/resource/women-in-peace-and-security-through-united-nations -security-resolution-1325-literature-review-content-analysis-of-national-action-plans -and-implementation/; Sahla Aroussi, ed., *Rethinking National Action Plans on Women, Peace and Security* (Amsterdam: IOS Press, 2017); Jan Maria Fritz, "Creating or Improving a National Action Plan Based on UN Security Council Resolution 1325," in *Gender, Conflict, Peace, and UNSC Resolution 1325*, ed. Seema Shekhawat (Lanham, MD: Lexington Books, 2018), 83–98; Mirsad M. Jacevic, "WPS, States, and the National Action Plans," in *The Oxford Handbook of Women, Peace, and Security*, ed. Sara E. Davies and Jacqui True (Oxford: Oxford University Press, 2018), 274–289. And in specific national contexts, see, again among many others, Helen Basini and Caitlin Ryan, "National Action Plans as an Obstacle to Meaningful Local Ownership of UNSCR 1325 in Liberia and Sierra Leone," *International Political Science Review* 37, no. 3 (2016): 390–403; Katrina Lee-Koo and Barbara K. Trojanowska, "Does the United Nations' Women, Peace and Security Agenda Speak With, For, or To Women in the Asia Pacific? The Development of National Action Plans in the Asia Pacific," *Critical Studies on Security* 5, no. 3 (2017): 287–301; Paula Drumond and Tamya Rebelo, "Global Pathways or Local Spins? National Action Plans in South America," *International Feminist Journal of Politics* 22, no. 4 (2020): 462–484; Diana Højlund Madsen and Heidi Hudson, "Temporality and the Discursive Dynamics of the Rwanda National Action Plans (NAPs) on Women, Peace and Security from 2009 and 2018," *International Feminist Journal of Politics* 22, no. 4 (2020): 550–571.

9. Heidi Hudson, "The Power of Mixed Messages: Women, Peace, and Security Language in National Action Plans from Africa," *Africa Spectrum* 52, no. 3 (2017): 12.

10. Alexander Betts and Phil Orchard, "Introduction: The Normative Institutionalization-Implementation Gap," in *Implementation and World Politics: How International Norms Change Practice*, ed. Alexander Betts and Phil Orchard (Oxford: Oxford University Press, 2014), 1–26.

11. Yasmin Chilmeran, "Women, Peace and Security Across Scales: Exclusions and Opportunities in Iraq's WPS Engagements," *International Affairs* 98, no. 2 (2022): 747–765.

12. David Campbell, *Writing Security: United States Foreign Policy and the Politics of Identity*, rev. ed. (Minneapolis: University of Minnesota Press, 1998), 5.

13. In the post-structuralist attitude, "How are practices orchestrated and interpretations oriented such that it becomes possible to constitute a multiplicity of political spaces, each understood as a self-evident realization of domestic society, each understood to be bounded and set apart from an external anarchy, and each subordinated to the sovereign presence of a state?" Richard K. Ashley, "The Powers of Anarchy: Theory, Sovereignty, and the Domestication of Global Life," in *International Theory: Critical Investigations*, ed. James Der Derian (Basingstoke, UK: Palgrave Macmillan 1995), 118–119. Ashley is a significant example for Patrick T. Jackson and Daniel H. Nexon, "Relations Before States: Substance, Process and the Study of World Politics," *European Journal of International Relations* 5, no. 3 (1999): 310. "Domestication" has also been used in the more direct sense of national implementation. See Josephine Beoku-Betts, "Holding African States to Task on Gender and Violence: Domesticating UNSCR 1325 in the Sierra Leone National Action Plan," *Current Sociology* 64, no. 4 (2016): 654–670.

14. Cf. R. B. J. Walker, *Inside/Outside: International Relations as Political Theory* (Cambridge: Cambridge University Press, 1992); Cynthia Weber, *Simulating Sovereignty: Intervention, the State, and Symbolic Exchange* (Cambridge: Cambridge University Press, 1995).

15. Over 2019–2021 period, the United Kingdom paid £2 million toward the development of a Jordanian NAP, and £200,000 toward an Egyptian one in 2020–2021, in both cases to UN Women. See Conflict, Stability and Security Fund, "Jordan: Internal Security Programme Summary, 2019–2020" (2020); Conflict, Stability and Security Fund, "Jordan: Security and stability Programme Summary, 2020 to 2021" (2021); and Conflict, Stability and Security Fund, "Egypt Programme Summary, 2020 to 2021" (2021). These are available online from the Government of the United Kingdom at https://www.gov.uk/government/publications/conflict-stability-and-security-fund-programme-summaries-for-middle-east-and-north-africa-2019-to-2020.

16. Hendricks, Cheryl, "Progress and Challenges in Implementing the Women, Peace and Security Agenda in the African Union's Peace and Security Architecture," *Africa Development/Afrique et Développement* 42, no. 3 (2017): 76.

17. Though, importantly, see Funmi Olonisakin and Awino Okech, eds., *Women and Security Governance in Africa* (Cape Town: Pambazuka Press, 2011); Hendricks, "Progress and Challenges"; Cheryl Hendricks, "Women, Peace and Security in Africa," *African Security Review* 24, no. 4 (2015): 364–375; Toni Haastrup, "WPS and the African Union," in Davies and True, *The Oxford Handbook of Women, Peace, and Security*, 375–387.

18. Angela Alchin, Amanda Gouws, and Lindy Heinecken, "Making a Difference in Peacekeeping Operations: Voices of South African Women Peacekeepers," *African Security Review* 27, no. 1 (2018): 10.

19. Lesley J. Pruitt, *The Women in Blue Helmets: Gender, Policing, and the UN's First All-Female Peacekeeping Unit* (Berkeley: University of California Press, 2016); Soumita Basu and Laura J. Shepherd, "Prevention in Pieces: Representing Conflict in the Women, Peace and Security Agenda," *Global Affairs* 3, nos. 4–5 (2017): 441–453; Sabrina Karim,

"Reevaluating Peacekeeping Effectiveness: Does Gender Neutrality Inhibit Progress?," *International Interactions* 43, no. 5 (2017): 822–847.

20. Soumita Basu, "The Women in Blue Helmets: Gender, Policing, and the UN's First All-Female Peacekeeping Unit; Equal Opportunity Peacekeeping: Women, Peace, and Security in Post-conflict States," *International Affairs* 94, no. 3 (2018): 663.

21. Pruitt, *The Women in Blue Helmets*, 30.

22. See, for example, UN Security Council, S/PV.8079 (October 27, 2017), https://undocs .org/en/S/PV.8079, 85; UN Security Council, S/PV.8382 (October 25, 2018), https:// undocs.org/en/S/PV.8382, 34; UN Security Council, S/PV.8649 (Resumption 2) (October 29, 2019), https://undocs.org/S/PV.8649%20(Resumption%202), 13.

23. Basu and Shepherd, "Prevention in Pieces," 447.

24. Rita Manchanda, "Introduction," in *Women and Politics of Peace: South Asia Narratives on Militarization, Power, and Justice*, ed. Rita Manchanda (New Delhi: SAGE, 2017), xv–xl, xxvii.

25. Akanksha Khullar, "A Lukewarm Commitment: India and Gender Equality in Security Affairs," *The Diplomat*, January 23, 2020, https://thediplomat.com/2020/01/a -lukewarm-commitment-india-and-gender-equality-in-security-affairs/.

26. UN Security Council, S/PV.8649 (Resumption 1) (October 29, 2019), https://undocs.org /S/PV.8649%20(Resumption%201), 17.

27. UN Security Council, S/PV.8649 (Resumption 2), 13, emphasis added.

28. Naomi Chazan, "Israel, Palestine, and UNSCR 1325: Then and Now," *Palestine-Israel Journal* 25, no. 3 and 4 (2020), https://pij.org/articles/2044/israel-palestine-and-unsc -resolution-1325-then-and-now; Fionnuala Ní Aoláin, "Rethinking the Women, Peace and Security Agenda Through the Lens of Resistance," *Just Security*, April 17, 2017, https://www.justsecurity.org/39982/rethinking-women-peace-security-agenda-lens -resistance/.

29. MIFTAH (Palestinian Initiative for the Promotion of Global Dialogue and Democracy), *Palestinian Women and Resolution 1325* (Ramallah, PS: Palestinian Initiative for the Promotion of Global Dialogue and Democracy, 2009), http://www.miftah.org /Publications/Books/Palestinian_Women_and_Resolution1325.pdf, 12, 12–13, 14.

30. MIFTAH, *Palestinian Women and Resolution 1325*, 22. See also MIFTAH, *A Vision for Palestinian Women's Rights Organisations Based on the Global Study on the Implementation of United Nations Security Council Resolution (UNSCR) 1325 (Ten Strategies for Tackling Issues Pertaining to Women, Peace and Security)*(Ramallah, PS: Palestinian Initiative for the Promotion of Global Dialogue and Democracy, 2017), http://www .miftah.org/Publications/Books/A_Vision_for_Palestinian_Women_on_the _International_Review_En.pdf.

31. "WCLAC and UNSCR 1325," WCLAC (Women's Centre for Legal Aid and Counselling), September 15, 2014, http://www.wclac.org/english/userfiles/WCLAC%20UNSR%20 1325%20final%20sept%2015%202014.pdf.

32. MIFTAH, *A Vision for Palestinian Women's Rights Organisations*.

33. Randa Siniora, "Statement at UN Security Council Open Debate on Women, Peace and Security," NGO Working Group on Women, Peace and Security, October 26, 2018. See

also Nadia Naser-Najjab, "The Challenge of Implementing UNSC Resolution 1325 Under Colonial Rule," *Palestine-Israel Journal* 25, nos. 3–4 (2020), https://www.pij.org /articles/2050/the-challenge-of-implementing-unsc-resolution-1325-under-colonial -rule, and Nivine Sandouka, "The Unique Case of Palestinian Women in East Jerusa-lem," *Palestine-Israel Journal* 25, nos. 3–4 (2020), https://www.pij.org/articles/2047/the -unique-case-of-palestinian-women-in-east-jerusalem.

34. Sarai B. Aharoni, "Internal Variation in Norm Localization: Implementing Security Council Resolution 1325 in Israel," *Social Politics: International Studies in Gender, State & Society* 21, no. 1 (2014): 1–25; "The Story of the Implementation of 1325 UN Security Council Resolution in Israel," Heinrich Böll Stiftung Gunda Werner Institute, accessed August 31, 2023, https://www.gwi-boell.de/en/2011/11/02/story-implementation-1325-un -security-council-resolution-israel.

35. In December 2014 the Israeli government announced a process for developing a NAP, but any draft floundered for years. See Sarai B. Aharoni, *Women, Peace and Security: United Nations Security Council Resolution 1325 in the Israeli Context* (Jerusalem: Van Leer Institute Press, 2015). As we were completing this manuscript, the plan was appar-ently on the verge of release.

36. Noa Furman, "Women in Peacekeeping Forces," Permanent Mission of Israel to the United Nations, April 11, 2019, https://embassies.gov.il/un/statements/security_council /Pages/women-peacekeeping-operations-noa-speech-0412-938.aspx.

37. Nelly Shiloh, "Women and Counterterrorism," Permanent Mission of Israel to the United Nations, September 9, 2015, https://embassies.gov.il/un/statements/committee _statements/Pages/Cons.-Nelly-Shiloh-on-Women-and-Counterterrorism.aspx.

38. Ron Prosor, "Women, Peace and Security," Permanent Mission of Israel to the United Nations, October 28, 2011, https://embassies.gov.il/un/statements/security_council /Pages/Women-and-Peace-and-Security.aspx. This motif has been repeated, for exam-ple, by Israeli ambassador David Roet at the Security Council open debate on WPS in 2014: "From the ancient prophetess Devorah to Miriam and Queen Esther, Jewish his-tory is rich with female leaders. More recently, courageous women from Hannah Senesh to Dorit Beinisch have left their mark on the Jewish people and the Jewish State. In fact, our Declaration of Independence was signed by two women—Golda Meir and Rachel Cohen—and Israel had a female Prime Minister before many other countries granted women the right to vote. In Israel, we understand that women's participation is a game changer. That is why two of the last three chief justices of our Supreme Court have been women and the current Israeli Parliament has more women than ever before. In recent years, Israel has welcomed its first female Major General, elected a female chairman to our federal bank, and three women were appointed to head our leading banks. Israeli women are agents of change, drivers of progress, and makers of peace." David Roet, "Women, Peace and Security," Permanent Mission of Israel to the United Nations, Octo-ber 30, 2014, https://embassies.gov.il/un/statements/security_council/Pages/Amb. -David-Roet-Addresses-the-Security-Council-on-Displaced-Women.aspx.

39. Paul Gilroy, "Colonial Crimes and Convivial Cultures," *Rethinking Nordic Colonial-ism*, April 22, 2006, http://rethinking-nordic-colonialism.org/files/pdf/ACT2/ESSAYS

/Gilroy.pdf. For a related argument on colonial amnesia and WPS, see Columba Achilleos-Sarll, "The (Dis-)Appearance of Race in the United Kingdom's Institution-alization and Implementation of the Women, Peace and Security Agenda," *International Studies Quarterly* 67, no. 1 (2023): sqad006, https://academic.oup.com/isq/article /67/1/sqad006/7033792.

40. We paraphrase a comment made by Anu Mundkur at an event on the horizons of WPS in September 2020, and thank her for permission to reuse it.

41. Derek Gregory, *The Colonial Present: Afghanistan, Palestine, Iraq* (London: Blackwell, 2004).

42. The United Kingdom for thematic WPS resolutions, the United States for those that deal primarily with sexual violence.

43. Neta C. Crawford and Catherine Lutz, "Human Costs of Post-9/11 Wars," Costs of War Project, November 13, 2019, https://watson.brown.edu/costsofwar/files/cow/imce /papers/2019/Direct%20War%20Deaths%20COW%20Estimate%20November%20 13%202019%20FINAL.pdf, 1.

44. Neta C. Crawford, "United States Budgetary Costs and Obligations of Post-9/11 Wars through FY2020 $6.4 Trillion," Costs of War Project, November 13, 2019, https://watson .brown.edu/costsofwar/files/cow/imce/papers/2019/US%20Budgetary%20Costs%20 of%20Wars%20November%202019.pdf. "Direct deaths" encompass killings of U.S. operatives, other allied forces, civilians, and journalists and humanitarians, some two-thirds of which were Iraqi civilians, perishing in Iraq alone. A further 179,000 have been killed in Syria, all but 50,000 of them combatants or state operatives. The expenditure figure covers the wider "Iraq and Syria" theater as a single zone, reflecting the metastasis of the original conflict. The figure does not include the financial costs of "homeland security" or veteran disability programs.

45. Twenty-three other NAPs mention Iraq, mostly from Europe (nineteen) or Australasia, with only Lebanon, Jordan, and Nigeria outside of the Global North, either in reference to refugees and returnees or in passing. For European plans, Iraq is commonly an object of "support" or "assistance," the 2003 war rarely if ever acknowledged.

46. Laura J. Shepherd, "Veiled References: Constructions of Gender in the Bush Administration Discourse on the Attacks on Afghanistan Post-9/11," *International Feminist Journal of Politics* 8, no. 1 (2006): 19–41; Zillah Eisenstein, *Sexual Decoys: Gender, Race, and War in Imperial Democracy* (Melbourne: Spinifex, 2007); Gargi Bhattacharya, *Dangerous Brown Men: Exploiting Sex, Violence and Feminism in the War on Terror* (London: Zed, 2008).

47. The tone is echoed in Iraq's NAP, which glosses over the agents of violence: "Iraqi society and Iraqi women in particular, have suffered difficult conditions and catastrophes after several wars and economic sanctions" (Iraq NAP I 2014, 3).

48. Philip Hammond, "Remarks at Launch of the UK National Action Plan on Women, Peace and Security," Government of the United Kingdom, June 12, 2014, https://www .gov.uk/government/news/launch-of-the-uk-national-action-plan-on-women-peace -and-security; Penny Mordaunt, "Speech at Launch of National Action Plan for Women,

Peace and Security," Government of the United Kingdom, January 17, 2018, https://www
.gov.uk/government/speeches/penny-mordaunt-speech-at-launch-of-national-action
-plan-for-women-peace-and-security.

49. See William Hague, "Remarks at Launch of the UK National Action Plan on Women,
Peace and Security," Government of the United Kingdom, June 12, 2014, https://www
.gov.uk/government/news/launch-of-the-uk-national-action-plan-on-women-peace
-and-security; Justine Greening, "Remarks at Launch of the UK National Action Plan
on Women, Peace and Security," Government of the United Kingdom, June 12, 2014,
https://www.gov.uk/government/news/launch-of-the-uk-national-action-plan-on
-women-peace-and-security; William Hague, "Written Statement on Women, Peace
and Security," 519 Parl. Deb. H.C. (2010) col. 50WS; Hammond, "Remarks at Launch of
the UK National Action Plan on Women, Peace and Security"; Mordaunt, "Speech at
Launch of National Action Plan for Women, Peace and Security."

50. See Hague, "Written Statement on Women, Peace and Security," and chapter 6.

51. Chilmeran, "Women, Peace and Security," 9.

52. Chilmeran, 13. See also Zeynep Kaya, *Women, Peace and Security in Iraq: Iraq's National
Action Plan to Implement Resolution 1325* (London: LSE Middle East Centre, 2016).
While some Iraqi women aligned themselves with the NAP and others with local action
plans (or LAPs, see chapter 6, pp. 172–175), both processes drew on out-of-country support, for the NAP from the Norwegian Embassy, the Euromed Feminist Initiative, and
the UN, and for LAPs from the Swedish Kvinna till Kvinna feminist fund. See Chilmeran, "Women, Peace and Security," 8, 15.

53. North American, European, and Australasian WPS, counting all NAPs as a proportion of the global total for 2000–2020.

54. To paraphrase Soumita Basu, "The Global South Writes 1325 (Too)," *International Political Science Review* 37, no. 3 (2016): 362–374.

55. Renata Avelar Giannini and Pérola Abreu Pereira, "Building Brazil's National Action
Plan: Lessons Learned and Opportunities," *Women, Peace and Security Working Paper
Series*, no. 24 (Centre for Women Peace and Security, London School of Economics and
Political Science, 2020), https://www.lse.ac.uk/women-peace-security/assets
/documents/2020/WPS24GianniniandPereira.pdf, 4; Paula Drumond and Tamya
Rebelo, "Implementing the 'Women, Peace and Security' Agenda in Brazil: An Assess-
ment of the National Action Plan," Strategic Paper 31 (Igarapé Institute, August 2019),
5. More contingently, several sources credit the woman leading the Foreign Ministry's
Peace and Security Division at the time. See Giannini and Pereira, "Building Brazil's
National Action Plan," 5; Tamya Rebelo and Paula Drumond, "Gender Entrepreneurs
in the Adoption of the Brazilian National Action Plan on Women, Peace and Security,"
Global Governance 27, no. 3 (2021): 343–365.

56. Rebelo and Drumond, "Gender Entrepreneurs." On the wider impact of Brazilian WPS,
see Caitlin Hamilton, Rhaíssa Pagot, and Laura J. Shepherd, "BRICS Countries and the
Construction of Conflict in the Women, Peace and Security Open Debates," *International Affairs* 97, no. 3 (2021): 739–757.

57. Interviewee I, 2021. See especially Paul Amar, *The Security Archipelago: Human-Security States, Sexuality Politics, and the End of Neoliberalism* (Durham, NC: Duke University Press, 2013).

58. By "historical women" we convey that gender has been deployed and negotiated differently according to time and context, creating space to acknowledge the potentially nonconformist identities of those who lived in the past. See the discussion in Patricia Owens and Katharina Rietzler, "Toward a History of Women's International Thought," in *Women's International Thought: A New History*, ed. Patricia Owens and Katharina Rietzler (Cambridge: Cambridge University Press, 2021), 9–11.

59. Maria Graham, *Journal of a Voyage to Brazil, and Residence There, During Part of the Years 1821, 1822, 1823* (London: Longman, Hurst, Rees, Orme, Brown and Green, 1824), 292–294. Graham's 1824 text includes an original drawing of Quitéria in full regalia, which served as the model for several subsequent paintings and reproductions, included that reprinted in the NAP.

60. Ivani Vassoler, "A Woman on the Front-Lines Against the Last Bastion of Colonialism in Brazil," *Latin American Essays* 18 (2005): 44–46.

61. Cited in Vassoler, "A Woman on the Front-Lines," 41–42.

62. Pedro dos Santos and Debora Thomé, "Women and Political Power in Brazil," in *Oxford Research Encyclopedia of Politics* (2020), https://oxfordre.com/politics/view/10.1093/acrefore/9780190228637.001.0001/acrefore-9780190228637-e-1744.

63. Cristina Ferreira-Pinto Bailey, " 'Compulsory' Whiteness and Female Identity: Race and Gender in Brazilian Women's Writings," *Letras Femeninas* 32, no. 1 (2006): 307.

64. Manuela Lavinas Picq, *Vernacular Sovereignties: Indigenous Women Challenging World Politics* (Tucson: University of Arizona Press, 2018), 4.

65. Interviewee I, 2021.

66. Interviewee H, 2021; Giannini and Pereira, "Building Brazil's National Action Plan," 6. See also Torild Skard, "Getting Our History Right: How Were the Equal Rights of Women and Men Included in the Charter of the United Nations?," *Forum for Development Studies* 35, no. 1 (2008): 37–60.

67. UN Security Council, S/PV.8234 (April 16, 2018), https://undocs.org/en/S/PV.8234, 30. Other invocations of Lutz include UN Security Council, S/PV.7533 (October 13, 2015), https://undocs.org/en/S/PV.7533, 68; UN Security Council, S/PV.8382, 75.

68. Written correspondence with interviewee I, 2021.

69. Rebelo and Drumond, "Gender Entrepreneurs," 360–361.

70. On visuality and NAPs, see Columba Achilleos-Sarll, " 'Seeing' the Women, Peace and Security Agenda: Visual (Re)Productions of WPS in UK Government National Action Plans," *International Affairs* 96, no. 6 (2020): 1643–1663; Toni Haastrup and Jamie J. Hagen, "Global Racial Hierarchies and the Limits of Localization Via National Action Plans," in *New Directions in Women, Peace and Security*, eds. Soumita Basu, Paul Kirby, and Laura J. Shepherd (Bristol, UK: Bristol University Press, 2020), 133–151.

71. UN Security Council, S/PV.7428 (April 15, 2015), https://undocs.org/en/S/PV.7428, 67.

72. Tomiak-Siemieniewicz is also a fixture on NATO's Instagram and YouTube social media channels.

73. O'Sullivan and Krulišová, "Women, Peace and Security in Central Europe."

74. Lila Abu-Lughod, "The Courage of Truth: Making Anthropology Matter," *Working Papers in Anthropology*, no. 7 (KU Leuven, September 2019), https://soc.kuleuven.be /immrc/paper_files/abu-lughod-wpa-2019-001, 8. See also Vasuki Nesiah, "Feminism as Counter-Terrorism: The Seduction of Power," in *Gender, National Security, and Counter-Terrorism Human Rights Perspectives*, ed. Margaret Satterthwaite and Jayne C. Huckerby (London: Routledge, 2013), 127–151; Negar Razavi, "NatSec Feminism: Women Security Experts and the US Counterterror State," *Signs: Journal of Women in Culture and Society* 46, no. 2 (2021): 361–386. We capitalize "White" (and "Black," "Indigenous") to stress its political coordinates. As Kwame Anthony Appiah explains, this "isn't to elevate. It is to *situate*." Quoted in Musab Younis, "To Own Whiteness," *London Review of Books* 44, no. 3 (2022): 15. Emphasis added.

75. Chamindra Weerawardhana, "Profoundly Decolonizing? Reflections on a Transfeminist Perspective of International Relations," *Meridians: Feminism, Race, Transnationalism* 16, no. 1 (2018): 195.

76. See, for example, Nicola Pratt, "Reconceptualizing Gender, Reinscribing Racial—Sexual Boundaries in International Security: The Case of UN Security Council Resolution 1325 on 'Women, Peace and Security,'" *International Studies Quarterly* 57, no. 4 (2013): 772–783; Basu, "The Global South Writes 1325 (Too)"; Maria Martín De Almagro, "Producing Participants: Gender, Race, Class, and Women, Peace and Security," *Global Society* 32, no. 4 (2018): 395–414; Swati Parashar, "The WPS Agenda: A Postcolonial Critique," in Davies and True, *The Oxford Handbook of Women, Peace, and Security*, 829–839; Haastrup and Hagen, "Global Racial Hierarchies"; Achilleos-Sarll, "The (Dis-)Appearance of Race."

77. We are grateful for comments from Michelle Lee Brown at the International Studies Association Convention in Toronto, March 2019, for spurring our further thinking on WPS and Indigeneity.

78. For rare exceptions, see Michelle Elizabeth Dunn, "Localising the Australian National Action Plan on Women, Peace and Security: A Matter of Justice," *Australian Journal of International Affairs* 68, no. 3 (2014): 285–299; Marjaana Jauhola, "Decolonizing Branded Peacebuilding: Abjected Women Talk Back to the Finnish Women, Peace and Security Agenda," *International Affairs* 92, no. 2 (2016): 333–351.

79. Australia, Brazil, Canada, Guatemala, and the United States, noting that definitions vary by context, and taking the lower bound for each case, using data from the last decade. For Australia: "Estimates of Aboriginal and Torres Strait Islander Australians—June 2016," Australian Bureau of Statistics, August 31, 2018, https://www.abs.gov.au /statistics/people/aboriginal-and-torres-strait-islander-peoples/estimates-aboriginal -and-torres-strait-islander-australians/latest-release. For all others: International Work Group for Indigenous Affairs, *The Indigenous World*, 34th ed. (Copenhagen: International Work Group for Indigenous Affairs, 2020), 360, 569, 418, and 580, respectively.

80. Fiona Harvey, "Activists Protest at 'Sidelining of Social Justice' at UN Climate Talks," *The Guardian*, December 12, 2019, https://www.theguardian.com/environment/2019 /dec/12/activists-protest-un-climate-talks; Indigenous Environment Network, "Native

American COP25 Delegation Removed from US Embassy While Honouring MMIW,"
Buffalo's Fire, December 10, 2019, https://www.buffalosfire.com/native-american-cop25
-delegation-removed-from-us-embassy-while-honoring-mmiw/.

81. Adrian Guelke, *Politics in Deeply Divided Societies* (Cambridge: Polity Press, 2012), 22.

82. Patrick Wolfe, *Settler Colonialism and the Transformation of Anthropology: The Politics and Poetics of an Ethnographic Event* (London: Cassell, 1999); Maile Arvin, Eve Tuck,
and Angie Morrill, "Decolonizing Feminism: Challenging Connections Between Settler Colonialism and Heteropatriarchy," *Feminist Formations* 25, no. 1 (2013): 8–34;
Lorenzo Veracini, " 'Settler Colonialism': Career of a Concept," *Journal of Imperial and
Commonwealth History* 41, no. 2 (2013): 313–333.

83. Wolfe, *Settler Colonialism*, 2.

84. It is worth remembering that according to some estimates, European powers colonized
up to 85 percent of the world's land mass in the period 1815–1914. See Edward W. Said,
Orientalism (London: Routledge and Kegan Paul, 1979), 41.

85. Sandrina de Finney, "Indigenous Girls' Resilience in Settler States: Honouring Body
and Land Sovereignty," *Agenda* 31, no. 2 (2017): 11.

86. Bonita Lawrence, "Gender, Race, and the Regulation of Native Identity in Canada and
the United States: An Overview," *Hypatia* 18, no. 2 (2003): 3–31.

87. Deborah Bird Rose, "Connectivity Thinking, Animism, and the Pursuit of Liveliness,"
Educational Theory 67, no. 4 (2017): 491–508; Deborah Bird Rose, "Cosmopolitics: The
Kiss of Life," *New Formations* 76 (2012): 101–113; Bawaka Country, Sarah Wright, Sandie
Suchet-Pearson, Kate Lloyd, Laklak Burarrwanga, Ritjilili Ganambarr, Merrkiyawuy
Ganambarr-Stubbs, Banbapuy Ganambarr, Djawundil Maymuru, and Jill Sweeny, "Co-
becoming Bawaka: Towards a Relational Understanding of Place/Space," *Progress in
Human Geography* 40, no. 4 (2016): 455–475; Lauren Tynan, "What Is Relationality?
Indigenous Knowledges, Practices and Responsibilities with Kin," *Cultural Geographies*
28, no. 4 (2021): 597–610.

88. Arvin, Tuck and Morrill, "Decolonizing Feminism," 10.

89. See, for example, the Pay the Rent movement in Australia, which encourages people,
especially White Australians, to "pay rent," or making donations to support Indigenous communities, under the slogan "Saying sorry isn't enough." Paying the rent is
articulated as a form of collective acknowledgment that Aboriginal land was stolen,
sovereignty never ceded, and the wealth generated from settlement has never been
evenly distributed.

90. Many of those NAPs that reference Indigeneity on our count do so simply because they
include 1325 as an appendix. See, for example, Côte d'Ivoire NAP I 2008, 24; Austria
NAP I 2007, 27.

91. There has also been occasional reference to Indigeneity from the WPS bureaucracy. See
UN Women, *Indigenous Women and the Women, Peace and Security Agenda*, research
brief (New York: UN Women, 2016).

92. Dunn, "Localising the Australian National Action Plan." Though Australian WPS
makes mostly passing reference to Indigeneity, the second NAP intriguingly lists the
2007 UN Declaration on the Rights of Indigenous Peoples as a key document of the

"Women, Peace and Security Architecture," which, along with the second Canadian plan, is to our knowledge the only times in the NAP corpus where this nexus is identified (see Australia NAP II 2021, 4; Canada NAP II 2017, 5).

93. The Guatemalan NAP includes 75 references to coloniality, Indigeneity, or race on our count; the first Palestinian NAP the same, and the second Canadian plan 33 (Canada NAP II 2017). Between them they provide over a third of the references in the NAP subset as a whole, made of 145 other documents.

94. Arturo Escobar, *Encountering Development: The Making and Unmaking of the Third World*, 2nd ed. (Princeton, NJ: Princeton University Press, 2012), 41–44.

95. Escobar, *Encountering Development*, 13.

96. John Briggs, "The Use of Indigenous Knowledge in Development: Problems and Challenges," *Progress in Development Studies* 5, no. 2 (2005): 100.

97. See Briggs, "The Use of Indigenous Knowledge," 108.

98. Taima Moeke-Pickering, Sheila Cote-Meek, and Ann Pegoraro, "Understanding the Ways Missing and Murdered Indigenous Women Are Framed and Handled by Social Media Users," *Media International Australia* 169, no. 1 (2018): 54–64.

99. Eileen Baldry and Chris Cunneen, "Imprisoned Indigenous Women and the Shadow of Colonial Patriarchy," *Australian & New Zealand Journal of Criminology* 47, no. 2 (2014): 279.

100. United Nations General Assembly and United Nations Security Council, *Conflict-Related Sexual Violence: Report of the Secretary-General*, A/66/657-S/2012/33 (January 13, 2012), https://undocs.org/S/2012/33, para. 17.

101. United Nations Security Council, *Report of the Secretary-General on Conflict-Related Sexual Violence*, S/2016/361 (April 16, 2016), https://undocs.org/S/2016/361, para. 32; United Nations Security Council, *Report of the Secretary-General on Conflict-Related Sexual Violence*, S/2018/250 (March 23,2018), https://undocs.org/S/2018/250, para. 33; United Nations Security Council, *Women and Peace and Security: Report of the Secretary-General*, S/2019/800 (October 9, 2019), https://undocs.org/S/2019/800, para. 37; United Nations Security Council, *Conflict-Related Sexual Violence: Report of the Secretary-General*, S/2020/487 (June 3, 2020), https://undocs.org/S/2020/487, para. 11.

102. UN Women, "Indigenous Women," 3.

103. Kimberlé Crenshaw, "Demarginalizing the Intersection of Race and Sex: A Black Feminist Critique of Antidiscrimination Doctrine, Feminist Theory and Antiracist Politics," *University of Chicago Legal Forum*, no. 1 (1989): 139–167; Kimberlé Crenshaw, "Mapping the Margins: Intersectionality, Identity Politics, and Violence against Women of Color," *Stanford Law Review* 43, no. 6 (1991): 1241–1299.

104. Avtar Brah and Ann Phoenix, "Ain't I a Woman? Revisiting Intersectionality," *Journal of International Women's Studies* 3, no. 5 (2004): 80.

105. Lawrence, "Gender, Race, and the Regulation of Native Identity," 8.

106. As many as three-quarters of all Native children in the United States were enrolled in residential schools, many closely linked to military installations and fulfilling a pacification function. See Nick Estes, "The U.S. Stole Generations of Indigenous Children to Open the West," *High Country News*, October 14, 2019, https://www.hcn.org/issues

/51.17/indigenous-affairs-the-us-stole-generations-of-indigenous-children-to-open-the-west.

107. See, for example, Lawrence, "Gender, Race, and the Regulation of Native Identity," 13–14; Glen Sean Coulthard, *Red Skin, White Masks: Rejecting the Colonial Politics of Recognition* (Minneapolis: University of Minnesota Press, 2014).

108. Brian R. Urlacher, "Introducing Native American Conflict History (NACH) Data," *Journal of Peace Research* 58, no. 5 (2021), https://doi.org/10.1177/0022343320987274.

109. The same may be said of Mexico, which in January 2020 declared a feminist foreign policy and has cochaired the Security Council's Informal Experts Group on WPS.

110. For discussion, see Lawrence, "Gender, Race, and the Regulation of Native Identity"; Coulthard, *Red Skin, White Masks*; Picq, *Vernacular Sovereignties*.

111. Aileen Moreton-Robinson, "The Discursive Nature of Citizenship: Indigenous Sovereign Rights, Racism and Welfare Reform," *International Journal of Critical Indigenous Studies* 2, no. 2 (2009): 2–9. For broader discussions of Indigenous sovereignty and self-determination, see Andrew Bear Robe, "First Nations and Aboriginal Rights," *Constitutional Forum* 2, no. 2 (1991): 46–49; Jodi A. Byrd, "Mind the Gap: Indigenous Sovereignty and the Antinomies of Empire," in *The Anomie of the Earth: Philosophy, Politics, and Autonomy in Europe and the Americas*, ed. Federico Luisetti, John Pickles, and Wilson Kaiser (Durham, NC: Duke University Press, 2015), 119–136.

112. Picq, *Vernacular Sovereignties*.

113. See, for example, Sherene H. Razack, "Gendered Disposability," *Canadian Journal of Women and the Law* 28, no. 2 (2016): 296.

114. Audra Simpson, "The State Is a Man: Theresa Spence, Loretta Saunders and the Gender of Settler Sovereignty," *Theory and Event* 19, no. 4 (2016), https://muse.jhu.edu/article/633280.

115. UN Women, "Indigenous Women." See Claudia Martin and Susana SáCouto, "Access to Justice for Victims of Conflict-Related Sexual Violence: Lessons Learned from the *Sepur Zarco* Case," *Journal of International Criminal Justice* 18, no. 2 (2020): 243–270.

116. Simpson, "The State Is a Man"; Razack, "Gendered Disposability"; Rauna Kuokkanen, "Globalization as Racialized, Sexualized Violence: The Case of Indigenous Women," *International Feminist Journal of Politics* 10, no. 2 (2008): 216–233. See also Jack Healy, "In Indian Country, a Crisis of Missing Women. And a New One When They're Found," *New York Times*, December 25, 2019, https://www.nytimes.com/2019/12/25/us/native-women-girls-missing.html.

117. UN Women, "Indigenous Women," 1. See also Dunn, "Localising the Australian National Action Plan," 294.

118. For a diagnosis and alternative, see Dunn, "Localising the Australian National Action Plan."

119. Following Coulthard, *Red Skin, White Masks*, 108–109.

120. Razack, "Gendered Disposability," 17.

121. Razack.

122. Greg Marks, "Sovereign States vs Peoples: Indigenous Rights and the Origins of International Law," *Australian Indigenous Law Reporter* 5, no. 2 (2000): 1–9.

123. Mazen Masri, "Colonial Imprints: Settler-Colonialism as a Fundamental Feature of Israeli Constitutional Law," *International Journal of Law in Context* 13, no. 3 (2017): 388–407.

124. Antony Anghie, "Finding the Peripheries: Sovereignty and Colonialism in Nineteenth-Century International Law," *Harvard International Law Journal* 40, no. 1 (1999): 1–72; Antony Anghie, *Imperialism, Sovereignty and the Making of International Law* (Cambridge: Cambridge University Press, 2004); Martti Koskenniemi, *The Gentle Civilizer of Nations: The Rise and Fall of International Law 1870–1960* (Cambridge: Cambridge University Press, 2001); Andrew Fitzmaurice, "Scepticism of the Civilizing Mission in International Law," in *International Law and Empire: Historical Explorations*, ed. Martti Koskenniemi, Walter Rech, and Manuel Jiménez Fonseca (Oxford: Oxford University Press, 2017), 359–384.

125. Sara R. Farris, *In the Name of Women's Rights: The Rise of Femonationalism* (Durham, NC: Duke University Press, 2017), 4.

126. Shweta Singh, "Re-thinking the 'Normative' in United Nations Security Council Resolution 1325: Perspectives from Sri Lanka," *Journal of Asian Security and International Affairs*, 4, no. 2 (2017): 225. See also Laura McLeod, "Back to the Future: Temporality and Gender Security Narratives in Serbia," *Security Dialogue* 44, no. 2 (2013): 165–181; Laura McLeod, *Gender Politics and Security Discourse: Personal-Political Imaginations and Feminism in "Post-conflict" Serbia* (Abingdon, UK: Routledge, 2015).

127. See especially Catherine Turner and Aisling Swaine, *At the Nexus of Participation and Protection: Protection-Related Barriers to Women's Participation in Northern Ireland* (New York: International Peace Institute, June 2021), and Aisling Swaine, "Resurfacing Gender: A Typology of Conflict-Related Violence Against Women for the Northern Ireland Troubles," *Violence Against Women* 29, nos. 6–7 (2022), https://doi.org/10.1177/10778012221149. Northern Ireland did finally appear in the fifth UK NAP, released as this manuscript was finalized. For background, see Paul Kirby, Hannah Wright, and Aisling Swaine, "The Future of the UK's Women, Peace and Security Policy," *Policy Brief Series*, no. 7 (LSE Centre for Women, Peace and Security, 2022). Strikingly, Northern Ireland appears often in Republic of Ireland plans as a fundamental and ongoing peace-building concern (Ireland NAP I 2011, 6, 13, 25; Ireland NAP II 2015, 5, 20–21; Ireland NAP III 2019, 8, 21, 34), and elsewhere in the ecosystem in historical celebrations of the women negotiators of the Good Friday Agreement (e.g., Philippines NAP I 2010, 5; U.S. NAP I 2011, 3).

128. Simpson, "The State Is a Man."

129. See again Achilleos-Sarll, "The (Dis-)Appearance of Race."

6. FRACTURES AND FRICTIONS OF A POLICY ECOSYSTEM

1. "Amnesty International Asks President Obama and President Karzai to Give Women a Role in Talks on Afghanistan's Future to Avert 'Catastrophe,' " Amnesty International, May 20, 2012, https://www.amnestyusa.org/press-releases/amnesty-international-asks

-president-obama-and-president-karzai-to-give-women-a-role-in-talks-on
-afghanistans-future-to-avert-catastrophe/.

2. In newspaper editorials promoting the shadow summit, the burqa would also feature
    prominently as the ur-symbol of women's oppression in Afghanistan and the promise
    of the international community to end it. See Jan Schakowsky, "The Burqa Reminder,"
    Chicago Tribune, May 18, 2012, https://www.chicagotribune.com/opinion/ct-xpm
    -2012-05-18-ct-oped-0518-women-20120518-story.html. Another Democratic Party
    congresswomen—Carolyn Maloney—had worn a burqa to link just war and women's
    rights on the floor of the House of Representatives in October 2001.

3. Vienna Colucci, "We Get It," *Human Rights Now* (blog), Amnesty International, May 19,
    2012, https://blog.amnestyusa.org/asia/we-get-it/.

4. Philip Rucker and Robert Costa, "'It's a Hard Problem': Inside Trump's Decision to Send
    More Troops to Afghanistan," *Washington Post*, August 21, 2017, https://www
    .washingtonpost.com/politics/its-a-hard-problem-inside-trumps-decision-to-send
    -more-troops-to-afghanistan/2017/08/21/14dcb126-868b-11e7-a94f-3139abce39f5_story
    .html.

5. Special Inspector General for Afghanistan Reconstruction, *Support for Gender Equal-
    ity: Lessons from the U.S. Experience in Afghanistan* (Arlington, VA: Special Inspector
    General for Afghanistan Reconstruction, 2021), 40.

6. Though our topic is not the nature of the Afghanistan War (encompassing the period
    from the Anglo-American invasion of September 2001 through the UN authorization
    of the International Security Assistance Force mandate to the departure of combat
    troops in 2014 and the end of in-country military support to the Afghan government
    in August 2021), it bears stressing that the anatomies of defeat that circulated in the
    Global North entrenched a dichotomy that placed women's rights with Western inter-
    vention and therefore opposition to Western intervention with a knowing or unwit-
    ting misogyny, an uncritical association of the war with feminist ends if not feminist
    methods.

7. Marsha Henry, "On the Necessity of Critical Race Feminism for Women, Peace and
    Security," *Critical Studies on Security* 9, no. 1 (2021): 22. See also chapter 5.

8. Sheri Lynn Gibbings, "No Angry Women at the United Nations: Political Dreams and
    the Cultural Politics of United Nations Security Council Resolution 1325," *International
    Feminist Journal of Politics* 13, no. 4 (2011): 522–538; J. Ann Tickner and Jacqui True, "A
    Century of International Relations Feminism: From World War I Women's Peace Prag-
    matism to the Women, Peace and Security Agenda," *International Studies Quarterly*
    62, no. 2 (2018): 221–233.

9. Charlotte Isaksson, "Integrating Gender Perspectives at NATO: Two Steps Forward,
    One Step Back," in *Women and Gender Perspectives in the Military: An International
    Comparison*, ed. Robert Egnell and Mayesha Alam (Washington, DC: Georgetown Uni-
    versity Press, 2019), 226.

10. One of the earliest guidelines was drafted by the Institute for Inclusive Security and
    the 2015 "scorecard" by the Women in International Security group and the Belgrade
    Centre for Security think tank with NATO funding. See NATO Committee on

Gender Perspectives, *How Can Gender Make a Difference to Security in Operations: Indicators* (2011), https://www.nato.int/issues/women_nato/2011/1869-11%20 Gender%20Brochure.pdf; Chantal de Jonge Oudraat, Sonja Stojanović-Gajić, Carolyn Washington, and Brooke Stedman, *The 1325 Scorecard: Preliminary Findings* (Washington, DC: Women in International Security and Belgrade Centre for Security Policy, 2015), https://wiisglobal.org/wp-content/uploads/2014/03/UNSCR-1325-Scorecard-Final -Report.pdf.

11.   Women's International League for Peace and Freedom, *Congress Report 2018* (Geneva: WILPF, 2019).

12.   On "Centres of Excellence," see Toni Haastrup and Jamie J. Hagen, "Racial Hierarchies of Knowledge Production in the Women, Peace and Security Agenda," *Critical Studies on Security* 9, no. 1 (2021): 27–30.

13.   See, for example, Jody M. Prescott, "NATO Gender Mainstreaming: A New Approach to War Amongst the People?," *RUSI Journal* 158, no. 5 (2013): 56–62; Robert Egnell, "Gender Perspectives and Military Effectiveness: Implementing UNSCR 1325 and the National Action Plan on Women, Peace, and Security," *PRISM* 6, no. 1 (2016): 73–89; Katharine A. M. Wright, "NATO's Adoption of UNSCR 1325 on Women, Peace and Security: Making the Agenda a Reality," *American Political Science Review* 37, no. 3 (2016): 350–361; Megan Bastick and Claire Duncanson, "Agents of Change? Gender Advisors in NATO Militaries," *International Peacekeeping* 25, no. 4 (2018): 554–577; Lisa A. Aronsson, *NATO Partnerships for Women, Peace and Security* (Washington, DC: Atlantic Council, 2021).)

14.   For example, True and Wiener describe NATO as one of the "early adopters and implementers of WPS." See Jacqui True and Antje Wiener, "Everyone Wants (a) Peace: The Dynamics of Rhetoric and Practice on 'Women, Peace and Security,'" *International Affairs* 95, no. 3 (2019): 564. NATO special representatives have traced NATO's gender experience further still to women who served in the alliance of the 1950s. See, for example, Annette Young, "Taking Up Arms: Campaigning for Equality in the Military." *The 51%*, France24, July 9, 2021, https://www.france24.com/en/tv-shows/the-51/20210709 -taking-up-arms-campaigning-for-equality-in-the-military.

15.   The nine NATO documents in our set include 103 mentions of sexual violence, 36 of sexual exploitation and abuse, 23 of human trafficking, and 12 of terrorism and extremism. Many other policy concerns—climate change, disasters, colonialism—receive no or just one reference.

16.   Katharine A. M. Wright, Matthew Hurley, and Jesus Ignacio Gil Ruiz, *NATO, Gender and the Military: Women Organising from Within* (London: Routledge, 2019), 60. Action plans tend to follow on the heels of policies and are in turn made operational in directives. For ecosystem purposes we have captured most of these documents, but not the first action plan, not publicly available but discussed in a report. See appendix 1.

17.   Cynthia Enloe, "NATO's Interest in Women: The Lesson Machine," in *Loaded Questions: Women in the Military*, ed. Wendy Chapkis (Amsterdam: Transnational Institute, 1981), 65–71; Cynthia Enloe, *Does Khaki Become You? The Militarization of Women's Lives* (Boston: South End Press, 1983), 131.

18. Wright, Hurley, and Gil Ruiz, *NATO, Gender and the Military*, 52.

19. Only three NATO member states do not currently have a NAP or prominent WPS pol-
     icy statement: Greece, Hungary, and Turkey.

20. Enloe, "NATO's Interest in Women," 68. Emphasis added.

21. Isaksson, "Integrating Gender Perspectives," 238; Wright, Hurley, and Gil Ruiz, *NATO,
     Gender and the Military*, 51. Today there are thirty member states and twenty partners,
     plus sundry other cooperating states ("partners across the globe" as distinct from the
     "partnership for peace"); the expanded "North Atlantic" alliance stretching as far as
     Colombia, Pakistan, Japan, and New Zealand. At the time of writing the membership
     of Sweden and Finland is all but assured.

22. Isaksson, "Integrating Gender Perspectives," 227; Katharine A. M. Wright, "Telling
     NATO's Story of Afghanistan: Gender and the Alliance's Digital Diplomacy," *Media,
     War & Conflict* 12, no. 1 (2019): 87–101.

23. On WPS, see UN Security Council, S/PV.6877 (November 30, 2012), https://undocs.org
     /en/S/PV.6877; UN Security Council, S/PV.7044 (October 18, 2013), https://undocs
     .org/en/S/PV.7044; UN Security Council, S/PV.7793 (October 25, 2016), https://undocs
     .org/en/S/PV.7793; UN Security Council, S/PV.8382 (October 25, 2018), https://undocs.org
     /en/S/PV.8382; UN Security Council, "Letter Dated 21 July 2020 from the President of
     the Security Council Addressed to the Secretary-General and the Permanent Repre-
     sentatives of the Members of the Security Council," S/2020/727 (July 21, 2020), https://
     undocs.org/S/2020/727. On sexual violence, see UN Security Council, S/PV.8234
     (April 16, 2018), https://undocs.org/en/S/PV.8234; UN Security Council, S/PV.8514
     (April 23, 2019), https://undocs.org/en/S/PV.8514; UN Security Council, "Letter Dated
     16 April 2021 from the President of the Security Council Addressed to the Secretary-
     General and the Permanent Representatives of the Members of the Security Council,"
     S/2021/375 (April 16, 2021), https://undocs.org/en/S/2021/375. The two special represen-
     tatives were Mari Skåre, former permanent representative of Norway to the alliance, and
     Marriët Schuurman, a Dutch diplomat who is now that country's human rights ambas-
     sador. The third special representative was Clare Hutchinson, a British-born Canadian
     citizen, was previously a gender adviser with the United Nations specializing in peace-
     keeping. In November 2021, Irene Fellin, an Italian with experience in the United Nations
     and formerly a senior gender adviser at NATO Headquarters, became the fourth.

24. NATO Committee on Gender Perspectives, *Summary of the National Reports of NATO
     Member and Partner Nations to the NATO Committee on Gender Perspectives 2018*
     (2020), https://www.nato.int/nato_static_fl2014/assets/pdf/2020/7/pdf/200713-2018
     -Summary-NR-to-NCGP.pdf, 65; NATO Committee on Gender Perspectives, *Summary
     of the National Reports of NATO Member and Partner Nations 2014* (Office of the Gen-
     der Advisor, 2016), https://www.nato.int/nato_static_fl2014/assets/pdf/pdf_2016_03
     /Summary.pdf, 18. The figures are taken from the earliest and latest available collations
     of national reports. The 2018 figure is likely significantly higher as six member states,
     including notably the United States, United Kingdom, Denmark, and Norway, failed
     to file their reports. For details on data collection and significant limits, see the dis-
     cussion in Wright, Hurley, and Gil Ruiz, *NATO, Gender and the Military*, 77–78, 123.

25. Helené Lackenbauer and Richard Langlais, eds., *Review of the Practical Implications of UNSCR 1325 for the Conduct of NATO-led Operations and Missions* (Kista: Swedish Defence Research Agency, 2013), 4. See also Louise Olsson, Johan Tejpar, and Johanna Valenius, "Introduction," in *Operational Effectiveness and UN Resolution 1325: Practices and Lessons from Afghanistan*, ed. Louise Olsson and Johan Tejpar (Stockholm: Swedish Defence Research Agency, 2009), 15–18. On how gender advisers negotiate their identity and institutional credibility, see Matthew Hurley, "The 'Genderman': (Re)negotiating Militarized Masculinities When 'Doing Gender' at NATO," *Critical Military Studies* 4, no. 1 (2018): 72–91.

26. See, for example, de Jonge Oudraat et al., *The 1325 Scorecard.*

27. See Marriët Schuurman, "NATO and the Women, Peace and Security Agenda: Time to Bring It Home," *Connections* 14, no. 3 (2015): 1.

28. See Anders Fogh Rasmussen, "Empowering Women in Peace and Security—Speech at the European Commission," NATO, January 27, 2010, https://www.nato.int/cps/en/natohq/opinions_61040.htm; de Jonge Oudraat et al., *The 1325 Scorecard.*; Schuurman, "NATO and the Women, Peace and Security Agenda," 6; Matthew Hurley, "Watermelons and Weddings: Making Women, Peace and Security 'Relevant' at NATO Through (Re)Telling Stories of Success," *Global Society* 32, no. 4 (2018): 436–456; Wright, "Telling NATO's Story."

29. Bastick and Duncanson, "Agents of Change?," 561–562.

30. Louise Olsson and Johan Tejpar, "How to Implement Resolution 1325: The Analysis," in Olsson and Tejpar, *Operational Effectiveness and UN Resolution 1325*, 115–127.

31. Robert Egnell and Mayesha Alam, "Gender and Women in the Military—Setting the Stage," in Egnell and Alam, *Women and Gender Perspectives in the Military*, 8. See also Synne L. Dyvik, "Women as 'Practitioners' and 'Targets': Gender and Counterinsurgency in Afghanistan," *International Feminist Journal of Politics* 16, no. 3 (2014): 410–429; Laleh Khalili, "Gendered Practices of Counterinsurgency," *Review of International Studies* 37, no. 4 (2011): 1471–1491. FETs were first deployed in Afghanistan following the example of "Lioness" teams in Iraq, though the first Human Terrain deployment had been to Afghanistan in 2007. Montgomery McFate and Steve Fondacaro, "Reflections on the Human Terrain System During the First 4 Years," *PRISM* 2, no. 4 (2011): 69.

32. "Integration" and "inclusiveness" are the first two catchwords of recent NATO WPS policy, referring, respectively, to the gender perspective in planning and women's participation at all levels. The third is "integrity," focusing on SEA within the alliance. See, for example, "NATO and the Women, Peace and Security Agenda: A Conversation with Clare Hutchinson," Women in Public Service Project, Wilson Center, June 27, 2018, https://www.wilsoncenter.org/event/nato-and-the-women-peace-and-security-agenda-conversation-clare-hutchinson.

33. Swanee Hunt and Douglas Lute, "Inclusive Security: NATO Adapts and Adopts," *PRISM* 6, no. 1 (2016): 13. See also Clare Hutchinson, "Statement at the United Nations Security Council Open Debate on Women, Peace and Security," NATO, October 25, 2018, https://www.nato.int/cps/en/natohq/opinions_159803.htm.

34. Wright, Hurley, and Gil Ruiz, *NATO, Gender and the Military*, 55.

35. David Kilcullen, "Twenty-Eight Articles: Fundamentals of Company-Level Counter-insurgency," *Military Review*, May–June 2006, 137. See also Dyvik, "Women as 'Practitioners.'"

36. Hannah Partis-Jennings, "The 'Third Gender' in Afghanistan: A Feminist Account of Hybridity as a Gendered Experience," *Peacebuilding* 7, no. 2 (2019): 178–193.

37. Sippi Azarbaijani-Moghaddam, "Seeking Out Their Afghan Sisters: Female Engagement Teams in Afghanistan" (Working Paper no. 1, Chr. Michelsen Institute, 2014), https://www.cmi.no/publications/5096-seeking-out-their-afghan-sisters.

38. Azarbaijani-Moghaddam, "Seeking Out Their Afghan Sisters," 10.

39. Azarbaijani-Moghaddam, 14.

40. Azarbaijani-Moghaddam, 4.

41. Olsson, Tejpar, and Valenius, "Introduction," 16.

42. David H. Ucko and Robert Egnell, *Counterinsurgency in Crisis: Britain and the Challenges of Modern Warfare* (New York: Columbia University Press, 2015), 21. On the euphemism of the "small war," see Tarak Barkawi, "On the Pedagogy of 'Small Wars,'" *International Affairs* 80, no. 1 (2004): 19–37.

43. Robert Egnell, "Gender Perspectives and Fighting," *Parameters* 43, no. 2 (2013): 33–41.

44. Egnell, "Gender Perspectives and Fighting," 39–40.

45. Robert Egnell, "Gender Perspectives and Military Effectiveness: Implementing UNSCR 1325 and the National Action Plan on Women, Peace, and Security," *PRISM* 6, no. 1 (2016): 74.

46. Lawrence of Arabia, cited in Egnell, "Gender Perspectives and Fighting," 37.

47. United States Department of the Army, *FM 3-24: Counterinsurgency* (Washington, DC: Department of the Army, 2006), 1. See also Khalili, "Gendered Practices." This much-quoted line was itself a quote, from an unnamed special forces officer in Iraq, and was chosen to open the first chapter of the field manual, though not in subsequent editions.

48. Clare Hutchinson, "NATO Statement at the United Nations Security Council Open Debate on Women, Peace and Security," NATO, October 20, 2020, https://www.nato.int/cps/en/natohq/opinions_179287.htm.

49. Hunt and Lute, "Inclusive Security," 9.

50. Bastick and Duncanson, "Agents of Change?," 557.

51. Marriët Schuurman, "The Women, Peace and Security Agenda: Integrating a Gendered Perspective Into Security Operations," *Fletcher Forum of World Affairs* 41, no. 1 (2017): 104.

52. Michael Miklaucic and Cathleen Pearl, "All the Elements of National Power," *PRISM* 6, no. 1 (2016): 2–5. The line is taken from the introduction to the special issue on "Women, Peace and Inclusive Security" of the U.S. National Defense University's in-house journal, *PRISM*, leading with a paper coauthored by Swanee Hunt, a significant personality in the 1325 origin story as founder of the Institute for Inclusive Security. The rationale for a special issue on 1325 was unabashedly geopolitical, bemoaning that the United States does not draw on the full talent of women, but that "our adversaries, including Boko Haram and ISIS, do not make the same mistake." See Miklaucic and

Pearl, "All the Elements," 2. See also the claim that "This is not political correctness; this is being prepared for the future." Miklaucic and Pearl, "All the Elements," 4.

53. See, for example, Egnell, "Gender Perspectives," 82.

54. Egnell has often objected to a "zero-sum" calculus that would force a choice between feminism and "traditional military values." See Egnell, "Gender Perspectives," 75. See also Egnell, "Gender Perspectives and Fighting," 38; Egnell and Alam, "Gender and Women in the Military," 8. There are voices of dissent, including those who characterize NATO's gender work as insufficiently linked to "kinetics"—deciding who should be killed and when. See Prescott, "NATO Gender Mainstreaming." On this account, gender advisers should operate at a higher and more integrated level of command to drive "demand" by demonstrating the utility of gender for psychological warfare, special operations, and "dynamic targeting." Prescott, "NATO Gender Mainstreaming," 59–61. For an insight into how gender already figures into targeting, see Khalili, "Gendered Practices."

55. See Wazhma Frogh, "Afghanistan's National Action Plan: 'A Wishlist of Many Dreams,'" *Women, Peace and Security Working Paper Series*, no. 10 (Centre for Women Peace and Security, London School of Economics and Political Science, 2017), https://www.lse.ac.uk/women-peace-security/assets/documents/2017/wps10Frogh.pdf, 9.

56. Isaksson, "Integrating Gender Perspectives."

57. Bastick and Duncanson, "Agents of Change?," 567.

58. Clare Hutchinson, "Statement at the UN Security Council's Open Debate on Sexual Violence in Conflict," NATO, April 14, 2021, https://www.nato.int/cps/en/natohq/opinions_183216.htm.

59. See also North Atlantic Military Committee, *Military Guidelines on the Prevention of, and Response to, Conflict-Related Sexual and Gender-Based Violence* (MCM-0009-2015, 2015), https://www.nato.int/issues/women_nato/2015/mcm-0009-2015_eng_pdp.pdf.

60. See Egnell, "Gender Perspectives," 76.

61. For discussion and examples, see Wright, Hurley, and Gil Ruiz, *NATO, Gender and the Military.*

62. On the latter, see Patricia Owens, *Economy of Force: Counterinsurgency and the Historical Rise of the Social* (Cambridge: Cambridge University Press, 2015).

63. Rachel Grimes, "Exclusive Interview with UNSCR 1325 as She Turns 19," *NATO Review*, October 31, 2019, https://www.nato.int/docu/review/articles/2019/10/31/exclusive-interview-with-unscr-1325-as-she-turns-19/index.html.

64. Magdalena Howland, "Harnessing the Power of Women in NATO: An Intersectional Feminist Perspective on UNSCR 1325," in *Women, Peace and Transforming Security: Visions of the Future of Women, Peace and Security for NATO*, ed. Office of the NATO Secretary General's Special Representative for Women, Peace and Security (2020), https://www.nato.int/nato_static_fl2014/assets/pdf/2020/10/pdf/201110-wps-essay-transforming-security-e.pdf, 19–20.

65. See Mari Skåre, "Having a Gender Perspective Matters in Defence and Security," *Diplomatic Courier*, July–August 2013, https://www.diplomaticourier.com/posts/having-a-gender-perspective-matters-in-defense-and-security-2.

66.   Schuurman, "The Women, Peace and Security Agenda," 110.

67.   Wilson Center, "NATO and the Women, Peace and Security Agenda," 21:02.

68.   Prescott, "NATO Gender Mainstreaming," 60.

69.   Egnell and Alam, "Gender and Women in the Military," 6.

70.   Aronsson, *NATO Partnerships*, 5.

71.   Clare Hutchinson, "Are We There Yet? Implementing the Women, Peace and Security Agenda: If Not Now, When?," *NATO WPS Bulletin*, no. 2 (2020): 3. Emphasis added.

72.   Clare Hemmings, *Why Stories Matter: The Political Grammar of Feminist Theory* (Durham, NC: Duke University Press, 2011).

73.   See Women's International League for Peace and Freedom, *WILPF Manifesto 2015* (Geneva: WILPF, 2015), 3.

74.   Fatma Alloo, "Remarks in 'Forum: The Events of 11 September 2001 and Beyond,'" *International Feminist Journal of Politics* 4, no. 1 (2002): 95–96; Sonali Kolhatkar, "'Saving' Afghan Women," *ZNet*, May 9, 2002, http://www.rawa.org/znet.htm; Nira Yuval-Davis, "Remarks in 'Forum: The Events of 11 September 2001 and Beyond," *International Feminist Journal of Politics* 4, no. 1 (2002): 99–103.

75.   Cynthia Cockburn, "Women Against NATO—Making a Feminist Case," *War Resisters' International*, September 20, 2010, https://wri-irg.org/en/story/2010/women-against-nato-making-feminist-case. See also "Snagged on the Contradiction: NATO, Resolution 1325, and Feminist Responses." *Women in Action* (2012): 48–57.

76.   "WILPF Statement Opposing NATO's Military and Nuclear Policies," Women's International League for Peace and Freedom, November 24, 2008, https://wilpf.org/wilpf_statements/wilpf-statement-opposing-natos-military-and-nuclear-policies/.

77.   Cynthia Cockburn, *Anti-militarism: Political and Gender Dynamics of Peace Movements* (Basingstoke, UK: Palgrave Macmillan, 2012), 136. The joint "No to War—No to NATO" statement—to which WILPF was party—was stronger still: "Our goal is to dissolve and dismantle NATO." See "The Strasbourg Declaration,' International Coordinating Committee, April 4, 2009, https://www.no-to-nato.org/2013/03/strasbourg-declaration/.

78.   Women's International League for Peace and Freedom, *The Nuclear Weapon Ban Treaty: A Resource Guide for WILPF* (Geneva: WILPF, 2018), 11.

79.   WILPF, *WILPF Manifesto 2015*, 5.

80.   "Disarmament," Women's International League for Peace and Freedom, accessed September 5, 2023, https://www.wilpf.org/global-programmes/disarmament/.

81.   WILPF, *Congress Report 2018*, 60–61.

82.   Women's International League for Peace and Freedom, *Congress Report 2015* (Geneva: WILPF, 2016), 41. See also "WILPF Resolutions, 21st Congress, Connecticut, USA, 1980," Women's International League for Peace and Freedom, 1980, https://www.wilpf.org/wp-content/uploads/2015/10/WILPF_triennial_congress_1980.pdf; "WILPF Resolutions, 22nd Congress, Gothenburg, Sweden, 1983," Women's International League for Peace and Freedom, 1983, https://www.wilpf.org/wp-content/uploads/2012/09/WILPF_triennial_congress_1983.pdf; Cynthia Cockburn, "Making Women's Opposition

Visible to NATO," *openDemocracy*, October 18, 2010, https://www.opendemocracy.net
/en/5050/making-womens-opposition-visible-to-nato/.

83. Madeleine Rees, "Open Letter to the UN Security Council," Women's International
League for Peace and Freedom, January 28, 2022, https://www.wilpf.org/war-over
-ukraine-militarism-is-killing-us-all/. The letter named NATO and the United States
but made no explicit reference to Russia. Though Rees charged co-optation, others have
noted the lack of WPS language. See Katharine A. M. Wright, "Where Is Women, Peace
and Security? NATO's Response to the Russia-Ukraine War," *European Journal of Politics and Gender* 5, no. 2 (2022): 275–277.

84. WILPF Sweden and WILPF Finland, "Sweden's and Finland's NATO Membership
Poses Great Risks," Women's International League for Peace and Freedom, May 16,
2022, https://www.wilpf.org/swedens-and-finlands-nato-membership-poses-great
-risks/. Though we cannot do justice to the dispute here, compare with the defense of
resistance, armed and unarmed, in the Ukrainian feminist–led "The Right to Resist:
A Feminist Manifesto," *Commons*, July 7, 2022, https://commons.com.ua/en/right-resist
-feminist-manifesto/.

85. "WILPF Resolutions, 18th Congress, New Delhi, India, December 1970–January 1971,"
Women's International League for Peace and Freedom, 1971, https://www.wilpf.org/wp
-content/uploads/2012/08/WILPF_triennial_congress_1971.pdf; Catia Cecilia Confortini, *Intelligent Compassion: Feminist Critical Methodology in the Women's International League for Peace and Freedom* (Oxford: Oxford University Press, 2012), 72–75.

86. See, for example, *WILPF Manifesto 2015*, 1, 10, 12.

87. NATO Committee on Gender Perspectives, *Summary of the National Reports of NATO
Member and Partner Nations to the NATO Committee on Gender Perspectives 2018*, 9.

88. Women's International League for Peace and Freedom, *UNSCR 1325 at 20 Years: Perspectives from Feminist Peace Activists and Civil Society* (Geneva: WILPF, 2020),
17–18.

89. Sarah Kenny Werner and Elena B. Stavrevska. *Where Are the Words? The Disappear-
ance of the Women, Peace and Security Agenda in the Language of Country-Specific UN
Security Council Resolutions* (London: Women's International League for Peace and
Freedom and LSE Centre for Women, Peace and Security, 2020).

90. The scorecard evaluates WPS commitments by the P5 states across several categories,
which are aggregated into an annual percentage score. As the PeaceWomen project
explains, "International actions addressed include the following: WPS-related statements and commitments at the Security Council, international gender and human
rights commitments and peacekeeping action. National action addressed are the following: financing of military versus gender equality, women's participation in parliament and judiciary, levels of sexual violence, and gendered post-conflict stabilisation
programmes." "WPS Scorecard: Implementation of the Women, Peace and Security
Agenda by the UN Security Council Permanent Members," PeaceWomen, accessed September 6, 2023, http://peacewomen.org/scorecards.

91. Women's International League for Peace and Freedom, *The Nuclear Weapon Ban
Treaty*, 13.

92. See, for example, Women's International League for Peace and Freedom, *WILPF Congress: Resolutions and Proposals 1919*, 2nd ed. (Geneva: WILPF, 2019), 5; Women's International League for Peace and Freedom, *WILPF International Programme 2018–2021* (Geneva: WILPF, 2018), 11.

93. This campaign is not to be confused with another under the same initials, the International Civil Society Action Network, which was active in the WPS space and was founded around the same time.

94. Treaty on the Prohibition of Nuclear Weapons, CN.476.2017.TREATIES-XXVI-9 (July 7, 2017) [certified true copy], https://documents-dds-ny.un.org/doc/UNDOC/GEN/N17/209/73/PDF/N1720973.pdf?OpenElement; Women's International League for Peace and Freedom, *The Nuclear Weapon Ban Treaty*.

95. Jennifer Nordstrom and Felicity Hill, "A Gender Perspective," in *Nuclear Disorder of Cooperative Security? U.S. Weapons of Terror, the Global Proliferation Crisis, and Paths to Peace: An Assessment of the Final Report of the Weapons of Mass Destruction Commission and Its Implications for U.S. Policy*, ed. Michael Spies and John Burroughs (New York: Lawyers' Committee on Nuclear Policy, 2007), 166.

96. Cockburn, "Making Women's Opposition Visible to NATO."

97. NATO, *NATO 2030: United for a New Era—Analysis and Recommendations of the Reflection Group Appointed by the NATO Secretary General* (November 25, 2020), https://www.nato.int/nato_static_fl2014/assets/pdf/2020/12/pdf/201201-Reflection-Group-Final-Report-Uni.pdf, 37.

98. NATO, *NATO 2030*, 43.

99. For an exception see Ray Acheson, "The Patriarchal Militarism of NATO's Reflection Group," in *Peace Research Perspectives on NATO 2030: A Response to the Official NATO Reflection Group*, ed. NATO Watch (Gairloch, UK: NATO Watch, 2021), 17–24.

100. On norm decay, see Richard Price, "Syria and the Chemical Weapons Taboo," *Journal of Global Security Studies* 4, no. 1 (2019): 37–52.

101. Stéfanie von Hlatky, *Deploying Feminism: The Role of Gender in NATO Military Operations* (Oxford: Oxford University Press, 2022), 3.

102. See, for example, von Hlatky, *Deploying Feminism*, 156.

103. Nicola Pratt, "Reconceptualizing Gender, Reinscribing Racial—Sexual Boundaries in International Security: The Case of UN Security Council Resolution 1325 on 'Women, Peace and Security,'" *International Studies Quarterly* 57, no. 4 (2013): 772–783; Swati Parashar, "The WPS Agenda: A Postcolonial Critique," in *The Oxford Handbook of Women, Peace, and Security*, ed. Sara E. Davies and Jacqui True (Oxford: Oxford University Press, 2019), 829–839; Toni Haastrup and Jamie J. Hagen, "Global Racial Hierarchies and the Limits of Localization via National Action Plans," in *New Directions in Women, Peace and Security*, ed. Soumita Basu, Paul Kirby, and Laura J. Shepherd (Bristol, UK: Bristol University Press, 2020), 133–151; Anna Stavrianakis, "Towards a Postcolonial and Anti-racist Feminist Mode of Weapons Control," in Basu, Kirby, and Shepherd, *New Directions in Women, Peace and Security*, 153–168.

104. Carol Cohn, Helen Kinsella, and Sheri Gibbings, "Women, Peace and Security: Resolution 1325," *International Feminist Journal of Politics* 6, no. 1 (2004): 130–140; Felicity

Hill, Mikele Aboitiz, and Sara Poehlman-Doumbouya, "Nongovernmental Organizations' Role in the Build-Up and Implementation of Security Council Resolution 1325," *Signs: Journal of Women in Culture and Society* 28, no. 4 (2003): 1255–1269; Dianne Otto, "A Sign of 'Weakness?' Disrupting Gender Certainties in the Implementation of Security Council Resolution 1325," *Michigan Journal of Gender and Law* 13, no. 1 (2006–2007): 113–176.

105. Laura J. Shepherd, *Gender, Violence and Security: Discourse as Practice* (London: Zed Books, 2008); Natalie Florea Hudson, *Gender, Human Security and the United Nations: Security Language as a Political Framework for Women* (London: Routledge, 2010).

106. Dianne Otto, "Securing the 'Gender Legitimacy' of the UN Security Council: Prising Gender from Its Historical Moorings," *Legal Studies Research Paper*, no. 92 (2004): 10.

107. See chapter 5, note 75.

108. Iris Marion Young, "The Logic of Masculinist Protection: Reflections on the Current Security State," *Signs: Journal of Women in Culture and Society* 29, no. 1 (2003): 1–25. See also Laura Sjoberg and Jessica Peet, "A(nother) Dark Side of the Protection Racket: Targeting Women in Wars," *International Feminist Journal of Politics* 13, no. 1 (2011): 163–182; Cecelia Åse, "Crisis Narratives and Masculinist Protection: Gendering the Original Stockholm Syndrome," *International Feminist Journal of Politics* 17, no. 4 (2015): 595–610; Laura Sjoberg, "Witnessing the Protection Racket: Rethinking Justice in/of Wars Through Gender Lenses," *International Politics* 53, no. 3 (2016): 361–384.

109. Jean Bethke Elshtain, *Women and War* (Chicago: University of Chicago Press, 1987).

110. Sjoberg and Peet, "A(nother) Dark Side," 172.

111. Young, "The Logic of Masculinist Protection," 2.

112. Chandra Talpade Mohanty, "Under Western Eyes: Feminist Scholarship and Colonial Discourses," *Feminist Review* 30, no. 1 (1988): 63.

113. See, for example, Young, "The Logic of Masculinist Protection"; Zillah Eisenstein, *Sexual Decoys: Gender, Race, and War in Imperial Democracy* (Melbourne, AU: Spinifex, 2007); Robin Riley, Chandra Talpade Mohanty, and Minnie Bruce Pratt, eds., *Feminism and War: Confronting US Imperialism* (London: Zed, 2013).

114. Gayatri Chakravorty Spivak, "Can the Subaltern Speak?," in *Marxist Interpretations of Culture*, ed. Cary Nelson and Lawrence Grossberg (Basingstoke, UK: Macmillan, 1988), 292.

115. Gargi Bhattacharyya, *Dangerous Brown Men: Exploiting Sex, Violence and Feminism in the War on Terror* (London: Zed, 2008).

116. Denise Maia Carter, "(De)constructing Difference: A Qualitative Review of the 'Othering' of UK Muslim Communities, Extremism, Soft Harms, and Twitter Analytics," *Behavioral Sciences of Terrorism and Political Aggression* 9, no. 1 (2017): 21–36; Madeline-Sophie Abbas, "Producing 'Internal Suspect Bodies': Divisive Effects of UK Counter-Terrorism Measures on Muslim Communities in Leeds and Bradford," *British Journal of Sociology* 70, no. 10 (2019): 261–262; Nadya Ali, "Seeing and Unseeing Prevent's Racialized Borders," *Security Dialogue* 51, no. 6 (2020): 579–596; Joel David Taylor, "'Suspect Categories,' Alienation and Counterterrorism: Critically Assessing PREVENT in the UK," *Terrorism and Political Violence* 32, no. 4 (2020): 851–873.

117. Caron E. Gentry, "Epistemological Failures: Everyday Terrorism in the West," *Critical Studies on Terrorism* 8, no. 3 (2015): 363.

118. Young, "The Logic of Masculinist Protection," 20.

119. Vasuki Nesiah, "Feminism as Counter-Terrorism: The Seduction of Power," in *Gender, National Security, and Counter-Terrorism Human Rights Perspectives*, ed. Margaret Satterthwaite and Jayne C. Huckerby (London: Routledge, 2013), 127–151.

120. Negar Razavi, "NatSec Feminism: Women Security Experts and the US Counterterror State," *Signs: Journal of Women in Culture and Society* 46, no. 2 (2021): 361–386.

121. Nesiah, "Feminism as Counter-Terrorism," x.

122. Razavi, "NatSec Feminism," 381.

123. Soumita Basu, "The Global South Writes 1325 (Too)," *International Political Science Review* 37, no. 3 (2016): 362–374.

124. Swati Parashar, "The WPS Agenda: A Postcolonial Critique," in Davies and True, *The Oxford Handbook of Women, Peace, and Security*, 833–834. See also Toni Haastrup and Jamie J. Hagen, "Racial Hierarchies of Knowledge Production in the Women, Peace and Security Agenda," *Critical Studies on Security* 9, no. 1 (2021): 27–30.

125. Basu, "The Global South Writes 1325."

126. Parashar, "The WPS Agenda," 832.

127. Parashar, 832.

128. Basu, "The Global South Writes 1325," 366.

129. Cf. Sheri Lynn Gibbings, "No Angry Women at the United Nations: Political Dreams and the Cultural Politics of United Nations Security Council Resolution 1325," *International Feminist Journal of Politics* 13, no. 4 (2011): 522–538; Sam Cook, "The 'Woman-in-Conflict' at the UN Security Council: A Subject of Practice," *International Affairs* 92, no. 2 (2016): 353–372.

130. Hill, Aboitiz, and Poehlman-Doumbouya, "Nongovernmental Organizations' Role," 1259.

131. Ndeye Sow quoted in Judy El-Bushra, "Feminism, Gender, and Women's Peace Activism," *Development and Change* 38, no. 1 (2007): 138.

132. "From Global Policies to Local Action," Global Network of Women Peacebuilders, accessed September 6, 2023, https://gnwp.org/what-we-do/global-policy-local-action/.

133. O'Sullivan and Krulišová, "Women, Peace and Security in Central Europe."

134. Charmaine Chua, "Against Localization: Rethinking Compliance and Antagonism in Norm Dynamics," in *Against International Relations Norms: Postcolonial Perspectives*, ed. Charlotte Epstein (Abingdon, UK: Routledge, 2017), 87–105.

135. Wright, Hurley, and Gil Ruiz, *NATO, Gender and the Military*, 14.

7. BORDERLANDS OF THE FEMINIST PEACE

1. Jack Donnelly, *International Human Rights*, 4th ed. (Boulder, CO: Westview Press, 2013), 3.

2. Roger Normand and Sarah Zaidi, *Human Rights at the UN: The Political History of Universal Justice* (Bloomington: Indiana University Press, 2008), 35.

3. See, for example, Susan Waltz, "Reclaiming and Rebuilding the History of the Universal Declaration of Human Rights," *Third World Quarterly* 23, no. 3 (2002): 437–448; Tarak Barkawi and Mark Laffey, "The Postcolonial Moment in Security Studies," *Review of International Studies* 32, no. 2 (2006): 329–352.

4. Convention on the Elimination of All Forms of Discrimination against Women, adopted and opened for signature, ratification, and accession by General Assembly resolution 34/180 of December 18, 1979, https://www.ohchr.org/Documents/Profession alInterest/cedaw.pdf, preamble.

5. Catherine O'Rourke and Aisling Swaine, "CEDAW and the Security Council: Enhancing Women's Rights in Conflict," *International and Comparative Law Quarterly* 67, no. 1 (2018): 167–199; Catherine O'Rourke and Aisling Swaine, "WPS and CEDAW, Optional Protocol, and General Recommendations," in *Oxford Handbook on Women, Peace and Security*, ed. Sara E. Davies and Jacqui True (Oxford: Oxford University Press, 2019), 669–679.

6. Interview N, 2019.

7. Niamh Reilly, *Women's Human Rights: Seeking Gender Justice in a Globalizing Age* (Cambridge: Polity, 2009), 3.

8. Donna Sullivan, "Women's Human Rights and the 1993 World Conference on Human Rights," *American Journal of International Law* 88, no. 1 (1994): 152; Jennifer Chan-Tiberghien, "Gender Skepticism or Gender-Boom: Poststructural Feminisms, Transnational Feminisms and the World Conference Against Racism," *International Feminist Journal of Politics* 6, no. 3 (2004): 454–484; Reilly, *Women's Human Rights*.

9. Vienna Declaration and Programme of Action, adopted by the World Conference on Human Rights in Vienna on June 25, 1993, https://www.ohchr.org/sites/default/files /vienna.pdf, art. 18.

10. Catherine Weaver, "The Strategic Social Construction of the World Bank's Gender and Development Policy Norm," in *Owning Development: Creating Policy Norms in the IMF and the World Bank*, ed. Susan Park and Antje Vetterlein (Cambridge: Cambridge University Press, 2010), 77.

11. Sanam Naraghi-Anderlini and Judy El-Bushra, "The Conceptual Framework: Security, Peace, Accountability and Rights," in *Inclusive Security, Sustainable Peace: A Toolkit for Advocacy and Action*, ed. International Alert and Women Waging Peace (London: Hunt Alternatives Fund and International Alert, 2004), 13.

12. Carlota Bustelo, "Reproductive Health and CEDAW," *American University Law Review* 44, no. 4 (1995): 1145–1156; Susanne Zwingel, "How Do Norms Travel? Theorizing International Women's Rights in Transnational Perspective," *International Studies Quarterly* 56, no. 1 (2012): 115–129; Eszter Kismödi et al., "Human Rights Accountability for Maternal Death and Failure to Provide Safe, Legal Abortion: The Significance of Two Ground-Breaking CEDAW Decisions," *Reproductive Health Matters* 20, no. 39 (2012): 31–39.

13. See Jennifer Thomson and Claire Pierson, "Can Abortion Rights Be Integrated Into the Women, Peace and Security Agenda?," *International Feminist Journal of Politics* 20, no. 3 (2018): 350–365.

14. Jutta Joachim, "Framing Issues and Seizing Opportunities: The UN, NGOs, and Women's Rights," *International Studies Quarterly* 47, no. 2 (2003): 268.

15. Sally Baden and Anne Marie Goetz, "Who Needs [Sex] When You Can Have [Gender]? Conflicting Discourses on Gender at Beijing," *Feminist Review* 56 (1997): 3–25; Doris Buss, "Robes, Relics and Rights: The Vatican and the Beijing Conference on Women," *Social & Legal Studies* 7, no. 3 (1998): 339–363; Jill Steans and Vafa Ahmadi, "Negotiating the Politics of Gender and Rights: Some Reflections on the Status of Women's Human Rights at 'Beijing Plus Ten,'" *Global Society* 19, no. 3 (2005): 227–245.

16. Baden and Goetz, "Who Needs [Sex]"; Elisabeth Jay Friedman, "Gendering the Agenda: The Impact of the Transnational Women's Rights Movement at the UN Conferences of the 1990s," *Women's Studies International Forum* 26, no. 4 (2003): 325–326.

17. Buss, "Robes, Relics and Rights," 348. It is profoundly dispiriting to acknowledge that we are now, twenty-five years later, having this same argument again, this time with other feminists who support the position outlined by the conservative coalition two and a half decades ago.

18. See Steans and Ahmadi, "Negotiating the Politics of Gender," 241–242.

19. UN Security Council, S/PV.7704 (June 2, 2016), https://undocs.org/en/S/PV.7704, 9.

20. United Nations, Rome Statute of the International Criminal Court, Volume 2187, 1–38544 (1998), https://treaties.un.org/doc/Treaties/1998/07/19980717%2006-33%20 p.m./volume-2187-I-38544-English.pdf, art. 7g.

21. See, for example, UN Security Council, *Report of the Secretary-General on Women, Peace and Security*, S/2007/567 (September 12, 2007), para. 31; UN Security Council, S/PV.7704, 9.

22. UN General Assembly/UN Security Council, *Sexual Violence in Conflict: Report of the Secretary-General*, A/67/792–S/2013/149 (March 14, 2013), https://undocs.org/A/67/792, para. 113.

23. For a thorough discussion, see Rosemary Grey, "Conflicting Interpretations of 'Sexual Violence' in the International Criminal Court," *Australian Feminist Studies* 29, no. 81 (2014): 273–288; Rosemary Grey, *Prosecuting Sexual and Gender-Based Crimes at the International Criminal Court: Practice, Progress and Potential* (Cambridge: Cambridge University Press, 2019); Felix Mukwiza Ndahinda, "The Bemba-Banyamulenge Case Before the ICC: From Individual to Collective Criminal Responsibility," *International Journal of Transitional Justice* 7, no. 3 (2013): 476–496; Jonneke Koomen, "WPS and the International Criminal Court," in *The Oxford Handbook of Women, Peace and Security*, ed. Sara E. Davies and Jacqui True (Oxford: Oxford University Press, 2019), 351–363; Nora Karsten, "Distinguishing Military and Non-military Superiors: Reflections on the Bemba Case at the ICC," *Journal of International Criminal Justice* 7, no. 5 (2009): 983–1004.

24. Sahla Aroussi, "'Women, Peace and Security': Addressing Accountability for Wartime Sexual Violence," *International Feminist Journal of Politics* 13, no. 4 (2011): 587–590.

25. For a brief but excellent overview, see Hilary Charlesworth, "Not Waving but Drowning: Gender Mainstreaming and Human Rights in the United Nations," *Harvard Human Rights Journal* 18 (2005): 1–18.

26. The literature on this is extensive, but see, among many equally excellent others, Fionnuala Ní Aoláin and Michael Hamilton, "Gender and the Rule of Law in Transitional Societies," *Minnesota Journal of International Law* 18, no. 2 (2009): 380–402; Christine Bell and Catherine O'Rourke, "Peace Agreements or Pieces of Paper? The Impact of UNSC Resolution 1325 on Peace Processes and their Agreements," *International and Comparative Law Quarterly* 59, no. 4 (2010): 941–980; Khanyisela Moyo, "Feminism, Postcolonial Legal Theory and Transitional Justice: A Critique of Current Trends," *International Human Rights Law Review* 1 (2012): 237–275; Mayesha Alam, *Women and Transitional Justice: Progress and Persistent Challenges in Retributive and Restorative Processes* (Basingstoke, UK: Palgrave Macmillan, 2014); Madeleine Rees and Christine Chinkin, "Exposing the Gendered Myth of Post-conflict Transition: The Transformative Power of Economic and Social Rights," *New York University Journal of International Law & Politics* 48, no. 4 (2016): 1211–1226.

27. Although we recognize that the Trump administration was something of an outlier in U.S. politics across the board, U.S. positioning vis-à-vis sexual and reproductive health rights is heavily partisan even in more normal times, and the country has a long history of exporting dangerous antiabortion policies. These include what is known as the "Mexico City policy" or the "global gag rule," which prevents global health organizations that receive U.S. funding from performing, or counseling pregnant people on the possibility of, abortions. It has been enacted by every Republican administration since Reagan held the presidency in 1984 and repealed by every Democratic president since. This and other measures have contributed to millions of unsafe abortions in low- and middle-income countries, leading to thousands of preventable maternal deaths each year. See Zosia Kmietowicz, "Abortion: US 'Global Gag Rule' Is Killing Women and Girls, Says Report," *BMJ* 365 (2019): l4118, https://doi.org/10.1136/bmj.l4118.

28. UN Security Council, *Conflict-Related Sexual Violence: Report of the Secretary-General*, S/2019/280 (March 29, 2019), https://undocs.org/S/2019/280, para. 19.

29. Jamie J. Hagen, "Queering Women, Peace and Security in Colombia," *Critical Studies on Security* 5, no. 1 (2017): 125–129; Jamie J. Hagen, "Queering Women, Peace and Security," *International Affairs* 92, no. 2 (2016): 313–332.

30. Rahul Rao, "The State of 'Queer IR,'" *GLQ: A Journal of Lesbian and Gay Studies* 24, no. 1 (2018): 147.

31. Cynthia Cockburn, *From Where We Stand: War, Women's Activism and Feminist Analysis* (London: Zed Books, 2007), 141. See also Sanam Naraghi Anderlini, *Women Building Peace: What They Do, Why It Matters* (Boulder, CO: Lynne Rienner, 2007); Sanam Naraghi Anderlini, "Civil Society's Leadership in Adopting 1325 Resolution," in Davies and True, *The Oxford Handbook of Women, Peace and Security*, 38–52; Annika Björkdahl and Johanna Mannergren Selimovic, "WPS and Civil Society," in Davies and True, *The Oxford Handbook of Women, Peace and Security*, 428–438.

32. It is perhaps worth noting that, within our ecosystem, the 2005 Council of the European Union document on implementing resolution 1325 (EU Policy I 2005) makes reference to "human rights defenders," although these are not defined as women either

in the document itself or in the EU Guidelines on Human Rights Defenders that the document references.

33.   UN Security Council, S/PV.5916 (June 19, 2008), https://undocs.org/en/S/PV.5916, 10.

34.   UN Security Council, S/PV.6196 (October 5, 2009), https://undocs.org/en/S/PV.6196, 6–7.

35.   UN Security Council, S/PV.6302 (April 27, 2010), https://undocs.org/en/S/PV .6302, 8.

36.   UN Security Council, *Report of the Secretary-General on Women, Peace and Security*, S/2011/598 (September 29, 2011), https://undocs.org/S/2011/598, 6.

37.   UN Security Council, *Report of the Secretary-General on Women, Peace and Security*, S/2015/716 (September 16, 2015), https://undocs.org/S/2015/716, para. 143.

38.   Interviewee F (civil society actor), 2014.

39.   Interviewee G, 2019.

40.   Gema Fernández Rodríguez de Liévana and Christine Chinkin, "Human Trafficking, Human Rights, and Women, Peace and Security: The Sound of Silence," in *New Directions in Women, Peace and Security*, ed. Soumita Basu, Paul Kirby, and Laura J. Shepherd (Bristol, UK: Bristol University Press, 2020), 193.

41.   "Resolutions Adopted by the International Congress of Women at the Hauge, May 1, 1915," in *Women at The Hague: The International Congress of Women and Its Results*, ed. Jane Addams, Emily G. Balch, and Alice Hamilton (Urbana: University of Illinois Press, 2003), 75. See also Harriet Hyman Alonso, "Introduction," in Addams, Balch, and Hamilton, *Women at The Hague*, xix.

42.   Jane Addams, "Women and Internationalism," in Addams, Balch, and Hamilton, *Women at The Hague*, 65.

43.   See, for example, Dianne Otto, "Women, Peace and Security: A Critical Analysis of the Security Council's Vision," *Women, Peace and Security Working Paper Series*, no. 1 (Centre for Women, Peace and Security, London School of Economics and Political Sciences, 2016), http://eprints.lse.ac.uk/69472/1/Otto_Women_peace_and_security_a _critical_analysis_WP1_2016.pdf.

44.   See Aiko Holvikivi, "What Role for the Security Sector? An SSR Approach to Implementing the Women, Peace and Security Agenda," *Connections* 14, no. 3 (2015): 31–44.

45.   Cora Weiss, then president of the Hague Appeal for Peace, made a speech in 2011 noting that efforts to eliminate conflict-related sexualized violence must not be motivated by a wish to "make war safe for women." Cora Weiss, "We Must Not Make War Safe for Women," *50:50 Inclusive Democracy*, May 24, 2011, https://www.opendemocracy.net /5050/cora-weiss/we-must-not-make-war-safe-for-women. This sentiment is often taken to represent or encapsulate WPS politics—the idea "that UNSCR 1325 and subsequent resolutions should not legitimise or normalise war, but rather the agenda should support the demilitarisation of society and facilitate the development of anti-militarist peace agenda." Laura J. Shepherd, "Making War Safe for Women? National Action Plans and the Militarisation of the Women, Peace and Security Agenda," *International Political Science Review* 37, no. 3 (2016): 332. Casting women in the role of heroine, however,

played against the pantomime villain of war, feeds a willful ignorance of the violence that is often perpetrated or condoned in the name of WPS and the extent to which feminisms and feminists have been complicit in such harm. See Swati Parashar, "Foreword: Waging the War on Wars: Feminist Ways Forward," in *Feminist Solutions for Ending War*, ed. Megan MacKenzie and Nicole Wegner (London: Pluto, 2021), xii–xvii; Swati Parashar, "The WPS Agenda: A Postcolonial Critique," in Davies and True, *The Oxford Handbook of Women, Peace, and Security*, 829–839.

46. On the history of ATT negotiations, see Brian Wood and Rasha Abdul-Rahim, "The Birth and the Heart of the Arms Trade Treaty," *Sur—International Journal on Human Rights* 22 (2015): 15–30; Ray Acheson and Maria Butler, "WPS and Arms Trade Treaty," in Davies and True, *The Oxford Handbook of Women, Peace and Security*, 690–703; Jessica Sutton, "Gender-Based Violence and the Arms Trade Treaty: Article 7(4) Under Fire," *New Zealand Journal of Public and International Law* 18, no. 1 (2020): 49–104.

47. United Nations, The Arms Trade Treaty (December 24, 2014), https://unoda-web.s3 -accelerate.amazonaws.com/wp-content/uploads/2013/06/English7.pdf, art 5(3).

48. Gender-based violence is also relevant to article 6, which bars transfer that would violate Security Council embargoes or where an exporter has "knowledge at the time of authorization" that the arms would be used in the commission of genocide, crimes against humanity, war crimes, or other breaches of the Geneva Conventions, each of which may have a gendered component. Though some have interpreted the separate article on gender as marginalizing harms against women, the precedent on treating gender-based violence as itself a violation of human rights and humanitarian law can be read as underscoring the permanent relevance of gender to export decisions. See, for example, Wood and Abdul-Rahim, "The Birth and the Heart," 22; Government of Ireland, "Working Paper Presented by Ireland to the Conference of State Parties to the Arms Trade Treaty: Article 7(4) and Gender-Based Violence Assessment," ATT/ CSP3/2017/IRL/183/Conf.WP (September 4, 2017), 2.

49. Sutton, "Gender-Based Violence," 64.

50. ATT Monitor, *ATT Monitor 2019* (New York: Control Arms, 2019), 23; Greenpeace Germany, *Exporting Violence and Inequality: The Link Between German Arms Exports and Gender-Based Violence* (Hamburg, DE: Centre for Feminist Foreign Policy on behalf of Greenpeace, 2020), 7.

51. ATT Monitor, *ATT Monitor 2019*, 31; Gender Action for Peace and Security UK, *Putting Women's Rights Into the Arms Trade Treaty* (London: GAPS, 2012), 12; Government of Ireland, "Working Paper," 4.

52. There are guidelines to assist. See ATT Monitor, *ATT Monitor 2019*, 26–35.

53. Caroline Green et al., "Gender-Based Violence and the Arms Trade Treaty: Reflections from a Campaigning and Legal Perspective," *Gender & Development* 21, no. 3 (2013): 553.

54. ATT Monitor, *ATT Monitor 2019*, 21.

55. See ATT Monitor, 19. Latvia was the conference president and noted its focus on GBV in its subsequent NAP on WPS (Latvia NAP I 2020, 5).

56. See, for example, Government of Ireland, "Working Paper," 5; Henri Myrttinen, *Connecting the Dots: Arms Control, Disarmament and the Women, Peace and Security Agenda* (Geneva: United Nations Institute for Disarmament Research, 2020).

57. Emile LeBrun, *Gender-Sensitive Ammunition Management Processes: Considerations for National Authorities* (New York: United Nations Office for Disarmament Affairs, 2021).

58. See, for example, Greenpeace Germany, *Exporting Violence*, 10.

59. ATT Monitor, *ATT Monitor 2019*, 28.

60. On overriding risk, see Sutton, "Gender-Based Violence," 61–63, 71; Wood and Abdul-Rahim, "The Birth and the Heart," 23. On reasonable foresight, see Women's International League for Peace and Freedom et al., "The Arms Trade Treaty: Security Women's Rights and Gender Equality—A United Call to Explicitly Include Gender-Based Violence in the Criteria," June 2012, https://www.peacewomen.org/assets/file/PWPublications/WILPF/joint_policy_paper_on_gender_and_the_arms_trade_treatyjunejuly2012.pdf, 4.

61. Women's International League for Peace and Freedom et al., "The Arms Trade Treaty"; Ray Acheson, "Starting Somewhere: The Arms Trade Treaty, Human Rights and Gender-Based Violence," *Human Rights Defender* 22, no. 2 (2013): 17–19; Sutton, "Gender-Based Violence," 56n60; Wood and Abdul-Rahim, "The Birth and the Heart," 26; GAPS UK, *Putting Women's Rights*, 1; Duncan Green and Anna Macdonald, "Power and Change: The Arms Trade Treaty," Oxfam Active Citizenship Case Study (January 2015), https://policy-practice.oxfam.org/resources/power-and-change-the-arms-trade-treaty-338471/. Amnesty and WILPF had also been members of the NGO Working Group on WPS. See chapter 4, pp. 94.

62. Sutton, "Gender-Based Violence," 59.

63. See Wood and Abdul-Rahim, "The Birth and the Heart," 16. See also chapter 4.

64. Beijing Declaration and Platform for Action, adopted at the 16th Plenary Meeting of the Fourth World Conference on Women, September 15, 1995, https://www.un.org/womenwatch/daw/beijing/pdf/BDPfA%20E.pdf, Strategic Objective E.2.

65. Economic and Social Council, *Commission on the Status of Women Report on the 57th Session*, E/2013/27 (March 4–15, 2013), https://undocs.org/E/2013/27, 5.

66. Formally, "women, disarmament, non-proliferation and arms control": A/RES/65/69 (2011), A/RES/67/48 (2013), A/RES/68/33 (2013), A/RES/69/61 (2014), A/RES/71/56 (2016). These are in addition to other General Assembly resolutions on the ATT that do not explicitly foreground gender—for example, A/RES/61/89 (2006), the first appeal for a treaty, and later examples such as A/RES/67/234 (2013).

67. Acheson and Butler, "WPS and Arms Trade Treaty," 691.

68. See Myrttinen, *Connecting the Dots*, 16.

69. Commission on the Status of Women, *Results of the Fifty-First, Fifty-Second and Fifty-Third Sessions of the Committee on the Elimination of Discrimination Against Women*, E.CN.6.2013.CRP.1 (December 3, 2012), https://www2.ohchr.org/english/bodies/cedaw/docs/E.CN.6.2013.CRP.1_en.pdf.

70. Committee on the Elimination of Discrimination Against Women, *General Recommen-dation No. 35 on Gender-Based Violence Against Women, Updating General Recom-mendation No. 19*, CEDAW/C/GC/35 (July 14, 2017), https://digitallibrary.un.org/record /1305057?ln=en, 14.

71. The three countries were Sweden, France, and Germany, though only in the case of Ger-many was the admonition explicitly put in WPS terms. Committee on the Elimination of Discrimination Against Women, *Concluding Observations on the Combined Eighth and Ninth Periodic Reports of Sweden*, CEDAW/C/SWE/CO/8–9 (March 10, 2016), https://undocs.org/en/CEDAW/C/SWE/CO/8–9, 7–8; Committee on the Elimination of Discrimination Against Women, *Concluding Observations on the Combined Seventh and Eighth Periodic Reports of France*, CEDAW/C/FRA/CO/7–8 (July 25, 2016), https:// undocs.org/en/CEDAW/C/FRA/CO/7–8, 9; Committee on the Elimination of Discrim-ination Against Women, *Concluding Observations on the Combined Seventh and Eighth Periodic Reports of Germany*, CEDAW/C/DEU/CO/7–8 (March 9, 2016), https://undocs.org/en/CEDAW/C/DEU/CO/7–8, 10. See also Acheson and Butler, "WPS and Arms Trade Treaty," 694.

72. CEDAW, preamble.

73. "Summary Analysis of the Arms Trade Treaty," Control Arms (May 2013), https://www .saferworld.org.uk/downloads/pubdocs/Control-Arms-Arms-Trade-Treaty-analysis .pdf, 1.

74. Jody Williams, "Women, Weapons, Peace and Security," *Sur—International Journal on Human Rights* 22 (2015): 31–38; ATT Monitor, *ATT Monitor 2019*, 35.

75. Wood and Abdul-Rahim, "The Birth and the Heart," 24.

76. See, for example, ATT Monitor, *ATT Monitor 2019*, 10.

77. Data on state parties to the ATT as of December 2, 2022, is available on the website dedicated to the Arms Trade Treaty at http://thearmstradetreaty.org. Many of the forty-five state parties without a NAP are microstates—for example, Antigua and Barbuda, Liechtenstein, Panama, Palau, San Marino, and Tuvalu. Twenty-six states with NAPs within our time frame are not parties to the ATT.

78. Shavana Musa, "The Saudi-Led Coalition in Yemen, Arms Exports and Human Rights: Prevention Is Better than Cure," *Journal of Conflict and Security Law* 22, no. 3 (2017): 433–462.

79. For example, in addition to article 7, the preamble states the following: "*Bearing in mind that civilians, particularly women and children, account for the vast majority of those adversely affected by armed conflict and armed violence.*" Arms Trade Treaty, 1. Empha-sis in original.

80. See, for example, Acheson, "Starting Somewhere." For an exception, see Sarah Mas-ters, "The Arms Trade Treaty: Why Women?," *openDemocracy*, May 19, 2011, https:// www.opendemocracy.net/en/arms-trade-treaty-why-women/.

81. See Women's International League for Peace and Freedom et al., "The Arms Trade Treaty," 2.

82. Acheson and Butler, "WPS and Arms Trade Treaty," 690.

83. See also Greenpeace Germany, *Exporting Violence*, 6, 15; Government of Ireland, "Working Paper," 2; Myrttinen, *Connecting the Dots*, 4.

84. See, for example, Williams, *Women, Weapons*; Green and Macdonald, "Power and Change,"

85. Wood and Abdul-Rahim, "The Birth and the Heart," 20; Gender Action for Peace and Security UK, *Putting Women's Rights*, 2–4.

86. ATT Monitor, *ATT Monitor 2019*, 27.

87. For example, Gender Action for Peace and Security UK, *Putting Women's Rights*, 12, 14; Myrttinen, *Connecting the Dots*.

88. In the days before the ATT, policy connections between WPS and small arms and light weapons control were similarly identified as a "missing link." See Cynthia Dehesa and Sarah Masters, *Joined-Up Thinking: International Measures for Women's Security and SALW Control* (London: International Action Network on Small Arms Women's Network, 2010).

89. WPS has latterly served as a model for how the ATT might be strengthened, especially through the Security Council. Sutton, "Gender-Based Violence," 95–97.

90. Beijing Declaration and Platform for Action, art. 28

91. United Nations, United Nations Charter (1945), https://www.un.org/en/about-us/un-charter/full-text, art. 47.

92. Srdjan Vucetic, "A Nation of Feminist Arms Dealers? Canada and Military Exports," *International Journal: Canada's Journal of Global Policy Analysis* 72, no. 4 (2017): 503–519.

93. In addition to the resources expended on NAPs, stand-alone initiatives, and earmarked foreign aid, see the list of contributors to such pools as the Women's Peace and Humanitarian Fund.

94. Small arms only: Japan NAP I 2015, 19; Japan NAP II 2019, 23; Philippines NAP I 2010, 12; Switzerland NAP III 2013, 18. More expansive (if only by not restricting to SALW) were Belgium NAP II 2013, 20; Finland NAP III 2018, 32–33; France NAP II 2015, 23; Ireland NAP III 2019, 31, 37; Latvia NAP I 2020, 5; Luxembourg NAP I 2018, 35; and Norway NAP IV 2019, 43. Denmark NAP III 2014 is somewhat ambiguous as it refers to the gender provision but only explicitly mentions small arms. Italy NAP II 2014, 10, merely welcomes adoption, while Poland NAP I 2018, 13, merely cites it. Outside of our time frame, the fourth Dutch NAP contains multiple expansive references to article 7(4). See NAP 1325 Partnership in the Netherlands 2021.

95. Stockholm International Peace Research Institute, SIPRI Arms Transfers Database, list of top fifty suppliers, generated November 3, 2021, at https://www.sipri.org/databases/armstransfers. The trend-indicator value is a measure of the production costs for a portfolio of weapons. Rather than showing the overall financial value of arms transfers, it instead allows comparisons of the underlying quantity and quality of military hardware. See "Sources and Methods" at https://www.sipri.org/databases/armstransfers/sources-and-methods; Vucetic, "A Nation of Feminist Arms Dealers?," 506–507.

96. There are 686 references to small arms in total against 131 to the wider trade and large weapons in the same period.

97. Myrttinen, *Connecting the Dots*, 54–55.

98. "Domestic Violence and Small Arms," Rutgers Center for Women's Global Leadership and International Action Network on Small Arms Women's Network, accessed September 6, 2023, https://www.wilpf.org/wp-content/uploads/2012/10/Domestic-Violence -Small-Arms.pdf; Gender Action for Peace and Security UK, *Putting Women's Rights*, 5. See also Sutton, "Gender-Based Violence," 54–56; Anna Stavrianakis, "Towards a Postcolonial and Anti-Racist Feminist Mode of Weapons Control," in Basu, Kirby, and Shepherd, *New Directions in Women, Peace and Security*, 153–168.

99. Greenpeace Germany, *Exporting Violence*, 7.

100. Again, see Stavrianakis, "Towards a Postcolonial."

101. See Musa, "The Saudi-Led Coalition"; Afrah Nasser, "Yemen's Women Confront War's Marginalization," *Middle East Report* 289 (2018): 12–15; Royal Courts of Justice, "Judgement: Campaign Against Arms Trade v. The Secretary of State for International Trade," T3/2017/2079 (June 20, 2019). In the former case, the alliance was weakened somewhat on the election of Joe Biden, as arms exports were frozen for a time, and the administration pledged to end the war. Joseph R. Biden, "Why America Must Lead Again: Rescuing U.S. Foreign Policy After Trump," *Foreign Affairs* 99, no. 2 (2020): 72. Congress had sought to use the War Powers Act, never previously invoked in the half century since it was passed in the depths of the Vietnam War, to break with the coalition in early 2019, forcing President Trump to use his veto power. See Danny Postel, "Progressive Surge Propels Turning Point in US Policy on Yemen," *Middle East Report* 289 (2018): 42–47. But within three years a $650-million missile deal had been authorized by the U.S. Senate, eschewing another opportunity to end American maintenance of Saudi warplanes. On the general softening of opposition, see Annelle R. Sheline and Bruce Riedel, "Biden's Broke Promise on Yemen," Brookings Institution, September 16, 2021, https://www.brookings.edu /blog/order-from-chaos/2021/09/16/bidens-broken-promise-on-yemen/.

102. See, for example, UN Human Rights Council, *Situation of Human Rights in Yemen, Including Violations and Abuses Since September 2014: Report of the Group of Eminent International and Regional Experts on Yemen*, A/HRC/48/20 (September 13, 2021), https://undocs.org/A/HRC/48/20, 3–6.

103. See Royal Courts of Justice, "Judgement: Campaign"; David Wearing, "Why Are We in Yemen?," *LRB Blog*, August 29, 2019, https://www.lrb.co.uk/blog/2019/august/why -are-we-in-yemen; European Centre for Constitutional and Human Rights et al., "Made in Europe, Bombed in Yemen: How the ICC Could Tackle the Responsibility of Arms Exporters and Government Officials," European Centre for Constitutional and Human Rights, accessed September 6, 2023, https://www.ecchr.eu/en/case/made-in-europe -bombed-in-yemen/; William Hartung, *Arming Repression: U.S. Military Support for Saudi Arabia, From Trump to Biden* (Washington, DC: Center for International Policy, 2021).

104. United Nations Office for the Coordination of Humanitarian Affairs (UNOCHA), *Global Humanitarian Overview 2021* (2020), https://2021.gho.unocha.org/, 111.

105. UNOCHA, *Global Humanitarian Overview 2022* (2021), https://2022.gho.unocha .org/, 115.

106.   Georgetown Institute for Women, Peace and Security (GIWPS), *Women, Peace and Security Index 2017/18* (Washington, DC: GIWPS, 2017), 22; GIWPS, *Women, Peace and Security Index 2019/20* (Washington, DC: GIWPS, 2019), 14; GIWPS, *Women, Peace and Security Index 2021/22* (Washington, DC: GIWPS, 2021), 2.

107.   Sana'a Center for Strategic Studies, *A Gendered Crisis: Understanding the Experiences of Yemen's War* (Sana'a, YE: Sana'a Center for Strategic Studies, 2019); UN Security Council, S/PV.8079 (October 27, 2017), https://undocs.org/en/S/PV.8079, 22; UN Security Council, S/PV.8234 (April 16, 2018), https://undocs.org/en/S/PV.8234, 24–25.

108.   UN Human Rights Council, *Situation of Human Rights*, 13–14.

109.   Sana'a Center for Strategic Studies, *A Gendered Crisis*, 65.

110.   Oxfam International, *The Gendered Impact of Explosive Weapons Use in Populated Areas in Yemen* (Oxford: Oxfam, 2019), 8.

111.   Cf. UN Security Council, "Letter Dated 18 July 2017 from the Permanent Representatives of Sweden, the United Kingdom of Great Britain and Northern Ireland and Uruguay to the United Nations Addressed to the Secretary-General," S/2017/627 (July 21, 2017), https://undocs.org/S/2017/627, 2–3; UN Security Council, "Letter Dated 17 March 2021 from the Permanent Representatives of Ireland, Mexico and the United Kingdom of Great Britain and Northern Ireland to the United Nations Addressed to the Secretary-General," S/2021/264 (March 17, 2021), https://undocs.org/S/2021/264, 4.

112.   UN Human Rights Council, *Situation of Human Rights*, 17.

113.   See especially Musa, "The Saudi-Led Coalition."

114.   Resolution 2216 followed the start of Operation Decisive Storm, so was not a formal authorization, but its exclusive focus on the Houthis and the political support lent by key P5 members has been understood as implicit acquiescence. See, for example, Luca Ferro and Tom Ruys, "The Saudi-Led Military Intervention in Yemen's Civil War—2015," in *The Use of Force in International Law: A Case-Based Approach*, ed. Tom Ruys, Olivier Corten, and Alexandra Hofer (Oxford: Oxford University Press, 2018), 899–911; Musa, "The Saudi-Led Coalition," 439–440.

115.   The nearest clue is this diagnosis: "The war escalated in March 2015, various types of weapons are used, and it was the last straw when it led to commit grave breaches to international law, causing the largest human-made humanitarian catastrophe." Yemen NAP I 2020, 9.

116.   UN Security Council, Resolution 2140 (2014), S/RES/2140 (February 26, 2014), https://www.undocs.org/S/RES/2140(2014).

117.   UN Security Council, Resolution 2564 (2021), S/RES/2564 (February 25, 2021), https://undocs.org/S/RES/2564(2021).

118.   See, for example, S/2020/487 2020, 21; S/2020/946 2020, 22.

119.   The Yemen Data Project lists 23,627 separate air war incidents, some of which involve several bombing raids, between late March 2015 and the end of September 2021. See "Data," Yemen Data Project, accessed September 6, 2023, http://yemendataproject.org/data.html; UN Human Rights Council, *Situation of Human Rights*, 4.

120.   "Yemen: 85,000 Children May Have Died from Starvation Since Start of War," Save the Children, November 20, 2018, https://www.savethechildren.org/us/about-us/media

-and-news/2018-press-releases/yemen-85000-children-may-have-died-from -starvation. Another study indicates a rise of 50 percent and growing in the child mortality rate in Yemen. See Dlorah Jenkins et al., "Estimating Child Mortality Attributable to War in Yemen," *International Journal of Development Issues* 17, no. 3 (2018): 372–383.

121. See, for example, European Centre for Constitutional and Human Rights et al., "Made in Europe."

122. Martha Mundy and Jeannie Sowers, "The Saudi Coalition's Food War on Yemen: An Interview with Martha Mundy," *Middle East Report* 289 (2018): 8–11; Alex de Waal, "Mass Starvation Is a Crime—It's Time We Treated It That Way," *Boston Review*, January 14, 2019, https://bostonreview.net/articles/alex-de-waal-starvation-crimes/. On starvation by all parties, see Mwatana for Human Rights, *Starvation Makers: The Use of Starvation by Warring Parties in Yemen* (Sana'a, YE: Mwatana for Human Rights, 2021), https://reliefweb.int/report/yemen/starvation-makers-use-starvation-warring -parties-yemen-method-warfare-enar.

123. Oxfam, *The Gendered Impact*.

124. Oxfam, 14–15.

125. UN General Assembly, *Human Rights Impact of Counter-Terrorism and Countering (Violent) Extremism Policies and Practices on the Rights of Women, Girls and the Family*, report of the special rapporteur on the promotion and protection of human rights and fundamental freedoms while countering terrorism, Fionnuala Ní Aoláin, A/ HRC/46/36 (January 22, 2021), https://www.ohchr.org/en/documents/thematic -reports/ahrc4636-human-rights-impact-counter-terrorism-and-countering-violent, para. 28.

126. UN General Assembly, *Human Rights Impact*, para. 6.

127. Anna Stavrianakis, "Legitimising Liberal Militarism: Politics, Law and War in the Arms Trade Treaty," *Third World Quarterly* 37, no. 5 (2016): 840–865.

8. FORGET WPS

1. Commission on the Status of Women, "Zero Draft: Achieving Gender Equality and the Empowerment of All Women and Girls in the Context of Climate Change, Environmental and Disaster Risk Reduction Policies and Programmes," draft agreed conclusions, March 14–25, 2022, https://www.unwomen.org/sites/default/files/2022-02 /CSW66%20Agreed%20Conclusions_zero%20draft_1%20February%202022.pdf; Carol Cohn and Claire Duncanson, "Women, Peace and Security in a Changing Climate," *International Feminist Journal of Politics* 22, no. 5 (2020): 742–762.

2. Lisa Sharland et al., *System Update: Towards a Women, Peace and Cybersecurity Agenda* (Geneva: United Nations Institute for Disarmament Studies, 2021); Sara E. Davies and Sophie Harman, "Securing Reproductive Health: A Matter of International Peace and Security," *International Studies Quarterly* 64, no. 2 (2020): 277–284; Marta Bautista Forcada and Cristina Hernández Lázaro, "The Privatization of War: A New Challenge for

the Women, Peace and Security Agenda," in *New Directions in Women, Peace and Security*, ed. Soumita Basu, Paul Kirby, and Laura J. Shepherd (Bristol, UK: Bristol University Press, 2020), 169–188.

3. Mila O'Sullivan and Katerina Krulišová, "Women, Peace and Security in Central Europe: In Between the Western Agenda and Russian Imperialism," *International Affairs* 99, no. 2 (2023): 625–643.

4. Kouvo and Pearson cited in Faye Bird, "'Is this a Time of Beautiful Chaos?' Reflecting on International Feminist Legal Methods," *Feminist Legal Studies* 28, no. 1 (2020): 180. Bird uses Margaret Jane Radin's theory of the feminist double bind to explore the "beautiful chaos" of feminist international legal encounters, which accommodates both ideal and nonideal visions and possibilities for feminist futures. In her persuasive and thoughtful account, Bird anchors the discussion in the case of the WPS agenda, because it so powerfully exemplifies the tension that is constitutive of the double bind. Methodologically, working with the concept of the feminist double bind requires holding space for both "nonideal structures and ideal feminist utopian thinking" (181), which seems in line with the oscillating valences we identify within the agenda, although the double bind is not a concept we work with in our analysis.

5. David Mosse, "Is Good Policy Unimplementable? Reflections on the Ethnography of Aid Policy and Practice," *Development and Change* 35, no. 4 (2004): 639–671.

6. Our forgetting mirrors efforts to move beyond objects that have come to weigh overbearingly on attempts to critique them. See, for example, Roland Bleiker, "Forget IR Theory," *Alternatives: Global, Local, Political* 22, no. 1 (1997): 57–85; Alison Howell, "Forget 'Militarization': Race, Disability and the 'Martial Politics' of the Police and the University," *International Feminist Journal of Politics* 20, no. 2 (2018): 117–136.

7. Judith Halberstam, *The Queer Art of Failure* (Durham, NC: Duke University Press, 2011), 4.

8. Soumita Basu, Paul Kirby, and Laura J. Shepherd, "Women, Peace and Security: A Critical Cartography," in Basu, Kirby, and Shepherd, *New Directions in Women, Peace and Security*, 4–6.

9. Gina Heathcote, *Feminist Dialogues on International Law: Successes, Tensions, Futures* (Oxford: Oxford University Press, 2019), 144–146. See also Karen Engle, Vasuki Nesiah, and Dianne Otto, "Feminist Approaches to International Law," in *International Legal Theory: Foundations and Frontiers*, ed. Jeffrey Dunoff and Mark Pollack (Cambridge: Cambridge University Press, 2022), 174–196.

10. Natalie Florea Hudson, *Gender, Human Security and the United Nations: Security Language as a Political Framework for Women* (London: Routledge, 2010), 144.

11. See, for example, Anne Marie Goetz and Natalie Florea Hudson, "Too Much That Can't Be Said: Anne Marie Goetz in Conversation with Natalie Florea Hudson," *International Feminist Journal of Politics* 16, no. 2 (2014): 338; Sam Cook, "Security Council Resolution 1820: On Militarism, Flashlights, Raincoats, and Rooms with Doors—a Political Perspective on Where It Came from and What It Adds," *Emory International Law Review* 23, no. 1 (2009): 125–140; Dianne Otto, "The Security Council's Alliance of Gender Legitimacy: The Symbolic Capital of Resolution 1325," in *Fault Lines of*

International Legitimacy, ed. Hilary Charlesworth and Jean-Marc Coicaud (Cambridge: Cambridge University Press, 2010), 239–275; Sam Cook, "Marking Failure, Making Space: Feminist Intervention in Security Council Policy," *International Affairs* 95, no. 6 (2019): 1289–1306.

12. Dianne Otto, "Power and Danger: Feminist Engagement with International Law Through the UN Security Council," *Australian Feminist Law Journal* 32, no. 1 (2010): 97–121.

13. Ian Hurd, *After Anarchy: Legitimacy and Power in the United Nations Security Council* (Princeton, NJ: Princeton University Press, 2007).

14. Otto, "The Security Council's Alliance."

15. On weapon talk, see Paul Kirby, "The Body Weaponized: War, Sexual Violence and the Uncanny," *Security Dialogue* 51, nos. 2–3 (2020): 211–230.

16. Soumita Basu, "Gender as National Interest at the UN Security Council," *International Affairs* 92, no. 2 (2016): 255–273. See also chapter 6, pp. 166–170.

17. Jennifer F. Klot, "The United Nations Security Council Agenda on 'Women, Peace and Security': Bureaucratic Pathologies and Unrealised Potential" (PhD diss., London School of Economics and Politics Science, 2015), 45–73.

18. Engle, Nesiah, and Otto, "Feminist Approaches to International Law," 175.

19. Lucy Delap, *Feminisms: A Global History* (London: Penguin, 2020), 20.

20. Heathcote, *Feminist Dialogues*, 145.

21. UN Security Council, S/PV.8886 (October 21, 2021), https://undocs.org/en/S/PV .8886, 22.

22. Marysia Zalewski, "Well, What Is the Feminist Perspective on Bosnia?," *International Affairs* 71, no. 2 (1995): 341.

23. Sam Cook, "The 'Woman-in-Conflict' at the UN Security Council: A Subject of Practice," *International Affairs* 92, no. 2 (2016): 353–372; Sheri Lynn Gibbings, "No Angry Women at the United Nations: Political Dreams and the Cultural Politics of United Nations Security Council Resolution 1325," *International Feminist Journal of Politics* 13, no. 4 (2011): 522–538.

24. Resolution 1820, for example, notes that "sexual violence . . . may in some instances persist after the cessation of hostilities," which blurs the temporal boundaries between conflict and "peace" (S/RES/1820 2008, preamble).

25. Sara Danius, Stefan Jonsson, and Gayatri Chakravorty Spivak, "An Interview with Gayatri Chakravorty Spivak," *boundary 2* 20, no. 2 (1993): 35. See also Sara de Jong, *Complicit Sisters: Gender and Women's Issues Across North-South Divides* (Oxford: Oxford University Press, 2017), 98.

26. Laura J. Shepherd, *Narrating the Women, Peace and Security Agenda: Logics of Global Governance* (New York: Oxford University Press, 2021), 152.

27. Seva Gunitsky, "Complexity and Theories of Change in International Politics," *International Theory* 5, no. 1 (2013): 36.

28. See, among other notable examples, Rebecca M. Hendrick and David Nachmias, "The Policy Sciences: The Challenge of Complexity," *Policy Studies Review* 11, nos. 3–4 (1992): 310–328; Mark Lubell, "The Ecology of Games Framework," *Policy Studies Journal* 41,

no. 3 (2013): 537–559; David Chandler, *Resilience: The Governance of Complexity* (London: Routledge, 2014); Christopher Ansell and Robert Geyer, " 'Pragmatic Complexity' a New Foundation for Moving Beyond 'Evidence-Based Policy Making'?," *Policy Studies* 38, no. 2 (2017): 149–167.

29.   Hubert Blalock and Peter Checkland cited in Hendrick and Nachmias, "The Policy Sciences," 315.
30.   Gunitsky, "Complexity and Theories of Change," 43.
31.   Janet Halley, *Split Decisions: How and Why to Take a Break from Feminism* (Princeton, NJ: Princeton University Press, 2006).

APPENDIX 1

1.   See Paul Kirby and Laura J. Shepherd, "Women, Peace and Security: Mapping the (Re) Production of a Policy Ecosystem," *Journal of Global Security Studies* 6, no. 3 (2021): ogaa45, https://doi.org/10.1093/jogss/ogaa045).

APPENDIX 2

1.   Being UN Security Council resolutions 1325, 1820, 1888, 1889, 1960, 2106, 2122, 2242, 2467, and 2493.

BIBLIOGRAPHY

Abbas, Madeline-Sophie. "Producing 'Internal Suspect Bodies': Divisive Effects of UK Counter-Terrorism Measures on Muslim Communities in Leeds and Bradford." *British Journal of Sociology* 70, no. 10 (2019): 261–282.

Abbott, Kenneth W., Jessica F. Green, and Robert O. Keohane. "Organizational Ecology and Institutional Change in Global Governance." *International Organization* 70, no. 2 (2016): 247–277.

Abu-Lughod, Lila. "The Courage of Truth: Making Anthropology Matter." *Working Papers in Anthropology*, no. 7. KU Leuven, September 2019. https://soc.kuleuven.be/immrc/paper_files/abu-lughod-wpa-2019-001.

Acharya, Amitav. "How Ideas Spread: Whose Norms Matter? Norm Localization and Institutional Change in Asian Regionalism." *International Organization* 58, no. 2 (2004): 239–275.

——. "The R2P and Norm Diffusion: Towards A Framework of Norm Circulation." *Global Responsibility to Protect* 5, no. 4 (2013): 466–479.

Acheson, Ray. "Starting Somewhere: The Arms Trade Treaty, Human Rights and Gender-Based Violence." *Human Rights Defender* 22, no. 2 (2013): 17–19.

——. "The Patriarchal Militarism of NATO's Reflection Group." In *Peace Research Perspectives on NATO 2030: A Response to the Official NATO Reflection Group*, edited by NATO Watch, 17–24. Gairloch, UK: NATO Watch, 2021.

Acheson, Ray, and Maria Butler. "WPS and Arms Trade Treaty." In *The Oxford Handbook of Women, Peace and Security*, edited by Sara E. Davies and Jacqui True, 690–703. New York: Oxford University Press, 2019.

Achilleos-Sarll, Columba. "The (Dis-)Appearance of Race in the United Kingdom's Institutionalization and Implementation of the Women, Peace and Security Agenda." *International Studies Quarterly* 67, no 1 (2023): sqad006. https://academic.oup.com/isq/article/67/1/sqad006/7033792.

———. " 'Seeing' the Women, Peace and Security Agenda: Visual (Re)Productions of WPS in UK Government National Action Plans." *International Affairs* 96, no. 6 (2020): 1643–1663.

———. "Women, Peace and Security Advocacy in the UK: Resisting and (Re)producing Hierarchies of Gender, Race and Coloniality." PhD diss., University of Warwick, 2020.

Achilleos-Sarll, Columba, Jennifer Thomson, Toni Haastrup, Karoline Färber, Carol Cohn, and Paul Kirby. "The Past, Present and Future(s) of Feminist Foreign Policy." *International Studies Review* 25, no. 1 (2023): viac068. https://doi.org/10.1093/isr/viac068.

Adams, Melinda. "Regional Women's Activism: African Women's Networks and the African Union." In *Global Feminism: Transnational Women's Activism, Organizing, and Human Rights*, edited by Myra Marx Ferree and Aili Mari Tripp, 187–291. New York: New York University Press, 2006.

Addams, Jane. "Women and Internationalism." In *Women at The Hague: The International Congress of Women and Its Results*, edited by Jane Addams, Emily G. Balch, and Alice Hamilton, 59–66. Urbana: University of Illinois Press, 2003.

Addams, Jane, Emily G. Balch, and Alice Hamilton, eds. *Women at The Hague: The International Congress of Women and Its Results.* Urbana: University of Illinois Press, 2003.

Åhäll, Linda. "Affect as Methodology: Feminism and the Politics of Emotion." *International Political Sociology* 12, no. 1 (2018): 36–52.

Aharoni, Sarai B. "Internal Variation in Norm Localization: Implementing Security Council Resolution 1325 in Israel." *Social Politics: International Studies in Gender, State & Society* 21, no. 1 (2014): 1–25.

———. *Women, Peace and Security: United Nations Security Council Resolution 1325 in the Israeli Context.* Jerusalem: Van Leer Institute Press, 2015.

Ahmed, Sara. *The Cultural Politics of Emotion.* Edinburgh: Edinburgh University Press, 2004.

Alaga, Ecoma. *"Pray the Devil Back to Hell": Women's Ingenuity in the Peace Process in Liberia.* Background brief. Ottawa, ON: Peacebuild, 2011.

Alam, Mayesha. *Women and Transitional Justice: Progress and Persistent Challenges in Retributive and Restorative Processes.* Basingstoke, UK: Palgrave, 2014.

Alchin, Angela, Amanda Gouws, and Lindy Heinecken. "Making a Difference in Peacekeeping Operations: Voices of South African Women Peacekeepers." *African Security Review* 27, no. 1 (2018): 1–19.

Alexander, Amanda. "A Short History of International Humanitarian Law." *European Journal of International Law* 6, no. 1 (2015): 109–138.

Ali, Nadya. "Seeing and Unseeing Prevent's Racialized Borders." *Security Dialogue* 51, no. 6 (2020): 579–596.

Alison, Miranda H. "Women as Agents of Political Violence: Gendering Security." *Security Dialogue* 35, no. 4 (2004): 447–463.

Allen, Louise. "The WPS Agenda Is Almost 20, But It's Not Time to Celebrate Yet." In *Women, Peace and Security: Defending Progress and Responding to Emerging Challenges*, edited by Lisa Sharland and Genevieve Feely, 12–13. Canberra: Australian Strategic Policy Institute, 2019.

Allison, Graham T. "Conceptual Models and the Cuban Missile Crisis." *American Political Science Review* 63, no. 3 (1969): 689–718.

Alloo, Fatma. "Remarks in 'Forum: The Events of 11 September 2001 and Beyond.'" *International Feminist Journal of Politics* 4, no. 1 (2002): 95–96.

Alonso, Harriet Hyman. "Introduction." In *Women at The Hague: The International Congress of Women and Its Results*, edited by Jane Addams, Emily G. Balch, and Alice Hamilton, vii–xl. Urbana: University of Illinois Press, 2003.

Alter, Karen J., and Sophie Meunier. "The Politics of International Regime Complexity." *Perspectives on Politics* 7, no. 1 (2009): 13–24.

Amar, Paul. *The Security Archipelago: Human-Security States, Sexuality Politics, and the End of Neoliberalism*. Durham, NC: Duke University Press, 2013.

Amsler, Sarah, and Sara C. Motta. "The Marketised University and the Politics of Motherhood." *Gender and Education* 31, no. 1 (2019): 82–99.

Anghie, Antony. "Finding the Peripheries: Sovereignty and Colonialism in Nineteenth-Century International Law." *Harvard International Law Journal* 40, no. 1 (1999): 1–72.

——. *Imperialism, Sovereignty and the Making of International Law*. Cambridge: Cambridge University Press, 2004.

Ansell, Christopher, and Robert Geyer. "'Pragmatic Complexity' a New Foundation for Moving Beyond 'Evidence-Based Policy Making?'" *Policy Studies* 38, no. 2 (2017): 149–167.

Aradau, Claudia, and Jef Huysmans. "Critical Methods in International Relations: The Politics of Techniques, Devices and Acts." *European Journal of International Relations* 20, no. 3 (2014): 596–619.

Armstrong, David, Theo Farrell, and Hélène Lambert. *International Law and International Relations*. Cambridge: Cambridge University Press, 2007.

Armstrong, Elisabeth. "Before Bandung: The Anti-imperialist Women's Movement in Asia and the Women's International Democratic Federation." *Signs: Journal of Women in Culture and Society* 41, no. 2 (2016): 305–331.

Aronsson, Lisa A. *NATO Partnerships for Women, Peace and Security*. Washington, DC: Atlantic Council, 2021.

Aroussi, Sahla, ed. *Rethinking National Action Plans on Women, Peace and Security*. Amsterdam: IOS Press, 2017.

——. "Strange Bedfellows: Interrogating the Unintended Consequences of Integrating Countering Violent Extremism with the UN's Women, Peace, and Security Agenda in Kenya." *Politics & Gender* 17, no. 4 (2020): 665–695.

——. "'Women, Peace and Security': Addressing Accountability for Wartime Sexual Violence." *International Feminist Journal of Politics* 13, no. 4 (2011): 576–593.

Arvin, Maile, Eve Tuck, and Angie Morrill. "Decolonizing Feminism: Challenging Connections Between Settler Colonialism and Heteropatriarchy." *Feminist Formations* 25, no. 1 (2013): 8–34.

Asante, Doris, and Laura J. Shepherd. "Gender and Countering Violent Extremism in Women, Peace and Security National Action Plans." *European Journal of Politics and Gender* 3, no. 3 (2020): 311–330.

Åse, Cecelia. "Crisis Narratives and Masculinist Protection: Gendering the Original Stockholm Syndrome." *International Feminist Journal of Politics* 17, no. 4 (2015): 595–610.

Ashley, Richard K. "The Poverty of Neorealism." *International Organization* 38, no. 2 (1986): 225–286.

——. "The Powers of Anarchy: Theory, Sovereignty, and the Domestication of Global Life." In *International Theory: Critical Investigations*, edited by James Der Derian, 94–128. Basingstoke, UK: Palgrave Macmillan, 1995.

Ashworth, Lucian. "Feminism, War and the Prospects for Peace: Helena Swanwick (1864–1939) and the Lost Feminists of Inter-war International Relations." *International Feminist Journal of Politics* 13, no. 1 (2011): 25–43.

ATT Monitor. *ATT Monitor 2019*. New York: Control Arms, 2019.

Australian Government. *Australian National Action Plan on Women, Peace and Security, 2021–2031*. Canberra: Ministry for Foreign Affairs, 2021.

Avant, Deborah D., Martha Finnemore, and Susan K. Sell, eds. *Who Governs the Globe?* Cambridge: Cambridge University Press, 2010.

——. "Who Governs the Globe?" In *Who Governs the Globe?*, edited by Deborah D. Avant, Martha Finnemore, and Susan K. Sell, 1–31. Cambridge: Cambridge University Press, 2010.

Axworthy, Lloyd, and Allan Rock. "R2P: A New and Unfinished Agenda." *Global Responsibility to Protect*, 1, no. 1 (2009): 54–69.

Azarbaijani-Moghaddam, Sippi. "Seeking Out Their Afghan Sisters: Female Engagement Teams in Afghanistan." Working Paper No. 1, Chr. Michelsen Institute, 2014.

Ba, Oumar. *States of Justice: The Politics of the International Criminal Court*. Cambridge: Cambridge University Press, 2020.

Bacchi, Carol. *Analysing Policy*. French's Forest, NSW: Pearson Australia, 2009.

Baden, Sally, and Anne Marie Goetz. "Who Needs [Sex] When You Can Have [Gender]? Conflicting Discourses on Gender at Beijing." *Feminist Review* 56 (1997): 3–25.

Badescu, Cristina G., and Thomas G. Weiss. "Misrepresenting R2P and Advancing Norms: An Alternative Spiral?" *International Studies Perspectives* 11, no. 4 (2010): 354–374.

Balakrishnan, Radhika, and Krishanti Dharmaraj. "WPS and Sustainable Development Goals." In *Oxford Handbook on Women, Peace and Security*, edited by Sara E. Davies and Jacqui True, 704–714. Oxford: Oxford University Press, 2019.

Baldry, Eileen, and Chris Cunneen. "Imprisoned Indigenous Women and the Shadow of Colonial Patriarchy." *Australian & New Zealand Journal of Criminology* 47, no. 2 (2014): 276–298.

Banda, Fareda. "Blazing a Trail: The African Protocol on Women's Rights Comes Into Force." *Journal of African Law* 50, no. 1 (2006): 72–84.

Barkawi, Tarak. "On the Pedagogy of 'Small Wars.'" *International Affairs* 80, no. 1 (2004): 19–37.

Barkawi, Tarak, and Mark Laffey. "The Postcolonial Moment in Security Studies." *Review of International Studies* 32, no. 2 (2006): 329–352.

Barker, Joanne. "Critically Sovereign." In *Critically Sovereign: Indigenous Gender, Sexuality, and Feminist Studies*, edited by Joanne Barker, 1–44. Durham, NC: Duke University Press, 2017.

Barkin, J. Samuel, and Bruce Cronin. "The State and the Nation: Changing Norms and the Rules of Sovereignty in International Relations." *International Organization* 48, no. 1 (1994): 107–130.

Barnes, Karen. "The Evolution and Implementation of UNSCR 1325: An Overview." In *Women, Peace and Security: Translating Policy Into Practice*, eds. 'Funmi Olonisakin, Karen Barnes, and Eka Ikpe, 15–34. London: Routledge, 2011.

Barnes, Karen, and 'Funmi Olonisakin. "Introduction." In *Women, Peace and Security: Translating Policy Into Practice*, edited by 'Funmi Olonisakin, Karen Barnes, and Eka Ikpe, 3–14. London: Routledge, 2011.

Barnett, Michael. "The UN Security Council, Indifference, and Genocide in Rwanda." *Cultural Anthropology* 12, no. 4 (1997): 551–578.

Barnett, Michael, and Raymond Duvall. "Power in Global Governance." In *Power in Global Governance*, edited by Michael Barnett and Raymond Duvall, 1–32. Cambridge: Cambridge University Press, 2005.

Barrow, Amy. "Operationalizing Security Council Resolution 1325: The Role of National Action Plans." *Journal of Conflict and Security Law* 21, no. 2 (2016): 247–275.

Basini, Helen, and Caitlin Ryan. "National Action Plans as an Obstacle to Meaningful Local Ownership of UNSCR 1325 in Liberia and Sierra Leone." *International Political Science Review* 37, no. 3 (2016): 390–403.

Bastick, Megan, and Claire Duncanson. "Agents of Change? Gender Advisors in NATO Militaries." *International Peacekeeping* 25, no. 4 (2018): 554–577.

Basu, Soumita. "Civil Society Actors and the Implementation of Resolution 1325 in India." In *Openings for Peace: UNSCR 1325, Women and Security in India*, edited by Asha Hans and Swarna Rajagopalan, 33–50. New Delhi: SAGE, 2016.

——. "Gender as National Interest at the UN Security Council." *International Affairs* 92, no. 2 (2016): 255–273.

——. "The Global South Writes 1325 (Too)." *International Political Science Review* 37, no. 3 (2016): 362–374.

——. "The United Nations' Women, Peace and Security Agenda." In *Handbook on Gender and War*, edited by Simona Sharoni, Julia Welland, Linda Steiner, and Jennifer Pedersen, 572–590. Cheltenham, UK: Edward Elgar, 2016.

——. "The Women in Blue Helmets: Gender, Policing, and the UN's First All-Female Peacekeeping Unit; Equal Opportunity Peacekeeping: Women, Peace, and Security in Postconflict States." *International Affairs* 94, no. 3 (2018): 663–665.

Basu, Soumita, and Catia C. Confortini. "Weakest 'P' in the 1325 Pod? Realizing Conflict Prevention Through Security Council Resolution 1325." *International Studies Perspectives* 18, no. 1 (2017): 43–63.

Basu, Soumita, and Laura J. Shepherd. "Prevention in Pieces: Representing Conflict in the Women, Peace and Security Agenda." *Global Affairs* 3, nos. 4–5 (2017): 441–453.

Basu, Soumita, Paul Kirby, and Laura J. Shepherd, eds. *New Directions in Women, Peace and Security*. Bristol, UK: Bristol University Press, 2020.

——. "Women, Peace and Security: A Critical Cartography." In *New Directions in Women, Peace and Security*, edited by Soumita Basu, Paul Kirby, and Laura J. Shepherd, 1–28. Bristol, UK: Bristol University Press, 2020.

Bautista Forcada, Marta, and Cristina Hernández Lázaro. "The Privatization of War: A New Challenge for the Women, Peace and Security Agenda." In *New Directions in Women, Peace and Security*, edited by Soumita Basu, Paul Kirby, and Laura J. Shepherd, 169–188. Bristol, UK: Bristol University Press, 2020.

Bawaka Country, Sarah Wright, Sandie Suchet-Pearson, Kate Lloyd, Laklak Burarrwanga, Ritjilili Ganambarr, Merrkiyawuy Ganambarr-Stubbs, Banbapuy Ganambarr, Djawundil Maymuru, and Jill Sweeny. "Co-becoming Bawaka: Towards a Relational Understanding of Place/Space. *Progress in Human Geography* 40, no. 4 (2016): 455–475.

Bear Robe, Andrew. "First Nations and Aboriginal Rights." *Constitutional Forum* 2, no. 2 (1991): 46–49.

Bell, Christine, and Sanja Badanjak. "Introducing PA-X: A New Peace Agreement Database and Dataset." *Journal of Peace Research* 56, no. 3 (2019): 452–466.

Bell, Christine, and Kevin McNicholl. "Principled Pragmatism and the 'Inclusion Project': Implementing a Gender Perspective in Peace Agreements." *Feminists@Law* 9, no. 1 (2019): 1–51.

Bell, Christine, and Catherine O'Rourke. "Peace Agreements or Pieces of Paper? The Impact of UNSC Resolution 1325 on Peace Processes and Their Agreements." *International and Comparative Law Quarterly* 59, no. 4 (2010): 941–980.

Bellamy, Alex J. "The Responsibility to Protect and the Problem of Military Intervention." *International Affairs* 84, no. 5 (2008): 615–639.

——. *Responsibility to Protect: The Global Effort to End Mass Atrocities.* Cambridge: Polity Press, 2009.

——. "UN Security Council." In *The Oxford Handbook of the Responsibility to Protect*, edited by Alex J. Bellamy and Tim Dunne, 249–268. Oxford: Oxford University Press, 2016.

Benjamin, Walter. *Illuminations: Essays and Reflections.* Translated by Harry Zohn. 1955. Reprint, New York: Schocken Books, 2007. Page references are to the 2007 edition.

Bennett, Colin J., and Michael Howlett. "The Lessons of Learning: Reconciling Theories of Policy Learning and Policy Change." *Policy Sciences* 25, no. 2 (1992): 275–294.

Beoku-Betts, Josephine. "Holding African States to Task on Gender and Violence: Domesticating UNSCR 1325 in the Sierra Leone National Action Plan." *Current Sociology* 64, no. 4 (2016): 654–670.

Betts, Alexander, and Phil Orchard. "Introduction: The Normative Institutionalization-Implementation Gap." In *Implementation and World Politics: How International Norms Change Practice*, edited by Alexander Betts and Phil Orchard, 1–26. Oxford: Oxford University Press, 2014.

Bhattacharyya, Gargi. *Dangerous Brown Men: Exploiting Sex, Violence and Feminism in the War on Terror.* London: Zed, 2008.

Biden, Joseph R. "Why America Must Lead Again: Rescuing U.S. Foreign Policy After Trump." *Foreign Affairs* 99, no. 2 (2020): 64–76.

Bigio, Jamille, and Rachel Vogelstein. "How Women's Participation in Conflict Prevention and Resolution Advances U.S. Interests." Council for Foreign Relations, October 2016. https://cdn.cfr.org/sites/default/files/pdf/2016/10/Discussion_Paper_Bigio_Vogelstein_Women%20in%20CPR_OR.pdf.

Bird, Faye. "'Is This a Time of Beautiful Chaos?': Reflecting on International Feminist Legal Methods." *Feminist Legal Studies* 28, no. 1 (2020): 179–203.

Bird Rose, Deborah. "Connectivity Thinking, Animism, and the Pursuit of Liveliness." *Educational Theory* 67, no. 4 (2017): 491–508.

——. "Cosmopolitics: The Kiss of Life." *New Formations* 76 (2012): 101–113.

Björkdahl, Annika, and Johanna Mannergren Selimovic. "WPS and Civil Society." In *The Oxford Handbook of Women, Peace and Security*, edited by Sara E. Davies and Jacqui True, 428–438. Oxford: Oxford University Press, 2019.

Bleiker, Roland. *Aesthetics and World Politics*. Basingstoke, UK: Palgrave Macmillan, 2009.

——. "Forget IR Theory." *Alternatives: Global, Local, Political* 22, no. 1 (1997): 57–85.

Bode, Ingvild. "Reflective Practices at the Security Council: Children and Armed Conflict and the Three United Nations." *European Journal of International Relations* 24, no. 2 (2018): 293–318.

Boserup, Esther. *Women's Role in Economic Development*. London: Earthscan, 1970.

Bousquet, Antoine, and Simon Curtis. "Beyond Models and Metaphors: Complexity Theory, Systems Thinking and International Relations." *Cambridge Review of International Affairs* 24, no. 1 (2011): 43–62.

Brah, Avtar, and Ann Phoenix. "Ain't I a Woman? Revisiting Intersectionality." *Journal of International Women's Studies* 3, no. 5 (2004): 75–86.

Breakey, Hugh. "Protection Norms and Human Rights: A Rights-Based Analysis of the Responsibility to Protect and the Protection of Civilians in Armed Conflict." *Global Responsibility to Protect* 4 (2012): 309–333.

——. "The Protection of Civilians in Armed Conflict: Four Concepts." In *Norms of Protection*, edited by Angus Francis, Vesselin Popovski, and Charles Sampford, 40–61. New York: United Nations University Press, 2012.

Brigg, Morgan, Mary Graham, and Martin Weber. "Relational Indigenous Systems: Aboriginal Australian Political Ordering and Reconfiguring IR." *Review of International Studies* 48, no. 5 (2022): 891–909.

Briggs, John. "The Use of Indigenous Knowledge in Development: Problems and Challenges." *Progress in Development Studies* 5, no. 2 (2005): 99–114.

Brighi, Elisabetta. "The Globalisation of Resentment: Failure, Denial, and Violence in World Politics." *Millennium: Journal of International Studies* 44, no. 3 (2016): 441–432.

Brittain, Victoria. "The Impact of War on Women." *Race & Class* 44, no. 4 (2003): 41–51.

Broome, André. "Stabilizing Global Monetary Norms: The IMF and Current Account Convertibility." In *Owning Development: Creating Policy Norms in the IMF and the World Bank*, edited by Susan Park and Antje Vetterlein, 113–136. Cambridge: Cambridge University Press, 2010.

Brown, Wendy. "The Impossibility of Women's Studies." *differences: A Journal of Feminist Cultural Studies* 9, no. 3 (1997): 79–101.

——. "Wounded Attachments." *Political Theory* 21, no. 3 (1993): 390–410.

Bueger, Christian, and Manuel Mireanu. "Proximity." In *Critical Security Methods: New Frameworks for Analysis*, edited by Claudia Aradau, Jef Huysmans, Andrew Neal, and Nadine Voelkner, 118–141. London: Routledge, 2014.

Bunch, Charlotte. "Women's Rights as Human Rights: Toward a Re-vision of Human Rights." *Human Rights Quarterly* 12, no. 4 (1990): 486–498.

Buss, Doris E. "The Curious Visibility of Wartime Rape: Gender and Ethnicity in International Criminal Law." *Windsor Yearbook of Access to Justice* 25, no. 1 (2007): 3–22.

——. "Robes, Relics and Rights: The Vatican and the Beijing Conference on Women." *Social & Legal Studies* 7, no. 3 (1998): 339–363.

Busse, Jan. *Deconstructing the Dynamics of World-Societal Order: The Power of Governmentality in Palestine.* London: Routledge, 2018.

Bustelo, Carlota. "Reproductive Health and CEDAW." *American University Law Review* 44, no. 4 (1995): 1145–1156.

Byrd, Jodi A. "Mind the Gap: Indigenous Sovereignty and the Antinomies of Empire." In *The Anomie of the Earth: Philosophy, Politics, and Autonomy in Europe and the Americas,* edited by Federico Luisetti, John Pickles, and Wilson Kaiser, 119–136. Durham, NC: Duke University Press, 2015.

Callahan, William A. *Sensible Politics: Visualizing International Relations.* New York: Oxford University Press, 2020.

Campbell, David. *Writing Security: United States Foreign Policy and the Politics of Identity.* Revised ed. Minneapolis: University of Minnesota Press, 1998.

Carter, Denise Maia. "(De)constructing Difference: A Qualitative Review of the 'Othering' of UK Muslim Communities, Extremism, Soft Harms, and Twitter Analytics." *Behavioral Sciences of Terrorism and Political Aggression* 9, no. 1 (2017): 21–36.

Chandler, David. *Resilience: The Governance of Complexity.* London: Routledge, 2014.

Chan-Tiberghien, Jennifer. "Gender Skepticism or Gender-Boom: Poststructural Feminisms, Transnational Feminisms and the World Conference Against Racism." *International Feminist Journal of Politics* 6, no. 3 (2004): 454–484.

Charlesworth, Hilary. "Not Waving but Drowning: Gender Mainstreaming and Human Rights in the United Nations." *Harvard Human Rights Journal* 18 (2005): 1–18.

Chazan, Naomi. "Israel, Palestine, and UNSCR 1325: Then and Now." *Palestine-Israel Journal* 25, nos. 3–4 (2020). https://www.pij.org/articles/2044/israel-palestine-and-unsc-resolution-1325-then-and-now.

Checkel, Jeffrey T. "International Institutions and Socialization in Europe: Introduction and Framework." *International Organization* 59, no. 4 (2005): 801–826.

Chilmeran, Yasmin. "Women, Peace and Security Across Scales: Exclusions and Opportunities in Iraq's WPS Engagements." *International Affairs* 98, no. 2 (2022): 747–765.

Chinkin, Christine, and Madeleine Rees. *Commentary on Security Council Resolution 2467: Continued State Obligation and Civil Society Action on Sexual Violence in Conflict.* London: LSE Centre for Women, Peace and Security, 2019.

Chowdhury, Arjun. "International Norms in Postcolonial Time." In *Against International Relations Norms: Postcolonial Perspectives,* edited by Charlotte Epstein, 106–122. Abingdon, UK: Routledge, 2017.

Chua, Charmaine. "Against Localization: Rethinking Compliance and Antagonism in Norm Dynamics." In *Against International Relations Norms: Postcolonial Perspectives,* edited by Charlotte Epstein, 87–105. Abingdon, UK: Routledge, 2017.

Chwieroth, Jeffrey M. "Normative Change from Within: The International Monetary Fund's Approach to Capital Account Liberalization." *International Studies Quarterly* 52, no. 1 (2008): 129–158.

Claude, Inis L. "Collective Legitimization as a Political Function of the United Nations." *International Organization* 20, no. 3 (1966): 367–379.

Clinton, Hillary. "Remarks on the Adoption of a United Nations Security Council Resolution to Combat Sexual Violence in Armed Conflict." U.S. Department of State Archive, September 30, 2009. https://2009-2017.state.gov/secretary/20092013clinton/rm/2009a/09/130041.htm.

Cockburn, Cynthia. *Anti-militarism: Political and Gender Dynamics of Peace Movements.* Basingstoke, UK: Palgrave Macmillan, 2012.

——. *From Where We Stand: War, Women's Activism and Feminist Analysis.* London: Zed Books, 2007.

——. "Making Women's Opposition Visible to NATO." *openDemocracy*, October 18, 2010. https://www.opendemocracy.net/en/5050/making-womens-opposition-visible-to-nato/.

——. "Snagged on the Contradiction: NATO, Resolution 1325, and Feminist Responses." *Women in Action* (2012): 48–57.

——. "Women Against NATO—Making a Feminist Case." *War Resisters' International*, September 20, 2010. https://wri-irg.org/en/story/2010/women-against-nato-making-feminist-case.

Cohn, Carol. "Mainstreaming Gender in UN Security Policy: A Path to Political Transformation?" In *Global Governance: Feminist Perspectives*, edited by Shirin M. Rai and Georgina Waylen, 185–206. Basingstoke, UK: Palgrave Macmillan, 2008.

Cohn, Carol, and Claire Duncanson. "Women, Peace and Security in a Changing Climate." *International Feminist Journal of Politics* 22, no. 5 (2020): 742–762.

Cohn, Carol, Helen Kinsella, and Sheri Gibbings. "Women, Peace and Security: Resolution 1325." *International Feminist Journal of Politics* 6, no. 1 (2004): 130–140.

Colucci, Vienna. "We Get It." *Human Rights Now* (blog), Amnesty International, May 19, 2012. https://blog.amnestyusa.org/asia/we-get-it/.

Conflict, Stability and Security Fund. *Egypt Programme Summary, 2020 to 2021.* London: CSSF, 2021.

——. *Jordan: Internal Security Programme Summary, 2019–2020.* London: CSSF, 2020.

——. *Jordan: Security and stability Programme Summary, 2020 to 2021.* London: CSSF, 2021.

Confortini, Catia Cecilia. *Intelligent Compassion: Feminist Critical Methodology in the Women's International League for Peace and Freedom.* Oxford: Oxford University Press, 2012.

Cook, Joana, and Vanessa Newby. "An Interview with NATO on Gender and Counter-Terrorism." International Centre for Counter-Terrorism, April 9, 2021. https://icct.nl/publication/an-interview-with-nato-on-gender-and-counter-terrorism/.

Cook, Sam. "Encountering Metis in the Security Council." *Women, Peace and Security Working Paper Series*, no. 15. London: Centre for Women Peace and Security, London School of Economics and Political Science, 2018. http://www.lse.ac.uk/women-peace-security/assets/documents/2018/wps15Cook.pdf.

——. "Marking Failure, Making Space: Feminist Intervention in Security Council Policy." *International Affairs* 95, no. 6 (2019): 1289–1306.

——. "Security Council Resolution 1820: On Militarism, Flashlights, Raincoats, and Rooms with Doors—a Political Perspective on Where It Came from and What It Adds." *Emory International Law Review* 23, no. 1 (2009): 125–140.

——. "The 'Woman-in-Conflict' at the UN Security Council: A Subject of Practice." *International Affairs* 92, no. 2 (2016): 353–372.

Coomaraswamy, Radhika, Patrick Cammaert, Anwarul Chowdhury, Liliana Andrea Silva Bello, Sharon Bhagwan Rolls, Leymah Gbowee, Julia Kharashvili et al. *Preventing Conflict, Transforming Justice, Securing the Peace: A Global Study on the Implementation of United Nations Security Council Resolution 1325*. New York: UN Women, 2015. https://wps .unwomen.org/pdf/en/GlobalStudy_EN_Web.pdf.

Coulthard, Glen Sean. *Red Skin, White Masks: Rejecting the Colonial Politics of Recognition*. Minneapolis: University of Minnesota Press, 2014.

Crawford, Kerry. *Wartime Sexual Violence: From Silence to Condemnation of a Weapon of War*. Washington, DC: Georgetown University Press, 2017.

Crawford, Neta C. *Argument and Change in World Politics: Ethics, Decolonization, and Humanitarian Intervention*. Cambridge: Cambridge University Press, 2002.

——. "United States Budgetary Costs and Obligations of Post-9/11 Wars Through FY2020 $6.4 Trillion." Costs of War Project, November 13, 2019. https://watson.brown.edu/costsofwar /files/cow/imce/papers/2019/US%20Budgetary%20Costs%20of%20Wars%20November%202019.pdf.

Crawford, Neta C., and Catherine Lutz. "Human Costs of Post-9/11 Wars." Costs of War Project, November 13, 2019. https://watson.brown.edu/costsofwar/files/cow/imce/papers/2019 /Direct%20War%20Deaths%20COW%20Estimate%20November%2013%202019%20 FINAL.pdf.

Crenshaw, Kimberlé. "Demarginalizing the Intersection of Race and Sex: A Black Feminist Critique of Antidiscrimination Doctrine, Feminist Theory and Antiracist Politics." *University of Chicago Legal Forum*, no. 1 (1989): 139–167.

——. "Mapping the Margins: Intersectionality, Identity Politics, and Violence Against Women of Color." *Stanford Law Review* 43, no. 6 (1991): 1241–1299.

Crossley, Noele "Is R2P Still Controversial? Continuity and Change in the Debate on 'Humanitarian Intervention.'" *Cambridge Review of International Affairs* 31, no. 5 (2018): 415–436.

Dahl-Eriksen, Tor. "R2P and the UN Security Council: An 'Unreliable Alliance.'" *International Journal on World Peace* 36, no. 1 (2019): 33–59.

Danius, Sara, Stefan Jonsson, and Gayatri Chakravorty Spivak. "An Interview with Gayatri Chakravorty Spivak." *boundary 2* 20, no. 2 (1993): 24–50.

Davies, Sara E., and Sophie Harman. "Securing Reproductive Health: A Matter of International Peace and Security." *International Studies Quarterly* 64, no. 2 (2020): 277–284.

Davies, Sara E., and Jacqui True. "Norm Entrepreneurship in Foreign Policy: William Hague and the Prevention of Sexual Violence in Conflict." *Foreign Policy Analysis* 13, no. 3 (2017): 701–721.

——, eds. *The Oxford Handbook of Women, Peace and Security*. Oxford: Oxford University Press, 2019.

——. "WPS: A Transformative Agenda?" In *The Oxford Handbook of Women, Peace and Security*, edited by Sara E. Davies and Jacqui True, 3–14. Oxford: Oxford University Press, 2019.

Dean, Mitchell. *Governmentality: Power and Rule in Modern Society*. London: SAGE, 1999.

de Carvalho, Benjamin, Halvard Leira, and John M. Hobson. "The Big Bangs of IR: The Myths that Your Teachers Still Tell You About 1648 and 1919." *Millennium: Journal of International Studies* 39, no. 3 (2011): 735–758.

de Finney, Sandrina. "Indigenous Girls' Resilience in Settler States: Honouring Body and Land Sovereignty." *Agenda* 31, no. 2 (2017): 10–21.

de Haan, Francisca. "Continuing Cold War Paradigms in Western Historiography of Transnational Women's Organisations: The Case of the Women's International Democratic Federation (WIDF)." *Women's History Review* 19, no. 4 (2010): 547–573.

Dehesa, Cynthia, and Sarah Masters. *Joined-Up Thinking: International Measures for Women's Security and SALW Control*. London: International Action Network on Small Arms Women's Network, 2010.

Deiana, Maria-Adriana, and Kenneth McDonagh. "'It Is Important, but . . .': Translating the Women, Peace and Security (WPS) Agenda Into the Planning of EU Peacekeeping Missions." *Peacebuilding* 6, no. 1 (2018): 34–48.

Deitelhoff, Nicole, and Lisbeth Zimmermann. "Norms Under Challenge: Unpacking the Dynamics of Norm Robustness." *Journal of Global Security Studies* 4, no. 1 (2019): 2–17.

de Jong, Sara. *Complicit Sisters: Gender and Women's Issues Across North-South Divides*. Oxford: Oxford University Press, 2017.

de Jonge Oudraat, Chantal, Sonja Stojanović-Gajić, Carolyn Washington, and Brooke Stedman. *The 1325 Scorecard: Preliminary Findings*. Washington, DC: Women in International Security and the Belgrade Centre for Security Policy, 2015. https://wiisglobal.org/wp-content/uploads/2014/03/UNSCR-1325-Scorecard-Final-Report.pdf.

Delap, Lucy. *Feminisms: A Global History*. London: Penguin, 2020.

d'Estaing, Sophie Giscard. "Engaging Women in Countering Violent Extremism: Avoiding Instrumentalisation and Furthering Agency." *Gender & Development* 25, no. 1 (2017): 103–118.

de Waal, Alex. "Mass Starvation Is a Crime: It's Time We Treated It that Way." *Boston Review*, January 14, 2019. https://bostonreview.net/articles/alex-de-waal-starvation-crimes/.

Dingworth, Klaus, and Philipp Pattberg. "World Politics and Organizational Fields: The Case of Transnational Sustainability Governance." *European Journal of International Relations* 15, no. 4 (2009): 707–743.

"Disarmament Programme." Women's International League for Peace and Freedom, accessed September 20, 2023. https://www.wilpf.org/global-programmes/disarmament/.

Doeland, Elin Martine, and Inger Skjelsbæk. "Narratives of Support and Resistance: A Political Psychological Analysis of the Implementation of UNSCR 1325 in Bosnia and Herzegovina." *Political Psychology* 39, no. 5 (2017): 995–1011.

Dolowitz, David P., and David Marsh. "Learning from Abroad: The Role of Policy Transfer in Contemporary Policy-Making." *Governance* 13, no. 1 (2000): 5–24.

——. "Who Learns What from Whom: Review of the Policy Transfer Literature." *Political Studies* 44, no. 2 (1996): 343–357.

"Domestic Violence and Small Arms." Rutgers Center for Women's Global Leadership and International Action Network on Small Arms Women's Network, accessed September 6,

2023. https://www.wilpf.org/wp-content/uploads/2012/10/Domestic-Violence-Small-Arms
.pdf.

Donnelly, Jack. *International Human Rights.* 4th ed. Boulder, CO: Westview Press, 2013.

dos Santos, Pedro, and Debora Thomé. "Women and Political Power in Brazil." In *Oxford Research Encyclopedia of Politics*, January 30, 2020. https://oxfordre.com/politics/view/10 .1093/acrefore/9780190228637.001.0001/acrefore-9780190228637-e-1744.

Doty, Roxanne Lynn, "Foreign Policy as Social Construction: A Post-positivist Analysis of US Counterinsurgency Policy in the Philippines." *International Studies Quarterly* 37, no. 3 (1993): 297–320.

——. *Imperial Encounters: The Politics of Representation in North-South Relations.* Minneapolis, MN: University of Minnesota Press, 1996.

Dowding, Keith. "Model or Metaphor? A Critical Review of the Policy Network Approach." *Political Studies* 43, no. 1 (1995): 136–158.

Drumond, Paula, and Tamya Rebelo. "Global Pathways or Local Spins? National Action Plans in South America." *International Feminist Journal of Politics* 22, no. 4 (2020): 462–484.

——. "Implementing the 'Women, Peace and Security' Agenda in Brazil: An Assessment of the National Action Plan." Strategic Paper 31, Igarapé Institute (August 2019). https:// igarape.org.br/wp-content/uploads/2019/07/2019-07-31_AE-31_Women-Peace-and -Security-National-Action-Plan.pdf.

Duncanson, Claire. "Beyond Liberal vs Liberating: Women's Economic Empowerment in the United Nations' Women, Peace and Security Agenda." *International Feminist Journal of Politics* 21, no. 1 (2019): 111–130.

——. *Gender & Peacebuilding.* Cambridge: Polity Press, 2016.

Dunn, Michelle Elizabeth. "Localising the Australian National Action Plan on Women, Peace and Security: A Matter of Justice." *Australian Journal of International Affairs* 68, no. 3 (2014): 285–299.

Dunne, Tim. "Good Citizen Europe." *International Affairs* 84, no. 1 (2008): 13–28.

Duriesmith, David. "Engaging Men and Boys in the Women, Peace and Security Agenda: Beyond the 'Good Men' Industry." *Women Peace and Security Working Paper Series*, no. 11. London: Centre for Women, Peace and Security, London School of Economics and Political Science, 2017. https://www.lse.ac.uk/women-peace-security/assets/documents/2017 /wps11Duriesmith.pdf.

Dyvik, Synne L. " 'Valhalla Rising': Gender, Embodiment and Experience in Military Memoirs." *Security Dialogue* 47, no. 2 (2016): 133–150.

——. "Women as 'Practitioners' and 'Targets': Gender and Counterinsurgency in Afghanistan." *International Feminist Journal of Politics* 16, no. 3 (2014): 410–429.

Eager, Paige Whalley. *From Freedom Fighters to Terrorists: Women and Political Violence.* London: Routledge, 2016.

Egnell, Robert. "Gender Perspectives and Fighting." *Parameters* 43, no. 2 (2013): 33–41.

——. "Gender Perspectives and Military Effectiveness: Implementing UNSCR 1325 and the National Action Plan on Women, Peace, and Security." *PRISM* 6, no. 1 (2016): 73–89.

Egnell, Robert, and Mayesha Alam. "Gender and Women in the Military—Setting the Stage." In *Women and Gender Perspectives in the Military: An International Comparison*, edited by Robert Egnell and Mayesha Alam, 1–21. Washington, DC: Georgetown University Press, 2019.

Eisenstein, Zillah. *Sexual Decoys: Gender, Race, and War in Imperial Democracy*. Melbourne, AU: Spinifex, 2007.

El-Bushra, Judy. "Feminism, Gender, and Women's Peace Activism." *Development and Change* 38, no. 1 (2007): 131–147.

Ellerby, Kara. "(En)gendered Security? The Complexities of Women's Inclusion in Peace Processes." *International Interactions* 39, no. 4 (2013): 435–460.

———. "A Seat at the Table Is Not Enough: Understanding Women's Substantive Representation in Peace Processes." *Peacebuilding* 4, no. 2 (2016): 136–150.

Elomäki, Anna, Johanna Kantola, Anu Koivunen, and Hanna Ylöstalo. "Affective Virtuosity: Challenges for Governance Feminism in the Context of the Economic Crisis." *Gender, Work and Organisation* 26, no. 6 (2019): 822–839.

Elson, Diane. *Male Bias in the Development Process*. Manchester, UK: Manchester University Press, 1991.

Emirbayer, Mustafa. "Manifesto for a Relational Sociology." *American Journal of Sociology* 103, no. 2 (1997): 281–317.

Engelbrekt, Kjell. "Responsibility Shirking at the United Nations Security Council Constraints, Frustrations, Remedies." *Global Policy*, 6, no. 4 (2015): 369–378.

Engle, Karen. "Judging Sex in War." *Michigan Law Review* 106, no. 6 (2008): 941–961.

Engle, Karen, Vasuki Nesiah, and Dianne Otto. "Feminist Approaches to International Law." In *International Legal Theory: Foundations and Frontiers*, edited by Jeffrey Dunoff and Mark Pollack, 174–196. Cambridge: Cambridge University Press, 2022.

Enloe, Cynthia. "NATO's Interest in Women: The Lesson Machine." In *Loaded Questions: Women in the Military*, edited by Wendy Chapkis, 65–71. Amsterdam: Transnational Institute, 1981.

Enloe, Cynthia. *Does Khaki Become You? The Militarization of Women's Lives*. Boston: South End Press, 1983.

Epstein, Charlotte. "Stop Telling Us How to Behave: Socialization or Infantilization?" In *Against International Relations Norms: Postcolonial Perspectives*, edited by Charlotte Epstein, 74–86. Abingdon, UK: Routledge, 2017.

Escobar, Arturo. *Encountering Development: The Making and Unmaking of the Third World*. 2nd ed. Princeton, NJ: Princeton University Press, 2012.

Estes, Nick. "The U.S. Stole Generations of Indigenous Children to Open the West." *High Country News*, October 14, 2019. https://www.hcn.org/issues/51.17/indigenous-affairs-the-us-stole-generations-of-indigenous-children-to-open-the-west.

"Estimates of Aboriginal and Torres Strait Islander Australians—June 2016." Australian Bureau of Statistics, August 31, 2018. https://www.abs.gov.au/statistics/people/aboriginal-and-torres-strait-islander-peoples/estimates-aboriginal-and-torres-strait-islander-australians/latest-release.

European Centre for Constitutional and Human Rights, Amnesty International, Campaign Against Arms Trade, Mwatana for Human Rights, Centre d'Estudis per la Pau J. M. Delàs, and Osservatorio Permanente sulle Armi Leggere e le Politiche di Sicurezza e Difesa. *Made in Europe, Bombed in Yemen: How the ICC Could Tackle the Responsibility of Arms Export- ers and Government Officials.* Berlin: European Centre for Constitutional and Human Rights, 2020.

Evans, Mark. "Policy Transfer in Critical Perspective." *Policy Studies* 30, no. 3 (2009): 243–268.

Farr, Vanessa. "UNSCR 1325 and Women's Peace Activism in the Occupied Palestinian Terri- tory." *International Feminist Journal of Politics* 13, no. 4 (2011): 539–556.

Farris, Sara R. *In the Name of Women's Rights: The Rise of Femonationalism.* Durham, NC: Duke University Press, 2017.

Fernández Rodríguez de Liévana, Gema, and Christine Chinkin. "Human Trafficking, Human Rights, and Women, Peace and Security: The Sound of Silence." In *New Directions in Women, Peace and Security,* edited by Soumita Basu, Paul Kirby, and Laura J. Shepherd, 189–206. Bristol, UK: Bristol University Press, 2020.

Ferreira-Pinto Bailey, Cristina. "'Compulsory' Whiteness and Female Identity: Race and Gen- der in Brazilian Women's Writings." *Letras Femeninas* 32, no. 1 (2006): 295–311.

Ferro, Luca, and Tom Ruys. "The Saudi-Led Military Intervention in Yemen's Civil War— 2015." In *The Use of Force in International Law: A Case-Based Approach,* edited by Tom Ruys, Olivier Corten, and Alexandra Hofer, 899–911. Oxford: Oxford University Press, 2018.

Finnemore, Martha. "International Organizations as Teachers of Norms: The United Nations Educational, Scientific, and Cultural Organization and Science Policy." *International Orga- nization* 47, no. 4 (1993): 565–597.

Finnemore, Martha, and Kathryn Sikkink. "International Norm Dynamics and Political Change." *International Organization* 52, no. 4 (1998): 887–917.

Fitzmaurice, Andrew. "Scepticism of the Civilizing Mission in International Law." In *Inter- national Law and Empire: Historical Explorations,* edited by Martti Koskenniemi, Walter Rech, and Manuel Jiménez Fonseca, 359–384. Oxford: Oxford University Press, 2017.

Ford Foundation. *Annual Report 2000: October 1, 1999 to September 30, 2000.* New York: Ford Foundation, 2000.

Foucault, Michel, in conversation with Alain Grosrichard, Gerard Wajeman, Jaques-Alain Miller, Guy Le Gaufey, Dominique Celas, Gerard Miller, Catherine Millot, Jocelyne Livi, and Judith Miller. "The Confession of the Flesh." In *Power/Knowledge: Selected Interviews and Other Writings, 1972–1977,* edited and translated by Colin Gordon, 194–228. New York: Pantheon, 1980.

Fox, Gregory H., Kristen E. Boon, and Isaac Jenkins. "The Contributions of United Nations Security Council Resolutions to the Law of Non-international Armed Conflict: New Evi- dence of Customary International Law." *American University Law Review* 67, no. 3 (2018): 649–732.

Frankell Pratt, Simon. "From Norms to Normative Configurations: A Pragmatist and Rela- tional Approach to Theorizing Normativity in IR." *International Theory* 12, no. 1 (2020): 59–82.

Friedman, Elisabeth Jay. "Gendering the Agenda: The Impact of the Transnational Women's Rights Movement at the UN Conferences of the 1990s." *Women's Studies International Forum* 26, no. 4 (2003): 313–331.

Fritz, Jan Maria. "Creating or Improving a National Action Plan Based on UN Security Council Resolution 1325." In *Gender, Conflict, Peace, and UNSC Resolution 1325*, edited by Seema Shekhawat, 83–98. Lanham, MD: Lexington Books, 2018.

Fritz, Jan Marie, Sharon Doering, and F. Belgin Gumru. "Women, Peace, Security and the National Action Plans." *Journal of Applied Social Science* 5, no. 1 (2011): 1–23.

Frogh, Wazhma. "Afghanistan's National Action Plan: 'A Wishlist of Many Dreams.'" *Women, Peace and Security Working Paper Series*, no. 10. London: Centre for Women Peace and Security, London School of Economics and Political Science, 2017. https://www.lse.ac.uk /women-peace-security/assets/documents/2017/wps10Frogh.pdf.

"From Global Policies to Local Action." Global Network of Women Peacebuilders, accessed September 16, 2023. https://gnwp.org/what-we-do/global-policy-local-action/.

Fujio, Christy. "From Soft to Hard Law: Moving Resolution 1325 on Women, Peace and Security Across the Spectrum." *Georgetown Journal of Gender and Law* 9, no. 1 (2008): 215–236.

Fukuda-Parr, Sakiko, and David Hulme. "International Norm Dynamics and the 'End of Poverty': Understanding the Millennium Development Goals." *Global Governance* 17, no. 1 (2011): 17–36.

Furman, Noa. "Women in Peacekeeping Forces." Permanent Mission of Israel to the United Nations, April 11, 2019. https://embassies.gov.il/un/statements/security_council/Pages /women-peacekeeping-operations-noa-speech-0412-938.aspx.

Gale, Ken, and Jonathan Wyatt. *Between the Two: A Nomadic Inquiry Into Collaborative Writing and Subjectivity*. Newcastle, UK: Cambridge Scholars Press, 2019.

Galtung, Johan. *Essays in Peace Research*, vol. 1. Copenhagen: Eljers, 1975.

——. "Violence, Peace and Peace Research." *Journal of Peace Research* 6, no. 3 (1969): 167–191.

Garcia, Denise. "Humanitarian Security Regimes." *International Affairs* 91, no. 1 (2015): 55–75.

Gender Action for Peace and Security UK. *Putting Women's Rights Into the Arms Trade Treaty*. London: GAPS, 2012.

Gentry, Caron E. "Epistemological Failures: Everyday Terrorism in the West." *Critical Studies on Terrorism* 8, no. 3 (2015): 362–382.

George, Nicole, Katrina Lee Koo, and Laura J. Shepherd. "Gender and the UN's Women, Peace and Security Agenda." In *Routledge Handbook of Gender and Security*, edited by Caron E. Gentry, Laura J. Shepherd, and Laura Sjoberg, 311–322. London: Routledge, 2019.

George, Nicole, and Laura J. Shepherd. "Women, Peace and Security: Exploring the Implementation and Integration of UNSCR 1325." *International Political Science Review* 37, no. 3 (2016): 297–306.

Georgetown Institute for Women, Peace and Security. *Women, Peace and Security Index 2017/18*. Washington, DC: GIWPS, 2017.

——. *Women, Peace and Security Index 2019/20*. Washington, DC: GIWPS, 2019.

——. *Women, Peace and Security Index 2021/22*. Washington, DC: GIWPS, 2021.

Giannini, Renata Avelar, and Pérola Abreu Pereira. "Building Brazil's National Action Plan: Lessons Learned and Opportunities." *Women, Peace and Security Working Paper Series*, no. 24. London: Centre for Women Peace and Security, London School of Economics and Political Science, 2020. https://www.lse.ac.uk/women-peace-security/assets/documents /2020/WPS24GianniniandPereira.pdf.

Gibbings, Sheri Lynn. "No Angry Women at the United Nations: Political Dreams and the Cultural Politics of United Nations Security Council Resolution 1325." *International Feminist Journal of Politics* 13, no. 4 (2011): 522–538.

Gilroy, Paul. "Colonial Crimes and Convivial Cultures." *Rethinking Nordic Colonialism*, April 22, 2006. http://rethinking-nordic-colonialism.org/files/pdf/ACT2/ESSAYS/Gilroy .pdf.

Glanville, Luke. "Does R2P Matter? Interpreting the Impact of a Norm." *Cooperation and Conflict* 51, no. 2 (2016): 184–199.

"Global Norms and Standards: Peace and Security." UN Women, accessed September 18, 2023. https://www.unwomen.org/en/what-we-do/peace-and-security/global-norms-and -standards.

Goetz, Anne Marie, and Natalie Florea Hudson. "Too Much that Can't Be Said: Anne Marie Goetz in Conversation with Natalie Florea Hudson." *International Feminist Journal of Politics* 16, no. 2 (2014): 336–346.

Goetz, Anne Marie, and Rob Jenkins. "Gender, Security, and Governance: The Case of Sustainable Development Goal 16." *Gender & Development* 24, no. 1 (2016): 127–137.

Gond, Jean-Pascal, Laure Cabantous, Nancy Harding, and Mark Learmouth. "What Do We Mean by Performativity in Organizational and Management Theory? The Uses and Abuses of Performativity." *International Journal of Management Reviews* 18, no. 4 (2016): 440–463.

Gooding, Francis. "Wolf, Turtle, Bear." *London Review of Books* 44, no. 10 (2022). https://www .lrb.co.uk/the-paper/v44/n10/francis-gooding/wolf-turtle-bear

Government of Ireland. "Working Paper Presented by Ireland to the Conference of State Parties to the Arms Trade Treaty: Article 7(4) and Gender-Based Violence Assessment." ATT/ CSP3/2017/IRL/183/Conf.WP, September 4, 2017.

Grady, Kate. "Sexual Exploitation and Abuse by UN Peacekeepers: A Threat to Impartiality." *International Peacekeeping* 17, no. 2 (2010): 215–228.

Graham, Maria. *Journal of a Voyage to Brazil, and Residence There, During Part of the Years 1821, 1822, 1823*. London: Longman, Hurst, Rees, Orme, Brown and Green, 1824.

Green, Caroline, Deepayan Basu Ray, Claire Mortimer, and Kate Stone. "Gender-Based Violence and the Arms Trade Treaty: Reflections from a Campaigning and Legal Perspective." *Gender & Development* 21, no. 3 (2013): 551–562.

Green, Duncan, and Anna Macdonald. *Power and Change: The Arms Trade Treaty*. Oxfam Active Citizenship Case Study. Oxford: Oxfam, 2015.

Green, Jessica F. "Hierarchy in Regime Complexes: Understanding Authority in Antarctic Governance." *International Studies Quarterly* 66, no. 1 (2022): sqab084. https://doi.org/10.1093 /isq/sqab084.

Greening, Justine. "Remarks at Launch of the UK National Action Plan on Women, Peace and Security." Government of the United Kingdom, June 12, 2014. https://www.gov.uk /government/news/launch-of-the-uk-national-action-plan-on-women-peace-and -security.

Greenpeace Germany. *Exporting Violence and Inequality: The Link Between German Arms Exports and Gender-Based Violence*. Berlin: Centre for Feminist Foreign Policy on behalf of Greenpeace, 2020.

Gregory, Derek. *The Colonial Present: Afghanistan, Palestine, Iraq*. London: Blackwell, 2004.

Grey, Rosemary. "Conflicting Interpretations of 'Sexual Violence' in the International Criminal Court." *Australian Feminist Studies* 29, no. 81 (2014): 273–288.

——. *Prosecuting Sexual and Gender-Based Crimes at the International Criminal Court: Practice, Progress and Potential*. Cambridge: Cambridge University Press, 2019.

Grimes, Rachel. "Exclusive Interview with UNSCR 1325 as She Turns 19." *NATO Review*, October 31, 2019. https://www.nato.int/docu/review/articles/2019/10/31/exclusive-interview-with-unscr-1325-as-she-turns-19/index.html.

Guelke, Adrian. *Politics in Deeply Divided Societies*. Cambridge: Polity Press, 2012.

Guerrina, Roberta, and Katharine A. M. Wright. "Gendering Normative Power Europe: Lessons of the Women, Peace and Security Agenda." *International Affairs* 92, no. 2 (2016): 293–312.

Guillaume, Xavier. "Collaboration." In *Critical Security Methods: New Frameworks for Analysis*, edited by Claudia Aradau, Jef Huysmans, Andrew Neal, and Nadine Voelkner, 189–207. London: Routledge, 2014.

Gunitsky, Seva. "Complexity and Theories of Change in International Politics." *International Theory* 5, no. 1 (2013): 35–63.

Haas, Peter M. "Introduction: Epistemic Communities and International Policy Coordination." *International Organization* 46, no. 1 (1992): 1–35.

Haas, Peter M., and Ernst B. Haas. "Learning to Learn: Improving International Governance." *Global Governance* 1, no. 2 (1995): 255–285.

Haastrup, Toni. "Creating Cinderella? The Unintended Consequences of the Women, Peace and Security Agenda for EU's Mediation Architecture." *International Negotiation* 23, no. 2 (2018): 218–237.

——. "WPS and the African Union." In *The Oxford Handbook of Women, Peace, and Security*, edited by Sara E. Davies and Jacqui True, 375–387. Oxford: Oxford University Press, 2019.

Haastrup, Toni, and Jamie J. Hagen. "Global Racial Hierarchies and the Limits of Localization via National Action Plans." In *New Directions in Women, Peace and Security*, edited by Soumita Basu, Paul Kirby, and Laura J. Shepherd, 133–151. Bristol, UK: Bristol University Press, 2020.

——. "Racial Hierarchies of Knowledge Production in the Women, Peace and Security Agenda." *Critical Studies on Security* 9, no. 1 (2021): 27–30.

Hagen, Jamie J. "Queering Women, Peace and Security." *International Affairs* 92, no. 2 (2016): 313–332.

——. "Queering Women, Peace and Security in Colombia." *Critical Studies on Security* 5, no. 1 (2017): 125–129.

Hagen, Jamie J., and Catherine F. O'Rourke. "Forum-Shifting and Human Rights: Prospects for Queering the Women, Peace and Security Agenda." *Human Rights Quarterly* 45, no. 3 (2023): 406–430.

Hague, William. "Remarks at Launch of the UK National Action Plan on Women, Peace and Security." Government of the United Kingdom, June 12, 2014. https://www.gov.uk/government/news/launch-of-the-uk-national-action-plan-on-women-peace-and-security.

——. "Written Statement on Women, Peace and Security." 519 Parl. Deb. H.C. (2010) col. 50WS. https://hansard.parliament.uk/commons/2010-11-25/debates/10112524000009/WomenPeaceAndSecurity.

Halberstam, Judith. *The Queer Art of Failure*. Durham, NC: Duke University Press, 2011.

Hall, Stuart. "The Narrative Construction of Reality: An Interview with Stuart Hall." *Southern Review* 17, no. 1 (1984): 3–17.

Halley, Janet. *Split Decisions: How and Why to Take a Break from Feminism*. Princeton, NJ: Princeton University Press, 2006.

Halley, Janet, Prabha Kotiswaran, Rachel Rebouché, and Hila Shamir. *Governance Feminism: An Introduction*. Minneapolis: University of Minnesota Press, 2018.

——, eds. *Governance Feminism: Notes from the Field*. Minneapolis: University of Minnesota Press, 2019.

Halley, Janet, Prabha Kotiswaran, Hila Shamir, and Chantal Thomas. "From the International to the Local in Feminist Legal Responses to Rape, Prostitution/Sex Work, and Sex Trafficking: Four Studies in Contemporary Governance Feminism." *Harvard Journal of Law & Gender* 29, no. 2 (2006): 335–423.

Hamilton, Caitlin, Rhaíssa Pagot, and Laura J. Shepherd. "BRICS Countries and the Construction of Conflict in the Women, Peace and Security Open Debates." *International Affairs* 97, no. 3 (2021): 739–757.

Hammond, Philip. "Remarks at Launch of the UK National Action Plan on Women, Peace and Security." Government of the United Kingdom, June 12, 2014. https://www.gov.uk/government/news/launch-of-the-uk-national-action-plan-on-women-peace-and-security.

Han, Yuna, and Sophie T. Rosenberg. "Claiming Equality: The African Union's Contestation of the Anti-impunity Norm." *International Studies Review* 23, no. 3 (2021): 726–751.

Hanieh, Adam. "Ambitions of a Global Gulf: The Arab Uprisings, Yemen and the Saudi-Emirati Alliance." *Middle East Report*, no. 289 (2018): 21–26.

Haraway, Donna J. "Situated Knowledges: The Science Question in Feminism and the Privilege of Partial Perspective." *Feminist Studies* 14, no. 3 (1988): 575–599.

Harding, Sandra. *The Science Question in Feminism*. Ithaca, NY: Cornell University Press, 1986.

——. *Whose Science? Whose Knowledge? Thinking from Women's Lives*. Ithaca, NY: Cornell University Press, 1991.

Hartung, William. *Arming Repression: U.S. Military Support for Saudi Arabia, from Trump to Biden*. Washington, DC: Center for International Policy, 2021.

Harvey, Fiona. "Activists Protest at 'Sidelining of Social Justice' at UN Climate Talks." *The Guardian*, December 12, 2019. https://www.theguardian.com/environment/2019/dec/12/activists-protest-un-climate-talks.

Healy, Jack. "In Indian Country, a Crisis of Missing Women. And a New One When They're Found." *New York Times*, December 25, 2019. https://www.nytimes.com/2019/12/25/us/native-women-girls-missing.html.

Heathcote, Gina. *Feminist Dialogues on International Law: Successes, Tensions, Futures*. Oxford: Oxford University Press, 2019.

——. "Security Council Resolution 2242 on Women, Peace and Security: Progressive Gains or Dangerous Development?" *Global Society* 32, no. 4 (2018): 374–394.

Hemmings, Clare. "Affective Solidarity: Feminist Reflexivity and Political Transformation." *Feminist Theory* 13, no. 2 (2012): 147–161.

——. *Why Stories Matter: The Political Grammar of Feminist Theory.* Durham, NC: Duke University Press, 2011.

Hendrick, Rebecca M., and David Nachmias. "The Policy Sciences: The Challenge of Complexity." *Policy Studies Review* 11, nos. 3–4 (1992): 310–328.

Hendricks, Cheryl. "Progress and Challenges in Implementing the Women, Peace and Security Agenda in the African Union's Peace and Security Architecture." *Africa Development/ Afrique et Développement* 42, no. 3 (2017): 73–98.

——. "Women, Peace and Security in Africa." *African Security Review* 24, no. 4 (2015): 364–375.

Henry, Marsha. "On the Necessity of Critical Race Feminism for Women, Peace and Security." *Critical Studies on Security* 9, no. 1 (2021): 22–26.

——. "Peacexploitation? Interrogating Labor Hierarchies and Global Sisterhood Among Indian and Uruguayan Peacekeepers." *Globalizations* 9, no. 1 (2012): 15–33.

Henshaw, Alexis L. *Why Women Rebel: Understanding Women's Participation in Armed Rebel Groups.* London: Routledge, 2017.

Hill, Felicity. "*How* and *When* Has Security Council Resolution 1325 (2000) on Women, Peace and Security Impacted Negotiations Outside the Security Council?" Master's thesis, Uppsala University, 2005. On file with authors.

——. "Women's Contribution to Conflict Prevention, Early Warning and Disarmament." *Disarmament Forum* 4 (2003): 17–24.

Hill, Felicity, Mikele Aboitiz, and Sara Poehlman-Doumbouya. "Nongovernmental Organizations' Role in the Build-Up and Implementation of Security Council Resolution 1325." *Signs: Journal of Women in Culture and Society* 28, no. 4 (2003): 1255–1269.

Hofferberth, Matthias. "Get Your Act(ors) Together! Theorizing Agency in Global Governance." *International Studies Review* 21, no 1 (2018): 127–145.

Holt-Ivry, Olivia. "Women Make Peace Stick." *Foreign Policy,* August 24, 2018. https://foreignpolicy.com/2018/08/24/women-make-peace-stick/.

Holvikivi, Aiko. "Gender Experts and Critical Friends: Research in Relations of Proximity." *European Journal of Politics and Gender* 2, no. 1 (2019): 131–147.

——. "What Role for the Security Sector? An SSR Approach to Implementing the Women, Peace and Security Agenda." *Connections* 14, no. 3 (2015): 31–44.

Holvikivi, Aiko, and Audrey Reeves. "Women, Peace and Security After Europe's 'Refugee Crisis.'" *European Journal of International Security* 5, no. 2 (2020): 135–154.

Holzscheiter, Anna. "Between Communicative Interaction and Structures of Signification: Discourse Theory and Analysis in International Relations." *International Studies Perspectives* 15, no. 2 (2014): 142–162.

Howell, Alison. "Forget 'Militarization': Race, Disability and the 'Martial Politics' of the Police and the University." *International Feminist Journal of Politics* 20, no. 2 (2018): 117–136.

Howland, Magdalena. "Harnessing the Power of Women in NATO: An Intersectional Feminist Perspective on UNSCR 1325." In *Women, Peace and Transforming Security: Visions of the Future of Women, Peace and Security for NATO*, edited by Office of the NATO Secretary General's Special Representative for Women, Peace and Security, 19–21. 2020.

Hudson, Heidi. "Gender, Peacebuilding and Post-conflict Reconstruction in Africa." In *The State of Africa: Post-conflict Reconstruction and Development*, edited by Dirk Kotzé and Hussein Solomon, 9–30. Pretoria: African Institute of South Africa, 2008.

——. "The Power of Mixed Messages: Women, Peace, and Security Language in National Action Plans from Africa." *Africa Spectrum* 52, no. 3 (2017): 3–29.

Hudson, Natalie Florea. *Gender, Human Security and the United Nations: Security Language as a Political Framework for Women*. London: Routledge, 2010.

Hudson, Valerie, and Patricia Leidl. *The Hillary Doctrine: Sex and American Foreign Policy*. New York: Columbia University Press, 2015.

Hunt, Swanee, and Douglas Lute. "Inclusive Security: NATO Adapts and Adopts." *PRISM* 6, no. 1 (2016): 6–19.

Hurd, Ian. *After Anarchy: Legitimacy and Power in the United Nations Security Council*. Princeton, NJ: Princeton University Press, 2007.

Hurley, Matthew. "The 'Genderman': (Re)negotiating Militarized Masculinities When 'Doing Gender' at NATO." *Critical Military Studies* 4, no. 1 (2018): 72–91.

——. "Watermelons and Weddings: Making Women, Peace and Security 'Relevant' at NATO Through (Re)Telling Stories of Success." *Global Society* 32, no. 4 (2018): 436–456.

Hutchinson, Clare. "Are We There Yet? Implementing the Women, Peace and Security Agenda: If Not Now, When?" *NATO WPS Bulletin*, no. 2 (2020): 2–3.

——. "NATO Statement at the United Nations Security Council Open Debate on Women, Peace and Security." NATO, October 20, 2020. https://www.nato.int/cps/en/natohq/opinions_179287.htm.

——. "Statement at the United Nations Security Council Open Debate on Women, Peace and Security." NATO, October 25, 2018. https://www.nato.int/cps/en/natohq/opinions_159803.htm.

——. "Statement at the UN Security Council's Open Debate on Sexual Violence in Conflict." NATO, April 14, 2021. https://www.nato.int/cps/en/natohq/opinions_183216.htm.

Hutchinson, Susan. "US Undermines UN Security Council Resolution Against Wartime Rape." *The Interpreter*. April 24, 2019. https://www.lowyinstitute.org/the-interpreter/us-undermines-un-resolution-against-wartime-rape.

Hutchison, Emma, and Roland Bleiker. "Theorizing Emotions in World Politics." *International Theory* 6, no. 3 (2014): 491–514.

Huvé, Sophie. *The Use of UN Sanctions to Address Conflict-Related Sexual Violence*. Washington, DC: Georgetown Institute for Women, Peace and Security, 2018.

Iileka, Nekwaya, and Julia Imene-Chanduru. "How Namibia Helped Birth UN Resolution 1325 on Women, Peace and Security." *Africa Renewal*, October 27, 2020. https://www.un.org/africarenewal/magazine/october-2020/how-namibia-helped-birth-un-resolution-1325-women-peace-and-security.

Inclusive Peace and Transition Initiative. *Case Study: Women in Peace and Transition Processes: Liberia (2003–2011)*. Geneva: Graduate Institute of International and Development Studies, 2018.

Indigenous Environment Network. "Native American COP25 Delegation Removed from US Embassy While Honouring MMIW." *Buffalo's Fire*, December 10, 2019. https://www .buffalosfire.com/native-american-cop25-delegation-removed-from-us-embassy-while -honoring-mmiw/.

International Commission on Intervention and State Sovereignty. *The Responsibility to Protect: Report of the International Commission on Intervention and State Sovereignty.* Ottawa, ON: International Development Research Centre, 2001.

International Women's Commission for a Just and Sustainable Palestinian-Israeli Peace. "Advancing Women's Leadership for Sustainable Peace in the Palestinian-Israeli Conflict and Worldwide." United Nations Development Fund for Women and International Women's Commission, Madrid, June 1–2, 2010. https://www.un.org/unispal/document/auto -insert-207967/.

——. "Charter of Principles." International Women's Commission, Istanbul, July 27, 2005. https://www.un.org/unispal/document/auto-insert-200863/.

——. "Political Vision—Paper of Understanding." International Women's Commission, August 30, 2008. https://www.un.org/unispal/document/auto-insert-197024/.

International Work Group for Indigenous Affairs. *The Indigenous World.* 34th ed. Copenhagen: International Work Group for Indigenous Affairs, 2020.

Isaksson, Charlotte. "Fighting for Gender Equality: Why Security Sector Actors Must Combat Sexual and Gender-Based Violence." *Fletcher Forum on World Affairs* 38, no. 2 (2014): 49–72.

——. "Integrating Gender Perspectives at NATO: Two Steps Forward, One Step Back." In *Women and Gender Perspectives in the Military: An International Comparison,* edited by Robert Egnell and Mayesha Alam, 225–251. Washington, DC: Georgetown University Press, 2019.

Jabri, Vivienne. "Disarming Norms: Postcolonial Agency and the Constitution of the International." *International Theory* 6, no. 2 (2014): 372–390.

Jacevic, Mirsad M. "WPS, States, and the National Action Plans." In *The Oxford Handbook of Women, Peace, and Security,* edited by Sara E. Davies and Jacqui True, 274–289. Oxford: Oxford University Press, 2018.

Jackson, Patrick T. *The Conduct of Inquiry in International Relations: Philosophy of Science and Its Implications for the Study of World Politics.* London: Routledge, 2010.

Jackson, Patrick T., and Daniel H. Nexon. "Relations Before States: Substance, Process and the Study of World Politics." *European Journal of International Relations* 5, no. 3 (1999): 291–332.

Jansson, Maria, and Maud Eduards. "The Politics of Gender in the UN Security Council Resolutions on Women, Peace and Security." *International Feminist Journal of Politics* 18, no. 4 (2016): 590–604.

Jauhola, Marjaana. "Decolonizing Branded Peacebuilding: Abjected Women Talk Back to the Finnish Women, Peace and Security Agenda." *International Affairs* 92, no. 2 (2016): 333–351.

Jenkins, Dlorah, Marcus Marktanner, Almuth D. Merkel, and David Sedik. "Estimating Child Mortality Attributable to War in Yemen." *International Journal of Development Issues* 17, no. 3 (2018): 372–383.

Joachim, Jutta. "Framing Issues and Seizing Opportunities: The UN, NGOs, and Women's Rights." *International Studies Quarterly* 47, no. 2 (2003): 247–274.

Joachim, Jutta, and Andrea Schneiker. "Changing Discourses, Changing Practices? Gender Mainstreaming and Security." *Comparative European Politics* 10, no. 5 (2012): 528–563.

Johnstone, Ian. *The Power of Deliberation: International Law, Politics and Organizations.* Oxford: Oxford University Press, 2011.

Jones, Alun. "Towards an Emotional Geography of Diplomacy: Insights from the United Nations Security Council." *Transactions of the Institute of British Geographers* 45, no. 3 (2019): 649–663.

Jones, Claudia. *Women in the Struggle for Peace and Security.* New York: National Women's Commission of the Communist Party, 1950.

Kabeer, Naila. *Reversed Realities: Gender Hierarchies in Development Thought.* London: Verso, 1994.

Kardam, Nüket. "The Emerging Global Gender Equality Regime from Neoliberal and Constructivist Perspectives in International Relations." *International Feminist Journal of Politics* 6, no. 1 (2004): 85–109.

Karim, Sabrina. "Reevaluating Peacekeeping Effectiveness: Does Gender Neutrality Inhibit Progress?" *International Interactions* 43, no. 5 (2017): 822–847.

Karim, Sabrina, and Kyle Beardsley. "Explaining Sexual Exploitation and Abuse in Peacekeeping Missions: The Role of Female Peacekeepers and Gender Equality in Contributing Countries." *Journal of Peace Research* 53, no. 1 (2016): 100–115.

——. "Female Peacekeepers and Gender Balancing: Token Gestures or Informed Policymaking?" *International Interactions* 39 (2013): 461–488.

Karsten, Nora. "Distinguishing Military and Non-military Superiors: Reflections on the *Bemba* Case at the ICC." *Journal of International Criminal Justice* 7, no. 5 (2009): 983–1004.

Katzenstein, Peter J., ed. *The Culture of National Security: Norms and Identity in World Politics.* New York: Columbia University Press, 1996.

Kaya, Zeynep. *Women, Peace and Security in Iraq: Iraq's National Action Plan to Implement Resolution 1325.* London: LSE Middle East Centre, 2016.

Keck, Margaret E., and Kathryn Sikkink. *Activists Beyond Borders: Advocacy Networks in International Politics.* Ithaca, NY: Cornell University Press, 1998.

Keohane, Robert O., and David G. Victor. "The Regime Complex for Climate Change." *Perspectives on Politics* 9, no. 1 (2011): 7–23.

Khalili, Laleh. "Gendered Practices of Counterinsurgency." *Review of international Studies* 37, no. 4 (2011): 1471–1491.

Khullar, Akanksha. "A Lukewarm Commitment: India and Gender Equality in Security Affairs." *The Diplomat*, January 23, 2020. https://thediplomat.com/2020/01/a-lukewarm-commitment-india-and-gender-equality-in-security-affairs/.

Kilcullen, David. "Twenty-Eight Articles: Fundamentals of Company-Level Counterinsurgency." *Military Review*, May–June 2006, 134–139.

Kincheloe, Joe L. "Describing the Bricolage: Conceptualizing a New Rigor in Qualitative Research." *Qualitative Inquiry* 7, no. 6 (2001): 679–692.

Kirby, Paul. "Acting Time; or, the Abolitionist and the Feminist." *International Feminist Journal of Politics* 17, no. 3 (2015): 508–513.

——. "The Body Weaponized: War, Sexual Violence and the Uncanny." *Security Dialogue* 51, nos. 2–3 (2020): 211–230.

——. "Ending Sexual Violence in Conflict: The Preventing Sexual Violence Initiative and Its Critics." *International Affairs* 91, no. 3 (2015): 457–472.

——. "Sexual Violence in the Border Zone: The EU, the Women, Peace and Security Agenda and Carceral Humanitarianism in Libya." *International Affairs* 96, no. 5 (2020): 1209–1226.

Kirby, Paul, and Laura J. Shepherd. "The Futures Past of the Women, Peace and Security Agenda." *International Affairs* 92, no. 2 (2016): 373–392.

——. "Women, Peace and Security: Mapping the (Re)Production of a Policy Ecosystem." *Journal of Global Security Studies* 6, no. 3 (2021): ogaa45. https://doi.org/10.1093/jogss/ogaa045.

Kirby, Paul, Hannah Wright, and Aisling Swaine. "The Future of the UK's Women, Peace and Security Policy." *Policy Brief Series*, no. 7. London: LSE Centre for Women, Peace and Security, 2022.

Kismödi, Eszter, Judith Bueno de Mesquita, Ximena Andión Ibañez, Rajat Khosla, and Lilian Sepúlveda. "Human Rights Accountability for Maternal Death and Failure to Provide Safe, Legal Abortion: The Significance of Two Ground-Breaking CEDAW Decisions." *Reproductive Health Matters* 20, no. 39 (2012): 31–39.

Klot, Jennifer F. "The United Nations Security Council Agenda on 'Women, Peace and Security': Bureaucratic Pathologies and Unrealised Potential." PhD diss., London School of Economics and Politics Science, 2015.

Klotz, Audie. *Norms in International Relations: The Struggle Against Apartheid.* Ithaca, NY: Cornell University Press, 1995.

Kmietowicz, Zosia. "Abortion: US 'Global Gag Rule' Is Killing Women and Girls, Says Report." *BMJ* 365 (2019): l4118. https://www.bmj.com/content/365/bmj.l4118.

Kolhatkar, Sonali. "'Saving' Afghan Women." *ZNet*, May 9, 2002. http://www.rawa.org/znet.htm.

Koomen, Jonneke. "WPS and the International Criminal Court." In *The Oxford Handbook of Women, Peace and Security*, edited by Sara E. Davies and Jacqui True, 351–363. Oxford: Oxford University Press. 2019.

Koskenniemi, Martti. *The Gentle Civilizer of Nations: The Rise and Fall of International Law 1870–1960.* Cambridge: Cambridge University Press, 2001.

Krasner, Stephen D. "Structural Causes and Regime Consequences: Regimes as Intervening Variables." *International Organization* 36, no. 2 (1982): 185–205.

Kratochwil, Friedrich, and John Gerard Ruggie. "International Organization: A State of the Art on an Art of the State." *International Organization* 40, no. 4 (1984): 753–775.

Krause, Jana, Werner Krause, and Piia Bränfors. "Women's Participation in Peace Negotiations and the Durability of Peace." *International Interactions* 44, no. 6 (2018): 985–1016.

Krook, Mona Lena, and Jacqui True. "Rethinking the Life Cycles of International Norms: The United Nations and the Global Promotion of Gender Equality." *European Journal of International Relations* 18, no. 1 (2012): 103–127.

Kuokkanen, Rauna. "Globalization as Racialized, Sexualized Violence: The Case of Indigenous Women." *International Feminist Journal of Politics* 10, no. 2 (2008): 216–233.

Lackenbauer, Helené, and Richard Langlais, eds. *Review of the Practical Implications of UNSCR 1325 for the Conduct of NATO-led Operations and Missions.* Stockholm: Swedish Defence Research Agency, 2013.

Lahoud, Nina J. "What Fueled the Far-Reaching Impact of the Windhoek Declaration and Namibia Plan of Action as Milestone for Gender Mainstreaming in UN Peace Support Operations and Where is Implementation 20 Years Later?" *Journal of International Peacekeeping* 24 (2020): 1–52. https://doi.org/10.1163/18754112-20200005.

Larner, Wendy, and William Walters, eds. *Global Governmentality: Governing International Spaces.* London, Routledge, 2004.

Latour, Bruno. "On Actor-Network Theory: A Few Clarifications." *Soziale Welt* 47 (1996): 369–381.

Law, John. *After Method: Mess in Social Science Research.* London: Routledge, 2004.

Law, John, and John Urry. "Enacting the Social." *Economy and Society* 33, no. 3 (2004): 390–410.

Lawrence, Bonita. "Gender, Race, and the Regulation of Native Identity in Canada and the United States: An Overview." *Hypatia* 18, no. 2 (2003): 3–31.

LeBrun, Emile. *Gender-Sensitive Ammunition Management Processes: Considerations for National Authorities.* New York: United Nations Office for Disarmament Affairs, 2021.

Lee-Koo, Katrina. "Implementing Australia's National Action Plan on United Nations Security Council Resolution 1325." *Australian Journal of International Affairs* 68, no. 3 (2014): 300–313.

Lee-Koo, Katrina, and Barbara K. Trojanowska. "Does the United Nations' Women, Peace and Security Agenda Speak With, For, or To Women in the Asia Pacific? The Development of National Action Plans in the Asia Pacific." *Critical Studies on Security* 5, no. 3 (2017): 287–301.

Legro, Jeffrey W. "Which Norms Matter? Revisiting the 'Failure' of Internationalism." *International Organization* 51, no. 1 (1997): 31–63.

Leiteritz, Ralf J., and Manuela Moschella. "The IMF and Capital Account Liberalization: A Case of Failed Norm Institutionalization." In *Owning Development: Creating Policy Norms in the IMF and the World Bank*, edited by Susan Park and Antje Vetterlein, 153–180. Cambridge: Cambridge University Press, 2010.

Lipschutz, Ronnie. "Global Civil Society and Global Governmentality: Or, the Search for Politics and the State Amidst the Capillaries of Social Power." In *Power in Global Governance*, edited by Michael Barnett and Raymond Duvall, 229–248. Cambridge: Cambridge University Press, 2005.

Lubell, Mark. "The Ecology of Games Framework." *Policy Studies Journal* 41, no. 3 (2013): 537–559.

Luck, Edward. *UN Security Council: Practice and Promise.* London: Routledge, 2006.

Lusenge, Julienne. "Statement at the UN Security Council Open Debate on Women, Peace and Security." NGO Working Group on Women, Peace and Security, October 13, 2015.

https://www.womenpeacesecurity.org/files/NGOWG_UNSC_OpenDebate_Statement
_Lusenge_10-2017.pdf.

Lyytikäinen, Minna, and Marjaana Jauhola. "Best Practice Diplomacy and Feminist Killjoys
in the Strategic State: Exploring the Affective Politics of Women, Peace and Security." In
New Directions in Women, Peace and Security, edited by Soumita Basu, Paul Kirby, and
Laura J. Shepherd, 83–90. Bristol, UK: Bristol University Press, 2020.

Maas, Heiko. "Speech by Federal Minister for Foreign Affairs Heiko Maas at the United Nations
Security Council—'Pledge of Commitment on Women, Peace and Security.'" Federal Foreign Office of Germany, April 23, 2019. https://www.auswaertiges-amt.de/en/newsroom
/news/maas-speech-security-council-pledge-of-commitment-on-women-peace-and
-security/2212520.

Mabee, Bryan, and Srdjan Vucetic. "Varieties of Militarism: Towards a Typology." *Security Dialogue* 49, nos. 1–2 (2018): 96–108.

Mabera, Faith, and Yolanda Spies. "How Well Does R2P Travel Beyond the West?" In *The
Oxford Handbook of the Responsibility to Protect*, edited by Alex J. Bellamy and Tim Dunne,
208–226. Oxford: Oxford University Press, 2016.

MacKenzie, Megan H. *Female Soldiers in Sierra Leone: Sex, Security, and Post-conflict Development.* New York: New York University Press, 2012.

MacKenzie, Megan H., and Mohamed Sesay. "No Amnesty from/for the International: The
Production and Promotion of TRCs as an International Norm in Sierra Leone." *International Studies Perspectives* 13, no. 2 (2012): 146–163.

Madsen, Diana Højlund, and Heidi Hudson. "Temporality and the Discursive Dynamics of
the Rwanda National Action Plans (NAPs) on Women, Peace and Security from 2009 and
2018." *International Feminist Journal of Politics* 22, no. 4 (2020): 550–571.

Mahdavi, Mojtaba. "A Postcolonial Critique of Responsibility to Protect in the Middle East."
Perceptions: Journal of International Affairs 20, no. 1 (2015): 7–36.

Malone, David. M. "The Security Council in the 1990s: Inconsistent, Improvisational, Indispensable?" In *New Millennium, New Perspectives: The United Nations, Security and Governance*, edited by Ramesh Thakur and Edward Newman, 21–45. New York: UN University Press, 2000.

Manchanda, Rita. "Difficult Encounters with the WPS Agenda in South Asia: Re-Scripting
Globalized Norms and Policy Frameworks for a Feminist Peace." In *New Directions in
Women, Peace and Security*, edited by Soumita Basu, Paul Kirby, and Laura J. Shepherd,
61–82. Bristol, UK: Bristol University Press, 2020.

——. "Introduction." In *Women and Politics of Peace: South Asia Narratives on Militarization,
Power, and Justice*, edited by Rita Manchanda, xv–xl. New Delhi: SAGE, 2017.

Manjoo, Rashida. "The Continuum of Violence Against Women and the Challenges of Effective Redress." *International Human Rights Law Review* 1, no. 1 (2012): 1–29.

Marchand, Marianne, and Anne Sisson Runyan, eds. *Gender and Global Restructuring: Sight-
ings, Sites and Resistances.* London: Routledge, 2010.

Marks, Greg. "Sovereign States vs Peoples: Indigenous Rights and the Origins of International
Law." *Australian Indigenous Law Reporter* 5, no. 2 (2000): 1–9.

Marsh, David, and Jason C. Sharman, "Policy Diffusion and Policy Transfer." *Political Studies* 30 no. 3 (2009): 269–288.

Martel, Stéphanie, Jennifer Mustapha, and Sarah E. Sharma. "Women, Peace and Security Governance in the Asia Pacific: A Multi-scalar Field of Discourse and Practice." *International Affairs* 98, no. 2 (2022): 727–746.

Martin, Claudia, and Susana SáCouto. "Access to Justice for Victims of Conflict-Related Sexual Violence: Lessons Learned from the *Sepur Zarco* Case." *Journal of International Criminal Justice* 18 (2020): 243–270.

Martín de Almagro, María. "Lost Boomerangs, the Rebound Effect and Transnational Advocacy Networks: A Discursive Approach to Norm Diffusion." *Review of International Studies* 44, no. 4 (2018): 672–693.

——. "Producing Participants: Gender, Race, Class, and Women, Peace and Security." *Global Society* 32, no. 4 (2018): 395–414.

Masri, Mazen. "Colonial Imprints: Settler-Colonialism as a Fundamental Feature of Israeli Constitutional Law." *International Journal of Law in Context* 13, no, 3 (2017): 388–407.

Masters, Sarah. "The Arms Trade Treaty: Why Women?" *openDemocracy*, May 19, 2011. https://www.opendemocracy.net/en/arms-trade-treaty-why-women/.

Maters, Karen. "The Nairobi World Conference." Supplement no. 24 to *Women of Europe*. Brussels: Commission of the European Communities, 1986.

Mawby, Briana, and Anna Appelbaum. "Addressing Future Fragility: Women, Climate, and Migration." In *New Directions in Women, Peace and Security*, edited by Soumita Basu, Paul Kirby, and Laura J. Shepherd, 207–222. Bristol, UK: Bristol University Press, 2020.

Mayntz, Renate. "New Challenges to Governance Theory." In *Governance as Social and Political Communication*, edited by Henrik Paul Bang, 27–40. Manchester, UK: Manchester University Press, 2003.

Mazower, Mark. *No Enchanted Palace: The End of Empire and the Ideological Origins of the United Nations*. Princeton, NJ: Princeton University Press, 2009.

McCourt, David. "Practice Theory and Relationalism as the New Constructivism." *International Studies Quarterly* 60, no. 3 (2016): 475–485.

McDermott, Rose. "The Body Doesn't Lie: A Somatic Approach to the Study of Emotions in World Politics." *International Theory* 6, no. 3 (2014): 557–562.

McDonald, Matt. "Human Security and the Construction of Security." *Global Society* 16, no. 3 (2002): 277–295.

McFate, Montgomery, and Steve Fondacaro. "Reflections on the Human Terrain System During the First 4 Years." *PRISM* 2, no. 4 (2011): 63–82.

McLeod, Laura. "Back to the Future: Temporality and Gender Security Narratives in Serbia." *Security Dialogue* 44, no. 2 (2013): 165–181.

——. *Gender Politics and Security Discourse: Personal-Political Imaginations and Feminism in "Post-conflict" Serbia*. Abingdon, UK: Routledge, 2015.

Mendlovitz, Saul. "On the Creation of a Just World Order: An Agenda for a Program of Inquiry and Praxis." *Alternatives* 7, no. 3 (1981): 355–373.

Merry, Sally Engle. *The Seductions of Quantification: Measuring Human Rights, Gender Violence, and Sex Trafficking*. Chicago: University of Chicago Press, 2016.

MIFTAH (The Palestinian Initiative for the Promotion of Global Dialogue and Democracy). *Palestinian Women and Resolution 1325.* Ramallah: MIFTAH, 2009. http://www.miftah.org /Publications/Books/Palestinian_Women_and_Resolution1325.pdf.

——. *A Vision for Palestinian Women's Rights Organisations Based on the Global Study on the Implementation of United Nations Security Council Resolution (UNSCR) 1325 (Ten Strategies for Tackling Issues Pertaining to Women, Peace and Security).* Ramallah: MIFTAH, 2017. http://www.miftah.org/Publications/Books/A_Vision_for_Palestinian_Women_on_the _International_Review_En.pdf.

Miklaucic, Michael, and Cathleen Pearl. "All the Elements of National Power." *PRISM* 6, no. 1 (2016): 2–5.

Miller, Barbara, Milad Pournik, and Aisling Swaine. "Women in Peace and Security Through United Nations Security Resolution 1325: Literature Review, Content Analysis of National Action Plans, and Implementation." Working Paper no. 13. Institute for Global and International Studies, George Washington University, Washington, DC, 2014. https://giwps .georgetown.edu/resource/women-in-peace-and-security-through-united-nations -security-resolution-1325-literature-review-content-analysis-of-national-action-plans -and-implementation/.

Mlambo-Ngcuka, Phumzile. "Foreword." In *Preventing Conflict, Transforming Justice, Securing the Peace: A Global Study on the Implementation of United Nations Security Council Resolution 1325,* edited by Radhika Coomaraswamy et al. New York: UN Women, 2015.

Moeke-Pickering, Taima, Sheila Cote-Meek, and Ann Pegoraro. "Understanding the Ways Missing and Murdered Indigenous Women Are Framed and Handled by Social Media Users." *Media International Australia* 169, no. 1 (2018): 54–64.

Mohanty, Chandra Talpade. "Under Western Eyes: Feminist Scholarship and Colonial Discourses." *Feminist Review* 30, no. Autumn (1988): 61–88.

——. " 'Under Western Eyes' Revisited: Feminist Solidarity Through Anticapitalist Struggles." *Signs: Journal of Women in Culture and Society* 28, no. 2 (2003): 499–535.

Monture, Patricia A. "Women's Words: Power, Identity, and Indigenous Sovereignty." *Canadian Women's Studies* 26, nos. 3–4 (2008): 153–159.

Moravcsik, Andrew. "The Origins of Human Rights Regimes: Democratic Delegation in Postwar Europe." *International Organization* 54, no. 2 (2000): 217–252.

Mordaunt, Penny. "Speech at Launch of National Action Plan for Women, Peace and Security." Government of the United Kingdom, January 17, 2018. https://www.gov.uk /government/speeches/penny-mordaunt-speech-at-launch-of-national-action-plan-for -women-peace-and-security.

Moreton-Robinson, Aileen. "The Discursive Nature of Citizenship: Indigenous Sovereign Rights, Racism and Welfare Reform." *International Journal of Critical Indigenous Studies* 2, no. 2 (2009): 2–9.

Mosse, David. "Is Good Policy Unimplementable? Reflections on the Ethnography of Aid Policy and Practice." *Development and Change* 35, no. 4 (2004): 639–671.

Moyo, Khanyisela. "Feminism, Postcolonial Legal Theory and Transitional Justice: A Critique of Current Trends." *International Human Rights Law Review* 1 (2012): 237–275.

Mundy, Martha, and Jeannie Sowers. "The Saudi Coalition's Food War on Yemen: An Interview with Martha Mundy." *Middle East Report*, no. 289 (2018): 8–11.

Musa, Shavana. "The Saudi-Led Coalition in Yemen, Arms Exports and Human Rights: Prevention Is Better than Cure." *Journal of Conflict and Security Law* 22, no. 3 (2017): 433–462.

Mwatana for Human Rights. *Starvation Makers: The Use of Starvation by Warring Parties in Yemen*. Sana'a, YE: Mwatana for Human Rights, 2021.

Myrttinen, Henri. *Connecting the Dots: Arms Control, Disarmament and the Women, Peace and Security Agenda*. Geneva: United Nations Institute for Disarmament Research, 2020.

——. "Locating Masculinities in WPS." In *The Oxford Handbook of Women, Peace and Security*, edited by Sara E. Davies and Jacqui True, 88–97. New York: Oxford University Press, 2019.

Myrttinen, Henri, Laura J. Shepherd, and Hannah Wright. *Implementing the Women, Peace and Security Agenda in the OSCE Region*. Helsinki and London: Organisation for Security and Co-operation in Europe and LSE Centre for Women, Peace and Security, 2020.

NAP 1325 Partnership in the Netherlands. *Women, Peace and Security NAP 1325-IV (2021–2025): Fourth Dutch National Action Plan on the Implementation of United Nations Security Council Resolution 1325 and Successive Related Resolutions*. NAP 1325 Partnership in the Netherlands, 2021.

Naraghi Anderlini, Sanam. *The A-B-C to UN Security Council Resolution 1325 on Women, Peace and Security*. London: International Alert, 2000.

——. "Civil Society's Leadership in Adopting 1325 Resolution." In *The Oxford Handbook of Women, Peace and Security*, edited by Sara E. Davies and Jacqui True, 38–52. Oxford: Oxford University Press, 2019.

——. *Women Building Peace: What They Do, Why It Matters*. Boulder, CO: Lynne Rienner, 2007.

Naraghi Anderlini, Sanam, and Judy El-Bushra. "The Conceptual Framework: Security, Peace, Accountability and Rights." In *Inclusive Security, Sustainable Peace: A Toolkit for Advocacy and Action*, edited by International Alert and Women Waging Peace, 5–13. London: Hunt Alternatives Fund and International Alert, 2004.

Naser-Najjab, Nadia. "The Challenge of Implementing UNSC Resolution 1325 Under Colonial Rule" *Palestine-Israel Journal* 25, nos. 3–4 (2020). https://www.pij.org/articles/2050/the-challenge-of-implementing-unsc-resolution-1325-under-colonial-rule

Nasser, Afrah. "Yemen's Women Confront War's Marginalization." *Middle East Report*, no. 289 (2018): 12–15.

NATO. "Comprehensive Report on the NATO/EAPC Policy on the Implementation of UNSCR 1325 on Women, Peace and Security and Related Resolutions." NATO, November 20, 2010. https://www.nato.int/cps/en/natohq/official_texts_68578.htm?selectedLocale=en.

——. "NATO and WPS: How an Unlikely Pair Became Inseparable." *NATO WPS Bulletin*, no. 2 (2020): 4–7.

——. *NATO 2030: United for a New Era—Analysis and Recommendations of the Reflection Group Appointed by the NATO Secretary General*. November 25, 2020. https://www.nato.int/nato_static_fl2014/assets/pdf/2020/12/pdf/201201-Reflection-Group-Final-Report-Uni.pdf.

NATO Committee on Gender Perspectives. *How Can Gender Make a Difference to Security in Operations: Indicators.* 2011. https://www.nato.int/nato_static/assets/pdf/pdf_topics /20120308_1869-11_Gender_Brochure.pdf.

——. *Summary of the National Reports of NATO Member and Partner Nations 2014.* Office of the Gender Advisor, 2016. https://www.nato.int/nato_static_fl2014/assets/pdf/pdf_2016_03 /Summary.pdf.

——. *Summary of the National Reports of NATO Member and Partner Nations to the NATO Committee on Gender Perspectives 2018.* 2020. https://www.nato.int/nato_static_fl2014 /assets/pdf/2020/7/pdf/200713-2018-Summary-NR-to-NCGP.pdf.

"NATO and the Women, Peace and Security Agenda: A Conversation with Clare Hutchinson." Wilson Center, June 27, 2018. https://www.wilsoncenter.org/event/nato-and-the -women-peace-and-security-agenda-conversation-clare-hutchinson.

Ndahinda, Felix Mukwiza. "The Bemba-Banyamulenge Case Before the ICC: From Individual to Collective Criminal Responsibility." *International Journal of Transitional Justice* 7, no. 3 (2013): 476–496.

Nesiah, Vasuki. "Feminism as Counter-Terrorism: The Seduction of Power." In *Gender, National Security, and Counter-Terrorism Human Rights Perspectives*, edited by Margaret Satterthwaite and Jayne C. Huckerby, 127–151. London: Routledge, 2013.

Neumann, Iver B., and Ole Jacob Sending. *Governing the Global Polity: Practice, Mentality, Rationality.* Ann Arbor: University of Michigan Press, 2010.

Nexon, Daniel H., and Vincent Pouliot. "'Things of Networks': Situating ANT in International Relations." *International Political Sociology* 7, no. 3 (2013): 342–345.

Ní Aoláin, Fionnuala. "Gutting the Substance of a Security Council Resolution on Sexual Violence." *Just Security*, April 24, 2019. https://www.justsecurity.org/63750/gutting-the -substance-of-a-security-council-resolution-on-sexual-violence/.

——. "Rethinking the Women, Peace and Security Agenda Through the Lens of Resistance." *Just Security*, April 17, 2017. https://www.justsecurity.org/39982/rethinking-women-peace -security-agenda-lens-resistance/.

——. "The 'War on Terror' and Extremism: Assessing the Relevance of the Women, Peace and Security Agenda." *International Affairs* 92, no. 2 (2016): 275–291.

Ní Aoláin, Fionnuala, and Michael Hamilton. "Gender and the Rule of Law in Transitional Societies." *Minnesota Journal of International Law* 18, no. 2 (2009): 380–402.

Nilsson, Desirée. "Anchoring the Peace: Civil Society Actors in Peace Accords and Durable Peace." *International Interactions* 38, no. 2 (2012): 243–266.

Nordås, Ragnhild, and Siri C. A. Rustad. "Sexual Exploitation and Abuse by Peacekeepers: Understanding Variation." *International Interactions* 39, no. 4 (2013): 511–534.

Nordstrom, Jennifer, and Felicity Hill. "A Gender Perspective." In *Nuclear Disorder or Cooperative Security? U.S. Weapons of Terror, the Global Proliferation Crisis, and Paths to Peace: An Assessment of the Final Report of the Weapons of Mass Destruction Commission and Its Implications for U.S. Policy*, edited by Michael Spies and John Burroughs, 165–168. Portland, OR: Lawyers' Committee on Nuclear Policy, 2007.

Normand, Roger, and Sarah Zaidi. *Human Rights at the UN: The Political History of Universal Justice.* Bloomington: Indiana University Press, 2008.

North Atlantic Military Committee. *Military Guidelines on the Prevention of, and Response to, Conflict-Related Sexual and Gender-Based Violence*. MCM-0009-2015, 2015.

Olonisakin, 'Funmi, Karen Barnes, and Eka Ikpe, eds. *Women, Peace and Security: Translating Policy Into Practice*. London: Routledge, 2011.

Olonisakin, 'Funmi, and Awino Okech, eds. *Women and Security Governance in Africa*. Cape Town: Pambazuka Press, 2011.

Olsson, Louise, and Theodora-Ismene Gizelis, eds. *Gender, Peace and Security: Implementing UN Security Council Resolution 1325*. London: Routledge, 2015.

Olsson, Louise, and Johan Tejpar. "How to Implement Resolution 1325: The Analysis." In *Operational Effectiveness and UN Resolution 1325: Practices and Lessons from Afghanistan*, edited by Louise Olsson and Johan Tejpar, 115–127. Stockholm: Swedish Defence Research Agency, 2009.

Olsson, Louise, Johan Tejpar, and Johanna Valenius. "Introduction." In *Operational Effectiveness and UN Resolution 1325: Practices and Lessons from Afghanistan*, edited by Louise Olsson and Johan Tejpar, 15–18. Stockholm: Swedish Defence Research Agency, 2009.

Onuf, Nicholas. "The New Culture of Security Studies." *Mershon International Studies Review* 42, no. 1 (1998): 132–134.

"Open Letter to Permanent Representatives to the United Nations on the Occasion of the 20th Anniversary of Resolution 1325 (2000)." NGO Working Group on Women, Peace and Security, October 1, 2020. https://www.womenpeacesecurity.org/wp-content/uploads/2020 -WPS-Civil-Society-Open-Letter-1-October-English.pdf.

O'Reilly, Marie. "Where the WPS Pillars Intersect." In *Oxford Handbook on Women, Peace and Security*, edited by Sara E. Davies and Jacqui True, 193–205. Oxford: Oxford University Press, 2019.

——. *Why Women? Inclusive Security and Peaceful Societies*. Washington, DC: Inclusive Security, 2015. https://www.inclusivesecurity.org/wp-content/uploads/2020/02/Why-Women -Brief-2020.pdf.

O'Reilly, Marie, Andrea Ó Súilleabháin, and Thania Paffenholz. *Reimagining Peacemaking: Women's Roles in Peace Processes*. New York: International Peace Institute, 2015.

O'Rourke, Catherine. "'Walk[ing] the Halls of Power'? Understanding Women's Participation in International Peace and Security." *Melbourne Journal of International Law* 15, no. 1 (2014): 128–154.

O'Rourke, Catherine, and Aisling Swaine. "CEDAW and the Security Council: Enhancing Women's Rights in Conflict." *International and Comparative Law Quarterly* 67, no. 1 (2018): 167–199.

——. "WPS and CEDAW, Optional Protocol, and General Recommendations." In *Oxford Handbook on Women, Peace and Security*, edited by Sara E. Davies and Jacqui True, 669–679. Oxford: Oxford University Press, 2019.

O'Sullivan, Míla, and Katerina Krulišová. "Women, Peace and Security in Central Europe: In Between the Western Agenda and Russian Imperialism." *International Affairs* 99, no. 2 (2023): 625–643.

Otto, Dianne. "Beyond Stories of Victory and Danger: Resisting Feminism's Amenability to Serving Security Council Politics." In *Rethinking Peacekeeping, Gender Equality and*

Collective Security, edited by Gina Heathcote and Dianne Otto, 157–152. Basingstoke, UK: Palgrave Macmillan, 2014.

——. "Power and Danger: Feminist Engagement with International Law Through the UN Security Council." *Australian Feminist Law Journal* 32, no. 1 (2010): 97–121.

——. "Securing the 'Gender Legitimacy' of the UN Security Council: Prising Gender from Its Historical Moorings." *Legal Studies Research Paper*, no. 92 (2004). https://genderandsecurity .org/sites/default/files/Otto_-_Securing_the_Gender_Legitimacy_of_the_Un_Security _Council-_Prising_Gender_from_Its_Historical_Moorings.pdf.

——. "The Security Council's Alliance of Gender Legitimacy: The Symbolic Capital of Resolution 1325." In *Fault Lines of International Legitimacy*, edited by Hilary Charlesworth and Jean-Marc Coicaud, 239–275. Cambridge: Cambridge University Press, 2010.

——. "A Sign of 'Weakness'? Disrupting Gender Certainties in the Implementation of Security Council Resolution 1325." *Michigan Journal of Gender and Law* 13, no. 1 (2006): 113–176.

——. "Women, Peace and Security: A Critical Analysis of the Security Council's Vision." *Women, Peace and Security Working Paper*, no. 1. London: Centre for Women, Peace and Security, London School of Economics and Political Sciences, 2016. http://eprints.lse.ac.uk /69472/1/Otto_Women_peace_and_security_a_critical_analysis_WP1_2016.pdf.

Owens, Patricia. *Economy of Force: Counterinsurgency and the Historical Rise of the Social*. Cambridge: Cambridge University Press, 2015.

Owens, Patricia, and Katharina Rietzler. "Toward a History of Women's International Thought." In *Women's International Thought: A New History*, edited by Patricia Owens and Katharina Rietzler, 1–25. Cambridge: Cambridge University Press, 2021.

Oxfam International. *The Gendered Impact of Explosive Weapons Use in Populated Areas in Yemen*. Oxford: Oxfam, 2019.

Paffenholz, Thania, Nick Ross, Steven Dixon, Anna-Lena Schluchter, and Jacqui True. "Making Women Count—Not Just Counting Women: Assessing Women's Inclusion and Influence on Peace Negotiations." Geneva: Inclusive Peace and Transition Initiative (Graduate Institute of International and Development Studies) and UN Women, 2016. https://www .unwomen.org/en/digital-library/publications/2017/5/making-women-count-not-just -counting-women.

Pantzerhielm, Laura, Anna Holzscheiter, and Thurid Bahr. "Power in Relations of International Organisations: The Productive Effects of 'Good' Governance Norms in Global Health." *Review of International Studie* 46, no. 3 (2020): 395–414.

Parashar, Swati. "Foreword: Waging the War on Wars: Feminist Ways Forward." In *Feminist Solutions for Ending War*, edited by Megan MacKenzie and Nicole Wegner, xii–xvii. London: Pluto, 2021.

——. *Women and Militant Wars*. London: Routledge, 2014.

——. "The WPS Agenda: A Postcolonial Critique." In *The Oxford Handbook of Women, Peace, and Security*, edited by Sara E. Davies and Jacqui True, 829–839. Oxford: Oxford University Press, 2019.

Park, Susan, and Antje Vetterlein. "Owning Development: Creating Policy Norms in the IMF and the World Bank." In *Owning Development: Creating Policy Norms in the IMF and the*

World Bank, edited by Susan Park and Antje Vetterlein, 3–26. Cambridge: Cambridge University Press, 2010.

Partis-Jennings, Hannah. "The 'Third Gender' in Afghanistan: A Feminist Account of Hybridity as a Gendered Experience." *Peacebuilding* 7, no. 2 (2019): 178–193.

Pauls, Evelyn. "Female Fighters Shooting Back: Representation and Filmmaking in Post-conflict Societies." *International Feminist Journal of Politics* 22, no. 5 (2020): 697–719.

Percy, Sarah. "What Makes a Norm Robust: The Norm Against Female Combat." *Journal of Global Security Studies* 4, no. 1 (2019): 123–138.

Peroni, Lourdes. "Women's Human Rights in Conflict: The WPS Agenda Twenty Years On." *Questions of International Law*, October 31, 2020. http://www.qil-qdi.org/womens-human-rights-in-the-wps-agenda-twenty-years-on/.

Pettman, Jan Jindy. "Feminist International Relations After 9/11." *Brown Journal of World Affairs* 10, no. 2 (2004): 85–96.

Picq, Manuela Lavinas. *Vernacular Sovereignties: Indigenous Women Challenging World Politics*. Tucson: University of Arizona Press, 2018.

Pison Hindawi, Coralie. "Decolonizing the Responsibility to Protect: On Pervasive Eurocentrism, Southern Agency and Struggles Over Universals." *Security Dialogue* 53, no. 1 (2022): 38–56.

Poirier, Sylvie. "Reflections on Indigenous Cosmopolitics—Poetics." *Anthropologica* 50, no. 1 (2008): 75–85.

Postel, Danny. "Progressive Surge Propels Turning Point in US Policy on Yemen." *Middle East Report*, no. 289 (2018): 42–47.

Pratt, Nicola. "Reconceptualizing Gender, Reinscribing Racial—Sexual Boundaries in International Security: The Case of UN Security Council Resolution 1325 on 'Women, Peace and Security.'" *International Studies Quarterly* 57, no. 4 (2013): 772–783.

Prescott, Jody M. "NATO Gender Mainstreaming: A New Approach to War Amongst the People?" *RUSI Journal* 158, no. 5 (2013): 56–62.

Price, Richard. "Syria and the Chemical Weapons Taboo." *Journal of Global Security Studies* 4, no. 1 (2019): 37–52.

Prosor, Ron. "Women, Peace and Security." Permanent Mission of Israel to the United Nations, October 28, 2011. https://embassies.gov.il/un/statements/security_council/Pages/Women-and-Peace-and-Security.aspx.

Prügl, Elisabeth. "Diversity Management and Gender Mainstreaming as Technologies of Government." *Politics & Gender* 7, no. 1 (2011): 71–89.

Pruitt, Lesley J. *The Women in Blue Helmets: Gender, Policing, and the UN's First All-Female Peacekeeping Unit*. Berkeley: University of California Press, 2016.

Puechguirbal, Nadine. "Women and Children: Deconstructing a Paradigm." *Seton Hall Journal of Diplomacy and International Relations* 5, no. 1 (2004): 5–16.

Qin, Yaqing. "A Relational Theory of World Politics." *International Studies Review* 18, no. 1 (2016): 33–47.

Rai, Shirin, and Georgina Waylen, eds. *Global Governance: Feminist Perspectives*. Basingstoke, UK: Palgrave Macmillan, 2008.

Ralph, Jason G., and James Souter. "Is R2P a Fully-Fledged International Norm?" *Politics and Governance* 3, no. 4 (2015): 68–71.

Rao, Rahul. "The State of 'Queer IR.'" *GLQ: A Journal of Lesbian and Gay Studies* 24, no. 1 (2018): 139–149.

Rasmussen, Anders Fogh. "Empowering Women in Peace and Security—Speech at the European Commission." NATO, January 27, 2010. https://www.nato.int/cps/en/natohq/opinions_61040.htm.

Raymond, Gregory A. "Problems and Prospects in the Study of International Norms." *Mershon International Studies Review* 41, no. 2 (1997): 205–245.

Razack, Sherene H. "Gendered Disposability." *Canadian Journal of Women and the Law* 28, no. 2 (2016): 285–307.

——. "Imperilled Muslim Women, Dangerous Muslim Men and Civilised Europeans: Legal and Social Responses to Forced Marriages." *Feminist Legal Studies* 12 (2004): 129–174.

——. "Settler Colonialism, Policing and Racial Terror: The Police Shooting of Loreal Tsingine." *Feminist Legal Studies* 28, no. 1 (2020): 1–20.

Razavi, Negar. "NatSec Feminism: Women Security Experts and the US Counterterror State." *Signs: Journal of Women in Culture and Society* 46, no. 2 (2021): 361–386.

Rebelo, Tamya, and Paula Drumond. "Gender Entrepreneurs in the Adoption of the Brazilian National Action Plan on Women, Peace and Security." *Global Governance* 27, no. 3 (2021): 343–365.

Rees, Madeleine. "Open Letter to the UN Security Council." Women's International League for Peace and Freedom, January 28, 2022. https://www.wilpf.org/war-over-ukraine-militarism-is-killing-us-all/.

Rees, Madeleine, and Christine Chinkin. "Exposing the Gendered Myth of Post-conflict Transition: The Transformative Power of Economic and Social Rights." *New York University Journal of International Law & Politics* 48, no. 4 (2016): 1211–1226.

Rehn, Elisabeth, and Ellen Johnson Sirleaf. *Women, War, Peace: The Independent Experts' Assessment of the Impact of Armed Conflict on Women and Women's Role in Peace Building.* New York: UN Women, 2002.

Reilly, Niamh. *Women's Human Rights: Seeking Gender Justice in a Globalizing Age.* Cambridge: Polity, 2009.

Richmond, Oliver. "Human Rights and the Development of a Twenty-First Century Peace Architecture: Unintended Consequences?" *Australian Journal of International Affairs* 73, no. 1 (2019): 45–63.

"The Right to Resist: A Feminist Manifesto." *Commons*, July 7, 2022. https://commons.com.ua/en/right-resist-feminist-manifesto/.

Riley, Robin, Chandra Talpade Mohanty, and Minnie Bruce Pratt, eds. *Feminism and War: Confronting US Imperialism.* London: Zed, 2013.

Robichau, Robbie Waters. "The Mosaic of Governance: Creating a Picture with Definitions, Theories, and Debates." *Policy Studies Journal* 39, no. 1 (2011): 113–131.

Roe, Emery. *Narrative Policy Analysis: Theory and Practice.* Durham, NC: Duke University Press, 1994.

Roet, David. "Women, Peace and Security." Permanent Mission of Israel to the United Nations, October 30, 2014. https://embassies.gov.il/un/statements/security_council/Pages/Amb. -David-Roet-Addresses-the-Security-Council-on-Displaced-Women.aspx.

"The Role of Women in Achieving Peace and Maintaining International Security—NGO Statement Read Out at the Arria Formula Meeting of the UNSC." International Alert, October 23, 2000. https://reliefweb.int/report/afghanistan/role-women-achieving-peace-and -maintaining-international-security.

Rosenau, James. "Governance, Order and Change in World Politics." In *Governance Without Government: Order and Change in World Politics*, edited by James Rosenau and Ernst Czempiel, 1–29. Cambridge: Cambridge University Press, 1992.

Royal Courts of Justice. "Judgement: Campaign Against Arms Trade v. The Secretary of State for International Trade." T3/2017/2079. June 20, 2019.

Rubin, Barnett R., and Bruce Jones. "Prevention of Violent Conflict: Tasks and Challenges for the United Nations." *Global Governance* 13, no. 3 (2007): 391–408.

Ruby, Felicity. "Security Council Resolution 1325: A Tool for Conflict Prevention?" In *Rethinking Peacekeeping, Gender Equality and Collective Security*, edited by Gina Heathcote and Dianne Otto, 173–184. Basingstoke, UK: Palgrave Macmillan, 2014.

Rucker, Philip, and Robert Costa. "'It's a Hard Problem': Inside Trump's Decision to Send More Troops to Afghanistan." *Washington Post*, August 21, 2017. https://www.washingtonpost .com/politics/its-a-hard-problem-inside-trumps-decision-to-send-more-troops-to -afghanistan/2017/08/21/14dcb126-868b-11e7-a94f-3139abce39f5_story.html.

Ruggie, John Gerard. "On the Problem of 'the Global Problematique': What Roles for International Organizations?" *Alternatives* 5, no. 4 (1980): 517–550.

——. "Reconstituting the Global Public Domain—Issues, Actors, and Practices." *European Journal of International Relations* 10, no. 4 (2004): 499–531.

Saeidi, Shirin, and Heather M. Turcotte. "Politicizing Emotions: Historicizing Affective Exchange and Feminist Gatherings." *International Studies Review* 13, no. 4 (2011): 693–695.

Said, Edward W. *Orientalism*. London: Routledge and Kegan Paul, 1979.

Salter, Mark. "Introduction: Circuits and Motions." In *Making Things International 1: Circuits and Motions*, edited by Mark Salter, vii–xxii. Minneapolis: University of Minnesota Press, 2015.

——. "#sorrynotsorry: A Well-meaning Response to PTJ." *Millennium: Journal of International Studies* 43, no. 3 (2015): 970–973.

Sana'a Center for Strategic Studies. *A Gendered Crisis: Understanding the Experiences of Yemen's War*. Sana'a, YE: Sana'a Center for Strategic Studies, 2019.

Sanders, Rebecca. "Norm Spoiling: Undermining the International Women's Rights Agenda." *International Affairs* 94, no. 2 (2018): 271–291.

Sandouka, Nivine. "The Unique Case of Palestinian Women in East Jerusalem." *Palestine-Israel Journal* 25, nos. 3–4 (2020). https://www.pij.org/articles/2047/the-unique-case-of -palestinian-women-in-east-jerusalem.

Särmä, Saara. "Collage: An Art-Inspired Methodology for Studying Laughter in World Politics." In *Popular Culture and World Politics: Theories, Methods, Pedagogies*, edited by Federica Caso and Caitlin Hamilton, 110–119. Bristol, UK: E-International Relations, 2015.

Schakowsky, Jan. "The Burqa Reminder." *Chicago Tribune*, May 18, 2012. https://www
.chicagotribune.com/opinion/ct-xpm-2012-05-18-ct-oped-0518-women-20120518-story
.html.

Schulz, Philipp, and Heleen Touquet. "Queering Explanatory Frameworks for Wartime Sexual Violence Against Men." *International Affairs* 96, no. 5 (2020): 1169–1187.

Schuurman, Marriët. "NATO and the Women, Peace and Security Agenda: Time to Bring It
Home." *Connections* 14, no. 3 (2015): 1–6.

——. "The Women, Peace and Security Agenda: Integrating a Gendered Perspective into Security Operations." *Fletcher Forum of World Affairs* 41, no. 1 (2017): 103–111.

Security Council Report. "S/2020/1054." 2020. https://www.securitycouncilreport.org/un
-documents/document/s-2020-1054.php.

Serrano, Mónica. "The Responsibility to Protect and Its Critics: Explaining the Consensus."
Global Responsibility to Protect 3, no. 4 (2011): 425–437.

Seyle, D. Conor. "Operationalizing Positive Peace: Canadian Approaches to International
Security Policy and Practice." In *The Palgrave Handbook of Global Approaches to Peace*,
edited by Aigul Kulnazarova and Vesselin Popovski, 193–213. Cham, CH: Palgrave Macmillan, 2019.

Sharland, Lisa, Netta Goussac, Emilia Currey, Genevieve Feely, and Sarah O'Connor. *System
Update: Towards a Women, Peace and Cybersecurity Agenda*. Geneva: United Nations Institute for Disarmament Studies, 2021.

Sharma, Ananya. "Decolonizing International Relations: Confronting Erasures Through
Indigenous Knowledge Systems." *International Studies* 58, no. 1 (2021): 25–40

Shawki, Noha. "Implementing the Women, Peace and Security Agenda." *Global Affairs* 3, nos.
4–5 (2017): 455–467.

Sheline, Annelle R., and Bruce Riedel. "Biden's Broke Promise on Yemen." Brookings Institution, September 16, 2021. https://www.brookings.edu/blog/order-from-chaos/2021/09/16
/bidens-broken-promise-on-yemen/.

Shepherd, Laura J. "Activism in/and the Academy: Reflections on 'Social Engagement.'" *Journal of Narrative Politics* 5, no. 1 (2018): 45–56.

——. "Advancing the Women, Peace and Security Agenda: 2015 and Beyond." NOREF: Norwegian Centre for Conflict Resolution, August 28, 2014. https://noref.no/Publications
/Themes/Gender-and-inclusivity/Advancing-the-Women-Peace-and-Security-agenda
-2015-and-beyond.

——. *Gender, UN Peacebuilding and the Politics of Space*. Oxford: Oxford University Press,
2017.

——. *Gender, Violence and Security: Discourse as Practice*. London: Zed Books, 2008.

——. "Listen to Women When Creating Peace Initiatives." In *Feminist Solutions for Ending
War*, edited by Megan MacKenzie and Nicole Wegner, 216–230. London: Pluto, 2021.

——. "Making War Safe for Women? National Action Plans and the Militarisation of the
Women, Peace and Security Agenda." *International Political Science Review* 37, no. 3 (2016):
324–335.

——. *Narrating the Women, Peace and Security Agenda: Logics of Global Governance*. New
York: Oxford University Press, 2021.

——. "Research as Gendered Intervention: Feminist Research Ethics and the Self in the Research Encounter." *Crítica Contemporánea: Revista de Teoría Política*, no. 6 (2016): 1–15.

——. "Sex, Security and Superhero(in)es: From 1325 to 1820 and Beyond." *International Feminist Journal of Politics* 13, no. 4 (2011): 504–521.

——. "Veiled References: Constructions of Gender in the Bush Administration Discourse on the Attacks on Afghanistan Post-9/11." *International Feminist Journal of Politics* 8, no. 1 (2006): 19–41.

Shepherd, Laura J., and Jacqui True. "The Women, Peace and Security Agenda and Australian Leadership in the World: From Rhetoric to Commitment?" *Australian Journal of International Affairs* 68, no. 3 (2014): 257–284.

Shields, Stephanie A. *Speaking from the Heart: Gender and the Social Meaning of Emotion.* Cambridge: Cambridge University Press, 2002.

Shih, Chih-Yu. "Affirmative Balance of the Singapore–Taiwan Relationship: A Bilateral Perspective on the Relational Turn in International Relations." *International Studies Review* 18, no. 4 (2016): 681–701.

Shilliam, Robbie, ed. *International Relations and Non-Western Thought: Imperialism, Colonialism, and Investigations of Global Modernity.* London: Routledge, 2011.

——. " 'Open the Gates Mek We Repatriate': Caribbean Slavery, Constructivism, and Hermeneutic Tensions." *International Theory* 6, no. 2 (2014): 349–372.

Shiloh, Nelly. "Women and Counterterrorism." Permanent Mission of Israel to the United Nations, September 9, 2015. https://embassies.gov.il/un/statements/committee_statements/Pages/Cons.-Nelly-Shiloh-on-Women-and-Counterterrorism.aspx.

Simmons, Beth A., and Hyeran Yo. "Measuring Norms and Normative Contestation: The Case of International Criminal Law." *Journal of Global Studies* 4, no. 1 (2019): 18–36.

Simpson, Audra. "The State Is a Man: Theresa Spence, Loretta Saunders and the Gender of Settler Sovereignty." *Theory and Event* 19, no. 4 (2016). https://muse.jhu.edu/article/633280.

Singh, Shweta. "Re-thinking the 'Normative' in United Nations Security Council Resolution 1325: Perspectives from Sri Lanka." *Journal of Asian Security and International Affairs* 4, no. 2 (2017): 219–238.

Siniora, Randa. "Statement at UN Security Council Open Debate on Women, Peace and Security," NGO Working Group on Women, Peace and Security, October 25, 2018. https://www.womenpeacesecurity.org/resource/statement-unsc-wps-open-debate-october-2018/.

Sjoberg, Laura. "Witnessing the Protection Racket: Rethinking Justice in/of Wars Through Gender Lenses." *International Politics* 53, no. 3 (2016): 361–384.

Sjoberg, Laura, and Caron Gentry. *Mothers, Monsters, Whores: Women's Violence in Global Politics.* London: Zed, 2007.

Sjoberg, Laura, and Jessica Peet. "A(nother) Dark Side of the Protection Racket: Targeting Women in Wars." *International Feminist Journal of Politics* 13, no. 1 (2011): 163–182.

Skard, Torild. "Getting Our History Right: How Were the Equal Rights of Women and Men Included in the Charter of the United Nations?" *Forum for Development Studies* 35, no. 1 (2008): 37–60.

Skåre, Mari. "Having a Gender Perspective Matters in Defence and Security." *Diplomatic Courier*, July/August, 2013. https://www.diplomaticourier.com/posts/having-a-gender -perspective-matters-in-defense-and-security-2.

Smith, Elizabeth Seymore. "Climate Change in Women, Peace and Security National Action Plans." *SIPRI Insights on Peace and Security*, no. 2020/7 (2020). https://www.sipri.org/sites /default/files/2020-06/sipriinsight2007.pdf.

Smith, Sarah. "Accountability and Sexual Exploitation and Abuse in Peace Operations." *Australian Journal of International Affairs* 71, no. 4 (2017): 405–422.

Smith, Sarah, and Elena B. Stavrevska. "A Different Women, Peace and Security Is Possible? Intersectionality in Women, Peace and Security Resolutions and National Action Plans." *European Journal of Politics and Gender* 5, no. 1 (2022): 63–82.

Smith, Steve. "The Discipline of International Relations: Still an American Social Science?" *British Journal of Politics and International Relations* 2, no. 3 (2000): 374–402.

——. "Singing Our World Into Existence: International Relations Theory and September 11." *International Studies Quarterly* 48, no. 3 (2004): 499–515.

Solis, Gary D. *The Law of Armed Conflict: International Humanitarian Law in War.* Cambridge: Cambridge University Press, 2012.

Somerville, Ian, and Sahla Aroussi. "Campaigning For 'Women, Peace and Security': Transnational Advocacy Networks at the United Nations Security Council." In *Gender and Public Relations: Critical Perspectives on Voice, Image and Identity*, edited by Christine Daymon and Kristin Demetrious, 156–176. London: Routledge, 2013.

Special Inspector General for Afghanistan Reconstruction. *Support for Gender Equality: Lessons from the U.S. Experience in Afghanistan.* Arlington, VA: Special Inspector General for Afghanistan Reconstruction, 2021.

Spivak, Gayatri Chakravorty. "Can the Subaltern Speak?" In *Marxist Interpretations of Culture*, edited by Cary Nelson and Lawrence Grossberg, 271–313. Basingstoke, UK: Palgrave Macmillan, 1988.

Stamnes, Eli, and Kari M. Osland. "Synthesis Report: Reviewing UN Peace Operations, the UN Peacebuilding Architecture and the Implementation of UNSCR 1325." *NUPI Report*, no. 2. Oslo: Norwegian Institute of International Affairs, 2016.

"Statement of Shared Commitments." Permanent Mission of Norway to the United Nations, April 4, 2022. https://www.norway.no/contentassets/1b036f2777f74bd3b8ff473555c63a98 /statement-of-shared-commitments-2022.pdf.

Staunton, Eglantine, and Jason Ralph. "The Responsibility to Protect Norm Cluster and the Challenge of Atrocity Prevention: An Analysis of the European Union's Strategy in Myanmar." *European Journal of International Relations* 26, no. 3 (2020): 660–686.

Stavrianakis, Anna. "Legitimising Liberal Militarism: Politics, Law and War in the Arms Trade Treaty." *Third World Quarterly* 37, no. 5 (2016): 840–865.

Stavrianakis, Anna. "Towards a Postcolonial and Anti-racist Feminist Mode of Weapons Control." In *New Directions in Women, Peace and Security*, edited by Soumita Basu, Paul Kirby, and Laura J. Shepherd, 153–168. Bristol, UK: Bristol University Press, 2020.

Steady, Filomina Chioma. *Women and Leadership in West Africa: Mothering the Nation and Humanizing the State.* New York: Palgrave Macmillan, 2011.

Steans, Jill, and Vafa Ahmadi. "Negotiating the Politics of Gender and Rights: Some Reflections on the Status of Women's Human Rights at 'Beijing Plus Ten.'" *Global Society* 19, no. 3 (2005): 227–245.

Steinberg, Donald. "Women and War: An Agenda for Action." In *Women and War: Power and Protection in the 21st Century*, edited by Kathleen Kuehnast, Chantal de Jonge Oudraat, and Helga Hernes, 115–130. Washington, DC: United States Institute for Peace, 2011.

Stimmer, Anette, and Lea Wisken. "The Dynamics of Dissent: When Actions Are Louder than Words." *International Affairs* 95, no. 3 (2019): 515–533.

Stone, Laurel. "Annex II: Quantitative Analysis of Women's Participation in Peace Processes." In *Reimagining Peacemaking: Women's Roles in Peace Processes*, edited by Marie O'Reilly, Andrea Ó Súilleabháin, and Thania Paffenholz, 34. New York: International Peace Institute, 2015.

——. "Women Transforming Conflict: A Quantitative Analysis of Female Peacemaking." SSRN Working Paper, May 13, 2014. https://papers.ssrn.com/sol3/papers.cfm?abstract_id =2485242.

"The Story of the Implementation of 1325 UN Security Council Resolution in Israel." Heinrich Böll Stiftung Gunda Werner Institute, accessed August 31, 2023. https://www.gwi-boell .de/en/2011/11/02/story-implementation-1325-un-security-council-resolution-israel.

Strange, Susan. "Cave! Hic Dragones: A Critique of Regime Analysis." *International Organization* 36, no. 2 (1982): 479–496.

Sullivan, Donna. "Women's Human Rights and the 1993 World Conference on Human Rights." *American Journal of International Law*. 88, no. 1 (1994): 152–167.

"Summary Analysis of the Arms Trade Treaty." Control Arms (May 2013). https://www .saferworld.org.uk/downloads/pubdocs/Control-Arms-Arms-Trade-Treaty-analysis .pdf.

Sutterlin, James. *The United Nations and the Maintenance of International Security: A Challenge to be Met*. 2nd ed. Westport, CT: Praeger, 2003.

Sutton, Jessica. "Gender-Based Violence and the Arms Trade Treaty: Article 7(4) Under Fire." *New Zealand Journal of Public and International Law* 18, no. 1 (2020): 49–104.

Swaine, Aisling. "Assessing the Potential of National Action Plans to Advance Implementation of United Nations Security Council Resolution 1325." *Yearbook of International Humanitarian Law* 12 (2009): 403–433.

——. "Resurfacing Gender: A Typology of Conflict-Related Violence Against Women for the Northern Ireland Troubles." *Violence Against Women* 29, nos. 6–7 (2023): 1391–1418. https:// doi.org/10.1177/10778012221114923.

Swanwick, Helena. *Women and War*. London: Union of Democratic Control, 1915.

Sylvester, Christine. *Feminist Theory and International Relations in a Postmodern Era*. Cambridge: Cambridge University Press, 1994.

Tamang, Dipti. "Rethinking 'Participation' in Women, Peace and Security Discourses: Engaging with 'Non-participant' Women's Movements in the Eastern Borderlands of India." *International Feminist Journal of Politics* 22, no. 4 (2020): 485–503.

Tannenwald, Nina. "The Nuclear Taboo: The United States and the Normative Basis of Nuclear Non-use." *International Organization* 53, no. 3 (1999): 433–468.

Taylor, Joel David. "'Suspect Categories,' Alienation and Counterterrorism: Critically Assessing PREVENT in the UK." *Terrorism and Political Violence* 32, no. 4 (2020): 851–873.

Taylor, Sarah. "Women, Peace, and Politics at the UN Security Council." *IPI Global Observatory*, July 17, 2013. https://theglobalobservatory.org/2013/07/women-peace-and-politics-at-the-un-security-council/.

Thomson, Jennifer, and Claire Pierson. "Can Abortion Rights Be Integrated Into the Women, Peace and Security Agenda?" *International Feminist Journal of Politics* 20, no. 3 (2018): 350–365.

Tickner, J. Ann, and Jacqui True. "A Century of International Relations Feminism: From World War I Women's Peace Pragmatism to the Women, Peace and Security Agenda." *International Studies Quarterly* 62, no. 2 (2018): 221–233.

Towns, Ann. *Women and States: Norms and Hierarchies in International Society.* Cambridge: Cambridge University Press, 2010.

Trithart, Albert. "The Women, Peace and Security Agenda Is Not Just for Straight Cisgender Women." *International Peace Institute Global Observatory*, October 13, 2020. https://theglobalobservatory.org/2020/10/the-women-peace-and-security-agenda-is-not-just-for-straight-cisgender-women/.

Trownsell, Tamara A., Arlene B. Tickner, Amaya Querejazu, Jarrad Reddekop, Giorgio Shani, Kosuke Shimizu, Navnita Chadha Behera, and Anahita Arian. "Differing About Difference: Relational IR from Around the World." *International Studies Perspectives* 22, no. 1 (2021): 25–64.

True, Jacqui. "Explaining the Global Diffusion of the Women, Peace and Security Agenda." *International Political Science Review* 37, no. 3 (2016): 307–323.

——. "A Tale of Two Feminisms in International Relations: Feminist Political Economy and the Women, Peace and Security Agenda." *Politics and Gender* 11, no. 2 (2015): 419–424.

True, Jacqui, and Yolande Riveros-Morales. "Towards Inclusive Peace: Analysing Gender-Sensitive Peace Agreements, 2000–2016." *International Political Science Review* 40, no. 1 (2019): 23–40.

True, Jacqui, and Antje Wiener. "Everyone Wants (a) Peace: The Dynamics of Rhetoric and Practice on 'Women, Peace and Security.'" *International Affairs* 95, no. 3 (2019): 553–574.

Tryggestad, Torunn L. "International Norms and Political Change: 'Women, Peace and Security' and the UN Security Agenda." PhD diss., University of Oslo, 2014.

——. "Trick or Treat? The UN and Implementation of Security Council Resolution 1325 on Women, Peace, and Security." *Global Governance* 15, no. 4 (2009): 539–557.

——. "The UN Peacebuilding Commission and Gender: A Case of Norm Reinforcement." *International Peacekeeping* 17, no. 2 (2010): 159–171.

Turner, Catherine, and Aisling Swaine. *At the Nexus of Participation and Protection: Protection-Related Barriers to Women's Participation in Northern Ireland.* New York: International Peace Institute, June 2021.

Tynan, Lauren. "What Is Relationality? Indigenous Knowledges, Practices and Responsibilities with Kin." *Cultural Geographies* 28, no. 4 (2021): 597–610.

Ucko, David H., and Robert Egnell. *Counterinsurgency in Crisis: Britain and the Challenges of Modern Warfare.* New York: Columbia University Press, 2015.

UN Women. *Indigenous Women and the Women, Peace and Security Agenda*. Research brief. New York: UN Women, 2016.

——. *Women's Participation in Peace Negotiations: Connections Between Presence and Influence*. New York: UN Women, 2012.

United States Department of the Army. *FM 3-24: Counterinsurgency*. Washington, DC: Department of the Army, 2006.

UNOCHA (United Nations Office for the Coordination of Humanitarian Affairs). *Global Humanitarian Overview 2021*. New York: UNOCHA, 2020.

——. *Global Humanitarian Overview 2022*. New York: UNOCHA, 2021.

Urlacher, Brian R. "Introducing Native American Conflict History (NACH) Data." *Journal of Peace Research* 58, no. 5 (2021): 1117–1125. https://doi.org/10.1177/0022343320987274.

Vassoler, Ivani. "A Woman on the Front-Lines Against the Last Bastion of Colonialism in Brazil." *Latin American Essays* 18 (2005): 38–54.

Veracini, Lorenzo. "'Settler Colonialism': Career of a Concept." *Journal of Imperial and Commonwealth History* 41, no. 2 (2013): 313–333.

Voiculescu, Cerasela. *European Social Integration and the Roma: Questioning Neoliberal Governmentality*. London: Routledge, 2017.

von der Lippe, Berit, and Tarja Väyrynen. "Co-opting Feminist Voices for the War on Terror: Laura Bush Meets Nordic Feminism." *European Journal of Women's Studies* 18, no. 1 (2011): 19–33.

von Hlatky, Stéfanie. *Deploying Feminism: The Role of Gender in NATO Military Operations*. Oxford: Oxford University Press, 2022.

Vucetic, Srdjan. "A Nation of Feminist Arms Dealers? Canada and Military Exports." *International Journal: Canada's Journal of Global Policy Analysis* 72, no. 4 (2017): 503–519.

Walker, R. B. J. *Inside/Outside: International Relations as Political Theory*. Cambridge: Cambridge University Press, 1992.

Waltz, Susan. "Reclaiming and Rebuilding the History of the Universal Declaration of Human Rights." *Third World Quarterly* 23, no. 3 (2002): 437–448.

"WCLAC and UNSCR 1325." Women's Centre for Legal Aid and Counselling, accessed September 6, 2023. http://www.wclac.org/english/userfiles/WCLAC%20UNSR%201325%20final%20sept%2015%202014.pdf.

Wearing, David. "Why Are We in Yemen?" *LRB Blog*, August 29, 2019. https://www.lrb.co.uk/blog/2019/august/why-are-we-in-yemen.

Weaver, Catherine. "The Strategic Social Construction of the World Bank's Gender and Development Policy Norm." In *Owning Development: Creating Policy Norms in the IMF and the World Bank*, edited by Susan Park and Antje Vetterlein, 70–89. Cambridge: Cambridge University Press, 2010.

Weaver-Hightower, Marcus B. "An Ecology Metaphor for Educational Policy Analysis: A Call to Complexity." *Educational Researcher* 37, no. 3 (2008): 153–167.

Weber, Cynthia. *Simulating Sovereignty: Intervention, the State, and Symbolic Exchange*. Cambridge: Cambridge University Press, 1995.

Weber, Martin. "The Normative Grammar of Relational Analysis: Recognition Theory's Contribution to Understanding Short-Comings in IR's Relational Turn." *International Studies Quarterly* 64, no. 3 (2020): 641–648.

Weerawardhana, Chamindra. "Profoundly Decolonizing? Reflections on a Transfeminist Perspective of International Relations." *Meridians: Feminism, Race, Transnationalism* 16, no. 1 (2018): 184–213.

Weiss, Cora. "We Must Not Make War Safe for Women." *50:50 Inclusive Democracy*, May 24, 2011. https://www.opendemocracy.net/5050/cora-weiss/we-must-not-make-war-safe-for-women.

Weiss, Cornelia. "Creating UNSCR 1325: Women Who Served as Initiators, Drafters, and Strategists." In *Women and the UN: A New History of Women's International Human Rights*, edited by Rebecca Adami and Dan Plesch, 139–160. London: Routledge, 2022.

Weiss, Thomas G. *Humanitarian Intervention*. Cambridge: Polity Press, 2007.

Weiss, Thomas G., and Ramesh Thakur. *Global Governance and the UN: An Unfinished Journey*. Bloomington: Indiana University Press, 2010.

Weiss, Thomas G., and Rorden Wilkinson. *Rethinking Global Governance*. Cambridge: Polity, 2019.

——. "Rethinking Global Governance? Complexity, Authority, Power, Change." *International Studies Quarterly* 58, no. 1 (2014): 207–215.

Weiss, Thomas G., Tatiana Carayannis, and Richard Jolly. "The 'Third' United Nations." *Global Governance* 15, no. 1 (2009): 123–142.

Werner, Sarah Kenny, and Elena B. Stavrevska. *Where Are the Words? The Disappearance of the Women, Peace and Security Agenda in the Language of Country-Specific UN Security Council Resolutions*. London: Women's International League for Peace and Freedom and LSE Centre for Women, Peace and Security, 2020.

Westendorf, Jasmine-Kim. *Violating Peace: Sex, Aid, and Peacekeeping*. Ithaca, NY: Cornell University Press, 2020.

——. "WPS and SEA in Peacekeeping Operations." In *The Oxford Handbook of Women, Peace and Security*, edited by Sara E. Davies and Jacqui True, 222–236. New York: Oxford University Press, 2019.

Westendorf, Jasmine-Kim, and Louise Searle. "Sexual Exploitation and Abuse in Peace Operations: Trends, Policy Responses and Future Directions." *International Affairs* 93, no. 2 (2017): 365–387.

"What Is UNSCR 1325? An Explanation of the Landmark Resolution on Women, Peace and Security." United States Institute of Peace, accessed September 18, 2023. https://www.usip .org/gender_peacebuilding/about_UNSCR_1325.

Wiener, Antje. *Contestation and Constitution of Norms in Global International Relations*. Cambridge: Cambridge University Press, 2018.

Wilén, Nina. "Female Peacekeepers' Added Burden." *International Affairs* 96, no. 6 (2020): 1585–1602.

Wilkinson, Rorden. "Global Governance: A Preliminary Interrogation." In *Global Governance: Critical Perspectives*, edited by Rorden Wilkinson and Steve Hughes, 1–14. Routledge: London, 2002.

Willett, Susan. "Introduction: Security Council Resolution 1325: Assessing the Impact on Women, Peace and Security." *International Peacekeeping* 17, no. 2 (2010): 142–158.

Williams, Jody. "Women, Weapons, Peace and Security." *Sur—International Journal on Human Rights* 22 (2015): 31–38.

"WILPF Resolutions, 18th Congress, New Delhi, India, December 1970-January 1971." Women's International League for Peace and Freedom, 1971. https://www.wilpf.org/wp-content/uploads/2012/08/WILPF_triennial_congress_1971.pdf.

"WILPF Resolutions, 21st Congress, Connecticut, USA, 1980." Women's International League for Peace and Freedom, 1980. https://www.wilpf.org/wp-content/uploads/2015/10/WILPF_triennial_congress_1980.pdf.

"WILPF Resolutions, 22nd Congress, Gothenburg, Sweden, 1983." Women's International League for Peace and Freedom, 1983. https://www.wilpf.org/wp-content/uploads/2012/09/WILPF_triennial_congress_1983.pdf.

"WILPF Statement Opposing NATO's Military and Nuclear Policies." Women's International League for Peace and Freedom, November 24, 2008. https://wilpf.org/wilpf_statements/wilpf-statement-opposing-natos-military-and-nuclear-policies/.

Wilson, Peter. "The Myth of the 'First Great Debate.'" *Review of International Studies* 24 (December 1998): 1–15.

Winston, Carla. "The Complex Nature of International Norms." Presentation, University of Sydney, Sydney, Australia, March 25, 2021.

Wolfe, Patrick. *Settler Colonialism and the Transformation of Anthropology: The Politics and Poetics of an Ethnographic Event.* London: Cassell, 1999.

Women's International League for Peace and Freedom. *Congress Report 2015.* Geneva: WILPF, 2016.

——. *Congress Report 2018.* Geneva: WILPF, 2019.

——. *The Nuclear Weapon Ban Treaty: A Resource Guide for WILPF.* Geneva: WILPF, 2018.

——. *UNSCR 1325 at 20 Years: Perspectives from Feminist Peace Activists and Civil Society.* Geneva: WILPF, 2020.

——. *WILPF Congress: Resolutions and Proposals 1919.* 2nd edition. Geneva: WILPF, 2019.

——. *WILPF International Programme 2018-2021.* Geneva: WILPF, 2018.

——. *WILPF Manifesto 2015.* Geneva: WILPF, 2015.

Women's International League for Peace and Freedom, International Action Network on Small Arms Women's Network, Amnesty International, and Religions for Peace International. "The Arms Trade Treaty: Security Women's Rights and Gender Equality—A United Call to Explicitly Include Gender-Based Violence in the Criteria." June 2012.

Women's International League for Peace and Freedom Sweden and Women's International League for Peace and Freedom Finland. "Sweden's and Finland's NATO Membership Poses Great Risks." Women's International League for Peace and Freedom, May 16, 2022. https://www.wilpf.org/swedens-and-finlands-nato-membership-poses-great-risks/

"Women's Participation in Peace Processes." Council on Foreign Relations, accessed September 16, 2023. https://www.cfr.org/womens-participation-in-peace-processes/.

Wood, Brian, and Rasha Abdul-Rahim. "The Birth and the Heart of the Arms Trade Treaty." *Sur—International Journal on Human Rights* 22 (2015): 15–30.

Wood, Michael C. "Security Council Working Methods and Procedure: Recent Developments." *International and Comparative Law Quarterly* 45, no. 1 (1996): 150–161.

"WPS Scorecard: Implementation of the Women, Peace and Security Agenda by the UN Security Council Permanent Members." PeaceWomen, accessed September 16, 2023. http://peacewomen.org/scorecards.

Wright, Hannah. "'Masculinities Perspectives': Advancing a Radical Women, Peace and Security Agenda?" *International Feminist Journal of Politics* 22, no. 5 (2020): 652–674.

Wright, Katharine A. M. "NATO's Adoption of UNSCR 1325 on Women, Peace and Security: Making the Agenda a Reality." *American Political Science Review* 37, no. 3 (2016): 350–361.

——. "Telling NATO's Story of Afghanistan: Gender and the Alliance's Digital Diplomacy." *Media, War & Conflict* 12, no. 1 (2019): 87–101.

——. "Where Is Women, Peace and Security? NATO's Response to the Russia-Ukraine War." *European Journal of Politics and Gender* 5, no. 2 (2022): 275–277.

Wright, Katharine A.M., Matthew Hurley, and Jesus Ignacio Gil Ruiz. *NATO, Gender and the Military: Women Organising from Within.* London: Routledge, 2019.

Yanow, Dvora. *How Does a Policy Mean? Interpreting Policy and Organizational Actions.* Washington, DC: Georgetown University Press, 1996.

"Yemen: 85,000 Children May Have Died from Starvation Since Start of War." Save the Children, November 20, 2018. https://www.savethechildren.org/us/about-us/media-and-news/2018-press-releases/yemen-85000-children-may-have-died-from-starvation.

Youde, Jeremy. "The Role of Philanthropy in International Relations." *Review of International Studies* 45, no. 1 (2019): 39–56.

Young, Annette. "Taking Up Arms: Campaigning for Equality in the Military." *The 51%*, France24, July 9, 2021. https://www.france24.com/en/tv-shows/the-51/20210709-taking-up-arms-campaigning-for-equality-in-the-military.

Young, Iris Marion. "The Logic of Masculinist Protection: Reflections on the Current Security State." *Signs: Journal of Women in Culture and Society* 29, no. 1 (2003): 1–25.

Youngs, Gillian. "Feminist International Relations in the Age of the War on Terror: Ideologies, Religions and Conflict." *International Feminist Journal of Politics* 8, no. 1 (2006): 3–18.

Younis, Musab. "To Own Whiteness." *London Review of Books* 44, no. 3 (2022): 15–16.

Yuval-Davis, Nira. "Remarks in 'Forum: The Events of 11 September 2001 and Beyond.'" *International Feminist Journal of Politics* 4, no. 1 (2002): 99–103.

Zalewski, Marysia. *Feminist International Relations; Exquisite Corpse.* London: Routledge, 2013.

——. "Forget(ting) Feminism? Investigating Relationality in International Relations." *Cambridge Review of International Affairs* 32, no. 5 (2019): 615–635.

——. "Well, What Is the Feminist Perspective on Bosnia?" *International Affairs* 71, no. 2 (1995): 339–356.

Zarakol, Ayşe. "What Made the Modern World Hang Together: Socialisation or Stigmatisation?" *International Theory* 6, no. 2 (2014): 311–332.

Zaum, Dominik. *The Sovereignty Paradox: The Norms and Politics of International Statebuilding*. Oxford: Oxford University Press, 2007.

Zwingel, Susanne. "How Do Norms Travel? Theorizing International Women's Rights in Transnational Perspective." *International Studies Quarterly* 56, no. 1 (2012): 115–129.

INDEX

World Summit, of 2005, R2P and, 58–59
WPS. *See* Women, Peace, and Security

Yemen, 204, 215; civil war and uprising in, 199; gendering of arms control by, 201;

Houthi or Ansarallah movement in, 199, 200; humanitarian crisis in, 199–200; IEG on sexual violence and GBV in, 200; NAP of, 200–201
Youth, Peace, and Security (YPS), 90

Printed in the USA
CPSIA information can be obtained
at www.ICGtesting.com
JSHW020909260524
63768JS00019B/95

9 780231 205139